MODERN INDIA: An Interpretive Anthology

MODERN INDIA
An Interpretive Anthology

Thomas R. Metcalf

Modern India: An Interpretive Anthology
©1990, Thomas R. Metcalf
First Edition 1990
Reprint 1994, 1997

STERLING PUBLISHERS PRIVATE LIMITED

Reprint in India.

Published by Sterling Publishers Pvt.

STERLING PUBLISHERS PRIVATE LIMITED
L-10, Green Park Extension, New Delhi-110016

Modern India: An Interpretive Anthology
©1990, Thomas R. Metcalf
First Edition 1990
Reprint 1992, 1994

PRINTED IN INDIA

Published by Sterling Publishers Pvt. Ltd., New Delhi-110016.
Printed at Crescent Printing Works (P) Ltd., New Delhi.

Preface

This anthology is an attempt to make readily available some of the better essays on the modern history of India written for the most part over the last twenty-five years. Inevitably any such collection must be selective, and this anthology makes no claims to comprehensiveness. Its only justification is the hope that it may encourage students to read more widely in the rich, and increasingly sophisticated, literature that has grown up in recent years on India's past.

The anthology is organised, on a roughly but not wholly chronological basis, in four parts. The first asks how Indians have shaped for themselves a distinctive culture, and how that past was shaped afresh by the country's British rulers. The second part examines those elements that formed the enduring structures of Indian society. The third assesses the nature of the transformation set in motion by the coming of British colonial rule, while the last examines the visions of the future put forward by Indians as they sought to refashion a society free from the bonds of colonialism.

To facilitate reading, footnotes and source references have been omitted in all except three selections where the notes may point the reader to the wider literature on the subject. A number of these essays were previously published under the same title in a volume released by Macmillan and Co., New York, in 1971. As that work has long been out of print, and much new scholarship has since appeared, a new and revised edition is appropriate.

Thomas R. Metcalf

Contents

Part IV — The Sense of the Future

PART I

The Creation of a Past

This first section of the volume poses the question: What is distinctive about India, and the Indian experience? How does their heritage shape the Indian people's view of themselves? The first two selections point to basic unifying threads in the subcontinent's civilization as interpreted by independent India's first Prime Minister and by a distinguished Sanskrit scholar. The latter two show how the British, as India's rulers for nearly two centuries, by their study of its ancient texts and its architecture created an enduring view of India's past.

1

It is fitting that we start with a brief selection written by Jawaharlal Nehru, for Nehru was not only a great political leader, but a sensitive intellectual forever asking what it meant to be an Indian, and what was basic to the Indian character. His Discovery of India, *written while he was in prison during the Second World War, is the product of this search for the "spirit of India". The view of India's past which the book contains, an intensely personal one shaped to a large extent by the enthusiasms of the nationalist struggle, should not be regarded as historically accurate in every detail. The volume has, however, helped mould the minds of a generation or more of young Indians, and thus itself forms part of contemporary India's view of itself.*

from

The Discovery of India: Part II, "The Quest"

JAWAHARLAL NEHRU

I. THE PANORAMA OF INDIA'S PAST

During these years of thought and activity my mind has been full of India, trying to understand her and to analyse my own reactions toward her. I went back to my childhood days and tried to remember what I felt like then, what vague shape this conception took in my growing mind and how it was moulded by fresh experience. Sometimes it receded into the background, but it was always there, slowly changing, a queer mixture derived from old story and legend and modern fact. It produced a sensation of pride in me as well as that of shame, for I was ashamed of much that I saw around me, of superstitious practices, of outworn ideas, and above all, our subject and poverty-stricken state.

As I grew up and became engaged in activities which promised to lead to India's freedom, I became obsessed with the thought of India. What was this India that possessed me and beckoned to me continually, urging me to action so that we might realise some vague but deeply felt desire of our hearts? The initial urge came to me, I suppose, through pride, both individual and national, and the desire, common to all men, to resist another's domination and have freedom to live the life of our choice. It seemed monstrous to me that a great country like India, with a rich and immemorial past, should be bound hand and foot to a faraway island which imposed its will upon her. It was still more monstrous that this forcible union had resulted in poverty and degradation beyond measure. That was reason enough for me and for others to act.

But it was not enough to satisfy the questioning that arose within me. What is this India, apart from her physical and geographical aspects? What did she represent in the past; what gave strength to her then? How did she lose that old strength, and has she lost it completely? Does she represent anything vital now, apart from being the home of a vast number of human beings? How does she fit into the modern world?

II. INDIA'S STRENGTH AND WEAKNESS

The search for the sources of India's strength and for her deterioration and decay is long and intricate. Yet the recent causes of that decay are obvious enough. She fell behind in the march of technique, and Europe, which had long been backward in many matters, took the lead in technical progress. Behind this technical progress was the spirit of science and a bubbling life and spirit which displayed itself in many activities and in adventurous voyages of discovery. New techniques gave military strength to the countries of western Europe and it was easy for them to spread out and dominate the East. That is the story not of India only but of almost the whole of Asia.

Why this should have happened so is more difficult to unravel, for India was not lacking in mental alertness and technical skill in earlier times. One senses a progressive deterioration during centuries. The urge to life and endeavour becomes less, the creative spirit fades away and gives place to the imitative. Where triumphant and rebellious thought had tried to pierce the mysteries of nature and the universe, the wordy commentator comes with his glosses and long explanations. Magnificent art and sculpture give way to a meticulous carving of intricate detail without nobility of conception or design. The vigour and richness of language, powerful yet simple, are followed by highly ornate and complex literary forms. The urge to adventure and the overflowing life which led to vast schemes of distant colonisation and the transplantation of Indian culture in far lands, all these fade away and a narrow orthodoxy taboos even the crossing of the high seas. A rational spirit of inquiry, so evident in earlier times, which might well have led to the further growth of science, is replaced by irrationalism and a blind idolatry of the past. Indian life becomes a sluggish stream, living in the past, moving slowly through the accumulations of dead centuries. The heavy burden of the past crushes it and a kind of coma seizes it. It is not surprising that in this condition of mental stupor and physical weariness India should have deteriorated and remained rigid and immobile while other parts of the world marched ahead.

Yet this is not a complete or wholly correct survey. If there had only been a long and unrelieved period of rigidity and stagnation, this might well have resulted in a complete break with the past, the death of an era, and the erection of something new on its ruins. There has not been such a break and there is a definite continuity. Also from time to time vivid flashes of renascence have occurred, and some of them have been long and brilliant. Always there is visible an attempt to understand and adapt the new and harmonise it with the old, or at any rate with parts of the old which were considered worth preserving. Often that old retains an external form only, as a kind of symbol, and changes its inner content. But something vital and living continued, some urge driving the people in a direction not wholly realised, always a desire for synthesis between the old and the new. It was this urge and desire that kept them going and enabled them to absorb new ideas while retaining much of the old. Whether there was such a thing as an Indian dream through the ages, vivid and full of life or sometimes reduced to the murmurings of troubled sleep, I do not know. Every people and every nation has some such belief or myth of national destiny, and perhaps it is partly true in each case. Being an Indian, I am myself influenced by this reality or myth about India, and I feel that anything that had the power to mould hundreds of generations, without a break, must have drawn its enduring vitality from some deep well of strength, and have had the capacity to renew that vitality from age to age.

Was there some such well of strength? And if so, did it dry up, or did it have hidden springs to replenish it? What of today? Are there any springs still functioning from which we can refresh and strengthen ourselves? We are an old race, or rather an odd mixture of many races, and our racial memories go back to the dawn of history. Have we had our day and are we now living in the later afternoon or evening of our existence, just carrying on after the manner of the aged quiescent, devitalised, uncreative, desiring peace and sleep above all else?

No people, no race continues unchanged. Continually it is mixing with others and slowly changing; it may appear to die almost and then rise again as a new people or just a variation of the old. There may be a definite break between the old people and the new, or vital links of thought and ideals may join them.

Behind the past quarter of a century's struggle for India's independence, and all our conflicts with British authority, lay in my mind and that of many others the desire to revitalise India. We felt that through action and self-imposed suffering and sacrifice, through voluntarily facing risk and danger, through refusal to submit to what we considered evil and wrong, we would recharge the battery of India's spirit and waken her from her long slumber. Though we came into conflict continually with the British government in India, our eyes were always turned toward our own people. Political advantage had value only in so far as it helped in that fundamental purpose of ours. Because of this governing motive, frequently we acted as no politician moving in the narrow sphere of politics, only, would have done, and foreign and Indian critics expressed surprise at the folly and intransigence of our ways. Whether we were foolish or not the historians of the future will judge. We aimed high and looked far. Probably we were often foolish, from the point of view of opportunist politics, but at no time did we forget that our main purpose was to raise the whole level of the Indian people, psychologically and spiritually and also, of course, politically and economically. It was the building up of that real inner strength of the people that we were after, knowing that the rest would inevitably follow. We had to wipe out the evil aftermath from some generations of shameful subservience and timid submission to an arrogant alien authority.

III. THE SEARCH FOR INDIA

Though books and old monuments and past cultural achievements helped to produce some understanding of India, they did not satisfy me or give me the answer I was looking for. Nor could they, for they dealt with a past age, and I wanted to know if there was any real connection between that past and the present. The present for me, and for many others like me, was an odd mixture of medievalism, appalling poverty and misery, and a somewhat superficial modernism of the middle classes. I was not an admirer of my own class or kind, and yet inevitably I looked to it for leadership in the struggle for India's salvation. That middle class felt caged and circumscribed and wanted to grow and develop itself. Unable to do so within the framework of British rule, a spirit of revolt grew against this rule, and yet this spirit was not directed against the structure that crushed us. It sought to retain it and control it by displacing the British. These middle classes were too much the product of that structure to challenge it and seek to uproot it.

New forces arose that drove us to the masses in the villages, and for the first time, a new and different India rose up before the young intellectuals who had almost forgotten its existence, or attached little importance to it. It was a disturbing sight, not only because of its stark misery and the magnitude of its problems, but because it began to upset some of our values and conclusions. So began for us the discovery of India as it was, and it produced both understanding and conflict within us. Our reactions varied and depended on our previous environment and experience. Some were already sufficiently acquainted with these village masses not to experience any new sensation; they took them for granted. But for me it was a real voyage of discovery, and while I was always painfully conscious of the failings and weaknesses of my people, I found in India's country folk something, difficult to define, which attracted me. That something I had missed in our middle classes.

I do not idealise the conception of the masses, and as far as possible I try to avoid thinking of them as a theoretical abstraction. The people of India are very real to me in their great variety, and in spite of their vast numbers I try to think of them as individuals rather than as vague groups. Perhaps it was because I did not expect much from them that I was not disappointed. I found more than I had expected. It struck me that perhaps the reason for this, and for a certain stability and potential strength that they possessed, was the old Indian cultural tradition which was still retained by them in a small measure. Much had gone in the battering they had received during the past two hundred years. Yet something remained that was worthwhile, and with it so much that was worthless and evil.

During the twenties my work was largely confined to my own provinces and I travelled extensively and intensively through the towns and villages of the forty-eight districts of the United Provinces of Agra and Oudh, that heart of Hindustan as it has so long been considered, the seat and centre of both ancient and medieval civilisation, the melting pot of so many races and cultures, the area where the great revolt of 1857 blazed up and was later ruthlessly crushed. I grew to know the sturdy Jat of the northern and western districts, that typical son of the soil, brave and independent-looking, relatively more prosperous; the Rajput peasant and petty landholder, still proud of his race and ancestry, even though he might have changed his faith and adopted Islam; the deft and skilful artisans and cottage workers, both Hindu and Moslem; the poorer peasantry and tenants in their vast numbers, especially in Oudh and the eastern districts, crushed and ground down by generations of oppression and poverty, hardly daring to hope that a change would come to better their lot, and yet hoping and full of faith.

During the thirties, in the intervals of my life out of prison, and especially during the election campaign of 1936-37, I travelled more extensively throughout India, in towns and cities and villages alike. Except for rural Bengal, which unhappily I have only rarely visited, I toured in every province and went deep into villages. I spoke of political and economic issues, and judging from my speech I was full of politics and elections. But all this while, in a corner of my mind, lay something deeper and more vivid, and elections meant little to it, or the other excitements of the passing day. Another and a major excitement had seized me, and I was again on a great voyage of discovery and the land of India and the people of India lay spread out before me. India with all her infinite charm and variety began to grow upon me more and more, and yet the more I saw of her, the more I realised how very difficult it was for me or for anyone else to grasp the ideas she had embodied. It was not her wide spaces that eluded me, or even her diversity, but some depth of soul which I could not fathom, though I had occasional and tantalising glimpses of it. She was like some ancient palimpsest on which layer upon layer of thought and revery had been inscribed, and yet no succeeding layer had completely hidden or erased what had been written previously. All of these existed together in our conscious or subconscious selves, though we might not be aware of them, and they had gone to build up the complex and mysterious personality of India. That sphinxlike face with its elusive and sometimes mocking smile was to be seen throughout the length and breadth of the land. Though outwardly there was diversity and infinite variety among our people, everywhere there was that tremendous impress of oneness, which had held all of us together for ages past, whatever political fate or misfortune had befallen us. The unity of India was no longer merely an intellectual conception for me: it was an emotional experience which overpowered me. That essential unity had been so powerful that no political division, no disaster or catastrophe had been able to overcome it.

It was absurd, of course, to think of India or any country as a kind of anthropomorphic entity. I did not do so. I was also fully aware of the diversities and divisions of Indian life, of classes, castes, religions, races, different degrees of cultural development. Yet I think that a country with a long cultural background and a common outlook on life develops a spirit that is peculiar to it and that is impressed on all its children, however much they may differ among themselves. Can anyone fail to see this in China, whether he meets an old-fashioned mandarin or a Communist who has apparently broken with the past? It was this spirit of India that I was after, not through idle curiosity, though I was curious enough, but because I felt that it might give me some key to the understanding of my country and people, some guidance to thought and action. Politics and elections were day-to-day affairs when we grew excited over trumpery matters. But if we were going to build the house of India's future, strong and secure and beautiful, we would have to dig deep for the foundations.

IV. BHARAT MATA

Often as I wandered from meeting to meeting I spoke to my audience of this India of ours, of Hindustan and of Bharata, the old Sanskrit name derived from the mythical founder of the race. I seldom did so in the cities, for there the audiences were more sophisticated and wanted stronger fare. But to the peasant, with his limited outlook, I spoke of this great country for whose freedom we were struggling, of how each part differed from the other and yet was India, of common problems of the peasants from north to south and east to west, of the *Swaraj,* the self-rule that could only be for all and every part and not for some. I told them of my journeying from the Khyber Pass in the far north-west to Kanyakumari or Cape Comorin in the distant south, and how everywhere the peasants put me identical questions, for their troubles were the same—poverty, debt, vested interests, landlord, moneylender, heavy rents and taxes, police harassment, and all these wrapped up in the structure that the foreign government had imposed upon us—and relief must also come for all. I tried to make them think of India as a whole, and even to some little extent of this wide world of which we were a part. I brought in the struggle in China, in Spain, in Abyssinia, in central Europe, in Egypt and the countries of western Asia. I told them of the wonderful changes in the Soviet Union and of the great progress made in America. The task was not easy; yet it was not so difficult as I had imagined, for our ancient epics and myth and legend, which they knew so well, had made them familiar with the conception of their country, and some there were always who had travelled far and wide to the great places of pilgrimage situated at the four corners of India. Or there were old soldiers who had served in foreign parts in World War I or other expeditions. Even my references to foreign countries were brought home to them by the consequences of the great depression of the thirties.

Sometimes as I reached a gathering, a great roar of welcome would greet me: *Bharat Mata ki Jai*——Victory to Mother India! I would ask them unexpectedly, what they meant by that cry, who was this *Bharat Mata*, Mother India, whose victory they wanted? My question would amuse them and surprise them, and then, not knowing exactly what to answer, they would look at each other and at me. I persisted in my questioning. At last a vigorous Jat, wedded to the soil from immemorial generations, would say that it was the *dharti*, the good earth of India, that they meant. What earth? Their particular village patch, or all the patches in the district or province, or in the whole of India? And so question and answer went on, till they would ask me impatiently to tell them all about it. I would endeavour to do so and explain that India was all this that they had thought, but it was much more. The mountains and the rivers of India, and the forests and the broad fields, which gave us food, were all dear to us, but what counted ultimately were the people of India, people like them and me, who were spread out all over this vast land. *Bharat Mata,* Mother India, was essentially these millions of people, and victory to her meant victory to these people. You are parts of this *Bharat Mata,* I told them, you are in a manner yourselves *Bharat Mata,* and as this idea slowly soaked into their brains, their eyes would light up as if they had made a great discovery.

V. THE VARIETY AND UNITY OF INDIA

The diversity of India is tremendous; it is obvious; it lies on the surface and anybody can see it. It concerns itself with physical appearances as well as with certain mental habits and traits. There is little in common, to outward seeming, between the Pathan of the north-west and the Tamil in the far south. Their racial stocks are not the same, though there may be common strands running through them; they differ in face and figure, food and clothing and, of course, language. In the North-Western Frontier Province there is already the breath of central Asia, and many a custom there, as in Kashmir, reminds one of the countries on the other side of the Himalayas. Pathan popular dances are singularly like Russian Cossack dancing. Yet with all these differences, there is no mistaking the impress of India on the Pathan, as this is obvious on the Tamil. It is not surprising, for these border lands, and indeed Afghanistan also, were united with India for thousands of years. The old Turkish and other races who inhabited Afghanistan and parts of central Asia before the advent of Islam were largely Buddhists, and earlier still, during the period of the Epics, Hindus. The frontier area was one of the principal centres of old Indian culture, and it abounds still with ruins of monuments and monasteries and especially of the great university of Taxila, which was at the height of its fame two thousand years ago, attracting students from all over India as well as different parts of Asia. Changes of religion made a difference but could not change entirely the mental backgrounds which the people of those areas had developed.

The Pathan and the Tamil are two extreme examples; the others lie somewhere in between. All of them have their distinctive features, all of them have still more the distinguishing mark of India. It is fascinating to find how the Bengalese, the Marathas, the Gujaratis, the Tamils, the Andhras, the Oriyas, the Assamese, the Canarese, the Malayalis, the Sindhis, the Punjabis, the Pathans, the Kashmiris, the Rajputs, and the great central bloc comprising the Hindustani-speaking people, have retained their peculiar characteristics for hundreds of years, have still more or less the same virtues and failings of which old tradition or record tells us, and yet have been throughout these ages distinctively Indian, with the same national heritage and the same set of moral and mental qualities. There was something living and dynamic about this heritage which showed itself in ways of living and a philosophical attitude to life and its problems. Ancient India, like ancient China, was a world in itself, a culture and a civilisation which gave shape to all things. Foreign influences poured in and often influenced that culture and were absorbed. Disruptive tendencies gave rise immediately to an attempt to find a synthesis. Some kind of a dream of unity has occupied the mind of India since the dawn of civilisation. That unity was not conceived as something imposed from outside, a standardisation of externals or even of beliefs. It was something deeper, and within its fold the widest tolerance of belief and custom was practised and every variety acknowledged and even encouraged.

Differences, big or small, can always be noticed even within a national group, however closely bound together it may be. The essential unity of that group becomes apparent when it is compared to another national group, though often the differences between two adjoining groups fade out or intermingle near the frontiers, and modern developments are tending to produce a certain uniformity everywhere. In ancient and medieval times the idea of the modern nation was non-existent, and feudal, religious, racial or cultural bonds had more importance. Yet I think that at almost any time in recorded history an Indian would have felt more or less at home in any part of India, and would have felt as a stranger and alien in any other country. He would certainly have felt less of a stranger in countries which had partly adopted his culture or religion. Those who professed a religion of non-Indian origin and coming to India settled down there, became distinctively Indian in the course of a few generations, such as Christians, Jews, Parsees, Moslems. Indian converts to some of these religions never ceased to be Indians in spite of a change of faith. All these were looked upon in other countries as Indians and foreigners, even though there might have been a community of faith between them.

Today, when the conception of nationalism has developed much more, Indians in foreign countries inevitably form a national group and hang together for various purposes, in spite of their internal differences. An Indian Christian is looked upon as an Indian wherever he may go. An Indian Moslem is considered an Indian in Turkey or Arabia or Iran or any other country where Islam is the dominant religion.

All of us, I suppose, have varying pictures of our native land and no two persons will think exactly alike. When I think of India, I think of many things: of broad fields dotted with innumerable small villages; of towns and cities I have visited; of the magic of the rainy season which pours life into the dry, parched-up land and converts it suddenly into a glistening expanse of beauty and greenery, of great rivers and flowing water; of the Khyber Pass in all its bleak surroundings; of the southern tip of India; of people, individually and in the mass; and above all, of the Himalayas, snow-capped, or some mountain valley in Kashmir in the spring, covered with new flowers, and with a brook bubbling and gurgling through it. We make and preserve the pictures of our choice, and so I have chosen this mountain background rather than the more normal picture of a hot, subtropical country. Both pictures would be correct, for India stretches from the tropics right up to the temperate regions, from near the equator to the cold heart of Asia.

2

The eminent American Sanskritist W.Norman Brown devoted his life to the study of the great texts that enshrine India's cultural heritage. Here he rises above the detailed analysis of texts to ask, What are the basic underlying unities that define Indian civilization? What has enabled it to retain its distinctive character over so many centuries?

The Content of Cultural Continuity in India

W. NORMAN BROWN

One of the problems recurring in the Buddhist Pali Texts is the question of what it is that transmigrates. Buddhism accepts as axiomatic the doctrine of rebirth, a process of "renewal of becomings" until the attainment of complete knowledge, whereupon the process terminates. At the same time, the Pali texts are committed to the doctrine that there is no soul. The two doctrines, held simultaneously, presented a difficulty of which the Buddhist monks were well aware. If there is no soul, no Ego, no self, and yet rebirth is a fact, what is reborn?

Of the many passages bearing upon the parts of this problem, one of the best known is that in which the Venerable Nagasena expounds the No-Soul doctrine to King Milinda. Nagasena had remarked to the king that, though he was called Nagasena, this was merely a convenient designation, an appellation, and any other designation would have done as well. There was no essential Nagasena, no Ego Nagasena.

This was more than the king could understand. "If there is no Ego", he objected, "who furnishes you monks with robes, medicine, and your other needs, who uses these things? Who observes the precepts, who undertakes meditation, who does evil? Without an Ego there can be no merit, no demerit; good and evil deeds can have no fruit. There can be no teacher. When you tell me that your fellow monks address you as Nagasena, what is this Nagasena? Is the hair of your head Nagasena?" "No, your majesty!" "The hair of your body?" "No!" "The nails, skin, teeth?" and he catalogued some thirty parts of the body. "Is it form,

Reprinted by permission from the *Journal of Asian Studies*, XX (August 1961), pp. 427-434.

sensation, perception, the predispositions, consciousness, or all of them together, or something besides them?" Always the answer was "No". Then the king said to Nagasena, "You are telling me a lie. There is no Nagasena."

In reply to the king, Nagasena resorted to a parable, using as its subject the chariot in which the king said he came to Nagasena's presence. "What is this chariot?" asked Nagasena. "Is it the pole, or the axle, or the wheels, or the chariot-body, or the banner-staff, or the yoke, or the reins, or the goad, or all of them together?" Each time the king answered, "No." "Then," said Nagasena, "king though you are, you are lying to me. There is no chariot!" Thus refuted, the king denied that he had lied, and then conceded that the word "chariot" was only a term, an appellation, a convenient designation, a name for all the parts mentioned. "Similarly," pointed out Nagasena, "must you understand the word 'Nagasena'. It is but an appellation, a convenient designation. But in the absolute sense there is no Nagasena to be found here."

Later, in the same text, King Milinda asked Nagasena the question which naturally followed: "If there is no Ego, what is it that is born in the next existence?"

"Your majesty," replied Nagasena, "it is name and form that is born in the next existence." By "name and form" (*namarupa*) the Pali means "individuality". Yet the individuality in the next existence, Nagasena went on to explain, is not the same individuality as that in this existence; "But with the individuality of this existence, your majesty, one does a deed—it may be good or it may be wicked—and by reason of this deed another individuality is born into the next existence."

"Reverend sir," said the king, "if it is not the same individuality that is born into the next existence, is not one freed from one's evil deeds?"

"If one were not born into another existence," answered Nagasena, "one would be freed from one's evil deeds; but, your majesty, inasmuch as one is born into another existence, therefore is one not freed from one's evil deeds."

Still puzzled, King Milinda asked for an illustration, and Nagasena gave him several, including the following:

"Your majesty, it is as if a man were to buy from a cowherd a pot of milk, and were to leave it with the cowherd, and go off, thinking he would come the next day and take it. And on the next day it were to turn into sour cream; and the man were to come back, and say, 'Give me the pot of milk.' And the other were to show him the sour cream; and the first man were to say, 'I did not buy sour cream from you. Give me the pot of milk.' And the cowherd were to say, 'While you were gone, your milk turned into sour cream'; and they, quarrelling, were to come to you. Whose cause, your majesty, would you sustain?"

"That of the cowherd, reverend sir."

"And why?"

"Because, in spite of what the man might say, the one sprang from the other."

"In exactly the same way, your majesty, although the individuality which is born into the next existence is different from the individuality which is to end at death, nevertheless, it is sprung from it. Therefore is one not freed from one's evil deeds?"

In other passages the simile of milk is extended to include the successive transformations into sour cream, butter, or ghee. The texts illustrate the point that there is continuity and causal connection, though not identity, of individuality.

And now arises a third question: what causes individuality to be reborn? In the Buddhist doctrine of the Chain of Dependent Origination, individuality is said to depend upon consciousness (Pali, *vinnana;* Sanskrit, *vijnana*), and the Buddha is represented as saying in the Mahanidanasutta of the Digha Nikaya, "Were consciousness not to descend in the maternal womb, name and form, that is individuality, would not consolidate in the maternal womb." And he goes on to say that were consciousness to be severed from a child, name and form would not attain growth, increase and development. "Accordingly," says he, "we have in consciousness the occasion, the origin, and the dependence of individuality...Verily this individuality coupled with consciousness is all there is to be born, or to grow old, or to die, or to leave one existence, or to spring up in another. It is all that is meant by any affirmation, predication, or declaration we may make concerning anybody. It constitutes knowledge's field of action. And it is all that is reborn to appear in its present shape." In short, we can see that consciousness is the only invariable, the one unalterable element, in the Pali Buddhist doctrine of rebirth.

I have used this bit of Buddhist doctrinal exposition because it presents a figurative analogy to the history of civilized man in India. Since the third millennium B.C. India has had a highly developed civilization, and we can see that this has had a continuity through successive periods with many variations from then to the present. The variation has often been great, so that today's phenomenon looks little like its antecedent, though caused by it, two or three or four thousand years ago, while there are also many differentiations in separate localities. Yet there must be something which in each successive periodic reincarnation of the civilization has caused the new existence of the civilization, something which in terms of the Buddhist doctrinal analogy corresponds to consciousness. To identify that something, assuming that it really is present, is the problem which I suggest deserves our attention. Its identification would contribute to our understanding of the process of Indian civilization, its past and its present, and give some hint, however slight or vague, of its future. The problem is essentially akin to that which Robert Redfield investigated in terms of the Great Tradition and the Little Tradition, or M.N. Srinivas treated under the heading of Sanskritization, or Milton Singer has recently been exploring as the relation between Text and Context. I hasten to say that I do not claim to have identified the vitalizing element, but I do wish to make a few remarks on the problem and shall be satisfied if I can help to define it more fully; even though I cannot achieve its solution.

The basic material for studying this problem is the mass of data available to us concerning the nature and development of civilization in India, the totality of items which reappear in altered form in the sequence of periods. Scholars have been assembling, synthesizing, and analyzing such material since the time of Christian Lassen, who published the first edition of his *Indishe Alterthumskunde* in 1847. Other treatments have been L.D. Barnett's *Antiquities of India* in 1914, A.A. Macdonell's *India's Past* in 1927, L. Renou and J. Filliozat's *L'Inde Classique* in 1947/1953. The most recent is A.L.Basham's *The Wonder That Was India*, which appeared in 1954. Such works easily establish the wide range of fields in which the continuity exists, the many aspects of life in which it is found.

These works and the specific researches on which they are based show us as well the great length of the continuity. There are, for example, certain items which appear throughout the entire 4,500 years of Indian civilization from the period of the Harappa culture in Western India in the third millennium B.C. to the present. Phallic worship is one of them; the use of the swastika symbol is another. A stylistic tradition in sculpture is still another, as Stella Kramrisch has pointed out. Though we have no interpretable data for ascertaining religious dogmas in the Harappa period, we see items in that culture which seem to indicate beliefs or practices similar to some now current. The pipal tree appears to have been honoured or valued by the Harappa people; it is sacred today. The Harappans depicted on their seal-amulets the bull and the tiger, both of which have religious connotations today. They portray a wide variety of hybrid animals; similar animal hybridization continues in Hindu religious art. They presumably honoured, perhaps worshipped, a three-faced anthropomorphic being whom they show seated in a yoga posture and surrounded by animals, recalling the god Shiva's aspect as the meditative ascetic deity and another of his aspects as Pasupati, "Lord of Animals". Unfortunately, we know nothing of the Harappa people's social structure and political organization, nor their language, nor their thought, and this, too, in spite of the fact that they left a script.

At a later period, when the Aryans had arrived in India and were producing the Vedic collections, in the second half of the second millennium B.C., roughly between 1500 and 1000, we see other culture items that have had a series of metamorphoses in the interval down to the present. The high value set upon the cow is one, which by the beginning of the Christian era had led to the doctrine of the cow's sanctity or inviolability. The joint family system seems to have existed in the time of the Rig Veda; it is still the typical Hindu pattern. A special view of truth appears in the Rig Veda also, where it is invested with a kind of magic power that should probably be considered the starting point of many later conceptions of the power of truth, down to Gandhi's mystical theory about *satyagraha*. The recorded history of speculative thought in India begins in the Rig Veda. Its start seems to have been the myth of the god Indra who slays the demon Vritra, releases the cosmic waters which were pregnant with the sun, and thus sets the stage for creation of the cosmos and the establishment of order in it. Out of this cosmological myth philosophy seems to have grown, with its subsequent manifold developments. The language of the Rig Veda, which is the earliest form of Sanskrit, served, as it developed into Classical Sanskrit, Pali, and the Prakrits, as the dominant vehicle of thought and culture in India until English superseded it in the nineteenth century, along with the body of western thought which it introduced. Even so Sanskrit is still remarkably alive and significant to Hindus.

A half a millennium after the Vedic period, Jainism and Buddhism put organized asceticism on a widely respected popular basis, where it still stands. These two faiths also promoted Ahinsa (*ahimsa*), "non-injury of living creatures", which remains to the present the most important ethical principle of Hinduism. They also accepted the joint doctrine of *karma* and rebirth, retribution for one's deeds in future existences, a doctrine already appearing in late Vedic thought, and popularized it until it was accepted as an axiom, and it continues to be so accepted in modern Hindu India.

At about the beginning of the Christian era, the social institution of caste, the rationalization of which was foreshadowed in Vedic literature as early as in the Purusa-sukta of the Rig Veda, had been developed and was firmly established. With two millennia of development it is still the basic feature of Hindu social structure.

It would be possible to compile a catalogue of many hundreds of cultural items appearing in ancient Indian civilization which are then reborn or at least reappear in constantly changing fashion in succeeding periods during centuries, even millennia. Such a catalogue doubtless would not answer the question of what has given Indian civilization its special character and vitality, the element corresponding to the "consciousness" of Buddhist thought, without which new existences would not come into being, existences which, though new, are yet dependent upon preceding existences. Nor is that element likely to be identified even if we could classify the details of Indian civilization into categories by ethnic source, that is determine which were developed by Indo-Aryans, or by Dravidians, or by some other ethnic group, hoping in this way to identify a given people as the author of characteristic Indian civilization.

When I have asked Indians their thoughts on the question of a vitalizing element in Indian civilization, I have always had the answer that such an element certainly exists, but I have found difference of opinion as to what that element is. As simple an answer as I have ever received is that it is a special feeling for the sanctity of water. Such a feeling can be deduced from the elaborate bathing and drainage systems of town planning and architecture in the Harappa culture, the reverence for the Cosmic Waters in the Rig Veda, the use of ceremonial ablution in Hinduism, the veneration of streams and springs, and other lesser religious practices or taboos associated with water.

Oftener than any other the answer is that the determining element is the Indian concern with religio-philosophical investigation and its application to life. This is the search for metaphysical truth, the nature of the cosmos, of god, of the human soul, and of the Absolute and man's relation to it. The answer is in line with the common Indian view today that India throughout its history, down to and including the present, has been engrossed in the quest for the spiritual—in contrast with the West, which is considered to be preoccupied with "materialism". Aside from this bit of cultural chauvinism there is support for the general idea of India's especially intensive interest in religio-philosophic activity in the long history of speculative thought and religious teaching, so voluminously recorded in Indian literature from its beginnings in the Rig Veda, its blossoming in the Upanishads and in the Jain and Buddhist scriptures, and its wide ramification and varying development thereafter until our own day, witness Gandhi and Vinoba Bhave as contemporary illustrations; others could be named.

Some Indians, on being pressed further, have reduced their stress on this facet of Indian civilization and instead have placed it on the prevalence of tolerance, and pointed to the wide, often contradictory, yet tolerated, variation in Hinduism of intellectual dogma, and the accompanying latitudinarianism in views of human behaviour. All these variations are accorded status in orthodox Hinduism.

This latter answer, or at least such a type of answer, seems to me to advance our investigation, but not to satisfy it. It carries us beyond material production in the arts, literature, and sciences; beyond skills, customs, political institutions, social institutions, social change and development, varying norms, and thought forms; into the field of values and attitudes; and thus to the basis of behaviour patterns.

Possibly we can take another step forward by looking at one of the values of Hinduism more closely. I am thinking of duty, and the unusual stress put upon correct action. Again, we can say nothing about this in the Harappa culture, but we can see it in the Rig Veda and still more markedly in the ritual worship described in the Yajur Veda and the Brahmanas. In this ritual every detail must be perfect, and the priests are a highly trained fraternity with specialized duties painstakingly learned and performed with the finest exactitude. The doctrine of rebirth and *karma*, the most characteristic of all Indian religious teachings, employs this notion to its fullest. Every person's slightest action is a determinant of his future state, and the literature in thousands of passages points out in minute detail the correspondence between deed and result. In caste practice, behaviour is the primary consideration; it must always accord with prescription, not only with respect to important matters such as marriage selection and birth and death ceremonies, but also with respect to such small ones as eating, speaking to or approaching others, or even the style of tonsure. Behaviour far outweighs dogma in Hinduism, which may vary widely even for members of the same caste without objection from one's fellows. But not so with action! Infringement there results in penalty, which may extend to expulsion from the caste, social death.

Correct or right behaviour is viewed as a personal responsibility or duty with a most significant meaning to Hindus, Buddhists, and Jains. Particular application of the idea of duty appears as early as in the Rig Veda. There it starts with the notion that our cosmos contains two opposing forces: that of ordered operation, progress, and harmonious cooperation of the parts; and that of disorder, chaos, destruction. The universe in which we live is held to operate under a code or set of principles to keep it going, and this code, this body of cosmic truth or order, has the name *satya* or *rta*: But disorder, anti-order, known as *anrita,* is ever beating at our universe, tending to disrupt or destroy it. To keep our universe operating smoothly, every being in it has a function. Gods have their specific functions; human beings have their functions. No two gods have the same function, and human beings' functions also differ. Each god and each human must assiduously devote himself to his function. If he fails in performing it, to that extent the operation of the universe is impaired. The word for this individual function is *vrata*, and so important is the concept that in post-Vedic times the word comes to mean a solemn, religious vow, to be undertaken with great seriousness and observed with unflagging zeal.

Human duty is differentiated in the Rig Veda for the four great classes of society: the Brahman (*brahmana*) or priest; the Rajanya or Kshatriya the temporal ruler or warrior; the Vaishya (*vaisya*) or commoner, peasant and artisan; and the Shudra (*sudra*) or slave. The Brahman celebrates the ritual, first performed at the time of creation by the gods, and this ritual gives the gods the help they need to counteract the destructive force of evil. The Kshatriya patronizes the sacrifice and protects it from harm. The Vaishya produces the economic means needed by the ruler and the Brahmasa. The Shudra does menial service for the other in their activities. In RV 10.90, creation is described figuratively as the primordial sacrifice by the gods of a being called Purusha (*purusa*), "male", a symbolic representation of all the materials needed to produced the universe. As he is dismembered, the parts of his body become the parts of the universe. There it is said that "the Brahmana was Purusha's mouth, the Rajanya was made into his arms; as for his thighs, that was what the Vaishya became; from his feet the Shudra was born." The symbolism is obvious.

After the caste system with its practice of endogamy and its ideas of pollution emerged by the beginning of the Christian era or earlier, it was artificially encased by orthodox Hindu priestly thought into the four-class system of Vedic society. Manu, author of the great and well-known legal text, ascribes the multiplicity of castes to mixture of the four original social groups, an evil practice in his opinion. Nevertheless, Hinduism eventually applied to the whole caste system the rationalizing theory that each caste has a specific function in the universe which it is duty bound to perform. Each individual member of a caste has as his personal duty that of fulfilling the function of his caste; if he avoids it, he commits sin.

Though this kind or rationalization is both bad anthroplogy and bad history, not to speak of dubious metaphysics, it has nevertheless had deep influence and led to important consequences, especially when it became associated with the doctrine of *karma* and rebirth. First, as we have already noticed, reward for doing one's duty or punishment for failure to do it were held to be experienced in rebirth and to determine the conditions of rebirth. Second, one's present caste status was considered to be the consequence of deeds done in previous existences. Birth in a high caste was a reward, birth in a low caste a punishment. Furthermore, the intellectual and spiritual, sometimes even the moral, endowments of a person at birth were regarded as a concomitant of his caste status. Hence a low caste person was expected to have a less sophisticated view of god, society, life and morality than a high caste person. That was part of his general lowly estate. He must therefore not be expected to comprehend what the high caste person was equipped to comprehend. So, too standards of behaviour were viewed as different. Normal conduct for a low caste man might be sin for a Brahman. All this was understood to be in accord with cosmic law. It constituted an acceptance of relativity concerning human capacity and human behaviour that is the basis of the Hindu tolerance mentioned above. There was no such thing as a single universal standard of duty. Not all people were or could rationally be expected to comprehend the same ideas or to live by the same codes. Each caste could quite legitimately frame its own rules for fulfilling its caste function—within limits, of course—so long as the observance of them did not interfere with another caste in the fulfilling of its function and the observance of its rules. This was the adjustment that made it possible for contradictory doctrines and conflicting codes to dwell side by side in peaceful coexistence. Divergency of duty was expected, accepted, and legtimized on what might seem to others to be a scale of astounding amplitude.

Other large or basic values of Indian civilization might be cited for examination, such as truth and Ahinsa, which have already been mentioned, or the attitude towards law as something not made by man, not even by the king—the Brhadaranyaka Upanished says law is "king over the king"—not invented by kings or by the gods or even by God, but existing before and independently of them all. Should we think that any such value or a whole set of values has constituted the feature giving Indian civilization its vitality throughout history? I repeat that I should not want to make a positive asseveration that it has, but I think the possibility may at least be worthy of consideration, and, in that case, the identification, description, and application of these values deserve deep study.

In viewing Indian civilization I am reminded of the banyan tree, a fig tree, in Sanskrit called *nyagrodha*, a word which means "the down-grower". Though this tree begins life with a single trunk rising from a minute seed, its wide-spreading branches send down air roots, some of which themselves reach the ground, penetrate it, and become secondary trunks, occasionally to rival in size the first trunk. Thus the tree may come to shade an acre or more of ground. One can imagine a banyan tree of such age and such coverage that it may have a number of secondary trunks capable of being confused at first glance with the primary trunk. Such, it seems to me, has been the history of Indian civilization. It arose from roots in the subsurface culture of India, the material of Redfield's Little Tradition or Singer's Contextual. It grew up and spread out into the Great Tradition and the Textual. As it grew it sent out branches, and these sent down air roots, some of which returned into the soil and so became the means of communication between subsurface roots and above-ground branches. This was always a two-way communication, though a selective one with respect to the items communicated, implementing a constant process of mutual feed and feedback, of reciprocal input and output.

But the animating principle of the Nyagrodha is not easy to discern. There is a passage in the Chandogya Upanished touching on that point. The setting is that of Svetaketu Aruneya being instructed by his father Uddalaka, after Svetaketu has come back from his twelve-year course of study, conceited and proud, thinking that he had mastered all knowledge. Uddalaka sets out to teach him something he has not learned, namely, how to know the one thing that gives knowledge of all other things. This is, it happens, the *atman* (Soul), which permeates all beings, is uniform, invariable, and indestructible. He teaches partly by parable, and one of the parables concerns the Nyagrodha fig tree, the banyan. Uddalaka speaks to his son:

"Bring hither a fig from there." "Here it is, sir." "Split it." "It is split sir." "What do you see there?" "These rather fine seeds, sir." "Please split one of these." "It is split, sir." "What do you see there?" "Nothing at all, sir." Then Uddalaka said to him, "Verily, my dear, the finest essence which you do not perceive—verily, my dear, from that finest essence this great *nyagrodha* tree thus arises." And he concludes by saying that the essence is the essence of the world, of Svetaketu himself; that it *is* Svetaketu.

Perhaps any efforts of ours to find the seed that has been the vitalizing essence of Indian civilization, its principle of consciousness, to use the Buddhist doctrinal analogy, may be as futile as Svetaketu's effort to see the essence of the banyan tree. Such a failure might still not convince an inquirer that a vitalizing element was not there, nor prevent the curious from seeking for it. Svetaketu, of course, had only his eyes with which to look.

3

*Although Hindu civilization remained a living presence throughout
India's history, all memory of the great empires and distinctive
religious culture of classical antiquity had been lost during the
intervening centuries. The recovery of this forgotten past was the
work of European Oriental scholarship. Begun by Warren
Hastings, the sympathetic governor-general (1772-1785) who also
set up the first organized British administration in India, this
scholarly activity was extended by a group of dedicated civil
servants in and around Calcutta during the subsequent half-
century. Although the work of these men owed much of its impetus
to the need of the new rulers for knowledge of the language and
culture of their subjects, the greatest beneficiaries were to be the
Indian people. Despite the fact that the British saw India's ancient
civilization as a golden age from whose heights India had
subsequently declined until it was ripe for conquest, the
resuscitation of their ancient past nevertheless gave the Indians a
sense of pride in a civilization whose rich history enabled it to stand
comparison with those of Europe and the Middle East. The
following selection describes the growth of Oriental scholarship in
the years just after Warren Hastings' departure from India.*

FROM

British Orientalism and the Bengal Renaissance: Chapter II, "The Orientalist in Search of a Golden Age"

DAVID KOPF

If the new elite of Company servants owed to Warren Hastings their
transformation in India from commercial adventurer to civil servant, the
basis of their thought and scholarship was the set of values, attitudes,
beliefs, and ideas of the eighteenth-century Enlightenment. Most of

them brought with them to Calcutta the conceptual baggage of the *philosophe*. In one sense, therefore, the remarkable historical breakthroughs of such men as William Jones and Henry Colebrooke are reminiscent of those of Gibbon and Voltaire—for all of them were products of the eighteenth-century world of ideas.

To appreciate fully the phenomenal Orientalist rediscovery of the Hindu classical age, it is necessary to isolate those components of the European Enlightenment that predisposed the Company servants in that direction. The intellectual elite that clustered about Hastings after 1770 was classicist rather than "progressive" in their historical outlook, cosmopolitan rather than nationalist in their view of other cultures, and rationalist rather than romantic in their quest for those "constant and universal principles" that express the unity of human nature. What made them an especially fertile field for Hastings's experiments in cultural interaction was the idea of tolerance, the mainspring of their historical and cultural relativism.

In one of his essays on the French Enlightenment in *The Party of Humanity,* Peter Gay characterized Voltaire as a "subversive anthropologist." "Voltaire was a real cosmopolitan," Gay concludes, "fond of England, impressed with China, attached to pagan Greece and Rome." This vew of Voltaire as representative of an age that combined an outgoing universalism with an appreciation for particularist diversity suggests a similar critical concept of twentieth-century scholarship. In the following passage from the *Essai sur les moeurs et l'esprit des nations,* Voltaire's "anthropological" attitude is very apparent:

> It follows from this survey of history that everything which pertains intimately to human nature is much the same from one end of the world to the other; that everything which depends on custom is different, and it is mere chance if there is any resemblance. The empire of custom is indeed much larger than that of nature. It extends over manners, over all usage; it spreads variety over the universal scene. Nature spreads unity; it establishes everywhere a small number of invariable principles: thus the foundation is everywhere the same, and culture produces diverse fruits.

This concept of unity and diversity, of process and pattern, viewed in historical perspective was perhaps one of the most significant ideas to emerge in the eighteenth-century philosophy of history. The belief that man, though culturally different, is basically the same everywhere enabled Voltaire, as Ferguson asserts, "to pave the way for a history of civilizations."

Voltaire and his contemporaries paved the way for a proper study of historical civilization, and they also felt a deep and lively interest in its classical form. "Whoever thinks, or whoever possesses taste," wrote Voltaire, "only counts four centuries in the history of the world." The four ages were all classical or neo-classical: Greece, Augustan Rome, Renaissance Italy, and the age of Louis XIV. To the men of the Enlightenment, therefore, the history of civilizations did not show uninterrupted progress toward Utopia, but was, on the contrary, cyclical in its discontinuous movements from greatness to decline.

Hence, what permeates Gibbon's masterpiece of eighteenth-century classicism, *The Decline and Fall of the Roman Empire*, is a kind of Greek sense of tragedy. Written between 1776 and 1788, it not only represented the cyclical interpretation of history but also expressed a profound identification with a remote age of antiquity. For Gibbon, the decline of the classical world was not so much a cause of jubilation as it was sufficient reason for despair. Referring to Gibbon's philosophy of history, Christopher Dawson has aptly pointed out: "Every man and every state have their hour, and though genius and virtue could realize the possibilities of that happy moment, they could not preserve it or make the wheel of fortune to stand still."

This mood of despair has provided since Petrarch the proper emotional receptiveness for a concept of dark ages. The ages of gold and the ages of darkness seem so closely interrelated that it is difficult to know whether—in the case of many European renaissance historians—those historians are exuberantly optimistic about the rebirth of the classical world in Italy or deeply fascinated by the decline of antiquity.

Cosmopolitanism, classicism, and rationalism were distinguishing features of the enlightened eighteenth-century mind, but it was the idea of tolerance that proved crucial to British Orientalists seeking to transcend alienation from another culture. The high intellectual regard for non-European peoples and cultures (even primitive ones) was presumably as prevalent in the 1700's as it was to become rare in the 1800's. In sharp contrast with the age of Kipling, the Age of Enlightenment believed, as Carl Becker tells us, "That far the greater part of mankind, during far the greater period of recorded history, had lived (except indeed, when oppressed and corrupted by Christian powers) more happily and humanely, under laws and customs more free and equitable, more in accord with natural relation and morality, than the peoples of Europe had done during the centuries of ecclesiastical ascendancy...."

It may be said that the *philosophes'* spirit of tolerance reached out to all but those guilty of intolerance. This seems to be Gay's explanation for Voltaire's low level of patience for Catholicism and its legacy of medieval "barbarism", with its "despicable faith steeped in superstition and stained with persecution." His high evaluation of Chinese mandarins, on the other hand, was due to "their admirable religion free from superstitions and the rage to persecute."

Both intolerance for the intolerant and a positive sympathy and appreciation for the histories of other cultures were regularly invoked "in the service of reason and common sense." In Gibbon's work, for example, the iconographical ritualism of medieval Catholicism was compared unfavourably with the puritanical simplicity of the Muslim faith. The special quality of the period that enabled historian-philosophers like Gibbon to combine a critical attitude toward one's own culture with an admiration for the virtues of another contributed to the birth of comparative history. In fact, this capacity for viewing history and culture relativistically, which is the key to understanding British Orientalist historiography, was strongly characteristic of Gibbon's thought. The following passage from *The Decline and Fall* could only have been written by an Orientalist: "More pure than the system of Zoroaster, more liberal than the law of Moses, the religion of Mahomet might seem less inconsistent with reason than the creed of mystery and superstition which in the seventh century disgraced the simplicity of the Gospel."

It seems evident, therefore, why many of the Company recruits who went to India were predisposed to adopt the basic tenets of Hastings's Orientalism. This is not to argue that they were necessarily influenced by European thought or that Orientalism was simply an intellectual extension of the West on Indian soil. At the other extreme, to argue that civil servants became Orientalists wholly as a result of their Indian experience, or that Orientalism was derived only from conditions of European rule in Asia, is to give too shallow an explanation for too complex a phenomenon.

It appears, rather, that the European climate of thought and opinion favoured an Orientalist movement in Asia. Judging from the Dutch experience in Indonesia, such a movement was not inevitable. On the other hand, later in the nineteenth century in England, when cosmopolitanism became less fashionable than nationalism and when tolerance for other peoples gave way to the intolerance of national self-adulation, the fitting atmosphere for an Orientalist movement or for a Warren Hastings himself largely disappeared.

The earliest Hastings-trained generation of officials was born between 1740 and 1765. As was customary in Company recruiting procedures, every man was originally sponsored by a relative or friends of the family. In many instances it was because of their impecunious circumstances and their desire to accumulate wealth rapidly that the men were prompted to apply. The majority of them began their ascent of the Company ladder in either commercial or revenue offices, and in true Horatio Alger fashion worked their way up through initiative and hard work.

The key to advancement, in most cases, was linguistic proficiency. Charles Grant, who moved from the post of resident in Malda to the Board of Trade in Calcutta, and on to greater heights in London, was an outstanding exception. When he met William Jones in 1785, the "variety and depth of learning" of the Orientalist filled Grant with the "shame of being unlearned." Grant's was a special kind of transformation. After the death of his two children from smallpox in 1776, Grant became deeply religious, and this attitude apparently served the same end for him as did the Orientalist commitment for other company employees.

In the era of Hastings, and for some time thereafter, the mastery of Indian languages opened the way to both professional advancement and the literary treasures of an Oriental civilization. Charles Wilkins, for example, who like Grant served in Malda and was at first unresponsive to the study of languages, suddenly applied himself to mastering Sanskrit. Wilkins's proficiency in the classical language of the Hindus not only endeared him to Hastings—who invited him to Calcutta—but also led to a major scholarly conversion. The same Wilkins who managed the first government press in Calcutta also translated the *Bhagavad Gita* in 1783, pioneered in the use of inscriptions to reconstruct the history of the Palas of Bengal, and was one of the charter members of the Royal Asiatic Society. His reputation as a "Sanskritist" earned him a D.C.L. from Oxford in 1805 and a knighthood in 1833.

Not all conversions conformed so neatly to this pattern. Henry T.Colebrooke—who was destined to be, next to Jones, the greatest of the Orientalists—prided himself at first on having resisted the temptation to join the translation game. "Translations," he wrote, "are for those who need to fill their purses." According to A.J.Arberry, not only did Colebroke ridicule the Hastings policy, but he spoke disparagingly of such Orientalists as Wilkins as "Sanskrit-mad" and described their early publications as "a repository of nonsense".

Colebrooke first came to India at the age of eighteen in 1783 as a writer in Madras. In the manner of Gibbon and like many of the more intellectually gifted men in company service, he experienced an "intoxicating" love for the classical civilization of Greece and Rome. In fact, Colebrooke was the type of eighteenth-century man who would prove most receptive to the Hastings ideal and was most likely to succeed as an Orientalist. In Madras, the youthful Colebrooke gained a reputation for eschewing both drinking and gambling and was concerned as little with illicit profiteering as he was in accumulating debts in order to keep up appearances. Instead, he spent long hours in his room studying the European classics.

The change in Colebrooke may well have been caused by the sudden depletion of the family fortune, which made a career in England impossible for him. When he turned finally to the study of Sanskrit, it was with the same sobriety and thoroughness that he had applied to the study of the classics and that were, as his German admirer Max Mueller has written, "the distinguishing features" of his later accomplishments. Colebrooke's subsequent service near the holy city of Benares afforded him an unusual opportunity to study at first hand the Sanskrit language and Sanskritic culture.

By 1794, his scholarly reputation in India was so generally acknowledged that he was chosen the logical successor to William Jones, who had died earlier that year. The scholarly reputation that Colebrooke continually reinforced by original research and brilliant articles not only won him laurels in Europe but contributed directly to his later career in Calcutta (1800-15), where he served in the highest offices of the state.

If officials such as Colebrooke, Wilkins, and Jones developed into great scholars as a result of the new Hastings spirit, it must be added that most of the other Orientalists proved mediocre scholars but outstanding civil servants. The pioneering achievements of a few men and the erudite aura of the Asiatic Society of Bengal have contributed to the mistaken impression that British Orientalism was made up of professorial individuals who spent most of their time on research and publication.

Jonathan Duncan, for example—for whom, unlike Colebrooke, no German ever thought of erecting a statue—nevertheless was closer to the Hastings ideal of a civil servant than perhaps anyone else in his generation. Though he was an able translator of Bengali and Persian and author of shcolarly articles in the *Asiatick Researches,* his bent was far more administrative than intellectual. Like Charles Metcalfe in the next generation, he expressed his Orientalist love and knowledge of India in programmes of social improvement that were relevant to urgent popular needs.

Duncan's career in India, 1772-1811, almost perfectly typifies that of the transformed civil servant. The Hastings policy opened up the attractive alternative of a non-commercial public-service career, and Duncan grasped the opportunity. The stages in his development are familiar, linguistic proficiency, translation of official documents, close relationships with the Hindu literati, exploration of and an ever-deepening appreciation for Hinduism, and charter member of the Asiatic Society of Bengal.

Professionally, Duncan ran the gamut of elitist positions in the administration. From a writership and a minor judicial position, he worked his way up through the ranks of the Revenue Department. He was one of three or four key aides whom Cornwallis inherited from Hastings and whom he greatly depended upon throughout his tenure of office. Duncan served Cornwallis as Persian interpreter, Secretary of the Public and Revenue Departments, Resident of Benares and Commissioner of Territories Ceded by Tipu Sultan. In 1795 he was appointed Governor of Bombay, a post he held until his death in 1811.

Duncan always coupled his duty to the Company with his responsibility to the people under his jurisdiction. In 1789, he took steps to abolish infanticide among the Rajkumars, a local grouping of Rajputs. As Resident of Benares, he might have legislated the evil out of existence. Instead, he met with the chiefs and discussed with them from various standpoints the deliberate starvation of their children. He pointed out that, for example, this practice contravened the dictates of the Hindu scriptures. Knowing that female children were an economic drain on many families, he offered government compensation if the Rajputs would agree to end the practice. In June of that year, the Rajkumars, apparently without coercion on the part of the government, complied with Duncan's wishes and put an end to infanticide.

In the Hastings manner, Duncan followed a consistent policy of encouraging the revitalization of Hindu learning and philosophy. While still at Benares, he proposed to his superiors in 1791 that a "Hindu College" be established "for the preservation and cultivation of the Laws, Literature and Religion of that Nation at this Centre of their Faith." In support of his proposal, Duncan pointed out that this institution, unlike the many smaller seminaries in Benares, would be a "public university" offering the Hindus a totally new concept of research and education. It would be both a centre for correcting existing texts and a "precious library of the most ancient and valuable learning and tradition." Finally it would prove "a Nursery of future Doctors and Expounders of the Law to assist European judges in...regular and uniform administration...."

While Duncan typified the ideal Orientalized civil servant and Colebrooke was one of the finest Oriental scholars produced in the same milieu, many of the Company employees who lacked the integrity of the one and the intellect of the other achieved a compromise between the values of the Clive generation and those of the new administration. At the same time that Duncan won approval for the Sanskrit university to be established in British India, another Scotsman, destined for Orientalist fame as a scholar of Hindustani language and literature, was engaged in some shady indigo operations in the vicinity of Benares.

This Scotsman, John B.Gilchrist represented a group of Company-recruited surgeons who subsequently established favourable reputations for themselves as skilled linguists. William Hunter, John Leyden, and H.H.Wilson also arrived in India as doctors and left as reputed philologists. Gilchrist was a shrewd man who seems to have turned to translation work as a means of augmenting his income after other means had failed. We first find him in Benares in 1787 buying land illegally for the cultivation of indigo. In 1793 Gilchrist had actually organized an army which went into combat against other Europeans also hoping to cultivate indigo in the same area. A year later he came to Calcutta and must have observed the opportunities beginning to open for anyone who was proficient in the Urdu language.

Whatever their intent upon arriving in India, whatever their motivation in mastering Indian languages and then translating them for profit, the first generation of Orientalists left India with a tradition of public service and cultural empathy which for the most part was lacking in the generation they replaced. More important, perhaps, the Hastings-inspired amateur scholars brought into being a new concept of the Hindu golden age as a legacy for the rising Indian intelligentsia.

The combination of a transplanted elite transformed on Indian soil and their eighteenth-century background helps to explain both the institutional genesis of the Asiatic Society and the nature of its intellectual values. The Asiatic Society was not properly the conception of any one man, be it Hastings or Jones, but the expression of a collective need. After a decade of studying facets of Hindu and Muslim civilization in India, the Hastings generation now required a more formal organization.

The Asiatic Society of Bengal was, until the nineteenth century, an association for an elite of Company officials in the Calcutta area meeting irregularly either in the Supreme court building or in private homes. Though the general membership had been well over 100 since 1790, the active core of members attending meetings was rather naturally limited to a small group of administrative and judicial figures stationed in Calcutta.

Apparently, the original intention of Society members was not so much to publish their findings as to make available English translations of Oriental classics. William Jones, their first president, contemplated the publication of one volume every year in a series to be entitled "Asiatick Miscellany". Unfortunately, lack of funds compelled him to abandon the scheme and instead he sought a publisher for the papers read at each meeting. In 1788, Manuel Cantopher agreed to publish the papers—on the condition that every Society member promise to buy each volume at 20 rupees per copy. The resulting journal, *Asiatick Researches,* was eagerly read by European scholars, who welcomed the first fruits of original research in India. Five volumes of the *Researches* were published by 1797 and one pirated edition appeared in Europe in 1798.

For William Jones, the most outstanding intellect in the Asiatic Society until his death in 1794, the decision to subordinate translation work to scholarship proved a turning point in his life. It was not his translation of *Sakuntala*, however well received, that established him as the great seminal figure of the Orientalist movement but rather his varied research, his brilliant analysis, and his broad, deeply suggestive generalizations on Asian antiquity. The papers that he read at Society seminars in the form of discourses were re-written for the edification of European scholars who conscientiously scanned the pages of the *Researches*. So anxious was Jones to integrate every finding into elaborate conceptual schemes that he reminded Max Mueller "of the dashing and impatient general who tries to take every fortress by bombardment and storm."

As soon as Jones reached Calcutta in 1783, he immediately concentrated upon applying his eighteenth-century ideals to an alien environment. His own vision of an Asiatic Society proved to be, as Garland Cannon has aptly pointed out, the crystallization of a new ideology of cultural encounter between Asia and the West. In Cannon's words: If it [the Asiatic Society] could stimulate Europeans to intellectual endeavour in regard to Asian culture, it would not just help prevent their indulgence in vice-ridden cities—a strong temptation against which Benjamin Franklin had warned Jones—but it would be promoting understanding between peoples, a condition necessary for a successful rule of the vast sub-continent.

In contrast to the Orientalism of the nineteenth century with its romanticist view of cultural diversity, the scholarship of Jones was universalist and rationalist. In his first presidential address to the Asiatic Society, Jones clearly stated that his "inquiry into the History, Civil and Natural, the Antiquities, Arts, Sciences and Literature of Asia" was a means to the end of discovering truths about "Man and Nature". Asian knowledge would add a new dimension to our understanding of human learning. Human learning, or knowledge, which was for Jones the true concern of the Asiatic Society, he divided into three parts: "History, Science and Art." In his own words:

> The first [history] comprehends either an account of natural productions, or the genuine records of empires and states; the second [science] embraces the whole circle of pure and mixed mathematics together with ethicks and law, as far as they depend on the reasoning faculty; the third [art] includes all the beauties of imagery and the chorus of invention, displayed in modulated language, or represented by colour, figure or sound.

William Jones was the man who, in 1786, may have been the first seriously to consider that India's golden period as a culture lay in a remote, unchartered period in world history. Moreover, this view was propounded in the very same discourse that outlined his remarkable rediscovery of a common source of the languages of the Indo-European peoples. Both these intellectual achievements were the work of a universalist who sought to explain cultural unity through common origins. In the following oft-quoted passage, Jones gives his reasons for maintaining that Sanskrit was the fountainhead of many languages:

> The Sanskrit language, whatever be its antiquity, is of a wonderful structure, more perfect than the Greek, more copious than the Latin, and more exquisitely refined than either, yet bearing to both of them a stronger affinity both in the roots of verbs and in the form of grammar, than could possibly have been produced by accident...there is a similar reason, though not quite so forcible, for supposing that both the Gothick and the Celtick, though blended with a very different idiom, had the same origin with the Sanskrit; and the old Persian might be added to the same family....

Indeed, what Jones actually accomplished, and which would have important repercussions in later generations, was that by linking Sanskrit, the language of the ancient Hindus, to the European language family he related Hindu civilization to that of Europe and reanimated the resplendent Hindu past. Jones responded in the same way to Indian philosophy. In contrast to the bias of German scholars who increasingly viewed the *Vedanta* as a unique manifestation of the "Aryan genius," Jones reacted to it by stressing similarities between it and other comparable works of philosophy. It was not possible for him, for example, "to read the Vedanta or the many fine compositions in illustration of it, without believing that Pythagoras and Plato derived their sublime theories from the same fountain with the sages of India."

In the 1786 discourse Jones admitted that, in the absence of authentic historical knowledge, his observations concerning the Indo-European period were impressionistic. His intellectual curiosity was whetted by extant fragments of a civilization which he understood incompletely. Bits and pieces of Sanskrit language and literature, the six schools of Indian philosophy, the Laws of Manu, the religious myths and symbols, and the varied sculptural and architectural remains all testified to a "people with a fertile and inventive genius." But these people had since then substituted astrological calculations for a viable chronological scheme and had buried their history in "a cloud of fables." For Jones, one thing seemed certain: "....how degenerate and abased so ever the Hindus may now appear, that in some early age they were splendid in arts and arms, happy in government; wise in legislation, and eminent in various knowledge...."

If Jones is to be remembered for those sweeping but none the less intuitively correct generalizations which portrayed a grandiose Indo-European world, H.T.Colebrooke should be recalled for his specialized interests and incisive monographic studies on Vedic India. Max Mueller, who admired Colebrooke far more than Jones, believed that "few scholars were able to go beyond Colebrooke." Whereas "Sir William explored a few fields," Mueller wrote, Colebrooke tackled "the really difficult works, the grammatical treatises and the commentaries, the philosophic systems, and before all, the immense literature of the Vedic period."

In his treatment of universal history Colebrooke, like Jones, displayed a typical intellect of the eighteenth century. Colebrooke viewed history not as a chronicle of political events but as a record depicting the growth of civilizations. In the tradition of Voltaire, he once said before the Royal Asiatic Society:

I do not refer merely to the succession of political struggles, national conflicts, and warlike achievements; but rather to less conspicuous, yet more important occurrences, which directly concern the structure of society, the civil institutions of nations. Their internal, more than their external relations, and the yet less prominent, but more momentous events which affect society universally, and advance it in the scale of civilized life.

Colebrooke also expressed the familiar argument of the eighteenth century in behalf of a liberal spirit between cultures. The West, he stated, "owes a debt of gratitude" to the civilizations of Asia for their contributions in the arts and science. In fact, "civilization had its origin in Asia." Now, whereas the West was taking large strides forward, Asia was in a state of decline. The way to help Asians, the Orientalist Colebrooke recommended, was to "investigate" the history of their cultures "with the hope of facilitating ameliorations of which they may be found susceptible."

Though Colebrooke held out hope for a rebirth of a declining East, his fascination with the rediscovery of a Hindu age of splendor drew him closer and closer to Gibbon's form of classicism. Far more than Jones, Colebrooke concentrated his research upon Vedic India, and by the end of his career, he had devised a new composite image of the Indo-Aryan period as an age of gold. As with Max Mueller, who continued Colebrooke's work, each discovery or rediscovery of Vedic India was dramatically and metaphorically contrasted with the peculiarities of contemporary Hindu society. It was Colebrooke, for example, approximately twenty years before Ram Mohan Roy's first tract on *sati,* who demonstrated from textual sources that the voluntary immolation of widows in Bengal was a departure from the authentic tradition. It was Colebrooke who first sought the historical origins of the Indian caste system and discovered the many discrepancies between ancient textual requirements and actual contemporary practices.

It was not until Colebrooke was brought to Calcutta by Governor-general Wellesley to be professor of Sanskrit at the College of Fort William (1800), that he was able to study the *Vedas* seriously for the first time. He used the college library to piece together the Vedic fragments which had been collected by Jones, Halhed, Martine, and Chambers. He collated their manuscripts with his own (which he had brought from Benares) and five years later published his results in the famous "Essay on the Vedas, or Sacred Writings of the Hindus." Though he never translated the *Vedas,* an arduous task performed by Max Mueller fifty years later, he did analyze their general contents, and placed them historically as dating prior to the age of the Puranas.

The significance of Colebrooke's "Essay on the Vedas," especially in the light of the later history of the *Brahmo Samaj,* was his discovery of "the unity of the Godhead," or a monotheistic tradition, in ancient India. In an earlier article he had already argued that the existence of polytheism and idolatry in present-day India suggested to him that "modern Hindus seem to misunderstand their numerous texts." In 1805 Colebrooke stated emphatically of the *Vedas* that "Most of what is there taught, is now obsolete; and in its stead new orders of religious devotees have been instituted; and new forms of religious ceremonies have been established. Rituals founded in the Puranas and observances borrowed from a *worse* source, the *Tantras,* have in great measure...[replaced] the Vedas."

The Jones-Colebrooke portrayal of the Vedic age to which a Mueller would add the finishing touches, and which today is widely accepted, depicted a people believed to have behaved very differently from present-day Hindus. It was the first reconstructed golden age of the Indian renaissance. The new view romanticized the virtues of the Aryan inhabitants of north India in the second millennium B.C. Instead of being introspective and other-worldly, the Aryans were thought to have been outgoing and non-mystical. They were pictured as a robust, beef-eating, socially equalitarian society. Instead of Oriental despotism, scholars discerned tribal republics. There were apparently no laws or customs to compel a widow to commit *sati*. There were no temples, and there was not the slightest evidence to suggest that Aryans concretized idolatrous images of their gods. And to round out the picture, also absent were the fertility goddesses, the evil personification of Kali, and the rites and rituals of later Tantrism.

In the first decade of the 1800's the work of the Orientalists seems to have been well received by the literate English public. The men of the Asiatic Society were not infrequently likened to the Italian humanists. They were regularly praised in the press for their gift of a new renaissance in the East. In one popular poem of the period, Hastings was wreathed as "father of India... saviour of the East," and on Wilkins was bestowed the double distinction of "Sanskritist" and the patient scholar "who gave to Asia typographic art." Jones was accorded the greatest honor of all: he was credited with restoring India to her rightful place among the civilizations of the world by rediscovering her golden age of arts and letters....

4

By the middle of the nineteenth century, convinced that they had mastered India's past, the British set out to press it into the service of the Raj. One central arena in which this took place was that of architecture, for the buildings erected by the British not only provided shelter but made visible their conception of empire. This selection shows how, rejecting the classical forms that had earlier defined a European past for the Raj, the British after 1860 turned to the forms of what they called "Indo-Saracenic" architecture to create a secure past for themselves in India.

Architecture and the Representation of Empire: India, 1860-1910

THOMAS R. METCALF

Speaking before the Society of Arts in 1873 on architectural art in India, T. Roger Smith, recently returned from Bombay, concluded his discussion by urging that

> as our administration exhibits European justice, order, law, energy, and honour—and that in no hesitating or feeble way—so our buildings ought to hold up a high standard of European art. They ought to be European both as a rallying point for ourselves, and as raising a distinctive symbol of our presence to be beheld with respect and even with admiration by the natives of the country.

No sooner had Smith taken his seat than William Emerson, who had just completed a design in an Indic style for a college in Allahabad, rose to dissent. The British, he maintained, should not carry into India a new style of architecture, but rather should follow the example of those whom they had supplanted as rulers, the Muslims, who "seized upon the art indigenous to the countries conquered, adapting it to suit their own needs and ideas". Indeed, he insisted, "it was impossible for the architecture of the west to be suitable to the natives of the east."

A debate was thus joined that was to rage unabated for over fifty years: whether in their building in India the British ought to look to their own, or to India's architectural traditions. The choice between styles did not reflect solely aesthetic concerns. As with the contest between Classical and Gothic in Britain, such decisions involved as well larger conceptions of national identity and purpose. Indeed, by providing a vocabulary for the consideration of those questions, the architectural debates themselves shaped and defined Britain's conception of its national purpose. In the colonial environment the bricks and mortar carried with them especially far-reaching significance. The choice of styles, the arrangement of space within a building, and of course the decision by the government to erect a particular monument, all testified as both Smith and Emerson were aware, to a vision of empire. Sometimes these conceptions moved the architect in the design of a building; at others they lay embedded beneath the surface. In either case the varied ways empire was represented in these buildings help us to understand the assumptions that shaped Britain's imperial enterprise. This paper is an examination of the meaning and implications of the use of Indian architectural styles by the British Raj.

Regardless of their commitment to a particular style, all architects who worked in the Empire shared a measure of common ground that set off their work from that at home. Most central was a concern with political effect. The classically-educated Briton, as he built his empire, invariably conceived of himself as following in the footsteps of the ancient Romans. With its roads, its system of law, and its monumental structures spread across the face of the ancient world, Rome stood always as an exemplar to spur the British on in their own imperial enterprise.

Were the British occupation of India to terminate tomorrow, the visible tokens of it would survive in our canals, and our railways, our ports, and our public buildings, or, at least, the remains of them for centuries to come.

Those like Smith, who rejected the emulation of indigenous styles took from Rome a further specific architectural precedent:

They unquestionably not only cut their roads and pitched their camps in Roman fashion, but put up Roman buildings wherever they had occasion to build,....The Roman governor of a province in Gaul or Britain continued to be as intensely Roman in his exile as the British collector remains British to the backbone in the heart of India.

But British builders in the Empire sought as well to take into account what they saw as the special demands that the climate, and with it the colonial style of life, imposed on architecture. As a result, all agreed that successful colonial building involved the incorporation or adaptation of some elements of indigenous design. For their private residences the colonial British adopted the single-storeyed bungalow, with pitched roof and expansive veranda, set in a spacious compound ringed with servants' quarters. This arrangement of space substantially altered the nature of the indigenous bungalow, but it at once secured the ventilation the English required in a hot climate and marked out their separateness as a colonial elite.

In public and monumental structures a number of indigenous structural features were regarded as essential for comfort. Even Smith, though he sought precedents for most of them in the "sunshiny regions" of Europe, could list what was required: walls of ample thickness to ward off the heat, an absence of vertical features such as buttresses that might interrupt the flow of air, a "constant preference" for horizontal cornices to cast shade, "frequent and ample" openings, piers and columns "frequent and numerous", a "constant use" of balconies and corbelled projections, roofs "sometimes flat, sometimes domical", and above all "an ample space allowed the whole building and its surroundings". Colonial architecture in sum, no matter of what elements particular buildings were constructed, remained always distinct. Neither European nor Indian, it made tangible, and helped define, the uniquely colonial culture of which it was part.

During the first decades of their rule in India, following the victories at Plassey (1757) and Buxar (1763), the British gave little thought to architecture. For the most part they were engaged in extending and consolidating their hold over the subcontinent, a task not completed until the mid-nineteenth century. Nor was the commercially-minded East India Company, ruler of Britain's eastern possessions, eager to expend its profits on what they regarded as the needless extravagance of showy buildings. Hence the presidency capitals of Madras, Bombay, and Calcutta were alone during the early years of British rule adorned with buildings of some architectural distinction. Each had at its core a massive fort, the seat of colonial government for the city and its hinterland; arrayed outside its ramparts were mercantile offices, civic buildings, churches, clubs, official residences and other structures required by the colonial elite.

In their architectural style these buildings transplanted contemporary European forms to Indian soil. Cities founded as trading outposts, and subsequently developed as centres of European commerce and government, the presidency capitals, with their substantial white populations and British forms of local self-government, to some degree were regarded as extensions of Europe in Asia, and their architecture inevitably reflected this conception. In Madras and Calcutta, which experienced sustained growth from the later decades of the eighteenth century onward, the predominant architectural motif was Classical. Madras buildings ranged in style from the Wren-inspired Renaissance of Fort St. George (c.1760) to the Greek revivalism of the Banqueting Hall (1802) and Collectorate (1817), while in Calcutta, proverbially a city of gleaming white "palaces", Wellesley's baroque Government House (1802) was surrounded by such classically proportioned structures as the Doric Town Hall (1813) and Metcalfe Hall (1840). By the time the western capital of Bombay had spurted to wealth and prosperity—in the middle decades of the nineteenth century—Gothic had triumphed in England's "battle of the styles". Hence Bombay's major civic structures were clothed in Gothic forms. Indeed so totally is Bombay's architecture a product of its mid-Victorian boom that the city retains to this day a distinctively Gothic appearance.

The colonial buildings of this era were not without political significance. As Sten Nilsson has pointed out, their Classical forms "began to contain forces that were not to be found in the prototypes; they stood as symbols of a conquering militarism and a culture and a race which considered themselves superior." Yet the demarcation of England's new role in Asia took the shape not of devising new architectural forms but rather of enhancing the impressiveness of the old. Lord Wellesley's Government House sought to project for the first time an image of British power: to make clear that India was now "to be ruled from a palace, not from a counting-house; with the ideas of a Prince, not with those of a retail dealer in muslins and indigo." But although it was an imposing structure with its stately central pile, curving wings, and ceremonial stairway, the building remained firmly rooted in the accepted conventions of the baroque idiom. It was no more than a grander version of the aristocratic country seat on which it had been modelled, Robert Adam's Kedleston Hall. In the days of the "Company Bahadur" up to mid-century, British buildings in India remains always, as Nilsson wrote of Calcutta and Madras, "projections of Greece and Rome".

In 1857 Britain's hold over India was shaken by a revolt, the so-called "Sepoy Mutiny", which, though originating in the armed forces, spread rapidly throughout northern India. The uprising was suppressed ruthlessly within little more than a year. Nevertheless the events of that year shattered British complacency. In 1858 the East India Company was abolished, and direct Crown rule instituted; at the time, determined to avoid any further challenge to their rule, the British undertook a more thorough and systematic governance of their vast Indian possessions. The white garrison was substantially increased, and a comprehensive network of railways was laid down. A central Public Works Department had already been established in 1854; a decade later consulting architects were appointed in each province, and the Government set on foot a building programme that spread new roads, irrigation canals, military cantonments, and civil stations across the face of India.

As the sinews of rule were strengthened, so too during these years did the British begin to formulate an ideology of empire. The construction of a conception of Britain as an imperial power, which lay at the heart of the late-century "new imperialism", first took shape in India in the 1860's and 1870's as the British grappled with the problem of post-Mutiny reconstruction. The capstone was Disraeli's proclamation in 1877 of Queen Victoria as Empress of India. Though subjected to much satirical criticism in an uncomprehending England, this act nevertheless at once defined, and inaugurated, Britain's self-conscious presentation of itself as an imperial power.

Effective imperial rule required not only troops and expressive symbols but knowledge. Throughout the late nineteenth century the British sought to comprehend, and thus to control, the colonial peoples and their past. In India this took the shape of such institutions as the Census (first taken on a nationwide basis in 1872), the Archeological Survey, and the production for each province of detailed gazetteers and ethnological surveys. In the process the range and character of India's architectural heritage became known in the West for the first time. Much of this was the work of James Fergusson (1808-1886). He began his studies, unsupported by government, in the 1830's while employed as an indigo merchant in Calcutta. In those days, as he told the Society of Arts in 1866, "the subject of Indian architecture had hardly been touched... No attempt had been made to classify them [India's buildings] and the vaguest possible ideas prevailed as to their age or relative antiquity." When he returned home in the early 1850's he found an unsympathetic public, "not then prepared for such works", and so for a time abandoned his enterprise. In the post-Mutiny years the more supportive climate of opinion, as the British sought a fuller understanding of their Indian subjects, gave Fergusson at last an audience, while the dissemination of photography during these same years helped make familiar India's novel architectural forms. Anyone, Fergusson wrote, "at a small expense may now make himself master of any branch of the subject." This self-confident sense of mastery informed above all Fergusson's own magisterial *History of Indian and Eastern Architecture,* first published in 1876, and for the subsequent half-century the final authority on the subject.

Britain's effort to grasp India was shaped by a search for those categories that would reveal the essential and enduring structure of its society. One such category was caste. A comprehensive but loose ordering of India's peoples based upon Hindu notions of purity and pollution, with countless local variations, caste was elaborated by the British into an intricate and rigid system of hierarchy, enforced by the courts and defined by the decennial censuses. Another, and for the British more central, marker of identity in India was religious affiliation. From the early days of British rule the entire population, apart from tiny scattered minorities, was fitted into two mutually exclusive, and comprehensive, categories: those of "Hindu" and "Muslim". In the process, as part of the larger transformation of India during the nineteenth century, localized identities in which religion was only one of many elements, and which itself took varied forms, gave way to membership of two all-embracing and India-wide communities.

British study of India's architecture at once reflected this colonial sociology and reinforced its hold. The "architecture indigenous to the soil" as Fergusson called it, that is, buildings erected in states with Hindu rulers, was labelled "Hindu," while the buldings of the Muslim dynasties that ruled between 1200 and 1800 A.D. were classed together as "Saracenic", a term for Islam derived from the European encounter with the Arabs of the early conquests. All scholars, and especially Fergusson whose work was devoted to its elaboration, recognized that India's architecture comprised a number of different styles corresponding to various "ethnological" and political divisions among its people; Fergusson himself counted thirteen distinct "Saracenic" styles. Yet it was accepted as a matter of course that "the division of the whole of India into two great classes—Hindoo and Saracenic—was undoubtedly happy and true". The insistence on the centrality of a religious identity, which took shape in fixed architectural styles, defined an India that was in effect an "Orientalist" construct: a timeless land of tradition bound-peoples for whom religion alone had meaning.

For the most part the British disdained the so-called "Hindu" style. Lord Napier, amateur student of architecture and Governor of Madras, in a speech in 1870 acknowledged that Hindu building "is imposing; it is even poetical...; yet, regarded both from a scientific and an aesthetic point of view, it is manifestly defective." The ruling feature of this style, he argued, was "the horizontal line: the wall or the column supports a beam, the beam supports a flat roof. When the building is lofty, the fabric ascends by successive horizontal stages, one succeeding another in diminishing proportions to the apex." Though such a structure might rise with a "certain measure of continuity and elegance", with its method of construction "ingeniously concealed" by decoration, still the inherent "mechanical deficiencies" of the style could always be discerned. Hence, Napier concluded, the Hindu style was "unavailable, under the present Government, for the purposes of the State, and ill-adapted for the common and public use of the collective people." It was alone suited to domestic building, where its princples of shade and seclusion fitted it ideally to social and climatic needs alike.

The arch and dome, the principal features of the "Saracenic" style were by contrast, in Napier's view, the "most beautiful, the most scientific, and the most economical" ways of covering large spaces. Saracenic forms were in consequence, he argued, as suitable for modern buildings—railway stations, theatres, galleries, and lecture halls—as for their traditional employment in mosques and tombs; and he even urged the Government of India to adopt this as its official architectural style. What made the Saracenic as a style so much more appealing? Part of the answer no doubt lies in its engineering, which managed stresses so as to avoid the "vast application of material in its most weighty and expensive form" that the horizontal style demanded. But most important surely was the association of the arch and dome with early Christendom, with the Roman and Byzantine empires, and with Renaissance notions of ideal beauty. Moreover, as the style associated with the Indian empire the British had themselves recently dispossessed, that the Mughals, its use would enhance their own sense of power and majesty. Of the indigenous styles the Islamic was, simply, the most suited for the representation of empire.

Lord Napier himself inaugurated the new era by employing R.F. Chisholm (1839-1915), the Government Architect, to design a building in the "Mussulman style" for the Madras Board of Revenue. With this design, Napier proudly proclaimed, Chisholm "has paid the first tribute to the genius of the past; he has set the first example of a revival in native art, which, I hope, will not remain unappreciated and unfruitful." Chisholm too saw his role as that of advocate for a new architecture. He told the Madras University Senate in 1869.

We have arrived at a most important period in the history of architecture in this country, and it will be decided in the course of the next five or ten years whether we are to have a style suited to the requirements of this country, or whether we are to be the mere copyists of every bubble which breaks on the surface of European art, and import our architecture, with our beer and our hats, by every mail-steamer which leaves the shores of England.

But the "Saracenic" style did not win any easy or an immediate public acceptance, nor were its elements elaborated without extended experimentation. Chisholm proposed to inaugurate the new era by establishing a professorship in architecture at the Madras University; the scheme was rejected by a unanimous vote of the Senate. Just a few years before, in 1860, Madras had celebrated its escape from the Mutiny by a Memorial Hall executed in a pure Greek style. This building was to be the last classically designed structure in Madras, and marked as well the end of the era of unselfconscious "projection" of European styles on to Indian soil. Yet its erection testified to the strength of established convention. Indeed the bulk of Chisholm's own building during the first decade in Madras owed little to Indic influence. He had initially been drawn to the city in 1864 from the Bengal Public Works Department by the announcement of a competition for new buildings for the Presidency College. His design not only won Chisholm the commission, but a prize of Rs. 3,000 and a permanent appointment as Consulting Architect to the Madras Government. The style was, however, "pure Italian" derived from Renaissance classicism. His design a few years later for the Senate House of the University, extravagantly idiosyncratic with a huge raised hall, was described as one that "leans to the Byzantine". Clearly, in his early work, apart from the Revenue Board building, which was in any case modelled on the existing "Saracenic"-styled Chepauk Palace of the Nawabs of the Carnatic, Chisholm moved but slowly toward his goal of developing a style "suited to the requirements of this country".

Yet these early buildings were not wholly unrelated to his larger concern. Though he deprecated the Gothic style as "parched and shrivelled" in India, the Italian, if not the equal of indigenous styles "as regards suitability to the climate and to oriental scenery", was still "distinguished for lightness and elegance". In the same way, so-called "Byzantine" styles, with their "quasi-Oriental" character, represented an effort to devise some sort of compromise between the familiarity of the European and the strangeness of the Indian. Lord Napier had urged the use of Byzantine styles in India especially for those types of buildings, such as Christian churches, where Europeans would feel uncomfortable in Saracenic surroundings. The two styles, he wrote, "have ever retained a certain family likeness, and the common possession of the dome constitutes a capital point of union." Besides, as the "most venerable" of Christian styles, Byzantine could never be "repugnant" in an ecclesiastical structure.

While Chisholm was developing an Indic style for colonial building in Madras, architects elsewhere in India were moving toward the same objective. Of these perhaps the most prominent was Major C.Mant (1839-1881) of the Royal Engineers. Mant first made his mark on Indian architecture with two Gothic designs in the Bombay Presidency: a high school in Surat (1868), and a town hall in Kolhapur (1872). These structures were "adapted to the requirements of the climate" by such devices as arcaded verandas running along the entire length of the building, but they remained otherwise obstinately European. From 1872, however, until his death by suicide a decade later—he was distraught at the possibility that one of his structures might collapse—Mant devoted himself wholly to elaborating an Indic style. He was fortunate in winning the patronage of Sir Richard Temple, successively Governor of Bengal and of Bombay. One of the most powerful Indian officials of his day, Temple prided himself on his connoisseurship of India's ancient architecture, and "warmly appreciated" Mant's efforts to incorporate such designs into his own building. Through Temple's influence Mant secured from Government of India in 1875 a commission—for the Mayo College, Ajmer—that was to announce the coming of age of what was to be called "Indo-Saracenic" architecture.

The Mayo College had its origin in a scheme by Lord Mayo as viceroy of India (1869-1872) to educate the sons and relatives of the ruling princes of Rajputana (now Rajasthan) in an environment as closely as possible resembling that of an English boarding school. Only in a proper public school, Mayo's Foreign Secretary wrote, could the young chief escape the intrigues of the palace *zenana* (women's quarters), where much of his boyhood education took place, and the "fawning parasitism, inseparable in the East from rank and coming power". Under the instruction of an English staff, these desert rulers, now attached to the Raj as its loyal "feudatories", would learn not only English and mathematics but games and discipline. Educated as "ordinary gentlemen", they would, so the British conceived, on their return home be in a position to "revolutionize" their states. A governing body of ranking European officials and Indian princes was formed under the viceroy to oversee the operation of the college. The Indian Government took upon itself responsibility for constructing the central college building, for lectures and academic functions, while the major princes each agreed, over the objection of officials who would have preferred English-style mixed boarding, to build a residence for the boys from his state.

The question of the appropriate architectural style for the college building provoked a controversy that raged for five years, involved the submission of seven separate designs, and delayed the start of construction until 1878. Not surprisingly, this protracted debate brought into the open the conflicting sets of assumptions, hitherto barely visible, as to how the Empire ought best to be translated into stone; hence it is worth looking at in some detail. Three alternate conceptions—which may be called the Classical, the mixed "Hindoo-Saracenic", and the "pure" Hindu—shaped the debate. The Classical was Lord Mayo's original preference. In the summer of 1871 he asked J.Gordon, Executive Engineer for the college, to prepare a plan for a "plain but handsome Hall, with classrooms surrounding a pillared verandah". The princes, when belatedly consulted over a year later, gave their support too, for reasons we will discuss presently, to this "Grecian" design. In the meantime, however, Mayo had changed his mind. In December 1871 he requested Gordon to prepare a "Hindoo" design. Mayo acknowledged that a Classical design might be "superior in beauty essentially", but it was, he had now decided, "less appropriate" for a princely boarding school than a design based on "Hindoo models". Exactly what a Hindu design ought to consist of, however, or where appropriate "Hindoo models" were to be found., was by no means clear. Two opposing views soon emerged : one found its inspiration in the deserted eighteenth-century Jat capital of Dig, near Agra; the other in the architecture of the ancient Hindu temple. Each depended upon detailed historical research, and carried with it the assumption that the British had mastered, and so could turn to their own purposes, India's architectural heritage.

In Mayo's view the best "Hindoo models" were those of Dig, which he instructed Gordon to visit and sketch before drawing up his revised plan for the college. Gordon visited not only Dig, but the nearby Mughal capitals of Agra and Fatehpur Sikri, and six months later submitted a design in what he called "a modern Hindoo or Indian saracene style" of architecture. It was, he insisted, "not a mere copy" of any historic building, but a design that embodied the "spirit of the style suggested to me", and was at the same time suited to the "requirements of a College and to the present age". The "best authority" on Hindu architecture was, however, perhaps not surprisingly, judged to be the Director of the Archeological Survey, General Alexander Cunningham; and so Mayo submitted Gordon's design to him for an opinion.

The palace at Dig, Cunningham asserted, in opposition to Mayo, though the residence of a Hindu prince, was in its architectural style "purely Mahomedan", with "very little if any trace of the real Hindu architecture about it, either in its outlines or in its details". Hence Gordon's design belonged, with Dig, to the "common class of modern Mahomedan garden architecture". The British knew, or rather he, General Cunningham, knew, even if the Rajas of Dig did not, what Hindu architecture consisted of. Its most striking feature, pronounced the self-assured archaeologist, was a "rich profusion of ornament, not a mere surface scratching intended to take the place of mouldings, but delicately carved lines of foliage, which cover the mouldings themselves..." Cunningham then proceeded to alter Gordon's design by adding a pair of small closed turrets, canopied balconies supported on brackets, and two open cupolas in the upper parapet; at the same time he struck out "the plain hemispherical or round domes", which, he said, were "purely Mahomedan". Hindus, he admitted, among them the Rajas of Dig, did occasionally make use of similar domes. So also, he argued, with a stupendous leap, "do they make use of English shoes; but no one has yet ventured to call them Indian shoes because they have been partially adopted by the Hindoos." Hindu domes, he explained, were constructed by layers of overlapping stones and thus presented externally a series of horizontal lines or steps, "of which the Hindoo architect availed himself in ornament". For Cunningham clearly the categories of "Hindu" and "Muslim", in keeping with the conventions of colonial sociology, were mutually exclusive. To be properly Hindu a building had to conform to certain stylistic principles which the archaeologist, who had studied the whole of India's past, was most competent to delineate. Furthermore, older structures built before the time of Muslim rule were by virtue of that antiquity regarded as authentically "Hindu"; later buildings, such as those of eighteenth-century Dig, were by contrast inevitably debased.

The viceroy, by now Lord Northbrook, acknowledged that "on the question of what is, and what is not, purely Hindu in architucture" he could not question the opinion of "so high an authority as General Cunningham". Nevertheless, while anxious always "to secure a thoroughly Hindu feeling throughout the design", he sought as well to make the proposed structure consistent with "the style of architecture affected by the Rajpootana chiefs themselves"; and there was no doubt, as the Secretary to the Public Works Department pointed out, that "in modern times the Hindoos have borrowed very much from the beauties of the Mussalman architecture." Hence there was no necessary barrier to the use of a "mixed"style. For inspiration Northbrook turned at this point to the work of Major Mant, who had just completed in the high school at Kolhapur his first Indian design. In early 1873 the hapless Gordon was dismissed, and an assistant engineer, R. Joscelyne, instructed to adapt the Kolhapur design to the requirements of the Mayo College. Joscelyne's scheme, submitted in March 1874, was ultimately judged unsatisfactory, so early in 1875 Northbrook commissioned Mant to draft an original design of his own. Although the first was rejected as too costly, the revised draft, approved by the viceroy, was unveiled in January 1877 on the occasion of the first meeting of the Mayo College Committee. Construction commenced in January 1878, and the building was finally completed in 1885.

What does this extended controversy tell us about the way empire took shape in architecture? Why, in the first place, did the government choose the mixed "Saracenic" style over the "pure" Hindu or the European Classical? In support of his design Mant argued that the "fusion" of Hindu and Muslim architecture that had grown up in Rajasthan and elsewhere was "admirably suited" to the needs of modern building, met the exigencies imposed by the climate, and "harmonizes with the traditions of the people". But, sensitive to Cunningham's criticism, he insisted further that great care has been taken, in preparing this design, to use only such Mohammedan features and forms as the Hindus of Rajputana have themselves universally adopted, and in using them, to so subordinate them to Hindu feeling and treatment, and to so supplement them by purely Hindu forms and details, that the whole building may be almost literally described, as being an adaptation of modern Hindu domestic architecture, and therefore thoroughly suitable, as far as architectural style is concerned, for a College in which the sons of Rajput Chiefs and Nobles are to be educated.

No doubt to some degree, in rejecting a purely "Hindu" style, the Government recognized that the endeavour to enforce such a style could lead only to the arid scholasticism of a Cunningham. The Hindu religious faith, they had to admit, like all others, had never carried with it a commitment to any particular style of architecture. The Rajas of Dig were by no means exceptional in drawing upon varied elements, reflecting the fashion or "taste" of the times, for their buildings without regard to the religious convictions of those who might first have used them. To have insisted upon the use of only "Hindu forms" would have been to be more Hindu than the Hindus. "Pure" Hindu architecture too, as Mant and others before him argued, "from its massive construction and elaborate ornamentation" was "scarcely capable of satisfactory adaptation to modern requirements". Yet there was surely more to it than this. Lord Northbrook, in announcing his preference for Gordon's over Cunningham's design, said that he did so "as a matter of taste". However, more than simply aesthetic considerations were involved. Lacking the dome and the arch, and overwhelmed with ornamentation, so-called "Hindu" architecture did not convey an adequate sense of sovereignty and majesty, and hence was politically unsatisfactory. An architecture primarily of temples, and a people conquered by both Muslim and British alike, it had of necessity to remain confined to its traditional domestic and sacral purposes.

The Indo-Saracenic style by contrast ideally suited the needs of British colonialism. In it not only could the distinct "Hindu" and "Saracenic" forms be melded, but the British, self-proclaimed masters of India's culture, could in the process shape a harmony the Indians themselves, communally divided, could not achieve. Indo-Saracenic thus found its widest application in buildings meant for Indians, but where the content and meaning of the structure were defined by the colonial ruler and embodied British definitions   of appropriate behaviour. Mayo College obviously served precisely this function. Indeed, a college of Indo-Sarcenic design encapsulated in itself the assumptions, and contradictions, of colonialism: the structure defined for the Indians their past, while the curriculum—based on European learning—laid out for them their future. In similar fashion, several of the most spectular Indo-Saracenic buildings were museums, among them the Albert Hall in Jaipur, the Prince of Wales Museum in Bombay, and the Victoria Memorial Hall in Madras. As a museum by its very nature was a showcase of India's past as organized and classified by its colonial rulers, an Indo-Saracenic structure—whose architectural forms reflected precisely the same enterprise—was altogether appropriate.

But why did the British reject with so little hesitation, when it was the princes' own preference, the Classical design Mayo had first proposed? Certainly once Mayo had abandoned the "Grecian" design there was no looking back. In large measure this decision reflected the considerations that underlay Chisholm's original objective in the 1860s: to derive from India's indigenous traditions an architecture suited to the needs of the British Raj. But there were further specific reasons that impelled the British to insist upon an Indic design for the Mayo College. The college was after all meant for the use of the sons of the princes of Rajputana. These princes, though now incorporated as "feudatories" within the British imperial system, represented some of India's most ancient ruling dynasties, and hence in themselves personified that link with India's past that the British sought for their own Raj. Thus it was unthinkable to set down a Grecian temple for their use in the middle of the Rajasthan desert. The princes might wish to emulate the West, and to enhance their own self-esteem by surrounding themselves with the architectural styles of their rulers. One might even argue that, as the curriculum of the new school was to be Western in character, as for that matter was the whole concept of a boarding school, surely the buildings in their style ought to reflect this orientation. As we shall see, the architecture of the College was by no means devoid of Western symbolism. But precisely because the princes had by the later nineteenth century become in such large measure creatures of the colonial order, it was for the British all the more essential that these men define their rulership in terms derived from India's past, and mark out visibly in architecture their distinctive status.

Nor did the princes raise a protest. Their continuing position as rulers was dependent upon the support of their colonial overlord: as "protected" princes they could ill-afford to defy their master. Furthermore, in so far as the princes defined themselves as traditional rulers—and they had of course no other claim upon legitimacy—the clothing of structures meant for their use in a traditional Indian idiom could only enhance their kingly role. They were in the end confined by the assumptions which alone gave validity to their rule. Although given the freedom to build their boarding houses according to their own designs, the princes for the most part simply handed over the money to the College Executive Engineer, who was then left in charge of the design and construction. Although the various states' houses are by no means identical, none ventures far from the Indo-Saracenic idiom of the main college building.

As the "Hindu-Saracenic" (or "Indo-Saracenic") established itself as a recognized colonial building style, the British turned for inspiration and models to the medieval cities of northern India. Dig was lavishly praised. Fergusson described its buildings as surpassing all the Rajput palaces in "grandeur of conception and beauty of detail", while Sir Richard Temple called its buildings "unsurpassed on earth" for "tasteful ornamentation, gracefully refined". The finish of details within the boldness of outline, Temple wrote:

> the chiaroscuro produced by the shadows from the projecting eaves; the arrangement of arched windows and doorways; the exquisitely projecting balconies; the balanced proportion between the whole and the parts; the combination of straight lines, curves, and angles; the adaptation of the stone material to the climatic surroundings—render it quite a study in the art of producing beauty. A school of architectural design could not do better than send out a class of students to note and mark this structure.

The British found other attractive examples of what they regarded as "Hindu-Saracenic" building in the capitals of several of the lesser Islamic states, above all Gaur, Bijapur, and Ahmedabad, where vigorous independent building traditions had grown up; in the Rajput capitals, above all Amber and Jaipur, whose architecture joined indigenous and Mughal styles; and to some extent in pre-Mughal Delhi. About the high Mughal architecture of Agra and Delhi the British were ambivalent. From first to last the "peerless" quality of such structures as the Taj Mahal was never questioned—indeed Temple spoke of the Great Mughal as "the greates architectural genius that ever lived"— though some skeptics did wonder whether Italian artists had not taken a large role in the decoration of Agra's monuments. The British nevertheless regarded these stupendous buildings, with their marble facades and inlay of semi-preious stones, as too, "florid" and "showy"; perhaps too they did not wish to have their own work judged next to that of Shah Jahan. For the Europeanized post-Mughal buildings of Lucknow and Hyderabad, on the other hand, they had nothing but contempt. The pseudo-classicism decked out in tawdry stucco favoured by the Nawabs of Oudh was not the kind of compliment India's colonial rulers sought from their subjects.

In applying the term "Indo-Saracenic" to this wide array of historic buildings, the British were not defining a coherent era in the history of Indian architecture. Rather, by lumping these historic structures under a common label together with their own, the British endeavoured to lay claim to a direct line of descent from the Rajputs and Mughals to themselves. James Ransome, Consulting Architect to the Government of India, in 1905 discussed, without any sense of incongruity, the Mughal tomb of Salim Chishti at Fatehpur Sikri (c. 1580), and the Albert Museum at Jaipur (1876) as being representative samples of "Saracenic work". As a term for scholarly analysis, "Indo-Saracenic" has in recent years been increasingly jettisoned as too vague and inclusive, and it now has no place in academic discourse on India's architecture. Yet as an artifact of colonialism the term remains useful as a way of describing British building that sought to model itself upon, or sought inspiration from, these earlier structures.

The balance of stylic elements, and the sites from which models were selected, varied for each building, depending on the objectives and interests of the architect. By and large the more remote and inaccessible sites such as Gaur and Mandu rarely figured in British building. Simply too little was known about them. By contrast, the Mughal buildings of Delhi and Agra, visited annually by thousands and mapped in detail, provided a rich source of stylic elements, from copings and plinths to pillars and brackets. In the Mayo College design, as we have seen, Mant endeavoured to draw the bulk of his stylistic elements from Rajput building. The plan nevertheless found room for a wide array of design elements. It included, among others, plain and cusped arches drawn from later Mughal work, several so-called Bengali, or "drooping", *chattris* (porticoes) of the same period, small domed entrance porches, an overhanging *chajja* or eave of pre-Mughal style, cupolas of varied forms at the angles, and two octagonal minarets at the front terminating at the roof level in cupolas crowned by "the well known Hindu 'Sikra' domes". Above it all soared a clock tower 94 feet high. The "most prominent feature in the design", the clock tower, wrote Mant.

> has a richly moulded and slightly spreading base, and is taken up as a square to the height of 22 feet from the ground. From this point it is chambered to an octagonal shaft, which at the height of 58 feet, corbels out again to the square form...Above the cobelling bold stone brackets support a narrow projecting balcony, with perforated stone railings, above which rises the square clock chamber (with marble angle shafts), terminating in a richly corbelled cornice and crowned by an iron guilded dome of ornamental design, the sides of which, being pierced by open arcading, will allow the sound of the gongs of the clock... to be heard freely below.

Even that pre-eminent symbol of British technology, the clock, was cast in an Indo-Saracenic form.

The profusion of design elements in the completed structure makes it clear that Mant had made no attempt to be faithful to the style—the "taste"—of any particular period of India's past. Clearly, one of the attractions of Indo-Saracenic for the British builder was the freedom it afforded to "mix and match" elements of design. Chisholm himself had no doubts as to how to proceed. The architect, he said, "may choose the comparatively easy archaeological road, copying piecemeal and wholesale structures of the past, or he may endeavour to master that spirit which produced such works, and select, reject, and modify the forms to suit the altered conditions." India's architectural heritages were as colours on a palette. Reflecting the Orientalist conceptions of the times, they were at the deepest level similar and interchangeable. Once mastered, they were available for any purpose the colonial ruler considered appropriate; none needed to be taken seriously on its own terms.

One unifying feature of much Indo-Saracenic architecture was a search for the :"picturesque". The cult of the picturesque was also a feature of Victorian Britain, but in India, where the British lived surrounded by the "exotic" and unfamiliar, it was an almost invariable accompaniment of art that sought to take the environment into account. Much of the attraction of remote and ruined capitals was to be found in their "picturesque" situation. In the space of a few pages James Fergusson, in his *History of Indian and Eastern Architecture* praises the "fairy-like" setting amidst lakes and hills of princely palaces from Udaipur and Bundi to Orccha and Amber. They are, he said, "seldom designed with much reference to architectural symmetry, but are nevertheless always picturesque and generally most ornamental objects in the landscape where they are found." The search for the picturesque could sometimes lead to extraordinary, if not absurd, results. The Mayo college tower, Mant proudly announced, "has been purposely placed at an angle and out of the centre of the building to obtain a picturesque effect" and to take the place of a massive central feature such as a dome. The bureaucrats in the central secretariat were not impressed. The clock tower, wrote back the Public Works Secretary, "is not only not quite consistent with the rest of the building but also gives it a lopsided effect", and so should be eliminated. Undaunted, Mant insisted that to omit the tower "would make the design somewhat tame and commonplace in its grouping, and wanting in spirit and picturesqueness of character". In the end the Government gave way. The tower, one official noted, "certainly is inconsistent, but as the rest of the design is by no means a pure style, and is a resultant of the combination of two or more styles, I do not think the addition of another style in the tower is objectionable, rather it is advantageous, as marking a further transition and the commencement of a new era."

In what way does the Mayo College tower mark "the commencement of a new era"? Mant does not tell us, but the symbolic meaning of such a tower is clear enough. The clock tower, frequently attached to the Victorian town hall, was a common feature of the urban landscape of provincial Britain. Nor were towers wholly unknown in precolonial India. But for the most part, following the precedent of the Qutab Minar set up by the first Muslim conquerors of Delhi about 1200, they told of conquest, not the hours. From the 1860s onward the British erected clock towers, usually free-standing, in the major cities of northern India. Delhi obtained one some 110 feet high opposite the town hall in Chandni Chowk, at the expense of the municipality, as one of the first "improvements" in the city following the devastation of the 1857 mutiny. In Lucknow the British induced the trustees of the Huseinabad Endowment, a Shia charitable body established by the rulers of Oudh, to meet the cost of a soaring tower some 221 feet in height adjacent to the burial ground of Nawab Mohammed Ali Shah. Set down in the two centres of the 1857 revolt, these structures can hardly be regarded as other than latter-day Qutab Minars, to mark out the presence of a new conqueror in the land. Lesser towers in cities like Ludhiana and elsewhere no doubt made the same point. Colleges were especially favoured with towers. Sometimes these reflected the munificence of large donors, like the Maharaja of Vizianagram, whose gift of £10,000 was commemorated with a 200-foot tall bell tower at Muir College, Allahabad. But political symbolism was surely never distant. It takes little imagination to see in the open iron dome which caps the Mayo College tower a symbolic representation of the British Crown: the Raj triumphant! The clock itself already had a symbolic significance as an element of "the new era". The British had always railed against the laziness and lethargy of their Indian subjects. With its hourly chiming gongs, the clock helped to remind the students and passersby not only of the supremacy of the Raj but of the virtues of punctuality. The modern world in India, as it had been for the peasant-become-factory-worker in Britain a half-century before, was to be marked by discipline and orderliness.

The crown surmounting the Mayo College was distinctive in yet another way; it was made of iron forged in a British foundry. The "new era"—and of this the British were in no doubt—was to be scientific and technological. Its "skin" might be of an ornate Indic design in marble, but the interior structure of the Mayo College incorporated the latest technology. In the roofs, Mant wrote:

> full advantage has been taken of the capabilities of cement concrete, which is to be used in flat slabs not exceedig twelve feet in span; spans of this size obtained by throwing arches across the rooms, where possible... and elsewhere (as in the main entrance porch and lecture hall) by provision of iron girders..

This unity of "European science" and "native art" was central to the conception of Indo-Saracenic architecture. Sir Richard Temple, in his eulogy of Mant, put the matter concisely. You may ask, he said,

> why, if the native architecture is so extremely good we should not follow it absolutely—follow it pure and simple—in our Anglo-Indian structures. Well, gentlemen, there is this particular reason: If you are to construct buildings which are perfect in respect of utility and convenience, then you must call in the aid of European science... [Mant's distinguishing merit] was this: that whereas some of his architectural and artistic predecessors transplaced European styles bodily into India... he tried instead to hit on some

style which should unite the usefulness of the scientific European designs together with the beauty, taste, grandeur and sublimity of the native style; and this style he called the Hindu-Saracenic.

Once the style had been elaborated, the question remained: how widely ought Indo-Saracenic to be used, and for what kinds of structures was it appropriate? The Public Works Member of the Viceroy's Council in 1877 wrote:

> There can be little doubt that buildings for native purposes, such as the following should be built in some style of native architecture: temples, mosques, palaces, colleges, schools, markets, hospitals, asylums; whilst those specially for the comfort and wants of Europeans, such as residence, churches, offices, railway buildings, etc., are more appropriate for some European style adapted to the various climates of India.

But the matter was not so simple as that. As a colonial regime the British had no intention of constructing mosques or temples. As we have seen, schools and colleges, with museums, were ideally suited for Indo-Saracenic architecture, and were commonly constructed in it. As the style became accepted in the later nineteenth century, public buildings meant for the joint use of Britons and Indians, including banks, railway stations, and even some government office blocks, were also frequently clothed in Indo-Saracenic forms. This was most strikingly the case in Madras. Here the influence first of R.F.Chisholm, and then of Henry Irwin, as Consulting Architects to the Government, was decisive in raising an array of imposing Indo-Saracenic buildings that dominate the Madras skyline to the present day. Among these are such diverse structures as the State Bank, the Law Courts and adjacent Law College, the Victoria Technical Institute, and the Egmore Railway Station. The Law Courts along the strand, capped by a tower used as a lighthouse, were designed by Irwin on the pattern of Chisholm's Revenue Board buildings. Like its predecessor, though on a much larger scale, the Law Court design incorporated arches extending from floor to ceiling; these "were borrowed from the designs of the Pathan buildings of the fifteenth century, where they were used in domed mosques, and were intended to throw light into the highest recesses of the domes, and shew their beautiful ornaments". The Egmore Station, designed a decade later in 1902, boasted a "Mogul style of architecture" with "intricate stone carving, fantastic shaped brackets, drip stones, and rich friezes that at once attract the attention of any observer to the excellence of the structure from an architectural point of view."

In buildings meant primarily for European use, especially in port cities such as Bombay where European forms continued in favour, Indo-Saracenic decorative motifs were frequently added to basically Gothic structures. Such a melded architecture reassured the public with its familiar forms while introducing a touch of the "exotic". F.W.Steven's stupendous Victoria Railway Terminal, for instance, and the Bombay, Baroda, and Central Indian Railway offices, though wholly Gothic in style, were decorated with Indic carving and details, carried out by students of the Bombay School of Art, that lent the structures a vaguely "Oriental feeling". But Bombay remained wedded to its Gothicized forms. Even though Chisholm in 1888 won the first prize in an open competition for new Bombay Municipal Offices, his Indo-Saracenic design was shelved, and the commission awarded to the trusted local builder F.W. Stevens.

Gothic and Indo-Sacrenic could also be joined in larger, if idiosyncratic conceptions, for the arches and ornamentation the two shared made them to some degree compatible. Perhaps the most notable mixture of the two, which made its author's reputation as an architect, was William Emerson's Muir College, Allahabad. In part in order to accommodate a large bell tower, Emerson

> determined not to follow too closely Indian art, but to avail myself of an Egyptian phase of Moslem architecture, and work it up with the Indian Saracenic style of Beejapore and the north-west, combining the whole in a western Gothic design. The beautiful lines of the Taj Mahal influenced me in my dome over the hall, and the Indian four-centred arch suggested itself as convenient for my purpose, as working in well with the general Gothic feeling.

He futher blended "Gothic tracery" with Indian geometrical perforated stone work, Gothic shafts and caps with Indian arches, and set his domes on "Gothicized Mohammedan pendentives and semi-circular arches".

The building of churches in an Indo-Saracenic style posed especially intractable problems. Like other public buildings of the same era, Indian churches in the late eighteenth and early nineteenth centuries followed contemporary English Georgian styles. The British modelled their Indian churches above all upon St. Martins in the Field, Trafalgar Square, for this church with its soaring tower not only was located at the heart of the Empire, but detailed published plans of the structure existed for the guidance of overseas engineer builders. By the 1840's, under the influence of Pugin and the "ecclesiologists", Gothic had become accepted in India as in England as the appropriate style for church architecture. Even in Calcutta, with its wholly Classical facade, the cathedral (1847) was put up in a Gothic style. In time the conventions that governed church architecture became so rigid that it was inconceivable to build an ecclesiastical structure in other than a Gothic style. Emerson's cathedral in Allahabad, though barely half a mile from Muir College, was strictly Gothic. Indeed, far from modelling the cathedral on the College, Emerson found in the proximity of the cathedral reason for refraining from "a rigorous adherence to the Saracenic style" in the college design. Likewise, the renowned Indo-Saracenic architect Swinton Jacob, while constructing the elaborate Albert Hall in Jaipur, put up the city's Anglican church in a severe early English style. The church, he wrote, must be "in keeping with a style with which all our feelings of devotion are associated". The only modifications he would allow were those dictated by a concern for climate: a high nave with clerestory windows protected by projecting sunshades to increase ventilation without heat and glare; and a flat ceiling with hooks to which a row of punkahs (fans) could be attached.

Any attempt to introduce Indo-Saracenic elements into a church structure at once provoked a fury of controversy. Mathura, a small north Indian district town adjacent to the sacred Hindu shrine of Brindaban, was graced, after its consecration in 1856, by an airy and elegant Anglican church in Italianate style for the use of the garrison. However, there was no Catholic church; this the Catholic officer in charge of the district in the 1870's, F.S.Growse, determined to set right. An enthusiast for Indian arts and crafts, Growse designed the ground plan and general proportions "in accordance with ordinary Gothic precedent", but then set out to make the rest of the church "purely Oriental in design". The carving in the doorways, the tracery in the windows, the kiosks set on the sides of the dome, all were "specimens of native art". He had futher intended, he wrote, to model the dome itself on the *shikara*, or spire, of a Hindu temple at Brindaban. Fearing opposition, however, Growse "altered it into a dome of the Russian type, which also is distinctly of Eastern origin and therefore so far in keeping with the rest of the building." As every compromise must, he sighed, "it fails of being entirely satisfactory."

Similar attempts at an Indo-Saracenic Christian architecture elsewhere fared little better. The building of the Madras Y.M.C.A. in a style consistent with the adjacent law courts provoked an outraged correspondent to ask *Indian Engineering* why "the authorities of this Christian Institute have ordered their architect to design this building in Heathen Architecture? It may have been so designed on the same principle that the Teetotal Preacher has a drunken man beside him, to emphasize the hideousness of the crime." Surely, the writer went on, echoing Napier's recommendation of some thirty years before, "there are plenty of Oriental Christian edifices, in and around Armenia, of Byzantine Oriental type which would have carried out that great and first principle of Architecture, I mean 'Fitness', better than the absurd caricature it now presents." When a storm of criticism broke around the Cambridge Mission for putting up their Delhi college in a "Mughal" style, the principal defended his decision by an appeal to the universal character of the Christian faith:

> I should have thought that it was somewhat late in the day for anyone to argue that a Christian College must necessarily be designed in some style of architecture already consecrated, so to say, to Christian use... [He could conceive] no nobler task for the Christian architect in this country than after patient sympathetic and accurate study of the best periods of Indian architecture, both Hindu and Mahomedan, to endeavour to fashion out of the models he has studied, new forms, not slavishly imitative of the old, but adapted to meet the needs of Christian worship and life.

At no time, even as a secular form, was Indo-Saracenic exempt from criticism. Always there were those who argued, with Roger Smith, that the British ought "proudly and truthfully [to] mark our sojourn in this country" with "an indelible history in brick and stone of the Anglo-Saxon rule," and not make "the noble art of architecture a living lie by affecting foreign styles". At home there was always grumbling at the Indian Government's commitment to the strange and unfamiliar Indo-Saracenic. *The Builder*, though upset at Chisholm's unfair treatment in the Bombay municipal competition, nevertheless found it difficult to share his—and Fergusson's—enthusiasms. The editors wrote in a leading article:

> You may learn to like anything if you try hard enough. Fergusson made Indian architecture his speciality, and managed to work himself up into an enthusiasm (not always communicated to his

readers) even over things that are like the architecture of nightmare, without form, proportion, or logic.

Of Indian buildings only the Taj Mahal was "marked by a purity of line and balance of proportion which may really be called quite Greek". They expressed their preference for a European style adapted to suit the climate and conditions of India, and lamented that British India's cities were still "much in want of their Norman Shaw".

Only a very few critics perceived that Indo-Saracenic was fundamentally flawed: a colonial style masquerading as a "national" one. E.B. Havell, critic and art school director associated with the burgeoning arts and crafts movement in England, argued that a true Indian architecture could only come about by encouraging its untutored master builders, and giving them a free hand to work within their own traditions. Of the British "Indo-Saracenic" architect, he wrote scornfully that he

> clothes his engineering with external paper-designed adornments borrowed from ancient buildings which were made for purposes totally foreign to those which he has in hand. The engineering is more or less real (according to the skill of the designer); the "style" is purely artificial... [The British did not] come as the Moguls did, to learn the art of building from the Indian master builder, but—on the false assumption that art in India vanished with the last of the Moguls—to teach the application of Indian archaeology to the constructive methods of the West, using the Indian craftsman only as an instrument for creating a make-believe Anglo-Indian "style".

In the end, in the years following 1912, Indo-Saracenic succumbed before the forceful genius of the man who was to be British India's "Norman Shaw"; Edwin Lutyens, the builder of New Delhi. Swinton Jacob's buildings, Lutyens reported to his collaborator Herbert Baker during his first tour of India, "are all made up of tit-bits culled from various buildings of various dates put together with no sense of relation or of scale. I do want," he insisted, "old England to stand up and plant her great traditions and good taste where she goes and not pander to sentiment and all this silly Moghul-Hindu stuff." A decade earlier, Indo-Saracenic had already been forced on to the defensive. From the late 1890's onward in Europe a resurgent Classicism had swept aside Victorian Gothic—as Lutyens wrote in 1903: "In architecture Palladio is the game..". As these changing patterns of taste altered architectural styles in Europe, they also affected imperial building. In India this Classical revival gained its first triumph with the 1905 Victoria Memorial in Calcutta. Although it was designed by William Emerson, the guiding hand was that of the Viceroy Lord Curzon, who insisted that "a structure in some variety of the Classical or Renaissance style was essential." James Ransome, the Government's Consulting Architect during this decade, for the most part too sought inspiration from European Classical deigns.

So it is not surprising that when the decision was made in 1912 to build a new capital at Delhi, the vision that informed it bore the impress of European and of classical forms. Elements of the older vision survived, above all in the placement of the new Delhi adjacent to the old Mughal capital. The British still sought to capture for their empire the majesty of their predecessors. The Viceroy Lord Hardinge also fought for a decorative schemes that would at least give an Indian appearance to the facades of these Classical structures. But henceforward Classical styles were to inspire Britain's building in India. They alone, as Herbert Baker wrote to *The Times*, "embody the idea of law and order which has been produced out of chaos by the British Administration."

The Indo-Saracenic, then, shaped Britain's conception of how its empire in India ought to be marked in stone for some fifty years, from 1860 to 1910. In so far as it involved repudiation of Western forms, this architecture sought to define Britain's empire in Indian terms. It endeavoured to draw upon the legitimacy of the Mughal Empire—and occasionally and ambivalently, of Hindu rulership. In so doing this architectural enterprise was part of a larger effort, in the years after the 1858 inauguration of Crown governance, to create for Britain in India a "secure and usable past". The elaboration of distinctive rituals and dress, the forging of special ties with India's princes, the proclamation of Victoria as Empress of India—all were directed to this same objective. As the Viceroy Lord Lytton wrote of the grand Imperial Assemblage he had convened in 1877 to proclaim Victoria's new title, it would conspicuously, "place the Queen's authority upon the ancient throne of the Moguls, with which the imagination and tradition of [our] Indian subjects associate the splendour of supreme power."

Yet at no time did the British ever cease to define themselves as above and apart from their Indian subjects. They never, for instance, built temples or mosques, acts by which previous rulers had sought to bond themselves to their subjects and make manifest the righteousness of their rule. The British after the 1850's vigorously disowned any involvement whatsoever with Indian religious institutions. They set out instead systematically to order and classify the elements of India's heritage. Its peoples, its languages, its philosophies, its styles of building, were all labelled and defined. Set apart from the West, India had become an object. In this respect the elaboration of Indo-Saracenic architecture was part and parcel of the contemporaneous listing of tribes and castes, the recruitment of "martial races" and award of princely gun salutes. Yet like colonialism itself, the buildings spoke with an inconsistent voice. The schools, office blocks, railway stations, and even clock towers the British built derived from Western models, and signified new values and new technologies at work in India. Yet their facades announced a "traditional" India—unchanging, stable, deferential, with a past defined for its people by its colonial masters. The Mayo College typifies the contradiction, for in it the architectural elements of the past defined a space within which a new learning took place.

The use of Indian forms to represent Empire testified in sum to a double claim. Buildings put up by the Raj for its purposes, these structures proclaimed the supremacy of the British as they sought to reshape India. At the same time they asserted a claim to knowledge, and hence to power, from within. Britain not only ruled, as the Romans had done, but had mastered the Orient. As the Viceroy Lord Hardinge wrote to Lutyens, when the latter wanted to use the round instead of the pointed "Saracenic" arch in New Delhi, "In your London surroundings you cannot feel the whisperings of the East, but I have lived fifteen years in the East, and I know and feel the language of Eastern buildings." New Delhi and the coming of Indian nationalism, were each in their own way to confound this claim.

PART II

The Structuring of a Society

In addition to its rich cultural heritage India possessed on the eve of the Western encounter a number of shared institutions which together formed its traditional social order. Among these the most prominent were the village community and the caste system. Often misunderstood by Westerners, who saw them as fixed and immutable, village and caste identity still gave the Indian at the most intimate level a sense of who he or she was. This section examines India's enduring social institutions, and shows how their varied character across the breadth of the subcontinent, along with their adaptability in British times as before, helped shape the complex society that is India today.

5

India's peasant villages, though open to invaders and often laid waste by rapacious officials, were not passive or defenceless. Rather they possessed an effective internal organization centering around the panchayat council and the village headman, and they were in large measure master of their own affairs. This essay describes the organization of rural society in one region of India, that of Maharashtra, in the early nineteenth century. Although it should not be taken as typical of all India—indeed the author is at pains to point out how Maharashtrian village social organization helped to reinforce a distinctive regional identity — this account illustrates many of the basic elements of enduring village life throughout the subcontinent.

Rural Life in Western India on the Eve of the British Conquest

RAVINDER KUMAR

The social organisation of rural life in traditional India is a subject of interest to the social historian. He has, therefore, devoted considerable time to an analysis of rural society, and he has focussed attention on the relations which subsisted between different social groups in the rural world. Yet his insights into rural society suffer from an inability to look upon the rural scene as an integrated world of institutions, groups interlocked into social relationships, values and modes of feeling. In this paper, therefore, I propose to dwell upon the organisation of rural society, and upon the quality of the social experience of the peasants of western India, before the British conquest of 1818 To highlight the world of the peasants, I shall ask myself a series of questions: How was rural society in western India organised on the eve of the British conquest? What were the important institutions within the village? How was social and economic power distributed between different individuals and social groups in rural society? What were the spiritual and secular values of the peasants? How were they integrated, intellectually, and through political and social institutions, with other

Reprinted by permission from *The Indian Economic and Social History Review*, Vol.II, No.3 (July 1965), pp.201-219, with omissions.

social groups in rural society? And finally, how did the peasants relate their identity to the sacred and the profane worlds around them?

The two outstanding features of the communities which comprised rural society in western India were their self-sufficiency, and their physical isolation from the rest of the world. It is easy to exaggerate both the isolation, and self-sufficieny of the villages of traditional India, and in the course of this paper I shall have occasion to highlight the economic, the political and the religious ties which integrated rural society. But despite the interdependence of the rural communities and despite the links which tied villages to one another, it is remarkable to what extent the rural world approached the romantic image of remote little communities, inhabited by proud and sturdy peasants, who conducted their affairs in a spirit of independence, and bowed their heads before no mortal man.

The very appearance of a village in Maharashtra set it apart as a miniature world, self-sufficient in itself, and geared to a style of life calling for a minimum of contact with the world outside. It would be located on a smoothly rolling mound, in close proximity to a stream, and surrounded by the fields which the villagers cultivated. From a distance the village had the appearance of a mass of crumbling grey walls, with a few stunted trees growing out amongst them, and here and there a structure standing out more conspicuously than the rest. All this was enclosed by a mud wall of irregular shape, and pierced by rude gates of wood at two or more points. On entering such a village appearances were no more prepossessing than from the outside. There was a complete lack of design in the layout of dwellings and streets. The crumbling walls would turn out to be the homes of the cultivators, and they were made of calcareous earth, with terraced tops of the same material. These dwellings were constructed without any attempt at order. They had narrow and crooked lanes winding amongst them, and dividing them into groups of two or three. While conforming to a basic pattern, the homes of the more substantial cultivators were slightly larger in size, and a little different in appearance, from those of the poorer cultivators. But the most conspicuous structures in the village were the *chowrie,* or the municipal hall, where the public concerns of the village were debated, and the temple, built either by a rich and repentant patil, or by a philanthropic deshmukh, in the hope of commuting their earthly sins. Conspicuous, too, were the dwellings of the untouchable castes like the mahars or the mangs, whose inferior social status prevented them from coming into physical contact with the rest of the community, and who, therefore, resided in little hamlets outside the walls of the village.

A majority of the inhabitants of the village were cultivators of the kunbi caste. They were grouped into *thulwaheeks,* or hereditary cultivators, and *uprees,* or peasants who did not possess any prescriptive rights in the soil. The *thulwaheeks* were descended from the first settlers of the soil, who had in periods of remote antiquity migrated in *jathas,* or family groups, to new sites, and had apportioned the available arable land between themselves. A *bakhar* setting out the circumstances connected with the establishment of the village of Muruda in south Konkan illustrates the ties which linked the *thulwaheeks* of a rural community to each other, and determined their property rights in the land of the village. Muruda originally formed a jungle, and it served as the *rudrabhumi,* or burning ground, of a neighbouring hamlet called Asuda. To Asuda in the 16th century came an enterprising Brahman called Gangadharbhatta, with two disciples in tow, and he decided to establish a new village. In the first instance, Gangadharbhatta asked the permission of the cultivators of Asuda to clear the jungle which served as their *rudrabhumi.* He next approached the raja of the region, a princeling of the Sekara dynasty called Jalandhra, for a grant of the land surrounding the village. The land gifted away by Jalandhra was then distributed among the thirteen families whom Gangadharbhatta had persuaded to migrate to the new settlement. The property of each *jatha* or family was marked off by stones called *Gadudus,* and *Kshetrapalas,* or tutelary deities, were appointed as divine witnesses to the allocation of fields. Besides providing them with holdings in land, Gangadharbhatta also defined the obligations and the prerogatives of the founding families of Muruda.

The *jathas* of a village like Muruda originally held their estates in joint ownership, and they were collectively responsible for the payment of the land-tax on the village. If the owner of one of the shares in a joint estate let his land fall waste, the family assumed responsibility for his share of the State's dues, and the fields belonging to him were taken over by his kinsmen for cultivation. Similarly, if a member of a *jatha* died without an heir, his portion was divided among the surviving relations. He was again free to dispose of his *baproti* or patronymic as he willed, but he was not permitted to sell his share outside the family if a kinsman was willing to buy it. Only if no one in the family was willing to purchase a field did it pass on to an outsider, who then entered the *jatha* on the same terms as the original incumbent, but was referred to as *birader bhaus,* or legal brother, instead of *ghar bhaus,* or house brother.

By the time Baji Rao Peshwa surrendered the Poona territories to the British Government in 1818, the *jathas* had lost some of their original cohesion, partly through inbuilt tensions, but partly also through the attempts of the Poona Government to undermine their authority in the distribution and collection of the land-tax in the village. Under the earlier Peshwas, once the tax to be paid by a village had been settled between the village headman and the revenue officials of the state, the internal distribution of this tax was left to the *jathas* of the village, and was accomplished on the basis of the customary or *rivaj* rates of the community. After the fateful defeat of Panipat, however, when the revenues of Maharashtra stood in desperate need of augmentation, Madhav Rao Peshwa introduced the *kamal* survey, which anticipated the *ryotwari* system of Sir Thomas Munro, and tried to undermine the autonomy of the *jathas* in the financial administration of the village, by obliging the kunbis to pay their dues directly to the state, instead of through the village community. But so powerful were the *jathas* in the village of Maharashtra, the the *kamal* survey proved abortive, for even after its execution the cultivators continued to pay their taxes on the basis of the *rivaj* rates, which differed significantly from the rates introduced by the *kamal* survey.

Despite the power wielded by the *jathas* over the villages of Maharashtra, and despite their ability to thwart Madhav Rao's attempt to regulate the finances of the state, the institution no longer functioned in full vigour at the time of the British conquest. The kunbis remembered the former basis of organisation only to the extent of entrusting the seniormost family in the community with the responsibility of collecting the land-tax for the entire village. However, joint responsibility for the payment of the land-tax was no longer rigidly enforced. The members of the oldest family in the village, who represented it in its dealings with the world outside, were styled patils, and their head was called the chief or *mukkadam* patil. Long after a village had been established, the cultivators descended from the patil families considered themselves higher in social status than other cultivators in the village, although their pretensions to superiority were not buttressed by any tangible social or economic privileges. The crucial difference within the cultivating community lay between the *thulwaheeks* and the *uprees*. The former had an inalienable right of cultivating their fields so long as they paid the land-tax. They could also sell or mortgage their property with the permission of other members of the *jatha*. In constrast, the *uprees'* connection with the village was tenuous. They leased the deserted holdings or the arable waste of the village, either on an annual basis, or on a lease running concurrently for a number of years.

The significant differences between the *thulwaheeks* and the *uprees* were expressed in social and not in economic differences. They were related to contrasting styles of life rather than to sharp economic differentials. In the village of Ambola in Poona district, for instance, the holdings of the *uprees* like Suntoojee Scindiah and Kundojee Scindiah were comparable in area and productivity to the holdings of the *thulwaheeks* of the same village. Besides, the *thulwaheeks* of Ambola like Beerjee Scindiah and Ambajee Scindiah paid a higher land-tax than the *uprees* of the village, even though their holdings were in no way superior to the holdings of the *uprees*. This was so because of the prevailing conditions in the labour market, and the scarcity of *uprees* for employment on waste land that was suitable for cultivation.

Because their connection with the land was tenuous, the *uprees* often wandered from one village to another in search of better leases. On the other hand, the *thulwaheeks* were deeply attached to their fields, and refused to migrate to a new village so long as they could make a bare subsistence on their ancestral fields. Their attachment to their land did not flow exclusively from a desire for acquisition. It was equally a result of the privileges which the *thulwaheeks* enjoyed in rural society, and the tremendous prestige which the possession of a *watan*, or right in land, bestowed on its owner in rural Maharashtra. The *thulwaheek* was an active member of the council which determined the public affairs of the village; he was exempted from a tax paid by other villagers on occasions of marriage; he did not pay any house-tax; and last but not least, he and his wife were entitled to precedence over the *upree* on all ceremonial occasions in the village.

The absence of sharp differences in incomes in the villages of Maharashtra created a climate devoid of conflict and strife which exercised a decisive influence on the behaviour of the cultivators. The kunbis possessed a mild and unobtrusive disposition, and they abhorred a want of gentleness in others. Yet for all their mildness, they had a latent warmth of temper, and if oppressed beyond a point, they could turn fiercely upon their tormentors, as indeed they did during the disturbances which broke out in the Deccan in 1875. A perceptive traveller in rural Maharashtra in the 1820's would have found the peasants surprisingly well informed about questions concerning agriculture, and the concerns of the little community of the village would immediately hold their interest. "On the whole," a British official observed, "they are far better informed than the lower classes of our own (British) population, and certainly far surpass them in propriety and orderliness of demeanour". That such a portrayal is not overdrawn is clear from the account we have of the distribution of holdings in the village of Ambola. Of the cultivating families of Ambola, more than half held fields which ranged between 15 and 30 *beeghas*. Holdings of this size yielded a reasonable income by the standards of the time, although they did not provide any insurance against involvement in debt. The three substantial cultivators in Ambola were the patil, Baboo Ram Scindiah, and Maroojee Scindiah and Bapoojee Scindiah, each of whom had a holding that was 60 *beeghas* in extent, and thrice as large as the holdings of the majority of cultivators in the village. In contrast to the three substantial cultivators of Ambola stood kunbis like Amruta Scindiah and Hykunt Scindiah, who found it difficult to keep body and soul together on the incomes derived from their miserable holdings. But such contrasts were rare, and by and large rural Maharashtra presented a picture of a mass of peasants who were neither ostentatiously affluent, nor miserably poor, and who held the balance between the few substantial cultivators, on the one hand, and the fringe of hopelessly impoverished peasants, on the other.

For all that the economic condition of the great body of cultivators was far from satisfactory. A stranger to the rural scene would have emerged with an unduly pessimistic notion of the actual state of affairs, since the cultivators were quick to suspect in any inquiry concerning their assets a potential enhancement of the burden of tax, and, therefore, presented an exaggerated picture of their debts and financial obligations. But the kunbis were by no stretch of imagination rolling in affluence. We get a precise idea of their condition from a close look into Lony, a substantial village, atypical only because it stood close to Poona. Of the 84 cultivating families of Lony, as many as 79 were indebted to the four jain and two marwari vanis, or moneylenders, who resided in the village. The total indebtedness of the kunbis of Lony amounted to the very considerable sum of Rs. 14,532, but this sum was split up into small loans ranging from Rs.50 to Rs.200. All this, however, does not take into consideration debts of Rs.2,000 and more which had been contracted by the three landed families of position which resided in Lony.

The kunbis of Lony had contracted debts either to purchase seed, food, or stock, or to defray expenses of marriage or caste observances. Each kunbi kept a running account with his vani, and he took a receipt for the sums which he paid in redemption of his debts from time to time. According to the principle of *dam dupat,* which was widely accepted, interests on loans accumulated only till it equalled the sum advanced in the first instance. Relations between the kunbi and the vani were thus conducted on an equitable basis, though it would be legitimate to have reservations about how the system worked in practice. For despite a natural liveliness of the mind, the kunbis were not very shrewd in the handling of money. Besides, in their role as borrowers they were pitted against individuals whose caste values made them grasping, and who specialised in the unlovely business of moneylending. However, the portrayal of the relationship between the kunbis and the vanis as one of tension and conflict would be untrue to the social temper of the times. For cultivation involved close and intimate cooperation between two social groups: the kunbis, who provided land and labour; and the vanis, who assisted with seed and capital. As a result of this partnership, the surplus produce of the cultivators was mortgaged to the vani even before the crop was reaped. But since the rural economy had worked out its own rationale, and because the vani had neither the inclination, nor the means, to appropriate the cultivator's holdings, the kunbis' dependence upon him did not lead to exploitation.

What prevented the exploitation of the kunbis was the manner in which social power was distributed in the villages of Maharashtra. The two key concentrations of power in the village were the office of the patil, and the judicial institution known as the panchayat. The patil, as already emphasised, was the head of the seniormost *jatha* of the village, besides which his position as the leader of the community was formally endorsed by the state. The patil, therefore, combined in his person facets of legal and traditional domination which made him the most important individual in the village, and invested him with sweeping powers of initiative. Like Baboo Rao Scindiah of Ambola, most patils were substantial landholders in their villages, besides which they enjoyed some freehold land as remuneration for their duties. So important was the patil's office, and so onerous the maintenance of its style, that many an incumbent who had fallen upon evil days was reduced to selling an office which he could no longer afford. However, the prerogatives attached to the patilship were considered so personal, that very often only a part of the rights of office were sold. Such transactions gave rise to the existence of two or even more patils in a village, with the seniormost amongst them retaining the rights of precedence.

The patil played his most important role in representing the village community in the crucial negotiations with the revenue officers of the Poona Government in which the quantum of tax on the village was settled. But in his dual capacity as a traditional leader of village society, and the official headman of the village, the patil was also entrusted with the task of extending the area of cultivation in the village, to which end he sought to encourage *uprees* to settle in the community. The patil attracted *uprees* to the village over which he presided by offering them attractive terms, either on the basis of the *cowl* tenure, whereby the *upree* paid a fraction of the rent in the first year, with annual increases leading to the full rent in the sixth year, or through the *muckta* tenure, whereby tenants were encouraged to clear the arable waste on the payment of a very nominal rent. More significant still was the patil's prerogative to grant *thulwaheek* status to those who wanted to purchase, and not just rent, land in the village. In bestowing such a right, however, he had to consult all the cultivators who had a permanent stake in the community. Any request for the purchase of land was, therefore, debated in the *chowrie* by the patil and the *thulwaheeks* of the village. A grant indicating the admission into their ranks of a kunbi called Kosajee by the patil and the *thulwaheeks* of the village of Multan vividly evokes the temper of such deliberations:

> We (the patil and the *thulwaheeks* of the village) being present, you Kosajee, son of Kosajee patil Taruh of Sowkee, came and presented a petition, if a letter of inheritance (*meeras puttah*) were granted for lands in the above village that you would labour and secure their prosperity. Having approved of your petition we give you...the field called San...

> We the village authorities have granted you this from our free will and pleasure...You and your children's children are to enjoy this right...

The admission of Kosajee to the community of Multan was clearly a collective decision of the patil and the *thulwaheeks* of the community. Since the patil's prerogatives flowed in a large measure from the acceptance of his authority and his leadership by the community, we can infer that similar consultations lay behind every important decision taken by the village, whether it was the question of the admission of a new member to the community, or the erection of a new temple or *chowrie,* or the adoption of an extra levy of tax to meet an emergency. Harking back once again to Ambola, it follows from the distribution of holdings in this village that patil Baboo Rao Scindiah would have proved completely ineffective, if in issues affecting the community, he did not consult kunbis like Madjee Scindiah and Raja Rao Scindiah, whose holdings in land were comparable to his holdings, and who, therefore, commanded considerable influence in the village. This is not to deny the special privileges enjoyed by the patil because of his status. For instance, even though the decision to accept a new member in Multan was a collective decision, this new member was still obliged to pay a cess called *meeras puttah* to the patil of the village before acquiring full-fledged membership into the community. But despite such privileges, the patil was not a law into himself, and he was guided in his decisions by the collective voice of all those kunbis who had a permanent stake in the village.

Indicative, too, of the manner in which the collective voice of the community was brought to bear on village administration was the way in which the panchayat, or the village court, functioned. Being the most influential individual in the village, the patil was invariably approached by the parties concerned when a dispute broke out in a rural community. The patil, in the first instance, tried to resolve the dispute through personal arbitration. But if he failed, which he often did, then the parties were referred to a panchayat, or ad hoc council, of the most intelligent and influential kunbis in the village. The panchayat was an informal institution. Its members, generally five in number, gathered in the open to hear the disputants argue their cases and to examine any witnesses that might appear. In the next stage the panchayat, after debating the issue, drew up an award which was communicated to the patil for execution. The panchayat's advantage over formal judicial institutions lay in the identity of values between its members and the parties to the dispute. Since its decisions were shaped by values which were shared by all the cultivators in the village, they were readily accepted by the disputants. However, the panchayat was by no means an ideal judicial institution. Its very constitution encouraged dilatoriness in the administration of justice, and it did not possess the means to execute its awards and was in this respect completely dependent upon the patil. Besides, it was not designed to resolve complicated cases, and often permitted complex disputes to drift unresolved, until it was no longer necessary to subject them to arbitration.

Since the panchayat was the only judicial institution in the village, and because it was completely dominated by the kunbis, the vanis in the rural communities of Maharashtra were unable to exploit the cultivators, despite the important role they played in the rural economy, and despite the extent to which the kunbis were dependent upon them for capital. It was open to the vanis to refer a recalcitrant debtor to a panchayat. but since the panchayat was made up of the kunbis of the village, it could be trusted to give decisions which showed more than legitimate concern for the interests of the cultivators involved. This was particularly true if the debtor happened to be a patil or a substantial kunbi. But even in ordinary cases, the vani had no chance of recovering his debt unless he could interest some powerful landed aristocrat on his behalf. More frequently, he took to incessant importunity, and by literally throwing himself on the threshold of his debtor, and refusing to budge till the debt was settled, he sometimes gained his objective. The vanis of Maharashtra had raised the practice of *dharna* to a fine art.

Apart from the vanis who provided them with capital to cultivate their fields, and the panchayats which protected them from the vanis,the kunbis of Maharashtra required the implements of agriculture, and a variety of goods for day-to-day consumption, before they could lay any claim to self-sufficiency within their little rural communities. Such goods and services were provided through the institution of the *bullotedars*. The *bullotedars* were artisans belonging to different castes, who possessed hereditary rights of service in a village, and who were compensated by the village community according to well-recognized scales of remuneration for performing these services. The most important *bullotedars* were those who contributed to the business of agriculture, and directly served the kunbi: for instance, the *sootar,* who fabricated the wooden plough of the cultivator, and kept it in a state of good repair; the *lohar,* who fashioned and repaired the ironwork associated with the plough, but could also press his skills to the tiring of a cart, or the shoeing of a horse; and the *chamar,* who made the leather holders, whips, ropes and bands required by the peasant. Also ranked as *bullotedars*, though they were not artisans, were the mahars, or the untouchable watchmen of the village. There were at least a dozen mahar families in a normal village, and they possessed an important voice in the community despite their low social ranking, since on them rested the important task of preventing encroachments upon the boundaries of the village, of which they possessed an accurate knowledge handed down to them by their forefathers. The mahars also served as the ears and the eyes of the community, always on the alert for any unusual happening which might spell danger for the village.

Though this account does not exhaust the list of artisans who lived in the village, enough has been said to indicate how the skills and services required for agriculture were to be found within the community, making it self-sufficient to a remarkable degree. But how were these artisans ranked? and how were they paid for their services? Reflection on these questions throws interesting light on the collective sentiment which prevailed in the village. It also reveals the gulf between the ritual ranking of a caste, and its actual status in the secular world. The *bullotedars* were not paid individually for the services they performed. Instead, they were allocated roughly one-eighth of the gross annual produce of the village. The fraction of this produce distributed to individual artisans was determined by the utility of the services they performed, and bore no relation to their caste status. Thus *bullotedars* of the first category, who received the maximum remuneration, not only included low castes like the *sootar* and the *lohar* but also the untouchable mahar. On the other hand, the Brahman priest who claimed to belong to the highest caste of all, and attended to the idols of the village Gods in substantiation of this claim, was ranked as a *bullotedar* of the third and lowest category and was hard put to make both ends meet. However, by and large the *bullotedars* made fairly substantial incomes. In the village of Kurmalla in the district of Sholapur, for instance, the *sootar* and the *lohar* had an annual income of Rs.24, which placed them in the same economic scale as the majority of the cultivators who owned landed property in the village.

Besides the kunbis who tilled the soil, the vanis who loaned them capital, and the *bullotedars* who provided the kunbis with goods and services, the villages of Maharashtra sheltered a number of Brahman families, which contributed in their own fashion to the life of the community. Both in their physical appearance, and in their intellectual sophistication, the Brahmans formed a separate group in the village, distinguishable from the kunbis and other castes in being 'fairer, better dressed, and more virtuous (sic) in their manners'. The two offices which belonged to them as of right were those of the joshi, or the village priest, and the kulkarni, or the village accountant. Because these offices required a level of education above the average, they admirably suited the Brahman style of life. They also conferred on those who held them considerable power and authority. The kulkarni, for instance, was an important member of the village community, and second only to the patil in the influence which he exercised, since he kept a record of the holdings of different cultivators in the village, the tax they paid to the state, and the terms on which they held their land. Because he was one of the few educated individuals in the village, the authority exercised by the kulkarni exceeded his formal status. Often he would instigate a split between the cultivators of a community, and lead a faction of kunbis against the patil of the village.

The influence of the Brahman families over the rural communities also stemmed from the fact that the joshi, who looked after the temple that was the pride of any respectable village, and attended to the ritualistic needs of the kunbis, provided some sort of link between the inhabitants of the village and the great tradition of Hinduism. It is true that the joshi was all too frequently an ignorant and bigoted person. But by relating the high culture of Hinduism to the crude idol of a Bhairav, or a Mahadev, or a Maruti, which adorned the village temple, he anchored the loyalty of the kunbis to the only tangible expression of Hinduism which they saw around them. Such bonds were reinforced on ritual occasions connected with births and deaths and marriages, when the joshi presided over the prayers addressed to the Gods, and invoked them to accept the offerings which the peasants gifted away in expectation of divine grace.

Yet the joshi did not rank as high in the rural community as his caste status, and his formal position, would lead us to assume. This was probably so because his dependence upon religion for his livelihood lowered him in the estimation of the cultivators. There was, however, yet another reason for the limited influence which the Brahman priest exercised over the rural communities of Maharashtra. Since the great tradition of Hinduism was expressed in a language, namely, Sanskrit, which the peasants could not follow, their interest in the values of orthodox Hinduism was marginal, and confined to ritual and practice.

The village joshi, through whom this interest sustained, was consequently looked upon as a functional member of the village community, and his ranking as a *bullotedar* of the third and lowest category reflects the inferior status he held in the eyes of the kunbis.

The Brahman priest who related the ritual life of the kunbi to the high culture of Hinduism, and institutions like the panchayats, the *jathas,* and the *thulwaheek* council, served to heighten the isolation of the village in an age in which means of communication were virtually non-existent and methods of transport primitive. But the identify of the village was not shaped exclusively by these institutions. The village acquired a personality of its own, and conferred a sense of belonging upon its residents through the communal life, social, religious and political, in which the villagers participated irrespective of distinctions in rank and status and wealth. While laying the foundations of Muruda, for instance, the shrewd Brahman Gangadharbhatta had ensured the dissemination of a sense of community among its residents by firmly setting down the festivals which the entire population of the village was to celebrate collectively. The ritual connected with the observance of the new year illustrates the purpose behind Gangadharbhatta's instruction:

The new year commences (according to the village *bakhar*) with the first of chaitra, which is the Varshapratipada, or the new year's day of the Saka year. On this day all the inhabitants assemble in a small temple of Devi, near the large temple dedicated to the same Goddess. The head village officers, before repairing to this village, proceed, in company with some other inhabitants, to pay visits of condolence to persons who have lost relatives during the last year, and conduct them to the great temple, with the flutes playing, and the drums beating. They are thence led to the small shrine...where the joshi or village astrologer reads the horoscope of the year, and foretells the events or fortunes of the year, as calculated or determined astrologically. The ceremony begins with the usual prayer to Ganapati, and ends with the customary benediction to the audience.

The congregation of the residents of Muruda for the changing of the sacred thread in the month of Sravana was equally evocative of the collective consciousness of the village. So strong were the ties of association forged among the members of a rural community by such observances, that they encouraged the villagers to defy the most rigid of social taboos, and even to violate the sanctity of the caste. In the several celebrations in Muruda, for instance, different castes partook of a common meal; while orthodoxy was flouted in an even more blatant fashion through the consummation of marriages between the Brahman sub-castes of Karhada and Chitpavan.

Although the social organisation of the villages of Maharashtra served to make them self-sufficient in most respects, it would be a mistake to look upon them as completely isolated from each other, or to dismiss the ties between different rural communities as irrelevant to the integration of rural society. Having already focussed attention on the institutions which were responsible for the isolation of the village, we shall now touch upon the bonds of religion and politics, and upon those interlocking economic roles, which shaped the regional identity of Maharashtra.

In portraying the role of the joshi in the village, we dwelt upon his inability to communicate the high culture of Hinduism to the kunbi, and the consequent contempt in which he has held the cultivators, who ranked him below the lowly mahar as a *bullotedar*. But although the joshi was unable to disseminate the great tradition of Hinduism among the peasants, a remarkable consensus between high and low castes shaped the ethos of Maharashtra, and linked the kunbi and the Brahman to a common corpus of religious values. This consensus stemmed from a religious philosophy which claimed the allegiance of the elite as well as the lower and middle castes, and which was instrumental in making Maharashtra the most closely integrated regional society in India.

The seminal intellectual influence on the Brahman castes of Maharashtra was the *advaita* philosophy of Sankara, who lived in the eighth century. Like other orthodox exponents of Hindu philosophy, in expounding his *advaitic* or monistic concept of the world, Sankara sought to initiate the individual into a state of existence called *moksha,* which represented the ultimate in spiritual realisation, and which protected the initiated from the trials and tribulations of the profane world. Also like other orthodox schools of Hindu philosophy, *advaitavada* claimed to be the true essence of the triple texts of Hinduism: the Upanishads, the Bhagavad Gita, and the Vedanta Sutras. The basic postulates of Sankara's philosophy were contained in a few propositions: the sole reality in the world was a principle called Brahman; the individual soul was a part and parcel of Brahman; and the phenomenal world was a reflection of Brahman upon the plane of human consciousness. But Sankara expounded these propositions with a skill and subtlety which made him the most distinguished figure in Hindu philosophy.

The vitality of *advaitavada* lay partly in its intellectual sophistication, and partly in the religious order organised by Sankara to provide a firm institutional basis for the dissemination of his ideas. However, the concepts expounded by Sankara were not directed towards social groups outside the Brahman pale, so that the values of Hindu orthodoxy did not in the first instance influence the lower and middle castes of Maharashtra. As a result of Sankara's proselytising activity, therefore, the community was divided into a small Brahman elite, and a host of lesser castes, which were only marginally influenced by the high culture of Hinduism. The integration of the lower castes with the Brahman elite was a task to which a remarkable coterie of religious leaders, the so-called Saints and Prophets of Maharashtra, addressed themselves in the centuries following the spread of Sankara's ideas among the Brahmans.

The initiators of the movement which sought to popularise Hinduism were Mukundraj and Jnaneshwar, who lived in the 12th and 13th centuries. Mukundraj was a Brahman by caste, a devotee of Shiva, and he wrote a number of philosophical works which expressed in simple Marathi poetry the *advaita* philosophy of Sankara. In deliberately choosing Marathi, the language of the people, instead of Sanskrit, the language of the intellectual aristocracy, for his writings in philosophy, Mukundraj set afoot a movement which aimed at influencing social groups outside the Brahman pale. Jnaneshwar, who was again a Brahman, was even more successful than Mukundraj in interpreting the great tradition of Hinduism to the lower and middle caste of Maharashtra. The most important composition of Jnaneshwar was a commentary on the Bhagavad Gita called the Jnaneshwari. In expounding the Gita for the masses, Jnaneshwar took as his principal theme the value of *bhakti* or devotion to God, and he is, therefore, looked upon as the founder of the *bhakti* school of Marathi poetry. He is in fact the coryphaeus of the devotional movement, which honoured Shiva as well as Vishnu, the two principal Gods of the Hindu pantheon, and followed Sankara in its philosophical outlook. Since Jnaneshwar started his spiritual career as a devotee of Shiva, and he was deeply influenced by the *advaita* doctrine of Sankara, his espousal of the Vaishnava principle of *bhakti* as a means to salvation was probably due to the teachings of Ramanuja, a Vaishnava philosopher of the 11th century, who is believed to be the principal opponent of the doctrines of Sankara. Jnaneshwar probably belonged to the Bhagawata cult, which recognised the worship of Shiva and Vishnu as equal and amounting to the same thing, and the whole devotional movement of Maharashtra is derived from this source.

Though it was initiated by Brahmans of high caste, the *bhakti* movement soon passed into the hands of lowly born individuals like Namadeva, a contemporary of Jnaneshwar, who was a man of the people, and who expressed religious and philosophical ideas in a simple and moving devotional poetry which exercised a great influence on the peasants of Maharashtra. The literature of the *bhakti* movement was permeated with the glorification of complete devotion to God. Besides preaching the superiority of devotional as opposed to intellectual realisation of God, the *bhakti* saints tried to undermine the obstacles which stood in the way of communication between the Brahmans and the lower castes, and to demolish the barriers which debarred the latter from access to spiritual salvation. But although they advocated the revolutionary doctrine of the spiritual equality of the different castes, the *bhakti* saints desisted from attacking secular distinctions of caste, partly in the interests of social harmony, and partly out of indifference to the secular world...

The spread of the *bhakti* movement in Maharashtra affiliated the kunbis to the great tradition of Hinduism, and bridged that gulf between popular and elite values which had reduced the joshi to a position of spiritual impotence. While the kunbi mechanically performed the rituals enjoined by orthodox Hinduism, it was the spiritual insights of the *bhakti* movement which enabled him to discern order and meaning in the drab and even harsh world which surrounded him. What reconciled the peasants of Maharashtra to a Brahmanical religious culture was the literature of the *bhakti* movement, which had remained alive in folk memory over the centuries through oral transmission from one generation to another. What embodied for the kunbis the values of Hinduism were the shrines of *bhakti* Gods, like the temple of Vithala at Pandharpur, to which thousands flocked every year to establish communion with the object of their devotion. The annual pilgrimage to Pandharpur brought together high and low castes, and kunbis hailing from remote villages, and it served as an institution for the transmission of religious values, and the spread of social cohesion...

However, it was not necessary to go to Pandharpur to gain initiation into the *bhakti* cult. For all over the countryside there flourished lay groups of devotees, led by a *guru* or spiritual leader, which met in the village *chowrie* to recite their favourite *abhangas,* and to ponder over the meaning of earthly existence, and the fate that lay beyond. Often, too, a wandering mendicant who had dedicated his life to the Gods of Pandharpur would visit the village, and hold a *harikirtan* or devotional congregation, to which all the villagers would flock, for Vithala made no distinction between Brahman and Shudra and rich and poor, but welcomed everybody to his fold. Thus *advaita* became a household concept in Maharashtra, and linked the people of the region in a close texture of values which transcended the tension between castes and communities and formed the basis of a popular culture flowing out of the great tradition of Hinduism.

The religious values which shaped the ethos of Maharashtra, and related the identity of kunbis in remote communities to the high culture of Hinduism were not the only influences which integrated rural society. For the administration of the Peshwas, too, was instrumental in creating cohesion in the rural world, and in forging ties of association between one village and another. It did this by linking remote communities to a central institution, the Government at Poona, which played a significant part in the life of the peasants, despite the institutions of self-government within the village.

Relations between the peasant and the State in traditional India revolved around a tax on the land, which the peasant was obliged to pay to the state, and in return for which he expected the ruler to maintain the social peace, and to protect him from external aggression. Since the rights and responsibilities of the state were so well-defined, and so simple, the system of administration created by the Peshwas was no more complex than was necessary for the performance of these functions. The territories of Maharashtra were divided into revenue districts, each one of which was placed under an officer called the mamlatdar, who also exercised judicial and magisterial authority. In the outlying districts an officer called the Sirsoobedar was interposed between the central government at Poona and the mamlatdars. The duties of the Sirsoobedar were ill-defined and his power and authority varied from place to place. In the Carnatic he was a provincial governor, who appointed his own mamlatdars, and who was held reponsible for the timely collection of land revenue. In Candesh, on the other hand, he merely supervised the administration, since the mamlatdars carried out their business under the direct control of the Poona authorities.

The mamlatdar was the lynch-pin of the administration, and he was, therefore, chosen from families which were bound in personal ties of loyalty to the Peshwa, or to a prominent member of his court. When he was appointed to a new district his first concern was to cultivate the friendship of the landed aristocrats of the region, whose knowledge of the district's revenues, and its tax bearing potential, added usefully to the information with which he equipped himself from the *daftar* at Poona before departing for his administrative charge.

The role of the deshmukhs, or the landed aristocrats of Maharashtra, in the collection of the tax on land was no less important than the role of the mamlatdars. But to understand this role, it is necessary to look into the relations between the deshmukhs and the state, on the one hand, and the peasant communities, on the other. The origin of the deshmukhs is shrouded in obscurity, and we do not know for certain whether they were petty chiefs, whose partial eclipse flowed from the establishment of a regional state in Maharashtra, or the officers of a central authority, who had gradually usurped hereditary status. Probably both these processes resulted in the creation of deshmukh families. However, whatever be the origin of the deshmukhs, when the Muslims invaded the Deccan in the 13th century, they found them solidly entrenched in rural society, and their authority was accepted without demur by the peasants. So strong were the ties between the deshmukhs and the peasants of their domain, that when the Muslim rulers appointed revenue officers to collect the land tax on their behalf, the peasants refused to pay this tax at the instigation of the deshmukhs. The Muslim rulers were consequently obliged to purchase the cooperation of the deshmukhs by recognising their traditional status, and by awarding them a percentage of the tax on land for the maintenance of their dignity. This compact was honoured by successive rulers of Maharashtra till the downfall of Baji Rao Peshwa in 1818, and the establishment of British rule over the region.

The relationship between the mamlatdar, who represented the authority of the Poona Government, and the deshmukhs, whose position rested on their traditional ties with the peasants, was characterised by a tension which often flared into the open. But this tension also ensured the efficiency of the Peshwa's administration, and prevented the mamlatdars from exercising arbitrary authority, despite the absence of legal restraints upon their behaviour. In apportioning the land-tax on each village, for instance, the mamlatdar consulted both the patil of the community concerned, and the deshmukh who presided over the region. The consultations between the mamlatdar, the patil and deshmukh were a great help in the evaluation of an equitable land-tax. For only through such consultations was it possible to reconcile the conflicting interests of the state and the peasants in the distribution of the profits of agriculture. A direct confrontation between the patil and the mamlatdar could possibly have led to oppressive taxation, ruinous for everybody concerned, because the mamlatdars were backed by the superior power of the state, and their revenue assessments were not governed by any rational principles. But the advice of the deshmukh assured a fair tax on the village. Nevertheless, if a mamlatdar insisted upon an exorbitant tax, then the patil and the village he represented could appeal to the central government at Poona through the deshmukh, who never failed to lend his good offices for such a purpose. The existence of an alternative channel of communication between the villages and the central government restrained the mamlatdars, and prevented them from oppressing the peasants.

Just as the system of administration set up a chain of command between the kunbis in remote villages, and the Peshwas in the court of Poona, similarly the economic organisation of rural life served to strengthen the ties between one rural community and another. These ties were geared to the dispersal of certain castes like the Marwari and Gujarati vanis, and they were shaped by the commercial style of these social groups. The Gujarati vanis, who were concentrated in the township of Supa near Poona, had migrated to Maharashtra in the first quarter of the 17th century, when Surat was the chief centre of trade in western India. They first arrived on the scene as itinerant dealers in foreign spices, but after a time they settled down, and took to the profession of moneylending, and became rich and influential. Two centuries later, they were still regarded as aliens by the kunbis, and for their own part went back to Gujarat to contract marriages, or to perform important religious ceremonies. Except for a few rich bankers in Poona, most vanis from this caste were employed in the rural districts.

The elite among the commercial castes were the Marwari vanis, who had come to Maharashtra after the Gujarati vanis. The Marwaris were looked upon by the peasants as aliens who took hoards of money to their homeland, and as vain heretics, whose temples were often taken away for worship of Brahmanical Gods. From the township of Vambori in Ahmednagar district, which was the seat of a large Marwari community, and the hub of its business and financial world, individual Marwaris fanned out into pergunnah towns, and from thence into isolated villages, where they soon established a monopoly over the business of moneylending. They invariably commenced their career in a humble capacity as clerks and servants of established caste-fellows, but the moment they had put aside sufficient capital, they moved to a new village or township which had not been opened up, and were soon found to be playing an important role in the economic life of the community.

The Marwaris, unlike the kunbis, possessed a strong acquisitive instinct, and they were shrewd and ruthless in their business dealings. Because such values were deeply ingrained in them, the vanis could always outwit the kunbis who were their clients in the rural districts. However, as we have already pointed out, the distribution of power in the villages of Maharashtra prevented them from embarking upon a career of exploitation. For the moment a vani set up his business in a village, he became an intimate part of the village community; and as such, he was subject to the executive authority of the patil, and the judicial authority of the panchayat, and was consequently rendered incapable of any mischief despite the importance of his social role, and the key part played in the economy of the village. Our account of the village of Lony shows how the kunbis were dependent upon the vanis for capital even before the conquest of Maharashtra by the British. But despite a relationship of dependence, it was the patil and the substantial peasants who lorded over the village, and shaped its social style.

Integration and cleavage were the twin foundations of stability and order in the rural society of traditional Maharashtra. Integration flowed from the great tradition of Hinduism, and from its popular expressions, the *bhakti* orders, which linked remote peasant communities in a close relationship, and established the social identity of the kunbis. It also stemmed from those social and political institutions which set up a chain of command between the kunbi and the Peshwas through the bureaucracy and the landed aristocracy, on the one hand, and the commercial castes, on the other. Cutting across these integrative influences, which embraced the whole of Maharashtra, existed institutions which split up the Marathi-speaking world into small and self-contained communities, namely, the village community, the *bullotedars,* and the village Gods. The counterposed institutions responsible for integration and cleavage in Maharashtra conjured into existence a society whose stability was related to its overall structure, rathern than to the specific position of any social group, or any individual, within it. The stability of such a society was reinforced, and not weakened, by the conflict and clash of interest between caste and caste, and social group, and the consequent jockeying for positions of power and influence within it contributed to, rather than detracted from, the overall state of equipoise.

6

The central importance of caste in Indian society has long been recognized. Indeed its importance has been exaggerated, if anything, and its character misunderstood. The four varna categories of Brahmin, Kshatriya, Vaishya, and Shudra have, for instance, often been mistaken for functioning caste groups when in fact they are collections of castes with a somewhat similar place in society. At the same time it has always been assumed that the prescriptions of caste imposed a rigid and inflexible barrier to change and mobility in traditional society. Despite this theoretical prohibition new groups—conquerors and the ambitious and wealthy of all sorts—did rise in the ritual hierarchy and others less fortunate sank in status. This mobility was legitimized and made acceptable by a process which has been called Sanskritization. In this selection the originator of the term, an eminent Indian anthropologist, discusses its significance and its connection with such related questions as caste formation and dominance, and the establishment of rural life styles.

FROM

Social Change in Modern India: Chapter 1, "Sanskritization"

M.N. SRINIVAS

Sanskritization is the process by which a "low" Hindu caste, or tribal or other group, changes its customs, ritual, ideology and way of life in the direction of a high, and frequently, "twice-born" caste. Generally such changes are followed by a claim to a higher position in the caste hierarchy than that traditionally conceded to the claimant caste by the local community. The claim is usually made over a period of time, in fact, a generation or two, before the "arrival" is conceded. Occasionally a caste claims a position which its neighbours are not willing to concede. This type of disagreement between claimed and conceded status may be not only in the realm of opinion but also in the more important realm of institutionalized practice. Thus Harijan castes in

Mysore will not accept cooked food and drinking water from the Smiths who are certainly one of the touchable castes and therefore superior to Harijans even if their claim to be Vishwakarma Brahmins is not accepted. Similarly Peasants (Okkaligas) and others such as Shepherds (Kurubas) do not accept cooked food and water from Marka Brahmins, who are certainly included among Brahmins. I remember talking to a Lingayat in north Coorg who referred to the Coorgs as "jungle people [kadu jana]", and this contrasted with the Coorg claim to be true Kshatriyas, and even "Aryans". The above instances are all from Mysore State, but parallels can be cited from every part of India.

Sanskritization is generally accompanied by, and often results in, upward mobility for the caste in question; but mobility may also occur without Sanskritization and vice versa. However, the mobility associated with Sanskritization results only in *positional changes* in the system and does not lead to any *structural change*. That is, a caste moves up, above its neighbours, and another comes down, but all this takes place in an essentially stable hierarchical order. The system itself does not change.

As I have already stated, Sanskritization is not confined to Hindu castes but also occurs among tribal and semitribal groups such as the Bhils of Western India, the Gonds and Oraons of Central India, and the Pahadis of the Himalayas. This usually results in the tribe undergoing Sanskritization claiming to be a caste, and therefore, Hindu. In the traditional system the only way to become a Hindu was to belong to a caste, and the unit of mobility was usually a group, not an individual or a family....

The first three *varnas* are called *dwija* or "twice-born" as only they are entitled to don the sacred thread at the ceremony of *upanayana* which is interpreted as a second birth. Only members of the first three *varnas* are entitled to the performance of Vedic ritual at which hymns *(mantras)* from one or other of the Vedas (excluding the Atharva Veda) are chanted. Among the "twice-born" *varnas* the Brahmins are the most particular about the performance of these rites, and they may therefore be regarded as "better" models of Sanskritization than the others. The cultural content of each *varna*, however, varies from one area to another, and from one period of time to another; and the diversity is generally far greater at the lower levels of the *varna* hierarchy than at the highest.

Let me begin with a brief consideration of the diversity in the Brahmin *varna*. In the first place, some elements of the local culture would be common to all the castes living in a region, from the highest to the lowest. Thus the Brahmin and Harijan (Untouchable) of a region would speak the same language, observe some common festivals, and share certain local deities and beliefs. I have called this "vertical solidarity", and it contrasts with "horizontal solidarity" which members of a single caste or *varna* have.

Some Brahmin groups such as the Kashmiri, Bengali, and Saraswat are non-vegetarians while Brahmins elsewhere are traditionally vegetarians. Some Brahmin groups are more Sanskritized in their style of life than others, and this is quite apart from the differences between *vaidika* (priestly) and *loukika* (secular) Brahmins. There is also considerable occupational diversity between different Brahmin groups. Brahmins in some areas such as Punjab and parts of Western Uttar Pradesh and Rajasthan have a low secular status, and several Brahmin groups in Gujarat (for example, Tapodhan), Bengal, and Mysore (Marka) are regarded as ritually low.

By and large it would be true to say that Kshatriya, Vaishya, and Shudra *varnas* would draw more of their culture from the local area than the Brahmins, and it follows from this that profound cultural differences exist between castes claiming to be Kshatriya and Vaishya in different parts of the country. In fact, while there seems to be some agreement in each area in India as to who are Brahmins and who Untouchables, such consensus is absent with regard to Kshatriyas and Vaishyas. Kshatriya and Vaishya status seems to be claimed by groups who have traditions of soldiering and trade respectively. Neither Kshatriyas nor Shudras in different parts of the country have a common body of ritual. Many of them do not undergo the essential sacraments (samskaras) characteristic of the twice-born *varnas*.

The historian K. M. Panikkar has maintained that there has been no such caste as the Kshatriya during the last two thousand years of history. The Nandas were the last "true" Kshatriyas, and they disappeared in the fifth century B.C. Since then every known royal family has come from a non-Kshatriya caste, including the famous Rajput dynasties of medieval India. Panikkar also points out that "the Shudras seem to have produced an unusually large number of royal families even in more recent times. The Palas of Bengal belonged undoubtedly to that caste. The great Maratha Royal House, whatever their function today, could hardly sustain their genealogical pretensions connecting them with Rajput descent." (One of the most important functions of genealogist and bardic castes was to legitimize mobility from the ranks of lower castes to the Kshatriya by providing suitable general logical linkage and myth.)

The lack of "fit" between the *varna* model and the realities of the existing local hierarchy is even more striking in the case of the Shudra. Not only has this category been a fertile source for the recruitment of local Kshatriya and Vaishya castes, as Panikkar has pointed out, but it spans such a wide cultural and structural arch as to be almost meaningless. There are at one extreme the dominant, landowning, peasant castes which wield power and authority over local Vaishyas and Brahmins, whereas at the other extreme are the poor, near-Untouchable groups living just above the pollution line. The category also includes the many artisan and servicing castes such as goldsmiths, blacksmiths, carpenters, potters, oil pressers, basket makers, weavers, barbers, washermen, watermen, grain parchers, toddy tappers, shepherds and swineherds.

Again, some castes in the omnibus category of Shudra may have a highly Sanskritized style of life whereas others are only minimally Sanskritized. But whether Sanskritized or not, the dominant peasant castes provide local models for imitation; and, as Pocock and Singer have observed, Kshatriya (and other) models are often mediated through them.

A feature of rural life in many parts of India is the existence of dominant, landowning castes. For a caste to be dominant, it should own a sizable amount of the arable land locally available, have strength of numbers, and occupy a high place in the local hierarchy. When a caste has all the attributes of dominance, it may be said to enjoy decisive dominance. Occasionally there may be more than one dominant caste in a village, and over a period of time one dominant caste may give way to another. This happened occasionally even in pre-British India, and has been an important aspect of rural social change in the twentieth century.

New factors affecting dominance have emerged in the last eighty years or so. Western education, jobs in the administration, and urban sources of income are all significant in contributing to the prestige and power of particular caste groups in the village. The introduction of adult franchise and panchayati raj (local self-government at village, *tehsil*, and district levels) since independence has resulted in giving a new sense of self-respect and power to "low" castes, particularly Harijans, who enjoy reservation of seats in all elected bodies from the village to Union Parliament. The long-term implications of these changes are probably even more important, especially in those villages where there are enough Harijans to sway the local balance of power one way or the other. In the traditional system it was possible for a small number of people belonging to a high caste to wield authority over the entire village when they owned a large quantity of arable land and also had a high ritual position. Now, however, in many parts of rural India power has passed into the hands of numerically large, landowning peasant castes; it is likely to remain there for sometime, except in villages where Harijans are numerically strong and are also taking advantage of the new educational and other opportunities available to them. Endemic factionalism in the dominant caste is also another threat to its continued enjoyment of power.

No longer is dominance a purely local matter in rural India. A caste group which has only a family or two in a particular village but which enjoys decisive dominance in the wider region will still count locally because of the network of ties binding it to its dominant relatives. What is equally important is that others in the village will be aware of the existence of this network. Contrariwise, a caste which enjoys dominance in only one village will find that it has to reckon with the caste which enjoys regional dominance.

The vast improvement in communications during the last fifty years has contributed to the decline in prestige of purely local styles of living. Rural leaders, or at least sons, now tend to borrow items from prestigious, urban ways of living, and the long-term effects of this process are a decrease in cultural diversity and an increase in uniformity.

Landownership is a crucial factor in establishing dominance. Generally, the pattern of landownership in rural India is such that the bulk of the arable land is concentrated in the hands of a relatively small number of big owners as against a large number who either own very little land or no land at all. The small number of big owners wield a considerable amount of power over the rest of the village population, and this situation is only made worse by rapid population growth. The big landowners are patrons of the bulk of the poor villagers. Each household from artisan and servicing castes provides goods and services to a certain number of landowning households; traditionally these ties have been stable, continuing from generation to generation. The former are paid in grain and straw during harvests. Ties between landlord and tenant or agricultural servant are also of an enduring kind, though in recent years they have become weaker. Tenants, labourers, artisans, and members of servicing castes stand in a relation of clientship to the landowning patron, and clientship involves a variety of duties.

Similar disparities in the pattern of landownership perhaps exist in other developing countries, but what is unique to the Indian situation is that owners, tenants, landless labourers, artisans, and those who provide services form permanent and hereditary caste groups. Landowners generally come from the higher castes while 35 per cent of Harijans are landless labourers, and the bulk of those who own land "have such small holdings that their condition is hardly better than that of agricultural labourers."

Landownership confers not only power but prestige, so much so that individuals who have made good in any walk of life tend to invest in land. If landownership is not always an indispensable passport to high rank, it certainly facilitates upward mobility. The existence of a congruence between landownership and high rank in the caste hierarchy has been widely observed, but it is important to remember that it is only of a general kind, and admits of exceptions in every area.

The power and prestige which landowning castes command affect their relations with all castes, including those ritually higher. This is true of parts of the Punjab where the landowning Jats look upon the Brahmins as their servants, and of Madhopur Village in eastern Uttar Pradesh where formerly the dominant Thakurs refused cooked food from all Brahmins except their *gurus* or religious teachers. In Rampura Village in Mysore State, the Brahmin priest of the Rama temple was a figure of fun; when, at a temple festival, he tried to distribute *prasada* (food consecrated by being offered to the deity) to the congregation, the peasant youths gathered there teased him by asking for more, and tugged at his *dhoti* when he did not comply....

But important as secular criteria are, ritual superiority has an independent existence and power of its own. Beidelman remarks rightly:

At the risk of inconsistency I must emphasize that there are many areas in which ritual ranks seems to operate independently of economic determinants. In Senapur and Rampur the Brahmins were not the powerful or economically superior caste, but were subordinate to the Jats and Thakurs. But by consensus the village would probably agree that these same Brahmins are ritually supreme. The village would not even find it paradoxical that Brahmins may refuse certain cooked foods and sometimes other social gestures from other castes, even from the economically powerful ones. They would recognize that these castes are all ritually impure to Brahmins.

The inconsistency stressed by Beidelman, of which the people themselves are aware, is an important aspect of caste ranking in which there is occasionally a hiatus between secular and ritual rank. On secular criteria alone a Brahmin may occupy a very low position, but he is still a Brahmin and as such entitled to respect in ritual and pollution contexts. A millionaire Gujarati Bania will not enter the kitchen where his Brahmin cook works, for such entry would defile the Brahmin and the cooking utensils...

Two distinct tendencies are implicit in the caste system. The first is an acceptance of the existence of multiple cultures, including moral and religious norms, in any local society. Such acceptance is accompanied by a feeling that some institutions, ideas, beliefs, and practices are relevant to one's group while others are not. A peasant takes a great deal of pride in his agriculture, and tells about its importance and difficulty and the skill and patience required. An artisan or a member of a servicing caste has a similar attitude toward his hereditary occupation. Occasionally, a man is heard making slighting remarks about the hereditary occupations of other castes.

The other tendency inherent in the caste system is the imitation of the ways of higher castes. Not any particular caste is imitated, or even the highest caste; Pocock is essentially right when he observes:

A non-Brahman caste of relatively low status does not (or did not before the advent of books) imitate an *idea* of Brahmanism nor did it have *general* notions of secular prestige. For it the models of conduct are the castes higher than itself with which it is in the closest proximity. Properly speaking, we may not even speak of one caste imitating another but rather *one local section of a caste imitating another local section* [Italics mine.]

It is necessary, however, to caution against treating the local, village system as completely independent from the wider, all-India system. Ideals of behaviour may be derived from sources of Great Traditions such as pilgrimages, *harikathas* and religious plays...

The elders of the dominant caste in a village were the watchdogs of a pluralistic culture and value system. Traditionally, they prevented the members of a caste from taking over the hereditary occupation of another caste whose interests would have been hurt by an inroad into their monopoly, the only exceptions being agriculture and trade in some commodities. The dominant caste probably ignored minor changes in the ritual and style of life of a low caste, but when the latter refused to perform the services, economic or ritual, which it traditionally performed, or when it appropriated an important high-cast symbol, then punishment followed swiftly. Pocock narrates an incident from his field area in Kaira District in Gujarat State in Western India:

A story is told in Motagam which relates events only thirty years old. At that time a Baria from Nanugam was seen walking through Motagam wearing his *dhoti* in the distinctive Patidar style, sporting a large handle-bar moustache which Patidars of the period cultivated, and smoking a portable hookah. A leading Patidar had him caught and forcibly shaved, and he was ordered, under pain of a beating, never to try to look like a Patidar again and to carry his hookah behind his back whenever he walked through a Patidar village...

Similar incidents have been reported from other parts of rural India during the last fifty years or so. William Rowe mentions that when, in 1936, the Noniyas ("low" caste of salt-makers now employed in digging wells, tanks and roads, and in making tiles and bricks) of Senapur Village in eastern Uttar Pradesh donned *en masse* the sacred thread,

the affronted Kshatriya landlords beat the Noniyas, tore off the sacred threads and imposed a collective fine on the caste. Some years later the Noniyas again began to wear the sacred thread but were unopposed. Their first attempt had been a direct, public challenge, but on the second occasion the Noniyas assumed the sacred thread quietly and on an individual basis.

Hutton has described a similar conflict between the Kallar, a dominant caste in Ramnad District in the extreme south of India, and the Harijans:

In December 1930 the Kallar in Ramnad propounded eight prohibitions the disregard of which led to the use of violence by the Kallar against the exterior Harijan castes, whose huts were fired, whose granaries and property were destroyed, and whose livestock was looted. The eight prohibitions were as follows:

(1)   that the Adi-Dravidas shall not wear ornaments of gold and silver;
(2)   that the males should not be allowed to wear their clothes above the hips;
(3)   that their males should not wear coats or shirts or *baniyans*;
(4)   no Adi-Dravida shall be allowed to have his hair cropped;
(5)   that the Adi-Dravidas should not use other than earthenware vessels in their houses;
(6)   their women shall not be allowed to cover the upper portion of their bodies by clothes or *ravukais* [blouses] or *thavanis* [upper cloths worn like togas];
(7)   their women shall not be allowed to use flowers or saffron paste;
(8)   the men shall not use umbrellas for protection against sun and rain, nor shall they wear sandals.

The dominant caste, then, maintained the structural distance between the different castes living within their jurisdiction. Many of the rules they upheld and enforced were local rules while a few—such as the ban on the donning of the sacred thread by a low caste—were the rules of the Great Tradition. However, it was likely that in those areas where the peasant castes enjoyed decisive dominance they had only a perfunctory knowledge of the Great Tradition. Since, in the traditional system, only the Brahmin priest was the repository of knowledge of the Great Tradition, the dominant caste was able to prevent cultural trespass by ensuring that the priest served only the high castes. Understandably enough, the priest had a healthy respect for the susceptibilities of the dominant caste and of his own caste fellows.

The role of the dominant caste was not, however, restricted to being the guardian of a pluralistic culture. It also stimulated in lower castes a desire to imitate the dominant caste's own prestigious style of life. The lower castes had to go about this task with circumspection—any attempt to rush things was likely to meet with swift reprisal. They had to avoid imitating in matters likely to upset the dominant caste too much, and their chances of success were much better if they slowly inched their way to their goals...

It is possible to prepare a map of rural India showing the castes dominant in each village, but it would require a great investment of labour. In the absence of a systematic map, the names of some of the more prominent dominant castes may be mentioned here. Villagers in North India speak of the *Ajgar*, which literally means "python" and testifies to the fear which the dominant castes rouse in the oppressed minority caste, *Ajgar* is an acronym in Hindi standing for the Ahir (cattle herder), Jat (peasant), Gujar (peasant) and Rajput (warrior). The Sadgop is a dominant caste in parts of West Bengal; Patidar and Rajput in Gujarat; Maratha in Maharashtra; Kamma and Reddi in Andhra; Okkaliga and Lingayat in Mysore; Vellala, Goundar, Padaiyachi, and Kallar in Madras; and finally, Nayar, Syrian Christian, and Izhavan in Kerala.

Dominant castes set the model for the majority of people living in rural areas including, occasionally, Brahmins. Where their way of life has undergone a degree of Sanskritization—as it has, for instance, among the Patidars, Lingayats and some Vellalas—the culture of the area over which their dominance extends experiences a change. Patidars have become more Sanskritized in the last hundred years or so, and this has had effects on the culture of all other groups in Kaira District in Gujarat including the Barias. The Lingayats and the Vellalas of South India also have a Sanskritized style of life, and from a much older period than the Patidars. The Lingayats have been a potent source of cultural and social change in Mysore State, especially in the region to the north of the Tungabhadra River. They have been able to do this because of their use of the popular language of Kannada instead of Sanskrit for the spread of their ideas, and the existence of a network of wealthy and prestigious monasteries. The monasteries have converted—and are still converting—people from different castes to the Lingayat sect.

The Marathas and Reddis, and in more recent years the Padaiyachis (who have changed their name to Vanniya Kula Kshatriyas), have laid claim to Kshatriya status. In pre-British times a claim to Kshatriya status was generally preceded by the possession of political power at the village if not higher levels, and a borrowing of the life style of the Kshatriyas. This set off a chain reaction among the low castes, each of which imitated what it considered to be the Kshatriya style of life. Thus present-day Barias in Kaira District don the red turban and sword in imitation of Patidars of thirty years ago. The Patidars themselves seem to have wanted to be classed as Kshatriyas until recently, when they changed their preference to Vaishya status. A variety of castes in modern Gujarat seek to be recognized as Kshatriyas. According to Pocock, "almost every caste in Charottar, including the Untouchable Dedh, has in its caste stories and legends a history of warrior and kingly origin; these claims can only become effective when supported by wealth suitably invested in Brahminic and secular prestige."

Brahmins, like Kshatriyas, have exercised dominance in rural as well as urban India. In strength of numbers they have rarely been able to compete with the peasant castes, but they have enjoyed ritual pre-eminence, and that in a society in which religious beliefs were particularly strong. In pre-British and princely India, a popular mode of expiating sins and acquiring religious merit was to give gifts of land, houses, gold, and other goods to Brahmins. The gifts were given on such occasions as the birth of a prince, his marriage, coronation, and death. In their roles as officials, scholars, temple priests (*pujaris*), family priests (*purohits*), and in some parts of the country, village record-keepers (*shanbhog, kulkarni, karnam*) also, they came to own land. Ownership of land further increased the great prestige Brahmins already commanded as members of the highest caste.

Centres of pilgrimage and monasteries were also sources of Sanskritization. Each pilgrimage centre had its own hinterland, the most famous of them attracting pilgrims from all over India, while the smallest relied on a few neighbouring villages. Even when a pilgrim centre had an all-India following, it probably attracted more pilgrims from one or a few areas than uniformly from every part of India. In the case of centres drawing from a small region, however, there were perhaps more pilgrims from particular castes or villages than from others. In spite of such limiting factors, a pilgrim centre as well as a monastery managed to influence the way of life of everyone in its hinterland. When a section of a dominant caste came under the influence of a centre or monastery, Sanskritization spread vertically to non-dominant castes in the area and horizontally to members living elsewhere. Such spreading has been greatly facilitated in recent years by a variety of forces, technological, institutional, and ideological.

Sanskritization has been a major process of cultural changes in Indian history, it has occurred in every part of the Indian subcontinent. It may have been more active at some periods than at others, and some parts of India are more Sanskritized than others; but there is no doubt that the process has been universal...

I have commented at some length on the ways in which the *varna* model of the caste system distorts our understanding of traditional Indian society. I have stressed the point that the traditional system did permit of a certain amount of mobility, and I shall pursue this further in this section.

There is, first of all, the process of Sanskritization itself. One of its functions was to bridge the gap between secular and ritual rank. When a caste or section of a caste achieved secular power it usually also tried to acquire the traditional symbols of high status, namely the customs, ritual, ideas, beliefs, and life style of the locally highest castes. It also meant obtaining the services of a Brahmin priest at various *rites de passage,* performing Sanskritic calendrical festivals, visiting famous pilgrimage centres, and finally, attempting to obtain a better knowledge of the sacred literature.

Ambitious castes were aware of the legitimizing role of the Brahmin. Even a poor Brahmin priest living in a village dominated by peasants had to be treated differently from poor people of other castes. Burton Stein, a student of medieval India, pointed out that even the powerful rulers of the Vijayanagar Kingdom (1336-1565) in South India had to acknowledge and pay a price for the legitimizing role of the Brahmin:

> These rulers identified and justified their own power in terms of the protection of Hindu institutions from Islam. The maintenance of proper caste duties and relationships (*varnashrama dharma*) was frequently cited as an objective of state policy in Vijayanagar inscriptions. The new warriors, then, did come to terms with the Brahman elite of South India. *On the basis of their continued support of Brahman religious prerogatives and high ritual rank— though not support of the earlier almost complete socio-political autonomy of landed Brahman communities—they won recognition from the Brahmans for their own ascendant military and political power.* [Italics mine]...

All over North India the bardic castes were traditionally a fruitful source of legitimization of the acquisition of political power. Thus Shah and Shroff observe,

> The Vahivanca is important to the Rajput not only as genealogist but also as mythographer. Anyone who wants to call himself Rajput should show that he is descended from an ancient Rajput dynasty,

and it is only the Vahivanca who is believed to be able to show this authoritatively. A Rajput's existence as a member of his caste depends upon the Vahivanca. Moreover, some of the most vital social and political institutions of the Rajputs are based on the belief that these have existed since time immemorial. The Vahivanca's records are, to the Rajput, proof of the antiquity of the institutions.

The Vahivanca provided the means of ligitimization not only for the Rajput but also for others, including the tribal Kolis. In Central Gujarat Rajputs marry girls from the lineages of the Koli chiefs, and this had provided the latter with a rope to pull themselves up with. Building upon the fact of the hypergamous marriage of Kolis with Rajputs, the Vahivancas are able to provide a charter to Koli mobility.

A caste group is generally endogamous, but occasionally endogamy is found to coexist with hypergamy. The caste considered to be lower has a one-sided relationship with the higher by which it gives its girls in marriage to the latter. This results in a scarcity of girls in the lower group, and of boys in the higher. Hypergamy occurs in several regions of India—Kerala, Gujarat, Bengal, and parts of Uttar Pradesh. And it provides evidence of the upward mobility of castes. In Pocock's terminology hypergamy corresponds to the "inclusive" aspects of caste while endogamy corresponds to its "exclusive" aspect. A caste would like to include itself with those it considers superior, and the existence of hypergamy provides an institutional basis for such inclusion. Similarly the practice of caste endogamy is an implicit repudiation of the claims of lower castes to equality...

Hypergamy was significant for mobility in yet another way. A caste or section of a caste would Sanskritize its way of life and then claim to be superior to its structural neighbours or to the parent section. Amma Coorgs, a section of the main body of the Coorgs, came under strong Brahminical influence in the first half of the nineteenth century and became vegetarians and teetotallers and donned the sacred thread. In course of time they became a distinct endogamous group even though they numbered only 666 individuals at the 1941 census. It may be presumed that throughout the history of caste new caste groups arose as a result of such fission from the parent body.

It is necessary to stress that the mobility characteristic of caste in the traditional period resulted only in *positional* changes for particular castes or sections of castes, and did not lead to a *structural* change. That is, while individual castes moved up or down, the structure remained the same. It was only in the literature of the medieval Bhakti (literally, devotion to a personal god) movement that the idea of inequality was challenged. A few sects even recruited followers from several castes in their early, evangelical phase, but gradually either the sect became an endogamous unit, or endogamy continued to be an attribute of each caste within the sect.

It is not my aim in this section to marshal systematically evidence to support the view that there was social mobility in every period of Indian history. i shall cite a few instances of mobility from ancient and medieval India while paying more attention to the period immediately prior to the establishment of British rule.

This institution of *varna* evolved gradually during the Vedic period (*circa* 1500-500 B.C.) the earliest for which any literary evidence is available. The Purusha Sukta, one of the later hymns of the earliest of the four Vedas, Rig Veda, gives a mythical account of the origin of the four *varnas*, Brahmana, Rajanya (that is, Kshatriya), Vaishya, and Shudra, and this is the first mention of the *varna* hierarchy as we know it today. The Brahmin's position began to strengthen during the latter part of the Vedic period, and this was linked up with the increasing importance and elaboration of the institution of sacrifice. By the end of the Vedic period the Brahmin's position had become impregnable, and his rival from an earlier period, the Kshatriya, had been pushed to a secondary place. Ghurye has stated that Jainism and Buddhism were both started by "Kshatriyas of exceptional ability preaching a new philosophy which was utilized by their immediate followers for asserting the social superiority of the Kshatriyas over the Brahmins. The Brahmin has a fresh cause for grudge. He comes forward as the saviour of the Vedic Brahminic culture."

The Vaishya occupied a low place in the hierarchy during the Rig Vedic period, and indeed, this *varna* figures singularly little in Vedic literature. The term Vaishya, in its earliest usage, referred to ordinary people, and Basham thinks that the caste "originated in the ordinary peasant triblesman of the Rig Veda." The conversion of Vaishyas to Buddhism and Jainism probably resulted in an improvement in their position.

Though the Brahmana literature gives Vaishya few rights and humble status, the Buddhist and Jaina scriptures, a few centuries later in date and of more easterly provenance, show that he was not always oppressed in practice. They mention many wealthy merchants living in great luxury, and powerfully organized in guilds. Here the ideal Vaishyu is not the humble tax-paying cattle breeder but the *astikotivibhava*, the man possessing eight million *panas*. Wealthy Vaishyas were respected by kings and enjoyed their favour and confidence.

Apart from the rise and fall of particular *varnas* over the centuries, the system seems to have enjoyed a degree of "openness". This is pointedly seen in the case of Kshatriyas who seem to have been recruited in ancient times from several ethnic groups including Greeks (*Yavana*), Scythians (*Shaka*), and Parthians (*Pahlava*). Panikkar has been quoted earlier as saying that in historical times there was no such caste as the Kshatriyas, and ever since the fifth century B.C. ruling families have come from a wide variety of castes:

Burton Stein considers the medieval period to be characterized by "widespread and persistent examples of social mobility". He emphasizes the contrast between theory and practice.

When the rank of persons was in theory rigorously ascribed according to the purity of the birth-group, the political units of India were probably ruled most often by men of very low birth. This generalization applies to South Indian warriors and may be equally applicable for many clans of "Rajputs" in northern India. *The capacity of both ancient and medieval Indian society to ascribe to its actual rulers, frequently men of low social origins, a "clean" or "Kshatriya" rank may afford one of the explanations for the durability and longevity of the unique civilization of India.* [Italics mine.]

A potent source of social mobility in pre-British India was the fluidity of the political system. Such fluidity was not limited to any particular part of India, but characterized the system everywhere. It constituted an important, through not the only, avenue to social mobility. In order to capture political power, however, a caste or its local section had to have a martial tradition, numerical strength, and preferably also ownership of a large quantity of arable land. Once it had captured political power it had to Sanskritize its ritual and style of life and lay claim to being Kshatriya. It had to patronize (or even create!) Brahmins who would minister to it on ritual occasions, and produce an appropriate myth supporting the group's claim to Kshatriya status. The establishment of *Pax Britannica* resulted in freezing the political system and blocked this avenue to mobility. That eventually British rule opened other avenues to mobility does not concern us here.

We are able to have a clearer understanding than before of the process of social mobility through the achievement of political power, thanks to the excellent studies of pre-British India by Bernard Cohn and Arvind Shah. Cohn has studied the Benares region in Eastern Uttar Pradesh, and Shah, the Central Gujarat region.

Cohn distinguishes four levels of the political system in eighteenth century India—imperial, secondary, regional, and local. The Mughals occupied the "imperial" level, and incidental to their efforts at ruling the entire subcontinent they had to have a loyal army and a bureaucracy. They succeeded so completely in monopolizing the symbols of legitimacy that in the eighteenth century even those groups "which were trying to free themselves of actual imperial control none the less turned to the remnants of the imperial authority for legitimizing their power..." The "secondary" level consisted of successor states such as Oudh which emerged after dissolution of Mughal power, and which exercised suzerainty over a major historical, cultural, or linguistic region. Each "secondary" system was made up of several "regional" systems, and at the head of the latter was an individual or family which had the status of hereditary official or ruler, a status conferred on it by the imperial or the secondary authority. "The leaders [of regional systems] were loosely incorporated through rituals of allegiance and financial obligation to the national power and were in competition with potential regional leaders." At the bottom of the power structure was the "local" system represented by lineages, an indigenous chief, a tax official turned political leader, or a successful adventurer. The heads of the local system were subordinate to the regional leader although they often derived their positions from the secondary authority. These heads controlled the local peasants, artisans, and traders, and offered them protection from outside interference. They collected from their subjects money or a share of the crop in return for their services.

In the Benaras region the Nawab of Oudh was nominally the political overlord, and he derived his authority from the Mughal Emperor in Delhi. The Nawab ruled this area through his officials from 1720 to 1740, and through his partially independent subordinate, the Raja of Benaras, from 1740 to 1775.

The Raja of Benaras in turn had to control, extract revenue or tribute from, and on occasion get military help from a large number of localized lineages, petty chiefs, and *jagirdars* (holders of revenue-free lands from the Nawab of Oudh or the Emperor of Delhi). Feuds within lineages, warfare between lineages, or warfare between lineages and the Raja of Benaras were frequent. Disputes often were settled by the direct use of force.

At the base of the social and political pyramid were the lower castes who actually cultivated the land as tenants, sharecroppers, serfs, and slaves. Above them were the members of the dominant castes, either Rajput or Bhumihar Brahmin, organized into corporate lineages controlling the land. The founders of the lineages were either conquerors or recipients of royal or other grants. By the end of the eighteenth century the lineages were large, corporate bodies often including over a thousand families related to each other by agnatic links. The corporate lineages realized from the actual tillers of land a share of the produce, a part of which they were forced to surrender to "subordinate political powers."...

Cohn traces the rise of Mansa Ram, a member of the landholding, dominant Bhumihar caste in a village in Jaunpur District, who worked for a local *amil* or tax collector, and eventually replaced the latter. His ability and lack of scruples enabled him to obtain from Safdar Jang, who succeeded his uncle to the Nawabship of Oudh, a royal grant making Mansa Ram's son, Balwant Singh, the Raja of Benaras and the Zamindar of the three districts of Benaras, Jaunpur and Mirzapur.

The Raja of Benaras had to pay tribute to the Nawab of Oudh, and also provide him with troops when necessary. The Raja had a dual role. He did not have the necessary administrative machinery to collect revenue directly from the people, bypassing the local chiefs and lineages. He was also dependent upon the latter for his troops without which he could not be independent from the Nawab of Oudh. In fact, he made a continuous effort to be completely independent from the control of the Nawab. He also needed to keep in check lineages and local chiefs who wielded power within his province. The more powerful of the chiefs posed a threat to his existence.

Cohn characterizes the political system of eighteenth century Benaras region as one of "balanced oppositions, each element in competition with the other, each dependent on the other, cultivator, corporate lineage, tax farmer, and Raja." The conflicts between lineages and between them and the local Raja or *jagirdar*, between the latter and the Raja of Benaras, enabled leaders of dominant groups to acquire political power, and through it a higher position in the hierarchy. In other words, the political system favoured social mobility.

Arvind Shah's description of the political system of eighteenth century Gujarat—or more correctly, central Gujarat—also emphasizes its fluidity...

The situation in the Benaras and Gujarat regions in the eighteenth century may be summed up by saying that the political system favoured mobility for the leaders of the dominant local groups such as the Bhumihar Brahmins, Rajputs, Patidars, and Kolis. It also favoured a few officials (for example, Mansa Ram in Benaras and Muslim officials in Gujarat) who drew on their official authority to establish principalities. (I suspect, however, that at some point their individual mobility became linked up with that of their castes.) The fact that the Mughal power was on the wane in the eighteenth century made the period particularly favourable to mobility, but the difference between it and earlier periods was only one of degree. Considering that pre-British India was characterized by primitive technology and poor communications, peripheral areas of large kingdoms were always likely to have considerable autonomy from the central power...

It is not necessary to labour further the point that the political system of pre-British India favoured mobility for some strategically situated individuals and groups. I shall now turn briefly to a secondary source of mobility in that system—the king or other acknowledged political head of an area. The latter had the power to promote or demote castes inhabiting his kingdom. The Maharaja of Cochin, for instance, had the power to raise the rank of castes in his kingdom, and the final expulsion of anyone from caste required his sanction. He is, in fact, reputed to have raised some "Charmas" [Cherumans?] to the status of Nayars for helping him and his allies, the Portuguese, against his traditional enemy, the Zamorin of Calicut. The power to raise the rank of castes living within their jurisdiction seems to have been enjoyed in South India by even some big *Zamindars*. During the British period, when their accounts were examined for the purposes of revenue assessment, they were found to include receipts on account of the privilege conferred by them on certain persons to wear the sacred thread.

The power to promote or demote castes stemmed from the fact that the pre-British Indian king, Hindu or Muslim, stood at the apex of the caste system. In the last analysis, the ranking of castes within the kingdom had the king's consent, and an individual who had been outcasted by his caste council for an offence had always the right of appeal to the king. The latter had the power to re-examine the evidence and confirm or alter the verdict. H.J.Maynard, a British official who served in the old Punjab area at the turn of the century, had the good fortune to witness the Rajput chief of a large region actually exercising his authority in caste matters. According to Maynard, "It appears that, even under the Mughal emperors, the Delhi Court was the head of all the Caste Panchayats, and the questions affecting a caste over a wide area could not be settled except at Delhi, and under the guidance of the ruler for the time being."

In settling disputes with regard to rank and in deciding the appropriate punishment for an offence, learned Brahmins were consulted by the king. But they only declared or expounded the law; it was the king who enforced their decision.

So far I have considered only mobility arising from the political system, and ignored mobility resulting from the pre-British productive system. In this connection it is necessary to emphasize that pre-British India did not suffer from overpopulation; Kingsley Davis, for instance, has argued that India's population was stationary between 1600 and 1800, and that it numbered about 125 million in 1800. In many parts of the country there existed land which, with some effort, could be rendered arable. This in turn meant that tenants and agricultural labourers enjoyed an advantage in their relations with their landowning masters. If the master was unusually oppressive and cruel, the tenants could move to another area and start new farms or work for another master. The fear of labourers and other dependents running away was a real one, and it served to restrain masters somewhat...

Burton Stein has argued cogently that the availability of "marginally settled land suitable for cultivation which permitted the establishment of new settlements and even new regional societies" imposed limitations

on the amount of tribute in the form of agricultural surplus, which local warriors could extract from peasant villages under their control, as well as on other forms of arbitrariness....Different branches of the Vellala community of Tamil-speaking South India, a respected and powerful cultivating caste, seem to have developed in this manner. This "looseness" in the agrarian order of medieval South India has been noted by historians, but there has been no systematic study of it. If a developing social system, characterized by such "openness" is seen as typical in many parts of South India during the medieval period, then the model of the contemporary competition of ethnic units for enhanced rank within a narrow, localized ranking system appears inappropriate for understanding the process of mobility in an earlier period. Much of the evidence we have on the nature of the medieval social order indicates that there was considerable opportunity for individual mobility in an earlier period.

According to Stein, then, social mobility in medieval India was closely bound up with spatial mobility; and the availability of potentially arable land along with other factors such as floods, droughts, epidemics, and excessive tribute demands stimulated migration. There were also obstacles to movement, but they were not insuperable. His mention of the existrence of subdivisions among the agrarian Vellalas is peculiarly apt, and subdivisions have similarly proliferated among other peasant castes such as Nayar, Kamma, Reddi, Okkaliga, and Maratha. A section which moved out became a separate endogamous *jati* after the lapse of several years, and true to caste tradition, each such *jati* claimed to be superior to the others. One division may change its occupation ever so slightly, or adopt a new custom, or become more or less Sanskritized in its style of life than the others. The forces released during British rule, and subsequently, have led to these *jatis* coming together to form large castes. The process is still active, and different sections of a *jati* are differently affected by it. I have called this an increase in "horizontal solidarity", but the *jatis* subsumed in the emergent entity are not, strictly speaking, equal.

Stein's other point—that "the model of the contemporary competition of ethnic units for enhanced rank within a narrow, local ranking system is inappropriate" for understanding social mobility in pre-British India—is also important in that it helps to account for cultural variations between sections of the same caste living in different areas. A family or group of families would have greater freedom to adopt the Sanskritic style of life in a new area where they were unknown than in their natal area where the locally dominant caste knew them. In other words, migration made "passing" possible, and the mobile group was able to assume new and prestigious cultural robes. But even within a narrow region the dominant caste of political chief did not have unlimited power, and this allowed low castes a certain amount of elbowroom. This is not to deny, however, that mobility within a localized ranking system, such as that described by Pocock, is the result of British rule.

Stein thinks that opportunities for "individual family mobility were great" in medieval India; also there was little need then for corporate mobility. Facilities such as the printing press which modern "corporate mobility" movements appear to require, as well as the political need for them, came into existence only recently. I presume that Stein is using "corporate" in the sense of "collective", and if I am right in so thinking, it is certainly true that collective movements are characteristic of modern times while "individual family movements" were characteristic of the medieval period. *But the latter have to be translated at some point into collective movements, and this necessity is forced on them by caste.* Where will the mobile family find brides for sons and grooms for daughters? Even in South India where the marriage of cross cousins and cross uncle and niece are preferred, a few families would be essential for the recruitment of spouses. Hypergamy also would enable a small group to be mobile, but that group must be much larger than an individual family.

7

Beneath the shared values of the Hindu social order lie a myriad of diverse regional customs and loyalties. The product of long historical evolution in a far-flung subcontinent, these regional differences are deeply rooted and often strikingly visible. No one would mistake a Punjabi for a Madrasi. For most Indians the sense of belonging to, and participating in, a greater Indian culture is complemented by a simultaneous participation in a regional culture defined in large part by language, literature, and a common past. This essay first asks how one defines a region in India, and then goes on to examine the growth of regional sentiment in modern India.

Regions Subjective and Objective: Their Relation to the Study of Modern Indian History and Society

BERNARD S. COHN

This will be a paper of questions and speculation, an attempt to look at some of the methodological and substantive issues common to the social scientists' endeavour to make empirical and theoretical sense out of modern Indian society. In the term "social scientists" I of course include historians, and in using the term "modern Indian society", I am talking not only about contemporary India, but India since the 18th century as well. The argument of this paper is a simple and probably self-evident one—there are regional differences in South Asia just as there is a reality to thinking about South Asia as a geographic and the historical entry, or Indian civilization as a cultural unity. The platitude "unity in diversity" is no less real than the reiteration of the differing structural and cultural features of regions, the differences in language and literature, of historical and ritual identities, in political and administrative styles and methods, and the variance from region to region of industrialization and modernization. The question is not one of the reality of region vs. the reality or significance of holistic entities

Reprinted by permission from R.I. Crane, ed., *Regions and Regionalism in South Asia,* Copyright © Committee on Southern Asian Studies, Duke University, Durham, N.C., 1966, pp. 5-37. Footnotes omitted.

like civilizations, but under what circumstances does it make sense to emphasize the total entity and under what circumstances does it make sense to emphasize the regional differences.

WHAT IS A REGION? PRELIMINARY DEFINITIONS

As Norton Ginsburg the geographer remarked, "There is no universally accepted definition of the region, except as it refers to some portion of the surface of the earth." There would seem to be as many definitions of regions as there are social science disciplines and problems that social scientists investigate. Most definitions of regions begin with a geographic component and develop out of the relationship between geographic features and man's adaptation to the physical environment. At one end of a continuum of definitions of regions would be the idea of a *natural region,* which would encompass only the physical basis of a region. For most purposes of research and analysis which concern us, I think the natural component, although important, can be assumed. For the last fifty years, human geographers have been developing techniques for the definition and analysis of various kinds of geographic regions, all of which involve synthetic or analytical efforts involving space relationships which encompass human as well as physical conditions. Most of us are familiar with John Brush's regional approach to Indian geography, in Norton Ginsburg, ed., *The Pattern of Asia,* or O.H.K.Spate's *India and Pakistan: A General and Regional Geography,* both sophisticated attempts to work out geographic regions for India. In more recent years, geographers, economists, planners, administrators, and political scientists have spent considerable time developing ideas and criteria for the establishment of *planning regions* in India; whether they be based on river valleys, metropolitan regions, intra-or inter-provincial areas based on some common economic/geographic variables, or transportation and communication variables. As these operations become more and more sophisticated methodologically and depend more and more on statistical and /or mathematical models, they seem less immediately useful to furthering the study of historical and / or cultural problems which engage most of us. It is clear, however, that although not immediately applicable to our current research interests, we need to hold a "watching brief" on these activities of our more quantitatively oriented colleagues in that they might discover relationships and be able to express them in a fashion we thus far haven't considered.

Although logically a definition of region "refers to some portion of the surface of the earth", and as important as these essentially geographic approaches are to the study of regions in India, they are the beginning point for us rather than an end in themselves. For most of us the conceptualization of regions involves basically non-physical phenomena, which I might term historical, linguistic, cultural, social structural, and / or the interrelations among these kinds of variables. I would offer the following definitions as a starting point of our discussions of regions and regionalism in India:

1. *"Historical" Regions:* A historical region is one in which there are sacred myths and symbols, held by significant groups within the area, regarding the relationship of people to their "past" and the geographical entity. Examples of such regions might be *Tamilnad,* the Tamil-speaking portions of the old Madras Presidency and the present state of Madras; *Bundelkhand,* the south-western portion of the present state of Utter Pradesh (the districts of Jhansi Jalaun, an Lalitpur), which geographically differs from the Gangetic portions of Uttar Pradesh and has a historical connection with a ruling caste, the Bundela Rajputs, who claimed and to some extent exercised suzerainty over the region, all of which to residents and outsiders give Bundelkhand its historical identity.

2. *Linguistic Regions:* A linguistic region is one in which there is a shared and recognized literary language, the standardized form of which is known and identified with by the educated groups within the area. As one reads through most attempts to empirically develop regional classifications for India, one keeps coming back to the distribution of languages. Language diversity is assumed as the necessary pre-condition for most attempts, not only to establish the criteria of linguistic regions, but to differentiate cultural and structural regions as well. It is usually difficult to differentiate the four types of regions, historical, linguistic, cultural, and structural, as it is assumed that there is concomitant variation among linguistic, cultural, historical, and structural variables. As Mrs. Karve points out:

> Intercommunication is easy within a linguistic region. The common language makes it the widest area within which marital connections are established and outside of which kinship hardly ever extends. It is a region over which the same folksongs and higher literature has spread.

If one starts, as does Mrs. Karve and most others, with the *literary standard*, e.g., Bengali, Tamil, Marathi, one can extend or expand linguistic classifications into much wider areas, into *language families,* e.g., Indo-European, Dravidian; or one may reduce the span and nature of regions by basing the classification on *regional standards* or *regional dialects*, e.g., Awadhi, Konkani, the dialect of Bengali spoken in Chittagong, East Pakistan.

3. *Cultural Regions:* A cultural region is one in which there are widely shared and recognized cultural traits and patterned behaviour, particularly among the common people. Descriptively, one or two kinds of behaviour, customs, or traits are taken as diagnostic of regional culture. Gods, goddesses, rituals, myths, and festivals are the most frequent diagnostic traits used to establish the "reality" of particular regions. For example:

> Bengalis do not worship the male incarnations of Vishnu and Shiva, but it is the female deities, manifestations of the supreme mother—such as Durga, Kali, Chandi, Lakshmi, Sarasvati, Sitala, and a number of others—who occupy the most prominent place in Bengal's folk religion; and especially, the worship of the Great Mother as Durga, with a protracted ceremonial, the Durga Puja which is the unique feature of the religious life of Bengal.

Other kinds of cultural items, which are sometimes thought to be diagnostic of a region are dress, style of turban, jewelry, agricultural implements, house types, or settlement patterns. House type and settlement pattern take one back to basic geographic determinants. (People build stone houses when they have stone available, or particular local climatic conditions might influence the type of house built.) The use of settlement pattern as a major variable for determining a regional culture also involves structural features as well.

4. *Structural Regions:* A structural region is one in which there are groups of associated structural variables which differentiate one structural area from another. The attempt to isolate and analyze social structural variables is the most recent attempt to establish a reasonable analytical basis for regional study. This form of regional analysis of course is inherent in some of the geographic and cultural attempts to develop a classification of the regions of India. In many ways McKim Marriott's "Caste Ranking and Community Structure in Five Regions of India and Pakistan" is the leading example of this approach. In the

study, Marriott argued that if one takes a structural view of caste and tries to explain the variation in the subcontinent of one major feature of the caste system, that of ranking, one can develop a scale of elaborateness from low to high, and then compare regions in regard to one major structural feature of the caste system. His aim:

> Some of the apparent uniqueness and seemingly fortuitous variety within caste in India and Pakistan become capable of regular analysis and understanding, however, when the phenomena of caste are examined, not historically in isolation, and not lumped together as a contemporary conglomerate of subcontinental scope, but locally and regionally with systematic regard for their contexts in peasant communities of differing social structure.

Marriott isolates deductively four variables which are the determinants of the elaboration of caste ranking, the number of ethnic groups (sub-castes) in the system, the degree and acceptance of overt inequalities of the groups as defined by attitudes and behaviour, the development of a consistent consensus among members of the community as to the standing of the ranked groups, and finally the need for relative isolation of one local ranking interacting series of groups from others.

The major part of Marriott's monograph is devoted to the application of the deductive framework of the significance of the four variables to an analysis of caste ranking in what Marriott terms regions. The regions compared are Kerala, Coromandel (both Telegu-and Tamil-speaking districts, but primarily Tamil speaking), the Upper Ganges (Uttar Pradesh—the 30 Gangetic Valley Districts), Middle Indus (the predominately Muslim districts of West Punjab, Pakistan), and the Bengal Delta. Marriott's selection and delimitation of the regions was partially based on the provincial classifications of the pre-Independence census volumes, in order to have quantitative data available for his analysis; and although criticism could be made at the empirical level of the "reality" of these regions for our purposes it is the approach in attempting to establish regions that matters, so that structural variables that are significant may be compared. This makes the study a significant development in the study of regions in India. Kolenda's work on the Jajmani system and the joint family are also significant demonstrations of the usefulness of comparison of structural regions. The use of structural regions as the unit of comparison merges at the more abstract end with the efforts of Bailey, Nicholas, and others in trying to establish types of political systems in India.

Having tried briefly to define and differentiate among some of the different types of definitions of regions which are prevalent today, I now would like to go back and discuss various problems which I think arise in attempting to set up the definitions.

Thus far, most attempts to establish a viable classification of regions have treated regions within their classifications as totally comparable as far as type is concerned. For example, in linguistic classifications, once having established the principal criteria of which level of the language was being used to establish the boundaries of the regions, it is assumed that the regions thus established are comparable. This, of course, ignores several central issues: the difference between literary and vernacular standards and their differential distribution between urban and rural areas: the presence of significant numbers of speakers of other than the dominant language within the circumscribed area, e.g., the presence of Mundari languages in Eastern India; the presence, as in much of the north, of two well established languages and associated cultural traditions, intertwined and side by side—i.e., Hindu and Urdu in U.P., Urdu and Telegu in Hyderabad. Most important, I think there are grounds to question the assumption of ease of intercommunication within the region. As Gumperz and others have shown, the level of mutual intelligibility within the "linguistic regions" at the village or rural level drops off rather rapidly, so that in many instances an illiterate villager speaking his local dialect is not understood when he travels one hundred miles and tries to communicate with his counterpart from that area. At the small town and bazaar level, where a regional dialect is spoken by the residents of the town, the spread is somewhat further than that of the villages. In the cities, in the 19th century, with the spread of primary and secondary education using the literary standards as the medium of instruction, the educated or city dweller had a speech community which was discontinuous but very widespread. The question of the use of linguistic criteria to establish a regional classification becomes a mixed linguistic and social one. The distribution of a language alone does not necessarily establish a tightly bordered or circumscribed region; rather one must think vertically as well as horizontally.

The introduction of printing necessitated the standardization of literary standards not common before. The availability of cheap, printed materials, particularly through the schools, points to another problem in the establishment of regions, and that is the time or historical factor. If we were establishing regional linguistic classifications in the mid-18th century we would draw our boundaries much differently than did some of those who deposed before the States Reorganization Commission in 1955. Not that there have been that many dramatic shifts of populations, although there have been some, bearing their languages with them, but I think we would be more inclined to use the regional standards or dialects as the significant boundary, rather than the literary standard as the criteria for the linguistic regional classification at earlier periods. The development of the literary standards or regional languages in the last century and a half as the basis of regionalism was clearly recognized by the States Reorganization Commission:

> One of the major facts of India's political evolution during the last 100 years has been the growth of our regional languages. They have during this period developed into rich and powerful vehicles of expression, creating a sense of unity among the peoples speaking them.

My cursory exploration of the problems of establishing linguistic regions raises certain general issues about regional classifications. On the surface the mapping of language distributions would seem simple and straightforward. Dialectologists and other linguists have simple techniques for going into the field, getting linguistic samples, and then plotting their samples on a map. But it is clear that where one draws his boundaries relates to how he defines a particular language. We can map the regional standards and then map the distribution of the regional dialects within the standards. Within the regional standard distribution there are enclaved languages as well. This very often is a function of human geography, e.g., speakers of Mundari languages are found in refuge hill regions. The question of the Mundari and other tribal languages is easier to handle than the presence of well developed differing linguistic and cultural traditions, particularly at the literary standard level within the regions. The best known and most interesting of the multiple language traditions within a linguistic region is of course Hindi and Urdu, where the distribution of what one identifies as his language is partially the distribution of Muslim and Hindu, but also in the 18th and 19th centuries a cultural marker of Persianization of both Hindus and Muslims. The distribution of Hindi and Punjabi in the Punjab is also correlated with the religious differences between Hindus and Sikhs. Linked with distribution of these kinds of multiples of language tradition is the question of urban vs. rural distribution. Again Hindi or Hindustani provides an example. One finds from Calcutta to Bombay and from Nagpur to Lahore native speakers of Hindi or Hindustani. In some cases as in Bombay and Calcutta the native speakers are fairly low in the social order and are recent migrants, often only temporary. In other instances the native speakers of Hindi or Hindustani, who are often bilingual in Hindustani and the regional dialect, have been resident for generations in the city, and may be the traditional commercial/administrative elites of the city, and are neither enclaved peoples like tribals or the Marwari business community of Calcutta, nor recent migrants, but represent a widespread urban style of life. Hence a linguistic classification, let us say, of much of Northern and Central India, which did not take into consideration the relationship between regional standard and regional dialect, the presence of multiple life styles of which language may be the central cultural marker, and above all the time/historical factor, would be doing considerable violence to the reality of Indian society and culture.

Since I am arguing that time and not the simple unidimensional distribution of phenomena is so crucial to regional classifications, let me turn to a consideration of *historical regions*. The establishment of what I would call historical regions lacks on the surface the definitiveness of the linguistic regions. We are not obviously plotting the distribution of a single diagnostic phenomenon like the language which a person or group of people speak, but at least two very differing but interrelated congeries of phenomena, symbols-myths and cultural-historical identities, and the relative persistence of political states and their boundaries.

Accepting the reality of *historical regions* as I do, it must be made clear at the outset that there is no one single type of *historical region*. I think it important to establish at the outset the different kinds of *historical regions* there are in a quasianalytical fashion, before looking at the substance of any regional classification. It is useful to think of *nuclear* or perennial *historical regions, shatter zones* or *route areas, cul de sacs,* and regions of *relative isolation.*

The perennial or nuclear regions are the principal river basins, which are major agricultural areas, the Indus, Ganges, Narmada, Tapti, Godavari, Krishna, and Cauvery. Although these areas have always attracted conquerors, they tended to maintain their identity through time, since they had the basic ecological-agricultural prerequisites for fairly large scale state formation and the maintenance of centres for the development and propagation of both the Great Tradition and regional variations. The lower basin of the Krishna and Godavari rivers, for example, is identifiable from early periods as Andhra; Kosala in the Ganges-Jamuna Doab was Awadh in the 18th century and is a large part of Uttar Pradesh of the present.

Shatter zones or route areas are the traditional regions through which large numbers of people passed either in military or peaceful invasion. In these areas which in effect connect the nuclear regions, there is no persistent political tradition. Socially and culturally the area tends to be more of a mosaic than a relative unitary kind of social structure, and the tendency is characteristic to some extent of both resions of relative isolation and the perennial nuclear regions. Malwa is an example of a shatter region or route region. Adrian Mayer summarizes the situation well:

> Malwa has had an eventful history, partly because it provides by far the best route from northern India to the Deccan and so has attracted conquerors, and partly because, when there has been peace, the fertility of the area has supported prosperous kingdoms...

States rose and fell in the region; at times they were independent in the region and at other times appendices to states established in the nuclear regions. In the 18th and early 19th centuries, warfare and movement was constant in the area. The result has been that many of the castes in the region are of "foreign" origin. In Ramkheri, the village Mayer describes, the village was itself completely reconstituted in the early 20th century.

> In 1899-1900 a famine decimated the village, causing some caste groups to die out completely, and others to leave the village in search of food...after the famine the Maharani encouraged settlers to come to fill the gaps caused by death or emigration. Of the 257 adult men in the village, 35 are themselves newcomers, and 109 have fathers or fathers' fathers who came to Ramkheri.

The facts of sociology and history notwithstanding, or perhaps because of them, the residents of Ramkheri as described by Mayer have a highly developed regional-historical sense. Mayer closes his discussion of the history of Malwa with the following:

> I have given this historical sketch for two reasons. First, I want to show that Malwa has its own history, which is known to the

villagers of Ramkheri. They look back to the golden age of Vikramaditya; they talk of the days of plenty under Raja Bhoja; they know of the great Muslim kings and of the palaces of Mandu, even if they have never been there. For them, Ujjain is the main ritual and cultural centre, and they compare its great twelve-yearly fair most favourably to anything occurring on the Ganges. They are, in short, conscious of being inhabitants of a specific province of India, which they consider to be superior to all others in climate and culture.

Malwa is not only a route region or shatter zone connecting the region around Delhi with Gujarat, the Deccan, and the West Coast of India, but also one of the routes into the mountain belt of central India. Hence, from early historic times waves of migrants have passed through the region and some have established themselves in Malwa. Venkatachar, in the census of the Central India Agency for 1931, lists 23 principal castes in the Central India Agency (which included parts of Malwa); of these, fifteen have traditions of migrations and this includes the bulk of the upper castes, Brahmans, Banias, and Rajputs. Many of the castes came with the Muslim invaders, e.g., the Khati, with Marathas; and the Baniyas, with the British. Others came because of famine and dislocation in their original home territories.

A subvariant of the route or shatter region might be termed the *march or ethnic frontier region.* Typically these are the transition zones or regions between plains and hills, in which the plains' Hindus are extending their political, economic, and cultural control over the hill people.

The possible complexities of a march region are described by S.C.Dube in his article, "A Deccan Village". Dewara, a village of slightly over 1,000 is on the fringe of the Northern edge of the Deccan Plateau, in a basically tribal area, but where "the culture areas of Telengana and Marathwada meet." The village has four distinct groups in it, Tribal (405), Telegu (446), Maratha (132), and Muslim (107). Each maintains linguistic and structural separateness. The tribe (in which there are three distinct groupings), the Telegu (13 castes represented), and the Maratha (5 castes) each has its own internal hierarchy. Each follows differing religious and other customs, each has arrangements for ordering relations within its ethnic groups. In addition, Dube states that there is a kind of "social symbiosis obtaining in the village (which) has led to a distinct type of inter group adjustment." It is in the nature of the social symbiosis and the distinct type of intergroup adjustment, the problem of distinct structures and cultures within one social system, which gives the *march region* its claim to be analytically a subvariant type of the *shatter or route region.*

The final type of a historical region is the region of *relative isolation* or the *cul de sac.* These are regions which because of their geographic ecological characteristics, which prevent easy access, have tended to be bypassed by processes and events which have affected the *nuclear* and *route* regions. Their location may be on the boundaries of South Asia, such as the Sub Himalayan regions, or in mountainous areas such as in Central India, where distinctive physical features and difficulties make them refugee areas into which people from outside have tended to migrate, but once there, have developed their own distinctive political and social forms. Gerald Berreman, in his *Hindus of the Himalayas,* describes such a situation. Another example of enclavement and elaboration of a separate social and cultural system in an area of physical inhospitality is Chattisgarh in Madhya Pradesh (see Bilaspur District Gazetteer). However, regions of relative isolation should not be thought of only in terms of mountain vastness and remoteness. Two areas which since the 10th century we have considered to be of central importance, Bengal and Kerala, I think should be subsumed under the category of relative isolation. Kerala, although having easy coastal communication with the west coast of India and since prehistoric times having been part of the Indian Ocean trade area, is relatively cut off from the rest of southern India by the western Ghats.

Seen from the west the Western Ghats present the appearance of a gigantic sea-wall, often rising in steps from the shore line—hence the name "ghats". They are a steep and rugged mass of hills, little more than 2,000 feet above sea-level at the northern end, rising to more than 4,000 feet about the latitude of Bombay, generally increasing in altitude towards the south and culminating in the Nilgiris with Dodabetta at a height of 8,760 feet where the Eastern Ghats meet the Western after making a sweep from the other side of the peninsula. Immediately south of the Nilgiri plateau lies the only break in the continuity of the Western Ghats, the Palghat or Coimbatore gap, which is about twenty miles from north to south and affords lowland access from the Carnatic to the Malabar coast at the level of about a thousand feet above the sea.

It was through the Coimbatore gap that trade flowed to and from the Malabar ports. The isolation of Kerala therefore is relative, but none the less, its relative isolation has contributed to the establishment and maintenance of a highly characteristic social and cultural system, including several unique structural features.

The claim for Bengal as a region of relative isolation, not a nuclear region, will raise the ire of the Bengalis and the Bengalists, but I would argue that until the 18th century, Bengal was isolated in a relative fashion from the nuclear region of the Ganges valley. James Rennell well conveys the situation in the late 18th century when he says:

> The natural situation of Bengal is singularly happy with respect to security from the attacks of foreign enemies. On the north and east it has no warlike neighbours; and has, moreover, a formidable barrier of mountains, rivers, or extensive wastes, towards those quarters; should such an enemy start up. On the south is a seacoast, guarded by shallows and impenetrable woods, and with only one port (and even that of difficult access), in an extent of three hundred miles. It is on the west only, that any enemy is to be apprehended, and even there the natural barrier is strong.

In the early 18th century, the Rajmahal hills were thought to be almost impassable and the Teligarhi pass, if properly guarded, was the strategic key to Bengal.

Our conception of Bengal as a central region is a function of the last 200 years and the reorientation under the British of the flow of authority and influence from land centres to the littoral of India, which brought the seaports of Madras, Bombay, and Calcutta into central commercial, political, and cultural importance. I will discuss below the consequences of British rule and modernization on the nature and conceptualization of regions, regional culture, and regionalism.

In conclusion of the discussion of historical regions, it is important to reiterate one of the basic arguments of the paper. Regions, even the assumed enduring ones subsumed under the concept "historical regions", are of a changing nature through time. Various kinds of circumstances can rapidly alter the boundaries and very nature and conception of a region. One need only think of Chota Nagpur and Chattisgarh in recent years. Both were thought of as remote, inhospitable, and from an economic point of view, relatively worthless regions, fit places for slash-and-burn agriculturalists and hunters and gatherers. Now both are of key economic importance because of the presence of ores, which provide the basis of two of India's most modern and complex industrial regions.

PROBLEMS IN THE ESTABLISHMENT OF CULTURAL REGIONS

For forty years anthropologists and other cultural scientists have struggled with the problem of establishing cultural areas. This effort largely grew out of attempts to order museum collections in some sort of rational fashion with some regard to the cultural context of material objects. Out of classificatory concerns in the establishment of culture areas also grew methodological and theoretical interests in the attempt to use culture areas as a basis from which to infer the history of societies and cultures without written records by plotting traits (specific items of material culture or custom, e.g., a particular kind of digging stick, cross cousin marriage) and trait complexes (e.g., the Sun Dance of the Plains Indians). Great energy, time, and meticulous care were lavished on the establishment of culture areas for North America and Africa.

From the beginning of systematic writing on Indian society and culture, in the middle of the 19th century, there was of course recognition of the significance of cultural variation in the subcontinent. Mountstuart Elphinstone in his *History of India: The Hindu and Mahometan Periods* was typical of his times in talking about cultural differences in India in terms of "Ten different civilized nations.... All these nations differ from each other, in manners and language, nearly as much as those inhabiting the corresponding portion of Europe." The ten nations are, not surprisingly, distinguished by their languages, the languages, spoken in the Punjab, Kanouj, Mithila, Bengal, Gujarat, and the five languages of Deccan, Tamil, Telegu, Kannada, and the languages spoken in Orissa and Maharastra. Elphinstone did not try to lay out systematically any regional-culture classification and as was typical of discussions on cultural classifications since his time, really talks about the differences between north and south:

> ...the religious sects are different; the architecture... is of different characters; the dress differs in many respects, and the people differ in appearance ... The northern people live much on wheat, and those of the south on ragi.

Elphinstone also differentiated between Hindustains and Bengalis thinking the difference was due to geographic factors:

...Bengal is moist, liable to inundation, and has all the characteristics of an alluvial soil; while Hindustan, though fertile, is comparatively dry, both in soil and climate. This difference may, by forming a diversity of habits, have led to a great dissimilitude between the people.

Elphinstone, one way or another, illustrates all the criteria which have been used to try to establish cultural regions, language, differences in religous sects, architecture (house types), physical appearance (race), subsistence base (wheat vs. ragi) climate, and geography.

Later in the 19th century, and into the 20th century, concerns about racial classification tended to supplant overriding interest in cultural-regional classifications. Two of the decennial census operations, 1901 and 1931, and their subsequent publications, collected great amounts of data on physical types in India. H.H.Risley, a distinguished civil administrator and one of the founders of systematic anthropology in India, contributed on the basis of his classification of measurements collected during the 1901 census the most persistent of racial-cultural classifications. As is typical with racial classifications of the period, there was a confusion of racial-lingustic and cultural criteria in the establishment of the classification. He believed that there were blocks of peoples, with similar head shapes, nose forms, and other measurements, occupying defined territories. He gave these racial types essentially linguistic labels, e.g., Turko-Iranian, Indo-Aryan, Aryo-Dravidian. Risley was concerned not only with the establishment of recial classifications in relation to culture, but was fumbling towards a racial history of India. This concern with racial and culture history reaches its apex in the 1931 census under J.H.Hutton and the distinguished Indian physical anthropologist, B.S.Guha, and has been a persistent theme in the research of D.N.Majumdar.

The attempt of Guha and Majumdar was to use data about physical types, derived from measurements or blood typing, to infer something about the long term cultural history of India. The Negrito type found only in traces of some of the tribal population, is thought to be the oldest strand in the racial history of India. The Negritos in the conventional view were supplanted by Australoids, who are represented by the majority of present day aborigines. When, however, the physical anthropologists come to infer anything about the history of civilized groups in Indian society they seem merely to echo well known facts about linguistic history.

Not unnaturally, the physical anthropologists tend to see a difference racially between northern and southern peoples of India but even this does not seem clear when seriological data are used in attempting to map the frequency of A and B blood types in India. "On the basis of our knowledge of blood groups data in India it may be assumed that the fluctuation of the percentages indicates considerable admixture between the various racial and culture groups."

It is safe to say that fifty years of trying to relate culture, race as defined by "scientific" criteria, and history have added very little to our understanding of regionalism in India, other than some self-evident propositions that the aborigines or tribals may represent a different racial strain than most of the rest of population. Such a statement, however, tells us little about culture.

In recent years there have been several attempts to revive earlier anthropological concerns with the development of culture areas in India. The most extensive and systematic of these was the survey on material culture carried out by the Department of Anthropology, Government of India, under the direction of Surajit Sinha and N.K. Bose. The objectives of the survey were the "drawing up of maps of zones and sub-zones of selected material traits which appear to have persisted over long historical periods. This will provide in a broad sweep, a comparable picture for the major cultural regions of India and will thus provide the background for detailed study of cultural processes in the future." Systematic data from every district in India were collected and plotted on maps for the following items of material culture: village settlement pattern, types of cottages, staple diet, kinds of fats and oils used, kinds of oil presses, types of plows, types of husking implements, men's dress, women's dress, foot gear, and bullock carts.

N.K. Bose in his introductory section to the study sees these eleven different traits grouped into a very broad pattern, a northern and a southern which tend to overlap in a broad zone running across India from Maharashtra to Bihar and in some cases Bengal and Orissa. However, as one scans the maps on which this data is plotted, it would seem that an argument for an east-west dividing of the subcontinent would be almost as tenable. Some idea of the difficulty of making generalizations on the basis of the maps given in the study can be seen from the listing as follows:

1. *Forms of villages:* There are three zones, the first including much of U.P.and Bihar, Madhya Pradesh, Punjab, and Rajasthan with a line running roughly in a NE-SW direction from the middle of Maharasthra into Assam. The second zone contains much of Bengal, all of Orissa, parts of Madhya Pradesh, most of Andhra, and some of Mysore. A third major zone is Tamilnad and the rest of Mysore. It tends to an east-west split.

2. *Types of cottages: roof and ground plan:* There is a basic similarity all over India with a zone running through Rajasthan in the north-west through Maharashtra into northern Tamilnad and southern Andhra. The basic split is an east-west one.

3. *Types of cottages: courtyard and parlour:* There is a clear three-zone pattern, northern, middle, and southern.

4. *Types of cottages: distribution of courtyard:* The distribution is a completely mixed one.

5. *Staple diet:* There are four zones, eastern rice—Bengal, Bihar, eastern U.P., Orissa, northern Andhra; central and northern wheat—most of U.P., Punjab, Madhya Pradesh, Gujarat, much of Maharashtra; a mixed millet-rice zone—Tamil and Telegu speaking areas. The eastern rice is replicated on the west coast with a coastal strip of rice area. There is a faint east-west split.

6. *Fats and oils:* There is a rough north-south, division.

7. *Oil presses:* There is a rough east-west division.

8. Types of plows: The division is roughly north-south, but with the demarcation running up a Nepal border with Bihar and some of Bengal having the type of plow found in much of the Peninsula.

9. *Husking implements:* There is a clear east-west division.

10. *Men's dress, lower garments*: Most of the sub-continent is the same, with the southern tip, the Punjab, and part of Rajasthan and Gujarat being different.

11. *Women's dress: sewn and unsewn garments*: Most of India with the exception of Kerala and everythingwest of a line from north of Bombay to Delhi is in one zone and the rest is mixed, making an east-west split.

12. *Foot gear: sandals other than wooden:* There is a clear three-zone distribution, northern, middle, and southern.

13. *Bullock carts: types of wheel:* There is a rough north-south split but with the lines coming far north of the middle mountain zone except in the east.

14. *Bullock carts: size of the wheel:* The distribution is mixed.

I would classify the distributions given on the fourteen maps as regards the major directions of splits in the following fashion:

East-west (6) maps numbered 1,2,5, 7,9,11
North-south (5) maps numbered 3,6,8,12,13
Mixed (3) maps numbered 4,10,14.

Another of Bose's conclusions is supported clearly by the distribution of the traits. "The boundaries of the culture area or sub areas do not tally with Grierson's boundaries of either linguistic families like Indo-Aryan and Dravidian or of the branches within either of these families.

The difficulty with the Bose-Sinha study would appear to be that they assumed the presence of clearcut cultural zones or areas and the data on material traits did not fall in any fashion to support their assumption.

WESTERNIZATION, MODERNIZATION AND REGIONALISM

The obvious distinction, conceptually, between the terms "region" and "regionalism" is sometimes overlooked. "Region" with all its difficulties as a concept refers to means of classification of a wide variety of kinds of data, which helps analyze particular or general situations. "Regionalism" refers usually to conscious or unconscious development of symbols, behaviours, and movements which will mark off groups within some geographic boundary from others in other regions for political, economic, or cultural ends. The term region relates to a form of analysis, regionalism to a call to action. The geographer, V.L.S.Prakasa Rao, points out that there is cycle of regionalism. The cycle begins with the revival of poetry and language and ends with plans for the economic invigoration of regional agriculture and industry, with proposals for more autonomous political life. In Europe, according to Rao, regionalism had different ends in various countries. In France, regionalism meant a protest against over-centralization of culture in Paris, and the movement was aimed at the free development of culture and local talent. In Germany the movement was aimed at reorganizing the old state boundaries. In Britain regionalism has meant administrative devolution and a new framework for local government. In Denmark it was directed to a folk revival combined with scientific agriculture. In India the cycle of regionalism begins with modernization and Westernization, intensified in the 20th century by the rise of the nationalist movement.

THE STRUCTURAL AND CULTURAL PREREQUISITES OF INDIAN REGIONALISM

Regionalism is a cultural phenomenon, but it is not inevitable and it does not just happen, but arises when certain conditions are present. The following is an attempt to specify in a preliminary fashion what these conditions or prerequisites might be.

1. *A Symbol Pool.* The first prerequisite of regionalism is what may be termed a pool of symbols which may be drawn upon and around which the content of the idea of regionalism can be formed for a particular region. In the Indian case the symbol pool has usually been made up of religious and/or literary and/or political historical symbols. The symbols may be couched in linguistic terms, that is, the language of a particular region is believed to be the main carrier and, to many, the rallying point for the regional movement. When, however, one gets behind the identification with the language *per se* and looks at the content of the particular set of symbols that make up the regional identification, it is apparent that it is literature, religion, and political history that are being called upon, not the language itself.

For Tamilians there appears to be a well developed hierarchy of kinds of symbols which at one and the same time set out Tamilnad from other parts of South India (the macro-region) and form the constituent parts of Tamilnad.

The Tamilian Scholar divided the country into five natural divisions according to their physical features. In his poetical imagination he carried such ideas into his daily life. It entered into the manners and customs of the people. In the course of time such divisions and attributes became conventional. If a poet dealt with a particular region in his poem, he always associated his thoughts to the particular sect of people who inhabited it, to the particular products growing in the tract, to the particular kind of song, amusement, festivity, food, dress, musical instruments and ideas connected with the region....The ancient scholar named such regions by the name of particular flower or plant which grew extensively in that region.

Internal political boundaries in Tamilnad never became fixed. It is in literature and the sacred geography in the culture of the ordinary people that a distinctive and fixed set of ideas of internal regions developed.

During the three centuries following the Saiva and Vaishnavite revival in the early part of the sixth century, Saints appeared in the country and revived the two great religions and suppressed the then prevalent Buddhism and Jainism. The four great Saivite saints and twelve Alwars travelled throughout the length and breadth of the land for the purpose of instilling religious spirit among the people, visited a large number of temples and have sung songs about them. While so doing they had mentioned the names of the divisions in the land. The other saints and poets who followed them developed the idea still further and have fixed the extent of the divisions while mentioning the temple which they visited. In this way the division of land into various sub-divisions on a religious basis became settled and was a vogue among the people.

It would appear that the set of well established literary religious symbols in Tamilnad concerning the region is the most extensive set found in India.

Maharastra is a region for which there has been claimed in the last seventy years a consistent historical-political tradition, reaching back hundreds of years. Not only is there the historical political tradition, but Maratha historians in particular and Indian historians in general see the tradition in terms of a Maratha state and nation from the time of Shivaji in the late 17th century until the early 19th century.

M.G. Ranade, the great Maharashtrian reformer, was the first to present the argument for a unique Maratha nation in his book, *Rise of Maratha Power*, originally published in 1900. In this book Ranade argued that the Maratha State was more than the expression of Shivaji's genius and the abilities of Marathas as free-booters:

The foundation (of the State and Maratha Confederacy of the 18th century) was laid broad and deep in the hearts of the whole people. Unlike the Subhedarships of Bengal, Karnatick, Oudh, and Hyderabad, the rise of the Maratha power was due to the first beginnings of what one may well call the process of nation-making. It was not the outcome of the successful enterprise of any individual adventurer. It was the upheaval of the whole population, strongly bound together by the common affinities of language, race, religion and literature, and seeking further solidarity by a common independent political existence... It was a national movement or upheaval in which all classes co-operated. The strength of the organization did not depend on a temporary elevation of the higher classes, but it had deeper hold on the vast mass of the rural population. Cowherds and shepherds, Brahmans and non-Brahmans, even Musalmans felt its influence and acknowledged its power.

Ranade and subsequent writers on Maratha history have made much of the Bhakti movements of the 15th and 16th centuries in establishing a religious ideology and style which bound the people of Maharashtra together. "This Religious Revival was not Brahmanical in its orthodoxy; it was heterodox in its spirit of protest against forms and ceremonies and class distinctions based on birth, and ethical in its preference of a pure heart, and the law of love, to all other acquired merits and good works. The religious values found their expression in the oral and written traditions of the mass of the people of Maharashtra.

This vein of rebellious sentiment runs through the vast Marathi literature of the three or four centuries that followed the extinction of the Yadavas of Deogiri; from the time of Mukundraj and Jnaneshwar to that of Tukaram and Ramdas, the whole range of Marathi literature accurately reflects the working of the popular mind... (The Maratha Saints and Holy Men) delivered orations and held *Harikirtans* which were avidly listened to, and which supplied the spiritual background to the political aims of workers like Shivaji.

Even the Bengali historian, Sir Jadunath Sarkar, saw religious literary movements as crucial to forming the ideology of the Maratha States. He makes the Marathas sound like an Indian version of the English Puritans—People of simplicity, who didn't have time for the polishing of their forms of expression. "Their poetry consisted of short jingles and apophthegms or monotonous metrical couplets like the epics,—with no lyric outburst, no long-flowing sonorous verses, no delicate play on the whole gamut of sounds."

There has been a distinguished line of Maharashtrian historians who have systematically and carefully explored Maratha history, and have produced a major historical school, their commitment to the proof of Maratha nationhood notwithstanding. Irawati Karve, a Maharashtrian, as an anthropoligist, has also been dedicated to the objective reality of a Maharashtrian culture, and has elevated her perception of the objective reality of Maharashtra as a cultural region to a theory of the presence in India of similar regions:

Ten years of field work in different parts of India has convinced us that a linguistic area is a culturally unified area. Its chief characteristic is that, (1) it is a stretch of contiguous territory where one language with its various dialects is spoken. Commonness of language, however, is not the only feature which distinguished such a region from others. On the other hand this commonness of language is only an outward and the most obvious symbol of an underlying cultural synthesis which embraces all aspects of social life. Such an area shows(2) common usages as regards marriage, kinship systems and family organization. (3) There is also a recognizable similarity in dress, utensils and food-preparations of the people. (4) They pay homage to the same saints, tell the same stories, sing the same songs and even show the same attitude towards certain situations in life.

2. *Selection, Standardization, and Transmission of Symbols.* The second prerequisite for the establishment and maintenance of regionalism is a means of selection, standardization, and transmission of symbols from the symbol pool. At any moment in the present or the recent past, or for that matter through much of the cultural history of India, the possible symbol pool in any region from which selection can be made seems to be, if not infinite, then vast. We have begun to recognize that valuable as such concepts as the Great and Little Tradition of Sanskritization have been in helping to sort and analyze data on Indian culture and society, they can do violence to complexity and variety on the ground and historically. The formation of and elevation of a relatively coherent view and articulation of one strand out of the symbol pool, religious, cultural, literary, or historical, does not just happen, but is the result of complex forces. The materials are at hand for some understanding of the process of the development of regional traditions both in the premodern and the modern period. It is one of the paradoxes of modern Indian history, that at the same time that British rule was establishing some of the pre-conditions of a national identity in the modern sense of the word, it also established the conditions for regionalism in the form that we have come to know it from the late 19th century.

As suggested above, one of these conditions was the establishment of printing in India. In order to print in the vernacular languages, decisions had to be made as to which dialects of the regional languages were the ones to be enshrined in the printed materials, the books, government regulations, teaching materials, and translations from English and European languages. The decision was made in a different fashion and by different groups for each of the languages. For the North Indian languages, particularly Bengali, Hindi, and Urdu, the establishment of the College at Fort William by Lord Wellesley was crucial. There James Gilchrist encouraged the publishing of Hindustani prose, and William Carey selected and encouraged Bengali pandits to writes textbooks and to publish versions of Bengali religious and their texts; such men helped standardize regional languages in such a fashion that educated Indians throughout the region could read the same materials. Although there were always *linguae francae* within the regions and across the regions, the standardizations of the languages through publishing and their disssemination through textbooks in the schools and colleges gave the regional languages a primacy for groups within the society that they may not before have had.

Although literacy may not have increased markedly in the 19th century in India, those who became literate tended to read standardized versions of the same texts. In each of the Presidency capitals at least, and later in the up country cities, voluntary associations were formed to further printing and distribution of vernacular materials. Typical of these societies was the Calcutta School Book Society, which distributed in the tens of thousands basic readers, arithmetic books, spellers, and grammars, as well as the famous weekly newspaper, *Digdarshan*.

Studies of social change in 19th century India give for obvious reasons prime attention to the rise of English language schools and colleges, but it must also be remembered that at the primary and secondary level vernacular education expanded somewhat and was standardized. At the same time that attention was focussed on the Anglo-Orientalist controversy, Lt. Governor Thomason was putting substantial resources into vernacular education in Upper India.

By the middle of the century even the elitist English-based higher education was having its effect, in an indirect fashion, on the establishment of regionalism in India. By the mid-19th century, some of the Western educated, particularly in Bengal and Bombay, were turning from their identification with Western values and ideals, from an admiration of things European, to an examination and admiration of things Indian. In this endeavour to find cultural superiority in Indian civilization, concerns with distinctive regional traditions were made coherent and were fixed.

In the last decades of the 19th century it was Bal Gangadhar Tilak in Maharashtra who developed methods for involving segments from the top to the bottom of the social order, regardless of literacy, in the glorification of regional traditions. Although Tilak's goal in a very real sense was nationalist, the vehicle of expression of nationalism was regional.

In 1893, Tilak along with Annasahib, an orthodox Brahman, organized as a public festival the worship over a ten-day period of the Hindu god Ganesh. The manifest reason for the celebrations was to prevent lower caste Hindus from participating in the Muhurram festival of the Muslims as had been the custom up until this time. Ganesh was one of the favourite gods of Western India, and the Ganapati festival had been celebrated as a household festival by the Peshwas, but had largely become a minor domestic event. Annasahib's and Tilak's actions "catapulted the Ganapati celebration from a purely private religious function to the most important and best attended public festival of Western India within a few years."

In 1896, Tilak and his followers sponsored a festival to honour the great Maratha Shivaji. As with many aspects of the regional and Hindu revivals of the 19th century, it was an Englishman who unwittingly provided the immediate stimulus for the establishment of the festival. James Douglas in a guide book on Bombay pointed out that Shivaji's *samadhi* (memorial stone) was lying unhonoured and in a state of disrepair. The Shivaji celebrations manifestly glorified Maharashtra and the festival was made available to the whole population.

The festival had all the trappings of a typical Hindu religious celebration with songs, dances, gymnastic events, readings from the scriptures, and distribution of sweets and betel leaves. In addition, however, ballads exalting Shivaji's heroic deeds, and lectures on the highlights of Maratha history were delivered. Symbolizing the joint political and religious character of the celebration, huge painted portraits of Shivaji and his Brahman guru Ramdas were carried side by side in procession up to the mount fortress, while the chant of devotional hymns blended contrapuntally with shouts of *"Shivaji Maharaj ki jai"*.

In his newspaper, *Kesari*, Tilak made it clear that through hero worship of Shivaji the ideal of Maratha self-rule and the glorification of Maharashtra would be reborn.

The late 19th century and the early 20th century were rich in movements which, in a significant fashion, standardized out of the symbol pool of various regions or parts of the country various articulations of regional cultures. The Andhra Movement and the Adi Dravida Movement in the South, and even the establishment of *Nagri Pracharini Sabha* in Benaras in 1890 to extend the revival of the Nagri alphabet, had the effect of furthering regionalism within their areas.

3.Establishment of Regional Elites. It is axiomatic that not only did British rule establish the conditions for changes or redefinitions in Indian cultural systems, but it also established the conditions for structural changes in the society. Up until fairly recently most discussion and research on structural changes in Indian society concentrated on the establishment of national elites in relation to the nationalist movement and the establishment of an All-India educational and administrative system. More recently, concomitant with the development of more behavioural approaches to the study of politics, the spread of social anthropological field work, and the regionalization of the modern historian of India, has come the realization of the significance of what are termed regional elites.

The concept of the elites has a long history in the historical and social scientific literature, and there is little consensus of what or whom are talking about except at the common sense level. In complex societies, there are hierarchies—some people are at the top and some at the bottom. Often those at the top, as a category or a group, exercise certain forms of leadership and have more control over or access to what is valued in the society, wealth, power, authority, the symbols of valued life styles, education, ritual purity, than do others. In some societies an elite can appear to monopolize almost all of that which appears to have value; in other societies elites may be segmented around particular valued activities or symbols. We can talk of a political elite, a commercial elite, an educated elite, and so forth. Elites, whether unitary or segmented, can be closed or open, and can be recruited by ascription or achievement. Elites may form hierarchies or may be pyramided; we can have rural and urban elites, local, regional, and national elites. Single individuals or small groups may play different elite roles at different levels in a hierarchical or pyramidal elite structure.

We are just beginning to perceive some of the complexities in analysis of elites in the study of Indian society and history, so that discussing elite formation as one of the functional prerequisites of the development of regionalism is a hazardous undertaking in the extreme. The first obvious caution in the discussion is that we should not look for identical categories of elites, playing identical kinds of roles in relation to the development of regionalism. "The Princes," the Bhadralog of Bengal, the Chitpavan of Maharashtra, the Tamil Brahman of Tamilnad, the Pattidar of Gujarat, the Parsi of Bombay, the Oudh Talukadar, and the Nayars of Malabar encompass analytically different kinds of things. These elites do fit on some kind of continuum in terms of their method of recruitment from elites whose origin might be termed composite such as the Oudh Talukadars, the "Princes", and the Bhadralog at one end to those who in origin have kin and caste ties to mark them off from other categories and groups in the regional society such as the Nayars and Chitpavans. The origin of a particular elite is important in that it can determine to a large extent the nature of internal ordering of the elite group. The Oudh Talukadars were in effect created as an elite by administrative action on the part of the British as part of the land settlement of Oudh in 1859. A Talukadar was anyone who was listed in the official list of Talukadars. The British wanted to create the Talukadars as an elite, but partially because of the method of recruitment which prevented any kind of common social and cultural solidarity from emerging within the elite category, they failed. (My view of the Oudh Talukadars is based on the work of Thomas Metcalf and Peter Reeves.)

The British even tried to establish educational institutions and to offer certain preferences to categories like the "Princes" and the Oudh Talukadars, in order to enable them to perform like elites. Colonel Walter, British Resident in Bharatpur, originally suggested the idea that an educational institution, "an Eton in India", be established, where the sons of the Rajputana chiefs, princes, and Thakurs could be "brought up as a gentleman should be". Walter believed that only if there was an educational institution devoted to the education of the Princes, where they could be educated by "English gentlemen, not mere bookworms, but men fond of field sports and outdoor exercise...can we hope to see the Native Princes of India occupying the position they ought to hold as the promoters of peace, prosperity and progress amongst their own people, and the hearty supports of British authority and power."

In 1879, the Viceroy Lord Lytton proposed that the Statutory Civil Service being established should "be confined to Indians selected from families of social standing... a 'native branch' of the civil service created for the employment by selection of those with inherited qualifications, early habits of authority and a commanding influence over large numbers of their fellow-countrymen." The Statutory Civil Service was never a success, and proved attractive neither to the "princes" nor to the educated classes. Within a region such as Rajasthan, the princes in a very real sense acted as an elite in terms of their economic and political power and in providing a life style and symbols for their own states. However, British efforts with both the princes and the Oudh Talukadars to establish an aristocratic elite for the society at large as a counter weight to other elites less favourable to their rule proved unsuccessful. The British of the late 19th century and scholars of the 20th century saw a new elite group being formed through the results of the British-introduced educational system. In Bengal in particular, a category of Western-educated was very much in evidence. British official society, increasingly through the latter 19th century, was unwilling to grant this category in the society access to authority, and to grant them roles and elite symbols, which in effect they were trained for by their university education in India. In Bombay and Bengal initially and then subsequently in other regions, at one and the same time the members of this educated group provided leadership in the national independence movement, leadership of regional movements for cultural identity, and in increasing numbers in the 20th century, as British policies changed, manned the covenanted civil service and the military.

The emergence in the late 19th century of distinctive regional elites, with connections to a forming educated national elite, in several regions led to counter-groupings in opposition to the emerging nationalist and civil service elites. The anti-Brahman movement in Maharashtra and the non-Brahman movement in Tamilnad are examples of such movements. The situation of elites and counter-elites in relation to regionalism became even more complex in the 1920's with the reorientation of the Congress party under Gandhi's leadership into a mass organization. In order to develop mass appeal and a mass organization, a new type of leadership was recruited, capable of organizing local and regional cadres of the Congress movement. Appeals were in vernaculars and regional cultures were glorified. Nationalism began to develop a regional flavour. Although, each in his own way, Gandhi and Nehru represented variants of a national ideal, lower echelons of the movement were regionally based and furthered regional styles. In post-Independence India this leadership and these styles have, in a significant fashion, become dominant.

The relationship between the rise of regional elites and their role in selection and standardization of symbols and values from the regional stock of symbols and values is a very complex one, relating to technology, education, access to civil and political roles, and the accidents of history and policy. In a very real sense we are just beginning to understand the complex relationship among the nature of the symbol pools of various regions, the mechanics and organization of standardization of regional cultures, and the interrelations between emerging national and regional elites.

COUNTERVAILING PROCESSES TO REGIONAL IDENTITY AND REGIONALISM

One of the oddities of current academic styles is that historians seem more prone than most to read history from the present to the past. Their growing concern with the study of regionalism has led them perhaps to overemphasize the study of regions. Historians of India seem at times to be about to take over the anthropologist's curse, the obsession with "my people". Not only in India, but in most parts of the world, anthropologists tend to see the tribe or village they have studied as the key region, and the processes and phenomena occurring in that particular region at the particular time with which they have been concerned as central to all of modern history. There is of course a real basis for the trend. Regions and regionalism are important to the study of Indian society and history. The concern is a healthy corrective to the previous almost exclusive concerns of historians with Indo-British history; but unless in our efforts we also look towards countervailing processes to regional identity and regionalism as they grew in the 19th century, we might well achieve the same sterility that much Indo-British historical research has reached. There is a pool of traditional Indian symbols, certainly Hindu symbols, which have been standardized through the nationalist movement and the emergence of an Indian nation state. There is a distinctive world view at an abstract level that is Indian; there certainly is rhetoric and style that is Indian which most of us recognize. There are languages, Sanskrit, Persian, Urdu, and English, which have been used or are used throughout India. In most periods of Indian history there have been definitive life styles which cut across regional life styles, the Brahmanic, the courtly-Persian, the modern or cosmopolitan. Since the rise of the Mughal empire there have been forms of a national administrative service. It could be argued that in some intermittent fashion there have been subcontinent-wide educational institutions, Madrassas, Pathshallas, and the Universities; even at the present when we are so aware of the regionalization of heigher education there is also the establishment of the I.I.T's and the conscious elevation of Delhi University into a national institution. Since Independence a large number of Indians have travelled overseas for higher education and technical training, where for a time, their identity as Indians rather than as Bengalis or Tamilians becomes primary. A "middle class" mass culture may be emerging in India, through the movies, and their attendant magazines, and publications like the *Illustrated Weekly of India*. One would like to know what impact, if any, the movies have on urban middle class women's sari styles, what effect the movies and "mass" magazines have on home furnishings, whether there is an emerging urban "modern" life style. We have tended to forget how rapidly regional cultures and styles were eroded and national cultures established in the history of the West. Less than one hundred years after we fought a civil war on regional grounds, and after sectionalism was thought to be a major factor in American history, most observers of American life comment on the uniformity at all levels in our society and culture. Cultures and regional/national styles can change with amazing rapidity. That which we think of as essentially Irish appears to have been formed in a brief time in the middle of the 19th century. The stereotype of the Scotsman as penurious and dour appears to have risen in the late 17th century with the rise of Presbyterianism.

The argument that I am trying to make throughout this paper is that regions are far from fixed, enduring things, especially if any historical perspective is taken. They are not absolutes and they are difficult, if not impossible, to define by objective criteria. Where one stands and for what purpose one is abserving or studying will determine the boundaries of the unit one is studying. For many purposes a region, which can be defined in a relative fashion for the purpose of the study, makes a logical unit; for other purposes a village, a city, or the civilization make the relatively important unit to be studied.

In recent years the study of regions and regionalism has become one of the prime concerns of all social scientists in the study of India and Indian culture. It should not be overlooked, however, that the phenomenon, no matter how we define it, exists through time and we must constantly be aware of the danger of reifying what might be a set of contingent choices by some individual or groups within the society we are studying and of elevating the contingent choices into an absolute.

8

Central to the growth of regionalism in modern India has been the rise of regional elites that embody and sustain the distinctive values of the area and shape its political life. Formed from those who successfully grasped the limited but still substantial opportunities for power and influence made available by the British, these elites gained positions of dominance during the nineteenth century. Later, with the extension of education and voting rights, aspiring counter-elites emerged. The result was lively political combat at the provincial level, beneath and even within the all-India nationalist struggle against British rule. In this provocative essay Professor Broomfield traces the process of elite formation in the various provinces of British India and shows how the nationalist movement itself bears the imprint of their political activity.

The Regional Elites: A Theory of Modern Indian History

J.H. BROOMFIELD

This paper will have served its purpose if it simply raises doubts as to the validity of some of the generally accepted assumptions underlying the interpretation of modern Indian history. It tries to expose a few of the current cliches, and if, in the reader's opinion, it merely trades old cliches for new, then I hope the resulting dissatisfaction will stimulate someone to offer fresh ideas to vary the rather stale fare of Indian historiography. The paper is full of grand sub-continental generalisations, but where I have paused to illustrate my argument I have chosen evidence from Bengal, which is my field of research.

1. One of the great social significances of the eighteenth century in the Indian international sub-system, with its internal political disorder and emerging power of the Europeans, was the destruction of the power of existing ruling groups. This was effected not simply by military and political means, but also through radical changes in such areas as trade, law and land-revenue assessment. It was accompanied for many of the displaced ruling groups by a loss of control over land.

Reprinted by permission from *The Indian Economic and Social History Review*, Vol.III, No.3 (September 1966),pp.279-290.

2. At the same time large opportunities opened up in various places in the international sub-system for those able to take advantage of them. There were special opportunities in the three initial areas of British intrusion, Bengal, Madras and Maharashtra, and the groups which grasped those opportunities became the elites in these societies in the nineteenth century.

3. The development of each of these elite groups was determined by the following factors:

A. *The group's experience before the British intrusion and its situation at that time:* This largely determined what 'cultural baggage' the group carried with it into the new situation.

At this point I would question the utility of the commonly-used metaphor of a British impact on India, with its implication of a dynamic force—expansive Europe—hitting a static object—Indian society. I believe that we are better able to understand the effects of the British intrusion if we take account of the fact that the pattern of relationships among Indian elites was subject to constant change in periods before the European arrival, as much as in the period of European dominance. We must recognize that in many areas, and certainly in the peripheral areas with which I am primarily concerned, there was considerable social mobility in pre-European times. Certainly the British presence affected the direction and possibly also the speed of movement, most directly by providing new opportunities for economic gain, but it is significant that the groups which took advantage of these new opportunities did so very largely in terms of their old methods of action.

To illustrate this let us look at Bengal. In that area before the British arrival there was fairly extensive international trade, considerable manufacturing in inland centres, and developed administrative and judicial organisation in the Mughal province and in the Hindu rajadoms, which occupied extensive areas of Bakarganj and Chittagong districts in the east, and Bankura and Burdwan districts in the west. Thus there were opportunities for enterprise in administration, law or commerce which paralleled those which were to be available after the British arrival, and it appears to have been the same group which took advantage of the opportunities in both periods. One sees in particular the movement of Brahmins, Baidyas and Kayasthas into the service of the East India Company from similar service under the Hindu rajas or in the Mughal system. They were able to move into the new system because they already possessed certain skills: experience in administration and law; entrepreneurial techniques and an accustomed readiness to work in an alien *lingua franca* (the talents of the *dubash:* the go-between); literacy, and experience in using that literacy in the service of organisation. The group's experience before the British intrusion and its situation at that time, I said earlier, largely determined what 'cultural baggage' it carried with it into the new situation. In the Bengal case, these skills were part of that baggage.

B. *The nature of the new opportunities offering*: Just as the experience and situation of the groups in the various regions differed, so did the opportunities of which they were able to take advantage.

For Bengal I would point to two in particular: the development of Calcutta as the British capital in India; and the opportunity for those who prospered in service to invest in landed property. Access to land for the new administrative elite was provided by the inequitable land revenue settlements of the period 1770 to 1790, the recognition by the law courts of the principle that land was saleable to realise debt, and the command of the legal system by the same group which had capital free for investment as a result of its success in service. By investing in land in preference to commerce, the elite revealed another piece of its cultural baggage: its belief in the superior prestige and security resulting from the possession of landed property.

C. *The manner in which the group came to terms with the new situation*: There are a number of points to be noted here:

(i)   some *modus vivendi* had to be reached with things European, whether through total acceptance, a synthesis, or rejection. I lump these three together for although they appear to be fundamentally different they were all possible responses to the European intrusion, and even among those elite groups which were to benefit from the new opportunities almost the whole range of response was to be found from individual members, or, perhaps, more significantly, from the group as a whole towards different items of the intruders' values. The range from total acceptance at one end to rejection at the other should be seen as a continuum. It is one of the unfortunate consequences of the impact on India metaphor that we have generally concentrated our attention on one end of that scale, where we have isolated a phenomenon which we have labelled 'westernisation', and in doing so have lost sight of its integral relationship to the whole range of actual response.

(ii)   the fact is important that the groups which had been able to grasp the opportunities and become elites were high caste, with pride in their roles as guardians of great cultural traditions.

As a consequence we see in all three regions—Bengal, Madras and Maharashtra—an articulate reconsideration of the local cultural tradition and a concern with its adaptation to the new intellectual situation. Each of the elites developed a new and distinct cultural synthesis, drawing in part upon European ideas but drawing as well upon their past experience.

(iii) the elite had not only to look upward to the European culture, it had to look downward to the lower strata of its own society, and work out for the new situation new relationships with them. Again the proud caste status of the elites was important. In Bengal, where there was a running discussion throughout the nineteenth century on the proper ordering of society, the elites justified their social dominance, at least to their own satisfaction, by a definition of their position which nicely combined their ascriptive caste ascendancy with their achievement. They called themselves *bhadralok:* the respectable people. Bhadralok was almost synonymous with high caste—Brahmin, Baidya and Kayastha—but not quite, for this was an open not a closed status group. A British government report of 1915 correctly, if rather tactlessly, described Bengali society as 'a despotism of caste, tempered by matriculation'. 'The school', wrote the Government of Bengal on another occasion, 'is the one gate to the society of *bhadralok.'* Education, especially English language education, the professional and clerical employment, and the literature culture to which that education gave access, as well as the acceptance of high-caste proscriptions, were the measures of *bhadralok* status.

The *bhadralok's* role was to lead. In their eyes it was proper that they should be the political class, that they should dominate the learned professions, that they should control the institutions of education, and that they should provide Bengal with its music, art and literature, as that they should be accorded honour in village and town as the respectable people. They were benevolent in their attitude to the lower orders, but it was as often a benevolent disdain as a benevolent paternalism.

4. Involved for each group in the process of coming to terms with the new situation was the process of forming a new identity. This new identity found its expression in distinct interpretations of the past, in distinct cultural values, in distinct styles of life, in distinct attitudes as to the proper organisation of society, in distinct institutions, and in the distinct use of language. Distinct that is to say, from other groups within the regional societies and also from the elites in other regions.

My last point, the distinct use of language needs no labouring. A moment's reflection will remind you of the role which the elites played in the nineteenth-century development of Bengali, Tamil and Marathi, and the immense significance to them of these achievements. I will select one other item from the Bengal experience further to illustrate my point: the *bhadralok's* distinct view of the past. By the 1880's and certainly by the time of Vivekananda's evangelism, the *bhadralok* had a generally accepted interpretation of their history which not only explained the foreign conquest of Bengal, but gave a sanction to the cultural division between elite and non-elite in the society, and provided direction for future *bhadralok* action. Bengal once strong in the classical age, it was said, had been emasculated by the quietist doctrines of Buddhism and the emotional popular cults of medieval Hinduism. The 'true Brahmanical virtues' of intellectual initiative and rational self-assertion had been neglected, and the degradation of the Muslim conquest was a natural consequence. 'Let us think for a moment of the fatal and universal weakness which had beset our people when the English first came to this land', Chittaranjan Das exhorted his fellow Bengal Congressmen in 1917. 'Our Religion of Power—the Gospel of "Sakti"—had become a mockery of its former self; it had lost its soul of beneficence in the repetition of empty formulas and the observance of meaningless memories...the Hindus of Bengal had lost strength and vigour alike in Religion, Science, and Life.' To Das, as to other *bhadraloks* of his own and the preceding generation, it was self-evident that it was their ordained mission, as Bengal's culture elite, to restore the glory of Bengal through strength in action. This interpretation of the past, with its implicit doctrine of elite action, as effectually separated the bhadralok from the mass of their fellow Bengalis, whether Muslims or Vaisnava Hindus, as it did from the Madrasi and Maharashtrian elites, whose historical reinterpretations were concerned with other places and directed to other problems.

Taking a general view of this process of identity formation it is important to note:

(a) the intense emotional attachment of the elite to each of the channels of expression of their new identity.

(b) the complexity and sophistication of these forms of expression. This fact has been badly played down, largely it seems as a consequence of that concept 'westernisation', which implies cultural borrowing or copying. Certainly these new Indian cultures were indebted to Europe, just as Europe in an earlier age had been indebted to western Islam, but they were not carbon copies—black, smudged, imperfect reproductions of an exotic original. They were themselves originals; distinct cultures with fairly complex institutional structures by the end of the nineteenth century.

(c) that they were regionally developed and regionally distinct.

5. The elites had social power but as subject people of a foreign imperialism they did not have satisfactory political power.

As a qualification to this statement, it is important to realize (as neither of the 'classical' schools of modern Indian history—British or nationalist—appears to have done) that the Indian elites did have *some* political power under the British. The major reason for the common failure to recognise this fact is that 'politics' appears to have been defined too narrowly. As a consequence of the classical schools' exclusive concern with the struggle between the nationalists and the British for control of the state, 'politics' and 'nationalism' have usually been equated, and 'non-nationalist' politics, if not totally disregarded, have been seen as 'anti-nationalist'. The failure to take account of the elites' political power has been a source of misinterpretation in a number of areas:

(a) the British are incorrectly represented as having been free agents in constitutional reconstruction.

(b) British attempts to use constitutional reform as a way to change the power relationships between elites and counter-elites have been largely underestimated and the consequent grave dangers to order have been overlooked.

(c) the leaders of the political elites have not been given due credit for the self-restraint and concern for the maintenance of order which they usually displayed in the exercise of their power. Nor conversely have the limitations imposed upon then by the responsibilities of power been recognised.

(d)   the contest between elites and counter-elites has normally been seen as a contest for future power, not for the control of present power.

With these qualifications in mind, we can return to the primary point that the elites did not have a *satisfactory* political power. Seeking to be master of its own political future and as a further expression of its identity, each elite developed a nationalism. For this the inspiration was European, most directly the struggles for unity in Italy and Germany, and according to the European ideal the nation to which it aspired was universal: the Indian nation. The existence under British control of a centrally-organised state called India was of equal importance in giving the elites a supra-regional nationalist vision. In the process of establishing hegemony over the sub-continent, the British had widened the horizons of ambition for the coastal elites, making it feasible for them to attempt an extension of their elite dominance beyond the confines of their regions. India was an exciting concept for them in the 1860's, and it was equally exciting for them in the eighties to discover that this concept gave them common ground for discussion with men elsewhere on the sub-continent, a discussion facilitated by the same alien *lingua franca* which had enabled them to work effectively outside their home region.

They defined their nationalism universally but they acted exclusively. Each elite, I have said, developed a nationalism as a means of political fulfilment and as a further expression of its identity. As with the other forms of expression many of the manifestations of this nationalism were in practice local and exclusive: regional institutions, regional leaders, regional languages, regional symbols, regional heroes and myths, and regional patriotism. In each case there was a passionate attachment to the particular nationalism, and, where the elites met as at the Indian National Congress sessions, the confident belief by each group that it supplied the initiative and the leadership for Indian nationalism.

This leads me to some general observations on our perception of Indian nationalism. Most historians have now rejected the concept of Indian nationalism as a 'monolith'—a solid, homogeneous bloc in opposition to the British, committed unquestioningly to one doctrine—but they have replaced that concept with another which is almost as misleading. Many of them have depicted Indian nationalism as some sort of 'container' in which were mixed more or less satisfactorily a variety of divergent views and aspirations. So may Indian nationalism appear to the detached observer floating above the affairs of the sub-continent on the magic carpet of historical research. So too it has appeared even to those involved on some occasions when the proponents of divergent views and aspirations have stood toe to toe to fight out points of disagreement.

Where the 'container' concept is misleading is that it distracts attention from the essential fact that for most of the time, for most of the groups and individuals to whom nationalism was important, it was and could be only one thing: what they perceived it to be. Most saw it as a 'monolith', not as a 'container'. Many would be offended at the suggestion that it was or should be a 'container'. This explains why on many of the occasions when events brought the proponents of divergent views face to face, they regarded one another with amazement, disbelief and incomprehension, and sometimes angrily rejected the other's claim even to rank as a nationalist. Discomfort and anger in this situation is understandable, for each individual concept of nationalism had been formed in the image of a particular interpretation of the Indian past, and this particular view of history was the core of each group's sense of identity. It is this intimate connection between identity and perception of nationalism which explains the emotional involvement of groups—their emotional vested interest—in the maintenance of their particular 'monolithic' nationalism.

Because of these factors myths have assumed extraordinary importance. To talk as many do of stripping away the mythology surrounding Indian nationalism to uncover the realities, is to overlook the fact that the myths are part of the reality, frequently the most passionately defended part. Without a healthy respect for potency of mythology and a willingness to give sympathetic attention to myth formation, the observer of the tension between the Indian elites and their rivals will find himself with little ability to comprehend what he sees. Much of the action before him must appear to be shadow play, for much of it will be the conflict of irreconcilable myths.

6. There are two points to be noted about timing in the development of the elites:

(a)   the coastal elites did not develop at equal pace, for example in politics the Tamil Brahmins lagged 20 odd years behind the Bengal *bhadralok*; nor were the elites which developed on the first beachheads of the British invasion to remain the only elite groups.

(b)   the situation for the elites was never static. For instance, their initial opportunities were extended as the British marched up-country conquering more territory, and members of the elites could follow with the baggage train: Tamil Brahmins through southern and eastern India; Maharashtrian Brahmins throughout the Deccan and into northern India; the Bengal *bhadralok* into Orissa and Assam, and right up the Gangetic valley. The result was the establishment by each of the elites of colonies beyond their regional frontier, colonies of English-speaking men who dominated the new professional life of the up-country towns. Then came the contraction of these opportunities with the growth of new regional elites in the hinterland, and with challenges from aspiring counter-elites beneath the old elites in their home regions. Changes in the economy of the sub-continent had opened opportunities for groups in new areas and for new groups in the old areas. Again the timing was not uniform for all three old elite groups, but each was faced at some stage by attacks on its position at home and in its colonies up-country.

The result in Bengal was that by the 1890's the *bhadralok* were faced with growing economic difficulties. What was already a serious situation as a result of population growth which had reduced the per capita income from landed rent holdings and increased the pressure on that limited area of 'while-collar' employment which the *bhadralok* considered respectable, was aggravated by job-competition from local Muslims and low-caste Hindus, who were now acquiring English language education in small but significant numbers, and by the emergence throughout the towns of north India of new indigenous educated groups, who demanded of the local Governments the exclusion of 'outsiders' from administrative employment. The very fact that they now distinguished the Bengalis as 'outsiders' is in itself significant, indicating the development, or at least a new expression, of regional consciousness.

7. For the old elites these challenges from without and within were both part of one crisis and the appearance of their inter-relation was enhanced by the fact that both the new up-country elites and the aspiring counter-elites at home repudiated the leadership of the old elites in the nationalist movement, scornfully pointing out the disparity between their universal protestations and their exclusive actions, and declaring that they had lost touch with the 'Indian nation' because of their 'Anglicisation'. They had gained their dominance through association with the British, it was said, and were irrevocably committed to the maintenance of the imperial structure, whether under British control or their own. New leaders from newly emerging groups were produced by the up-country areas, with new concepts of nationalism and an appeal aimed at all the new aspiring groups. Thus Gandhi, a *banya* from Gujarat, attempting to influence Bengal politics in 1920 directed his appeal for a mass movement to the Muslims and low-caste Hindus, the aspiring counter-elites in Bengal.

The vulnerability of the old elites to criticism and the difficulty which they had in countering the influence of the new nationalists points to a significant fact: that those administrative and entrepreneurial skills which had carried them so successfully into the British system, and which had become formal measures of elite achievement as the new cultures were given structure in the nineteenth century, were no longer of great advantage — if indeed they were not of positive disadvantage — in the changed political conditions of the twentieth century. The skills which political leaders had to command if they were to be effective in the new situations were those of brokerage and communication. They had to be capable of articulating and aggregating interests, of manipulating popular symbols and imagery to give expression to wider political identities. The old elites were ill-fitted and ill-inclined to perform these roles.

8. The connection between the two challenges to the old elites' dominance—the challenges from up-country and at home—was not in fact as close as it appeared to be, for the aspiring counter-elites in the old areas did not readily accept the proffered leadership from outside or the proffered redefinition of nationalism. They had their own definitions, and, as with the elites they were trying to displace, the context of these definitions was regional. The aspiring counter-elites valued the home ground as much as did the old elites and were determined to battle with them for its possession. In each of these areas,

elite and counter-elite became engaged in bitter in-fighting, and they were left struggling on the periphery of a nationalist movement which was henceforth directed from the new areas by a leadership which had far less regional commitment.

This suggests two points:

(a) that in the old areas there were strong regional identifications by the second decade of the twentieth century, resulting from the development of complex social structures with internal centres of power, status and wealth, the control of which was keenly contested.

(b) that similar regional identification had not developed in what I have called the new areas, and apparently as a consequence the new nationalist-leadership could act as well as talk universally.

9. Looked at from one angle, the 'universalist' nationalism of the post-1920 leadership can be understood as a result of the development of nationalist sentiment among more sections of society in widespread areas of the sub-continent, who could respond to attacks on the regional and exclusive disposition of the old elites. This does not, however, explain how the new leadership could define their nationalism universally, nor how they could escape primary involvement in regional affairs. For that explanation I believe we must look at the character of the three areas which supplied most of the nationalist leadership from the twenties into the early sixties: the U.P., Bihar and Gujarat.

I see four reasons for *Gujarat's* production of 'universalist' nationalists:

(a) the Maharashtrian elite had previously dominated the institutions of this area of Bombay province, as they had all other areas outside Bombay city.

(b) Gujarati families with political ambitions could satisfy those ambitions in the service of the native states which were thick on the ground in this area. It is significant, I think, that Gandhi's family was in this line of business.

(c) the splintering of Gujarat between the native states and a conglomerate British Indian province like Bombay, with its cosmopolitan coastal capital, discouraged the development of regional consciousness.

(d) the *banyas* who became so prominent in the Gujarati Congress had a supra-regional culture (Vaisnavism-Jainism) and most had family connections throughout India's trading centres.

Bihar is a comparable case:

(a)   this was a 'colonial' area for the Bengal *bhadralok* into the first decade of this century and an indigenous elite had difficulty raising its head as a consequence.

(b)   Bihar was but one part of a wider cultural and linguistic region, embracing the U.P., Delhi and sections of the Punjab, Rajputana and Central India. Most important, for the U.P. as well as Bihar, this was the seat of the classical Indian imperial tradition. If the idea of a universal India had any historic home this was surely it.

There are special and particularly interesting features in U.P. case. Here, it appears, the continued dominance of the great landholders from the Mughal period into the British period, as a result of the protective policy of the 'Oudh School', prevented the rise of an elite of the Bengal-Maharashtrian variety. The great landholders, with their Indo-Persian 'husk culture' (as Anthony Low has called it), their social dominance, and their control of political institutions, were in fact the elite at least until the 1920s, and those who then challenged them could best do so through that universalist and 'anti-dominant' nationalism of the new elites and counter-elites. The Nehrus, Tandon, Kidwai and their ilk; in shaking themselves off the coattails of the great holders could use local discontents to advantage (viz. their use of the *kisans)* but they were not embarrassed by detailed regional commitments.

10. The effect of this extra-regional stance on the part of the nationalist opponents of the great landholders was to leave the U.P. without one clearly dominant group as the power of those landholders declined in the 1930's. The regional struggles from the late thirties to the present have been concerned as much with the contest between rival caste and class groups over the redistribution of power, as with the task of wresting that power from the great landholders.

In Maharashtra and Tamilnad new, relatively stable counter-elite were firmly in power by the 50's. In West Bengal the partition had allowed the *bhadralok* to reassert themselves in a remnant of their former domain. But in the U.P. no one clearly dominant elite has yet emerged. The struggle goes on and the political bosses of Congress balance dexterously but dangerously on the rolling balls of the struggle.

9

Europeans have often ascribed India's economic backwardness to the constraints of the Hindu social order, which is thought to value spirituality and resignation to one's fate above entrepreneurship and a "Puritan ethic" congenial to capitalism. An American economic historian here examines the role of the "Hindu value system" in India's economic development and argues that not only were such values much less of a hindrance than is usually supposed but that, in some areas at least, India's economic growth was greater than is often assumed.

Values as an Obstacle to Economic Growth in South Asia: An Historical Survey

MORRIS D. MORRIS

There are two widely held explanations for South Asia's failure to attain the level of economic performance achieved by the now developed countries of world: One is that British imperial policy frustrated economic growth after 1750; the other is that the Indian value system and the social structure that reflected that value system were obstacles to economic growth. It is worthy of note that both interpretations tend to visualize pre-1750 South Asia at a level a of economic organization and performance at least equal to that of western Europe in 1750, with the economic gap appearing only subsequently.[1]

As South Asia's colonial past recedes and the rate of economic growth of the now independent nations remains disappointing, there is a strong tendency to view the traditional value system and social structure as the decisive obstacles to satisfactory economic performance. The widely read and extremely influential volume by Kusum Nair, *Blossoms in the Dust,* expresses this view.[2] The economic historian Vera Anstey had come to the same conclusion before Independence when she wrote that the "religious tenets and practices of Hinduism and Muhammadanism have strictly limited economic development in the

Reprinted by permission from *The Journal of Economic History,* Vol.XXVII, No. 4 (Dec. 1967),pp. 588-607.

past...."[3] The same view was expressed in 1821 by the distinguished French scholar, the Abbé Dubois, after three decades in South India.[4] And in 1838 Charles Trevelyan wrote:

> [The] Hindu system of learning contains so much truth as to have raised the nation to its present point of civilization and to have kept it there for ages without retrograding, and so much error as to have prevented it from making any sensible advance during the same period....The peculiar wonder of the Hindu system is, not that it contains so much or so little knowledge, but that it has been so cleverly contrived for arresting the progress of the human mind, as to exhibit it at the end of two thousand years fixed at nearly the precise point at which it was first moulded.[5]

But for the definitive statement and classic analysis, we must turn to Max Weber. Concerned to explain differential levels and rates of economic achievement not only within Europe but between Europe and the great civilizations of the East, Weber initially raised the problem in his study of Protestantism. He pointed out that various manifestations of "capitalism and capitalistic enterprises" existed all through history, notably in China and India, but it was only in western Europe that "sober bourgeois capitalism with its rational organization of free labour" developed. Why, he asked, "did not...the economic development there [in China and India] enter upon that path of rationalization which is peculiar to the Occident?"[6]

For India, Weber's answer was that the effects of Hinduism on South Asian economic progress were "essentially negative". These adverse effects did not flow from any specific religious institution or ritual which "every one of the great religious systems in its way has placed, or has seemed to place, in the way of the modern economy. The core of the obstruction was rather imbedded in the 'spirit' of the whole system."[7]

It seems fairly clear that Weber believed that South Asia was, in earlier periods, a society organizationally, intellectually, and in terms of output per capita, at least the peer of Europe. It was only because of a special conjuncture of historical circumstances that capitalism and its productive consequences appeared in the West but did not develop in India. In this sense, Weber did not visualize a specific turning point, the Protestant Reformation, as decisive. Rather, he saw two quite different lines of development—one associated with the triumph of Hinduism over Buddhism and Jainism in the first thousand years of our era, and the other identified with specific consequences flowing from Judeo-Christian theology.

What is particularly striking in Weber's position is not the proposition that the ideological characteristics of Hinduism prevented the independent creation of modern bourgeois capitalism but that they raised serious doubts about the ability of South Asia (unlike Japan) even to be a successful follower.[8] Here the phenomenon of ideology was not the decisive factor; it was the restrictions imposed by the complex interdependence of Hindu ideology and the peculiarly rigid Brahamanic social structure embodied in the institution of caste that precluded the transformation to a capitalist economic structure and the achievement of high rates of economic growth.

But, obviously, South Asia is not entirely Hindu. Apart from Islam, it comprises a large number of other religious traditions: Jainism, Sikhism, Buddhism, Christianity, Zoroastrianism, as well as a variety of tribal animisms. In this context of religious diversity, can one appropriately speak of a single system of values? Can the effects of Hindu values be carried over to other religious traditions?

For Weber the answer was simple. He argued that Hinduism was an "almost irresistible social force", that its assimilative powers have been so great "that it tends even to integrate social forms considered beyond its religious borders....Islam, too, succumbed in India to the engulfing tendency toward caste formation....."[9] In these terms, Weber's judgements about Hinduism and its effects on economic activity are intended to apply with virtually no exception to the whole of South Asia.

Viewed in terms of its purported influence on socio-economic behaviour through time, what are the major characteristics of Hinduism, the carrier of the South Asian value system? For purposes of this essay, a most general statement will suffice. The decisive doctrinal features are *samsara,* the belief in rebirth; *karma,* the belief that actions in one life determine fortune and status in the next; and *dharma,* the definition of what one's behaviour must be in the life status to which one's *karma* has brought one.

The universe is seen as an enormously complex system, each part having a specific function which must be performed by a specific group of beings, a special *varna* or caste. Brahmans, the highest caste, perform the religious functions; Kshatriyas provide protection, "fighting in war and governing in peace"; Vaishyas, the third *varna* but still included among the "twice-born," are the commercial class; while Shudras, the lowest *varna,* are created to serve all the rest.[10]

By the working of *karma,* the iron law of retribution, man is born into a specific caste with a specific function in this life. His *dharma* dictates that he perform the specific role set for his caste, a role supported by an array of ritual practices and safeguards. It is a violation of his *dharma* to aspire to perform a function which properly lies within the *dharma* of another caste. As the *Bhagavad Gita* warns: "For there is more joy in doing one's own duty badly/than in doing another man's duty well./ It is joy to die in doing one's duty,/ but doing another man's duty brings dread."[11] If one is to improve his socio-economic position, he must do his duty and only that, aspire to no one else's status, and relate by proper ritual and behaviour to all other castes. The reward will come in the next reincarnation.

One other characteristic of the value system is economically relevant—the stress on asceticism. The highest goal in Hinduism is *moksha,* salvation by release from *karma,* the wheel of eternal rebirths. The concept of *moksha* set as the ultimate value the ideal of perfect asceticism, of absolute wantlessness. For ordinary people the Hindu system, of course, imposes specific sumptuary notions for each caste. Moreover, the hierarchy of castes favours those—Brahman and Kshatriya—whose functions are unconcerned with direct productive activity or accumulation of wealth.

Certain historical consequences purportedly flowed from the Hindu value system and its dependent social structure. Put most generally, the notions of *karma* and *dharma* lowered the levels of human aspiration and placed "a premium on passive acceptance rather than on amelioration of the human situation whether by hard work or social reform".[12] The combination of theology and caste organization supposedly froze people into the occupation or narrow cluster of occupations traditional to each caste to which its members were restricted by custom, by relations with other caste groups, and by the pressures of ritual and magic.

Caste puts a premium on traditional occupations by preventing the development of personal initiative; it works against the emergence of a relationship between individual aptitude, performance and earnings. Caste may even be said to restrict and determine consumption standards which are open to each individual in accordance with various caste rules.... Caste may thus be said to achieve what Western advertising aims at: it differentiates demand schedules and makes them less elastic.[13]

What is being suggested, generally, is that over time and at any equivalent level of resources and organization South Asian society produced a smaller quantum of output than a society with a different system of values. Moreover, at any given level of savings, the rate of economic growth over time would be lower in South Asia because incentives to invest would be lower.[14]

The traditionalism of the artisan, great everywhere, was stiffened "to the extreme" by Hinduism. The "magical fear of innovation" worked harshly against technical improvement. In many cases, the tools of the artisan were worshipped as quasi-fetishes and this stereotyping of tools "was one of the strongest handicaps to all technical development".[15]

The system, while not completely unresponsive to change, tended to encapsulate it. More than a passive barrier, Hinduism had its own built-in devices for deterring the potential threat. Any change of place, occupation, or even the merest change in work technique could precipitate caste schism, and a new caste created by such deviation was invariably ranked lower than its parent group on the ritual and status scale. As Weber concluded, caste "sustains tradition no matter how often the all-powerful development of imported capitalism overrides it."[16]

The system not only generally slowed down change and its consequences but tended to restrict the groups through which economic change of the modern sort could occur. It is claimed that only traditional trading caste groups moved into modern commerce and then into modern industrial entrepreneurship, where, because of their traditional orientation to commerce, they retained a "speculative mentality". Handicraftsmen, for reasons already suggested, tended neither to accumulate capital nor to become industrial entrepreneurs. In general, the implication is that to the extent that groups did modify their economic activities, they succeeded only as they sustained traditional value systems. They did not bring to new activities the rational outlook of modern capitalism.[17]

The growth of modern industry was handicapped, it is contended, not only by the ritually limited supply of entrepreneurship but also by the enormous difficulties of recruiting labour. Artisans, despite the competition of foreign and domestic factory production, struggled to stay in their traditional occupations. The magical barriers to geographical mobility, to undertaking new occupations, to working in novel relationships with other castes, all served as inhibitions to the flow of craftsmen into industry. Labour came "not from the ancient industrial castes, but predominantly from rural migrants, declassed and pariah castes, and declassed members of certain higher castes."[18] Low castes as well as high were infected with the sense of ritual appropriateness, the notion of limited aspirations, the doctrine of wantlessness which pervades the civilization. The obvious consequence of this even in the new occupations was a backward supply curve of labour.[19]

I have presented in this very gross fashion a widely accepted interpretation of how Hindu values and social structure have inhibited the economic performance of South Asian society through time. Most views, whatever the variation in presentation, seem to suggest that the rigidity, the incapacity of the economy to respond to novel and very productive opportunities, was most explicitly revealed after 1750-1800. To what extent does the historical evidence confirm such a hypothesis for the nineteenth and twentieth centuries?

An initial caution needs stating. The amount of satisfactory historical research that can be brought to bear on this range of problems is truly insignificant. The paucity is not for want of materials. South Asia is supplied with a range and quality of data that are in some ways quite impressive. Unfortunately, little of that material has been used to amplify our knowledge of the economic history of South Asia.[20] As a result, it is possible to examine only certain questions but these ultimately cast rather serious doubts on what, for simplicity's sake, I will call the Weberian hypothesis.

One important characteristic of South Asia, which tends to be dismissed in most discussions, is its sheer size. The area of what is now Pakistan and India is almost equal to the whole of Europe excluding the Soviet Union, and the most distinctive feature of the entire pre-British historical record is the evidence of political fragmentation and economic distinctiveness of the separate regions. I for no other reason than the sparseness of interregional communications during the entire period before 1800, it is impossible to conceive of any economic integration of South Asia in terms relevant even for early modern Europe or China.[21] It is, of course, possible to argue, as Weber did, that despite political and economic fragmentation, Hinduism imposed an overriding ideological unity that shaped socio-economic behaviour, but how valid is the notion of a unified "Hindu value system" in any sense significant to the economic historian?

The idea of an all-pervasive "Indian" value system has been derived from a scholarly dependence on the grand corpus of Brahmanical doctrinal literature. Even accepting the representativeness of this source, we must ask whether a single, monolithic ideology emerges. The moment the question is raised, the negative answer becomes obvious. As Weber himself recognized, within the format of this theology the range of possible, relevant value systems is enormous.[22] There is no single "Hindu"—and therefore no single Indian—ideological position to shape social behaviour. Not only does the Brahmanical literature contain enormous philosophical diversity; there is no single "book" and no formal church apparatus to elicit and impose any single dominating tradition of values.

Apart from the diverse "orthodox" value systems derivable from the Brahmanical literature itself, substantial doubt arises whether that literature is entirely representative of the traditional outlook.[23] A far more varied range of philosophical positions and theological concerns seems to have existed than could have been derived from the Brahmanical sources alone.

There is the further problem of establishing the link between expression and behaviour. The formal system of ideas and values was, after all, the property of an incredibly small elite.[24] Even assuming a monolithic Hindu theology in South Asia, can we ask how important was the effect of formal religious thought on actual behaviour? Moreover, if, as I have suggested, Hindu theology contained many strands, it is certainly possible that these could have been extracted and combined in a variety of ways to rationalize or stimulate variety of economic behaviours ranging from the most passive and otherworldly to the most aggressive and profit-maximizing. When this potential and actual philosophical diversity is further linked with the historical reality of geographical fragmentation, it is hard to sustain the idea that any single system of values could have influenced all South Asian economic behaviour in any single coherent direction.[25]

One further matter relating to the notion of a Hindu value system is worth mentioning in this brief essay. Weber was aware that the Brahmanic ideology had not established its domination over the subcontinent at one fell swoop. It spread from a small region in northern India, only gradually embracing various non-Hindu groups. The process of diffusion he described is not unlike M.N.Srinivas' "sanskritization" phenomenon, and it continues into our own time. While Weber saw the process as incorporating groups into a system of Brahmanical values with a fundamental ideological unity, recent fieldwork by anthropologists suggests that the values to which lower status groups aspire may not be Brahmanical at all. These groups, just coming into the Hindu system or striving to raise their status, tend to be responsive to the values and practices of the dominant group in their immediate locality, Brahman, Kshatriya, or even Vaishya. The implications of this recent work suggest once again that there are a number of "Hindu" value systems to which groups can respond.[26]

Weber's position was, of course, far more complex than the simple minded dependence on a value system which is so frequently trotted forth to explain the behaviour of South Asian society. As I have already indicated, for him the "cause" of India's failure to modernize is the value-supported rigidity of the caste system. I shall deal later with this view of caste. Bet let me first ask whether the *purported* slow economic growth of South Asia after 1800 is satisfactory historical evidence that Indians were less responsive to economic incentives than were others.[27] The obvious implication is that specific economic opportunities existed, that there were no significant discriminatory institutional barriers, and Englishmen were taking advantage of opportunities while Indians were not. In fact, the British record of investment in India is not a particularly distinguished one. Not only was the per capita amount low, but the bulk went into a limited block of activities—railroads, general trading enterprises, plantations, jute manufacturing, and mining.[28] In effect, "it concentrated on extractive industries and processing for export, on international trade, and on ancillary services," activities requiring a specific and detailed knowledge of foreign markets.[29] Natives were certainly at a disadvantage as against the Europeans in these enterprises.

It is true that Indians did not invest in railway shares. In 1870 there were 51, 519 British shareholders and only 368 Indians. But the rate of return guaranteed by the government was only 5 per cent and, as

Buchanan said, that sort of investment "appealed to conservative Europeans."[30] In other words, it may be incorrect to say that Indians did not invest in railway and other such enterprises because they lacked the entrepreneurial instinct or because they preferred traditional commercial or landed investments. It is entirely probable that Indian capital did not flow into railroads because the real rate of return to capital in India for alternative uses (net of risk) was much higher.[31]

If one looks specifically at modern factory industry, the British created only one substantial model, the jute industry, and that was also oriented to the export market. It cannot even be said that the British here gave a lead to Indian entrepreneurs in the development of factory industry. The first jute mill was started in 1854, but so were the first cotton textile mills in Bombay. Although Englishmen were modestly involved in the financing of these early Bombay enterprises, it is quite clear that the cotton mills were essentially native enterprises. It was not until 1874, after seventeen locally financed mills had been established in Bombay, that the first British mill was projected. In that same year, when British capital was cautiously projecting one cotton textile factory, ten more native mills were started. By 1914 the Indian cotton textile industry had become the fourth largest in the world and it was almost entirely Indian-financed and managed.

One of the fascinating aspects of the aggressiveness of Indian entrepreneurs in the cotton industry is that they poured capital into the very sector where it would seem that competition with Britain was sharpest, where political pressures from Manchester were destined to be very great, and where they had to function with no tariff protection (or virtually none). In this sense, the career of the cotton textile industry suggests the reverse of the point usually made. In India, it was British capital that was cautious; native capital and entrepreneurship were aggressive, rational, and creative.[32]

But in one sense the issue is not the responsiveness of Indian entrepreneurs to profit opportunities but the "rationality" of their involvement. A good deal has been said about the short-run speculative mentalities of native entrepreneurs, but little suggested about their behaviour could not be said equally of British and United States businessmen in similar circumstances.[33] Again we feel the almost total lack of detailed studies. My own work on the Bombay cotton textile industry suggests that from the beginning one sees a pattern of behaviour indicating economically rational responsiveness to available technology and to factor-price relationships differing little from that in the West.[34]

Is it possible that my evidence is biased by preoccupation with Western India and the cotton textile industry? After all, these are a region and an industry in which the specific value and group characteristics are consistent with the Weberian hypothesis.[35] Although one can point to the growth of native-owned cotton mills elsewhere in India, dispersion of the industry was a relatively slow process before 1914. Immediately the question of the purported regional differences in levels of native entrepreneurship arises. This is a very complicated matter on which virtually no helpful large-scale research has yet been done. Therefore, let me comment on only one small aspect—the claim that the pre-1914 native enterprise involved itself in the modern sector mainly in Gujarat, while in Bengal it seems to have devoted itself mainly to agriculture, government employment, and intellectual pursuits.[36]

It is not entirely clear to me that Bengali capital completely deserted the modern sector at some date before the mid-nineteenth century. This matter, too, needs research. However, the argument seems not concerned with the flow of capital but with the flow of entrepreneurship. Bengalis were not becoming the promoters of jute mills as Gujaratis were becoming promoters of cotton factories. At this point a peculiar analytic bias manifests itself. The plaint that this kind of active entrepreneurship was lacking in Eastern India rests on the implicit assumption that only this kind of activity is really modern. Somehow, investments and activities in rural marketing, small-scale (workshop) industry, or agriculture (except plantation agriculture) are not counted as an expression of the modern outlook. No thought has been given to the possibility, in fact the likelihood, that Bengali capital turned to investments in agriculture and other rural activities (as it seems to have done) because the profitability of these sectors expanded greatly after about 1830. While scholars will occasionally suggest that rural investment was profitable, they invariably pass over the implications.[37]

What I am suggesting by way of reinterpretation is that investment in modern factories should not be treated as something special. If we view all investment opportunities, except for the anticipated rate of return, as essentially the same to the entrepreneur, then the behaviour of Bengali investors would seem perfectly explicable to an economic historian without appealing to any special cultural characteristics. If my hunch is correct, nineteenth century Bengali enterprise seems to have responded precisely to those outlets for its talents and capital for which the rate of return was higher than in industry.[38] Under such circumstances, the first test to explain the varied directions of Indian investment in Bengal and in Gujarat would most faithfully examine the differences in production possibilities. I am suggesting, in other words, that one does not have to refer to anything as elusive as a "Hindu value system" to explain regional variations in economic performance in nineteenth-and twentieth-century South Asia. Opportunity and specific, identifiable political and economic barriers are probably sufficient.[39]

The same argument appears applicable elsewhere in the economy. It seems fairly clear that Indian agriculture has been generally responsive to the market. Although the detailed historical evidence we have relates only to the twentieth century, it seems consistent with what we do know about the nineteenth century—the growing regional specialization and changes in types of crops cultivated.[40] However, the responsiveness I note may not have permeated the entire agricultural sector. As Kusum Nair has suggested, we may merely be observing the reactions of specific groups whose traditional value systems happen to be compatible with certain possibilities the market generated.

> Throughout India... the best farmers are to be found not necessarily in communities most favourably endowed with material resources, but in those that are traditionally agriculturist by caste, such as the *Sadgops* in West Bengal, the *Jats* in the Punjab and the *Patidars* in Gujarat. It is so mainly because these castes have an inherited respect for agricultural work and they are not precluded by religion or tradition from working on the land.[41]

Again, briefly, I can only suggest that superior explanations will be found by referring, among other features, to the complex systems of land tenures, the distribution of power and control of economic resources associated with tenurial arrangements, and the effects of all these on rewards, incentives, and decision making in the countryside.

Weber wrote of the difficulty of recruiting labour for modern factories, "even in those manufacturing industries with the highest wages". The Hindu system of values with its sumptuary characteristics supposedly generated a backward-sloping supply curve of labour.[42] The historical studies consistently run counter to such a view. The careers of the Bombay cotton textile industry and the Jamshedpur iron and steel enterprise both indicate that labour recruitment presented no problems and the labour supply curves sloped in the orthodox fashion in the relevant ranges.[43] Here, as elsewhere, specific features of economic development are readily explainable without calling into account any concept of a Hindu value system—at least, as so far developed.

Let me now turn to the crucial area in which the value system functions through the social structure. Limited by space to a few categorical statements, I will attempt to focus on the claimed influences of caste on the performance of the Indian economy. We lack hard historical evidence, a fact which in itself raises an interesting question. Given the overwhelming social importance attributed to the institution of caste, one would expect to find a good deal of attention to caste relations in the history books. But the reverse is the case. It is almost as if the institution is irrelevant when change is being described.[44]

A careful examination of the material pertinent to economic change indicates that what purport to be references to caste are, in fact, usually references either to *varna* or "community", much vaguer and analytically less useful terms. This is not the place to attempt a precise definition of caste. It is only necessary to indicate that in economic terms the relevant unit is what are called subcastes, *jati*, endogamous groups invariably confined to limited territories. The *jati* is the functional social unit in the countryside; the *jati* exhibits whatever ritualized and religiously determined behaviour we will find; only the *jati* embodies those notions of belief, bulwarked by specific concepts of pollution, which could have any systematic effect on economic behaviour. It is, therefore, not analytically appropriate to lump discrete *jati* into larger groups merely because of similarity of function or name. With this in mind, it becomes obvious that the *varna* categories used by Weber and others are entirely irrelevant for the evaluation of the major features of economic or social change. I think there would be little disagreement on this point among those who have worked most intimately on the problem.[45]

The notion of "community" is even less satisfactory. Here there is a widespread tendency to confuse regional or other gross characteristics with caste. I have shown elsewhere how such imprecision has led to incorrect conclusions about the historical development of the labour force.[46] The same confusion seems to bear heavily on discussions about entrepreneurship. For example, one invariably finds reference to the various great South Asian business "communities"—Gujarati, Marwari, Bania, Chettiar,Muslim, Jain, Parsi, etc. Not one of these is, in fact, a *jati*. Typically, the community embraces a very large number of endogamous groups (except in the case of the Parsi). The Gujarati and Marwari communities are geographical classifications which incorporate all the main *jati* and religious groups that do business in these areas.[47] Terms like Bania and Chettiar are also collective categories embracing a very great number of *jati;* these terms are particularly confusing since, while ostensibly defining specific *jati* or *varna* groups, they tend to be used as functional descriptions (anyone who trades!) and thus become quite meaningless. For example, in a recent article Bania was defined as "a member of a *traditional* merchant caste." The group considered in the sample embraced at least three and possibly thirteen (or more) jati. Moreover, groups identified as Bania in the study included elements which in the countryside had artisan or other non-merchant designations—*Teli* (oil pressers); *Kalvar* (distillers); *Bhuj* (grain parchers); and so on. The justification for including them as Banias was that "these groups also sell these products and commonly operate shops." While possibly true, this certainly does not make them members of any "traditional merchant caste".[48]

Not only are *varna* and "community" hopelessly confusing terms, but the fact that they rather than *jati* are used in itself seems to imply something significant—that *jati* as such is not the economically or historically relevant category. Here two behavioural characteristics can be documented historically. First, there is widespread evidence, at least among the Ahmedabad and Bombay enterprisers, of inter-jati cooperation. It is not only a matter of cooperation in the modern sector; there is evidence of cooperation in traditional business activities. Let me illustrate the point with only two of many examples I have culled. The Walchand Hirachand family is now a major industrial force. They are Digambar Jains who migrated from north Gujarat to Maharashtra about 1840. Walchand himself was apprenticed by his father to a Marwari commission agent for experience, early in his career cooperated with a Muslim contractor, and later went into partnership with a Brahman.[49] The Tata family, is, of course, the most distinguished of the Parsi industrial enterprisers. The father of the great J. N. Tata was apprenticed (in the 1830's or early 1840's) to a "Hindu banker and general merchant." Somewhat later he went into business with the Brahman, Premchand Roychand. J. N. Tata, of course, was noted for the variety of his business connections.[50]

These are not special cases; similar ones can be found scattered throughout the nineteenth-century records. They are paralleled by the inter-*jati* collaboration within the labour force. This, of course, appears in modern industry[51] Moreover, the same system of apprenticeship which provided training in commerce was apparently also at work among rural artisans. In Jamshedpur I found considerable evidence that people employed as skilled masons were frequently not from "traditional" mason *jati*. On inquiry, I discovered that most of these had obtained their village-generated skill by working with a caste mason in the village from which they came. I have encountered evidence suggesting that in this same way new groups came into handloom weaving in the countryside in the nineteenth century.

A second feature worth mentioning is that the *jati* concept does not guarantee purity of function. One will constantly encounter in the literature reference to "traditional" caste occupations. The implication is that the group was traditionally found in this activity, and further that to the extent that census data report something less than 100 per cent employed in that "traditional" employment. But let me remark that the notion of a "traditional" occupation we are seeing the evil consequences of "modernization". I do not want to deal with the obvious logical fallacy that neglects the impact of differential rates of population growth on the possibilities of engaging in a "traditional" employment. But let me remark that the notion of a "traditional" occupation to which members of a *jati* are tried is a very confused one which hides a great deal of interesting development. For example, in research that I am doing on handicraft weaving in the seventeenth century and after, there is very clear evidence that many groups in so-called traditional weaving castes were really cloth merchants and financiers.[52] The actual weavers frequently were recruited from non-traditional *jati*. Without going into details, let me merely make the point that even in the rural sector and under circumstances not obviously related to the "modernization" process, castes "traditionally" identified with specific occupations were often found in other activities, socially both higher and lower.[53] Moreover, there is evidence that groups classified as "traditionally"linked with a specific occupation will frequently be found to have come into that occupation within an historically recent period. Thus, to attempt to link occupation and *jati* rigidly is to find one's self operating in a universe of exceptions. The Indian society historically has exhibited a reasonably high degree of fluidity. This explains why so little can be said definitively about the influence of caste on economic change. Once one leaves the formal world represented by the Laws of Manu and the static analysis of the anthropologist, one enters a realm where caste and *jati* seem to be as fluid as change requires.

This essay has concluded that there is no precise definition of a "Hindu value system" that can be identified as a significant obstacle to economic growth or change. Nor does the value system working through the caste system exhibit any decisive impact on the process of change. While *jati* seems to be the operative unit, it behaves historically as extended kin groups have done elsewhere. For example, the descriptions of entrepreneurial behaviour in nineteenth- and early twentieth-century India resemble similar activities in Renaissance Europe and seem to reflect primarily the limited scope of economic opportunities rather than any specific form of social structure.

I confess I find these conclusions disturbing. What I am saying is that for the economic historian there seem to be no analytically significant differences between Indian *civilization* and any other. While this ability to generalize is what the social scientist struggles for, my conclusion "feels" as if it violates the "sense of things". But all I can suggest is that we must occasionally re-examine the evidence and our categories in the hope that we will be able to resolve this intellectual anxiety. Until then, we will have to push research along lines which assume that values have not been a significant obstacle to economic change and growth.

Notes and References

1. M.D. Morris and Burton Stein, "The Economic History of India; A Bibliographic Essay", *The Journal of Economic History*, XXI(June 1961), 182-183, 192 ff.; and M.D. Morris, "Towards a Reinterpretation of Nineteenth Century Indian Economic History", *Journal of Economic History*, XXIII, Dec, 1963, 607-8.

2. Kusum Nair, *Blossoms in the Dust*, New York; Frederick A. Praeger, 1962, particularly pp. 192-93.

3. Vera Anstey, *The Economic Development of India*, 3d. ed., London: Longmans Green and Company, 1936, p. 47.

4. J.A. Dubois, *Hindu Manners, Customs and Ceremonies*, Henry K. Beauchamp, ed. 3d. ed., Oxford: At the Clarendon Press, 1906, pp. 5, 96-97.

5. Charles E. Trevelyan, *On the Education of the People of India* (London: 1838), pp. 83-84.

6. Max Weber, *The Protestant Ethic and the Spirit of Capitalism*, New York: Charles Scribner's Sons, 1958, pp. 19-25.

7. Max Weber, *The Religion of India*. Translated and edited by H.H. Gerth and D.Martindale, Glencoe, III: The Free Press, 1958, pp. 111, 112.

8. ibid., p. 325. Weber quoted with obvious approval the judgement of "some eminent English students of the land" that even though "the penetration of Indian society by [British] capitalistic interest is already so extensive that they can no longer be eliminated.... the removal of the thin conquering strata of Europeans and the Pax Brittannica enforced by them would open wide the life and death struggles of inimical castes, confessions, and tribes; the old feudal robber romanticism of the Indian Middle Ages would again break forth" (ibid).

9. ibid., pp. 18-20.

10. ibid., p. 55; he very explicitly accepts the four-class *varna* scheme as the "picture of historical social reality". While most modern descriptions see the caste system fragmented into many more units than this, the historical consequences seem to be about the same as those described by Weber. See, for example, K. William Kapp, *Hindu Culture, Economic Development and Economic Planning in India*, New York: Asia Publishing House, 1963, ch. ii. Kapp stresses the psychological manifestations and consequences. ibid., chs.i-iii. Weber, *in Religion of India*, pp. 339-40, explicitly denies the usefulness of a psychological analysis of the problem.

11. From A.L. Basham's translation, *The Wonder That Was India*, London: Sidgwick and Jackson, 1954, p.341.

12. Kapp, *Hindu Culture*, p. 16.

13. ibid., pp. 46-47.

14. ibid., p. 17. This last consequence seems to be somewhat at odds with the view earlier mentioned that the great performance gap between South Asian and Western economic systems manifested itself after about 1750. There are a number of possible interpretations of this. This most popular seems to be based on the assumption of "the strong preference of Hindu wealth for commercial investment..." *Weber, Religion of India*, p. 117. Within the *varna* system there is provision for commercial groups, vaishyas, who would be vigorously responsive to traditional types of investment opportunity but were not at all responsive to the much more productive (but novel) investment opportunities in the modern industrial sector.

15. Weber, *Religion of India*, p. 99.

16. ibid., pp. 11-123. See, also, Kapp, pp. 46 ff.

17. Weber, *Religion of India, (passim)*. Cf. particularly pp. 102-117, 334 ff; Kapp, *Hindu Culture*, chs. i-iii; and Nair, *Blossoms*, particularly the comment about traditional agricultural castes, pp. 190-91. See, also, Helen B. Lamb, "The 'State' and Economic Development in India", in Simon Kuznets, Wilbert E. Moore, and Joseph Spengler, eds., *Economic Growth: Brazil, India, Japan*, Durham: Duke University Press, 1955, p. 479.

18. Weber, *Religion of India;* pp. 104-5.

19. ibid., particularly p. 114. Weber suggests that the one advantage to entrepreneurs "is that the caste division of workers has so far made any trade union organization and any real 'strike' impossible."

20. For a general survey of the state of the field of Fourth Asian economic history, see Morris and Stein, *Economic History*, pp. 179-207. I know of only one explicit attempt to relate the Hindu value system to economic change through time: V.Mishra, *Hinduism and Economic Growth*, Bombay: Oxford University Press, 1962. The result is unsatisfactory.

21. Morris, *Reinterpretation*, pp. 606-18. For this alone, it strikes me that any attempt to compare South Asian economic performance with that of Britain or Japan in the nineteenth and twentieth centuries is far from the mark.

22.   This ignores for the time being the fact that each *varna* necessarily had its distinctive set of values associated with and appropriate to its *dharma*.

23.   This is suggested in W. Norman Brown, "Traditional Culture and Modern Developments in India", *Report of the XIth International Congress of the Historical Sciences, Stockholm, 1960,* Paris: Mouton & Co. 1960, particularly pp. 129-35.

24.   Weber, *Religion of India,* pp. 326-28. See, also, M.N. Srinivas, *Social Change In Modern India* Berkeley: University of California Press, 1967, pp. 5-6.

25.   Basham, *Wonder That Was India,* ch. vii, particularly pp. 322 and 340 ff., suggests some of the possibilities of reinterpretation. The point about philosophical diversity becomes even more relevant when we recall that Weber's intellectual system usually derived its distinctive results from relatively minor ideological differences, e.g., differences among the various Protestant sects or between Protestantism and Catholicism. See also Marion J. Levy, Jr., "Contrasting Factors in the Modernization of China and Japan", *Economic Development and Culture Change,* II, Oct. 1953, pp. 161-97, for the significance of the notion of small differences.

26.   Weber, *Religion of India,* pp. ff; and M. Singer, "The Social Organization of Indian Civilization", *Diogenes,* Winter, 1964, 84-119. Srinivas, *Social Change,* p. 5, referring to the Brahmanical *varna* theology, commented: "The claims which the Brahmans made for themselves and their view of the caste hierarchy are understandable, but not so the fact that many scholars, Indian as well as foreign, have regarded them as representations of historical reality." Cf. Srinivas, *Social Change,* pp. 3ff.

27.   I stress my doubt about the slowness of Indian economic growth in the nineteenth century. There have been no very helpful studies of the period. The rate of growth (if any) is unknown but a reasonable case can be made for rather substantial per capita growth between 1800 and 1914. The counter-argument is based on the somewhat dubious assumption that the level of Indian economic performance about 1700-1750 was approximately equal to that in Western Europe. For a brief examination of these issues, see Morris, *Reinterpretation.*

But even if, when ultimately compiled, all-Indian data would confirm the more traditional view that no per capita growth occurred during the nineteenth century, one would still have to avoid the danger arising out of the aggregation procedure. For an example of the importance of regional diversity, see the effects of Greater Bengal on the all-Indian results in G. Blyn's *Agricultural Trends in India, 1891-1947: Output, Availability, and Productivity,* Philadelphia: University of Pennsylvania Press, 1966, pp. 219ff. It is certainly clear on the basis of the qualitative data that some regions—Punjab, Assam, and most probably, Gujarat—grew very rapidly. If I am correct about this, we have a level of economic performance superior to many areas of Europe, Latin America, and Africa during the same period. Obviously, this would raise some very serious doubts about the meaningfulness of the "Hindu values" discussion. But even if such comparison cannot be made, the fact that there were very distinct variations in the rates of economic growth between one part of India and another would still raise very substantial issues. In this event one could possibly rationalize diverse regional economic performance with the notion of a "Hindu" value system by referring to the proposition that each *varna* had its specific *dharma.* If one could relate regions of more rapid expansion with higher proportions of Vaishyas in the population, the differences might just be justifiable. This is what Weber, in *Religion of India,* pp. 91-92, seems to have had in mind. At any rate, an obvious early task for scholars interested in South Asian economic history is an attempt to derive some estimates of rates of growth by region for the nineteenth century.

28. Arun Bose, "Foreign Capital", in V.B. Singh, ed., *Economic History of India: 1857-1956*, (Bombay: Allied Publishers Private Limited, 1965), pp. 492ff. See also L.H. Jenks, *The Migration of British Capital to 1875*, New York: Alfred A. Knopf, 1927, pp. 206ff.; and D.H. Buchanan, *The Development of Capitalistic Enterprise in India*, New York: The Macmillian Company, 1934, pp. 148ff.

29. Michael Kidron, *Foreign Investments in India*, London: Oxford University Press, 1965, p.3.

30. Buchanan, *Development*, p. 152.

31. This is hinted at by Vera Anstey, "Economic Development", in L.S.S. O'Malley, ed., *Modern India and the West*, London, Oxford University Press, 1941, p. 272, and by Buchanan, *Development*, p. 146.

It is worth mentioning that the discussions of Indian investment behaviour during the nineteenth century almost invariably neglect the matter of comparative rate of return between one form of investment and another. This is the case whether the stress is on Indian preference for investment in commerce rather than industry or in land rather than in industry. The same failure to consider the nature of alternative opportunities and rates of return appears in the discussions of the purported unwillingness of Indians to shift from literary to technical education in the later nineteenth century. See Robert. I. Crane, "Technical Education and Economic Development", in C.A. Anderson and M.J. Bowman, eds., *Education and Economic Development*, Chicago; Aldine Publishing Company, 1965, pp. 167-201. Still the best discussion of this entire problem is Henry G. Aubrey, "Industrial Investment Decisions: A Comparative Analysis", *Journal of Economic History*, XV (Dec. 1955), 335-51. For a useful essay directly on the Indian situation see S. Bhattacharya, "Cultural and Social Constraints on Technological Innovation and Economic Development: Some Case Studies", *The Indian Economic and Social History Review*, III (Sep, 1966), 240-67.

32. For the history of jute and cotton industries, see Buchanan, *Development*, chs, x and xi; and S.C. Mehta, *The Cotton Mills of India, 1854-1954*, Bombay: The Textile Association (India), 1954. For the estimate of India's role in world cotton manufacturing see Anstey, *Economic Development*, p. 262. For a brief comment on investment in the Bombay industry, see M.D. Morris, *The Emergence of an Industrial Labour Force in India*, Berkeley: University of California Press, 1965, pp. 22ff. For an example of the caution of British investors, see the report of John Robertson reproduced in Bombay Millowners' Association, *Report of the Bombay Millowners Association for the Years 1875 and 1875-76*.
British prudence showed itself not only in the cotton textile industry. In the steel industry, also, it was native enterprise that took on the task. See William A. Johnson, *The Steel Industry of India*, Cambridge: Harvard University Press, 1966, pp. 243-50 and references found there. See also Kidron, *Foreign Investments*, p. 41.

33. Aubrey, *Investment Decisions*.

34. Morris, *Emergence of an Industrial Labour Force*, pp. 31-38 and *passim*. The notion is widespread that Indians were technically and organizationally entirely dependent on Britain dating the nineteenth and early twentieth centuries. But if one examines the Indian cotton textile industry, it becomes obvious that very early and in important ways the Indians developed their own solutions that took

them down independent paths. Of course, as one would expect, labour-to-equipment ratios were quite different than those in Lancashire. But there were other substantive differences. Unlike Manchester, the Indian mills very quickly shifted out of mule and into ring spindles. Almost from the beginning of their history they integrated spinning and weaving departments, differing here, too, from British practice. And of course, the managing agency device was a different technique for administering the companies than was employed in Britain.

35. Weber, *Religion of India*, particularly pp. 91-92, 192-204, and 314-16.

36. Morris, *Emergence of an Industrial Labor Force*, pp. 15-16. While it is popular to explain the situation in Bengal by reference to imperial policy, this does not explain why the response seems to have been different on the two sides of the subcontinent.

37. See, for example, N.C.Sinha, *Studies In Indo-British Economy A Hundred Years Ago*, Calcutta: A. Mukerjee & Co., 1946, pp. 27-46. The fact that certain kinds of investments, as in modern factories, might ultimately have yielded some derivative benefits, some socio-economic externalities, is no reason to imply either that the native entrepreneur was forced to choose rural investments or that his system of values made him unresponsive to the modern investments. It merely suggests that knowledge was not perfect. But this is not a defect only of the Hindu value system.

38. Buchanan, *Development*, p. 146, suggests this same possibility. It can, of course, be argued that the phenomenon flowed from patterns of discrimination against native enterprises in the modern sector. While this possibility cannot be ignored, the answer will only be found when scholars have studied the rates of return from rural investments in the nineteenth century.

39. Unfortunately, space limitations force me to advance my argument in cruder form than I would like. While my proposition possibly explains the differences that distinguish Gujarat from Bengal, it does not immediately respond to the claim that it was Marwaris rather than Bengalis who moved in on the expanding rural opportunities of the nineteenth century. All I can say at this point is that categories such as "Bengali" and "Marwari" are far too gross to be analytically useful. My casual examination of some relevant data leaves me with the impression that when the details inherent in these categories are properly reconsidered, we will uncover a much different story than is now usually accepted.

40. Dharm Narain, *The Impact of Price Movements on Areas Under Selected Crops in India 1900-1939*, Cambridge, (Eng.): At the University Press, 1965; and Morris, "Reinterpretation." p. 612.

41. Nair, *Blossoms*, pp. 190-91.

42. Weber, *Religion of India*, p. 114.

43. Morris, *Emergence of an Industrial Labor Force;* M.D. Morris, "The Labor Market in India", in W.E. Moore and A.S. Feldman, eds., *Labour Commitment and Social Change in Developing Areas*, New York: Social Science Research Council, 1960, pp. 173-200; and M.D. Morris, "Order and Disorder in the Labour Force: The Jamshedpur Crisis of 1958", *Economic Weekly*, November 1, 1958, pp. 1387-95.

44. See A.M. Shah, "Social Anthropology and the Study of Historical Societies", *The Economic Weekly* (Special Number), July 1959, p. 959. I have examined a good deal of the travel literature and the records of the European companies that traded in India after 1600. The references to caste are amazingly few. In fact, most of them strike me as being occupational designations rather than caste references. It is true that these reporters were not trained social scientists. Nevertheless, one

would assume that had caste been a decisive factor affecting their economic relationships it would have been commented upon. The silence of the records is, I suggest, analytically significant.

The only study I know of that seems to deal specifically with caste in history is Leon Sinder, *Caste Instability in Moghul India*, Seoul, Korea: Chung-ang University, 1964. Unfortunately, I have been unable to obtain a copy of it.

45. Irawati Karve, "What is Caste?" *The Economic Weekly*, X, Jan., Mar., and July 1958, pp. 125-38, 401-07, 881-88; and ibid., XI, Jan. 1959, 149-63; Srinivas, *Social Change*, pp. 3-9; and D.R. Gadgil, "Notes on the Rise of the Business Communities in India", a mimeographed memorandum prepared for the Institute of Pacific Relations, April 1951. Gadgil states (p.v): "It is my belief that the bulk of positions of administrative responsibility and especially positions of profit in an Indian business are held by persons belonging to the sub-caste [*jati*] of its owner or managing agent. The sub-caste thus tends to determine, in a large measure, the distribution of wealth and economic power."

Weber recognized that each *varna* category incorporated many subgroups. He knew, for example, that there were socially degraded Brahman subcastes. See, especially, Weber, *Religion of India*, pp. 9ff. However, his analysis required that these distinctions be ignored.

46. M.D. Morris, "Caste and the Evolution of the Industrial Workforce in India", *Proceedings of the American Philosophical Society*, CIV, Apr. 1960, 124-133; and Morris, *Emergence of an Industrial Labour Force*, pp. 71-83.

47. D.P. Pandit, "Creative Response in Indian Economy: A Regional Analysis", *The Economic Weekly*, IX, Feb. 23 and Mar. 2, 1957, 283-86, 315-17; Hemlata Acharya, "Creative Response in Indian Economy: A Comment", *The Economic Weekly*, IX, Apr. 27, 1957, 547-49; and Howard Spodek, "The 'Manchesterisation' of Ahmedabad", *The Economic Weekly*, XVII, Mar. 13, 1965, 483-90. These three references refer to Brahmans, Rajputs, Patidars, Bhatias, Patels, Jains, Kapol Banias, Muslims, and Parsis, as well as others, all involved in the Ahmedabad cotton textile industry. The same phenomenon can be traced in Bombay. See, for a beginning, S.M. Rutnagar, *Bombay Industries: The Cotton Mills*, Bombay: *The Indian Textile Journal Limited*, 1927.

48. Richard G. Fox, "Family, Caste, and Commerce in a North Indian Market Town", *Economic Development and Cultural Change*, XV, Apr. 1967, 297-314, particularly pp. 297, 301, 304-8. My comments are not necessarily intended as a reflection on Fox's article. His purposes may have been satisfied by the Bania category he used. I am merely trying to point out that economic relationships and behaviour are obviously not explicitly linked with any notion of caste that is operationally meaningful to the economic historian.

49. *Walchand Diamond Jubilee Commemoration Volume*, Bombay: Published by B.D. Sardesai, Walchand Diamond Jubilee Celebration Committee, 1942, pp. 3ff. It is interesting to mention that while the women of the family still speak Gujarati and dress in Gujarati style, the male members have become culturally Maharashtrian. ibid, pp. 4-5.

50. F.R. Harris, *Jamsetji Nusserwanji Tata*, 2d. ed.; Bombay: Blackie & Son, 1958, ch. i. There is a tendency to assume that Parsis were particularly cosmopolitan. What is neglected is the fact that they had to be cosmopolitan with someone! It is my own impression that the economic significance of Parsis as a group has been exaggerated. Among the Parsis only a few families are decisive. If their role is important, it is more a reflection of the small scale of economic action in India than of any specific system of values. Otherwise, one has difficulty explaining

action in India than of any specific system of values. Otherwise, one has difficulty explaining why the Parsis, so influential in Bombay, were insignificant in Ahmedabad.

51. See references in footnote 43.

52. Buchanan, *Development*, pp. 113, makes specific reference to a case in which part of a weaver *jati* took over merchant functions. The phenomenon, which seems to have occurred in many other occupations, is important for at least two reasons. It makes clear that handicraft workers were not all being driven into the state of landless labour in the nineteenth and early twentieth centuries. It also reveals a process of economic differentiation not unlike that which occurred in Europe and suggests the possibility that artisans, after moving into commerce, might well have functioned as merchant manufacturers with all the developmental possibilities inherent in such a process. I am convinced that there was a good deal of modern activity built up in the rural sector in this way in the last 150 years. But we will only be able to find out what happened when scholars give up the notion that planting, harvesting, and money-lending were the only activities occurring in the rural sector. Buchanan, in *Development*, chs. v-vii, says more about these possibilities than almost any other source I know.

53. Nair, in *Blossoms*, pp. xviii-xix, has a passage which indicates some of the categorical confusions which exist in the literature and which tends to blur the presence of change. "The words 'cultivator' and 'agriculturist' do not imply that the peasant necessarily tills the land himself. They may merely indicate that he lives mainly by income from agriculture. Then there are certain communities in India that are agriculturist by caste. They are like other professional castes, such as those of blacksmiths or weavers. The majority of the people who actually work on the land belong to what are known as the scheduled castes of *Harijans*."

PART III

The Sense of Urgency

The coming of the British caught India up in a flood of change. Sometimes changes were introduced in the interests of an increased tax revenue, or, with new law courts and legal procedures, to secure what the British perceived as a fair and efficient governance. Other changes, particularly after the 1820's, reflected the critical spirit and reforming zeal that were transforming England, and could, it was thought, as easily make of India a modern liberal society. Yet changes in ideology cannot easily measure changes in practice. Much of the old order survived, and much indeed was incorporated into the new as the British sought to consolidate their imperial order. The extent of change was never as dramatic and far-reaching as historians commonly assumed. The first two articles in this section attempt overall assessments of the impact of colonial rule on India in the days of the East India Company. The others examine one of the most portentous of Britain's reforming measures—the introduction of Western education—and the ways this new schooling set in motion among Indians a searching re-evaluation of their own cultural heritage.

10

*In this selection Eric Stokes argues that while older accounts
exaggerated the abruptness of the transition to a modern India,
recent historians have gone too far in arguing that British rule
brought no change at all. Change, in his view, was slow and
uneven, and felt far sooner in the upper reaches of Indian society,
but by the middle of the ninteenth century it had extended itself
throughout the land.*

The First Century of British Colonial Rule in India: Social Revolution or Social Stagnation?

ERIC STOKES

The science of history proceeds no doubt as the detailed criticism of
sociological generalisations, but of generalisations so rudimentary and
so little analysed that they constitute primitive archetypal images
lurking in the background of the historian's consciousness rather than a
formed system of ideas. In South Asian studies such images are the
simple dichotomies of East and West, tradition and modernity,
continuity and change, status and contract, feudalism and capitalism,
caste and class; and the historian and social scientist conduct their
increasingly technical and sophisticated studies in the form of an
implicit critique of these conceptual polarities. Nineteenth-century
sociological thought, with its evolutionary and therefore historical bias,
founded itself squarely and unabashedly upon such polarities, but today
few read James Mill, or Hegel, or Maine, or Lyall, or even, one
suspects, Weber, on India. To strike the primitive images into our
consciousness there was needed a synthesising mind of genius who
could throw the sociological generalisations of his time into memorable
epigrammatic phrase and fire them with political passion. That is one
reason at least why Marx's occasional journalism on India is still read
and pondered, even though his more academic studies have remained
neglected until quite recently.

World copyright : the Past and Present Society, 175 Banbury Road, Oxford, England. This
article is reprinted with the permission of the society and the author's executor from *Past
and Present*, No. 58 (February 1973), pp. 136-60.

Marx recognised that the pre-conditions of Western conquest lay in Indian rather than in British society. His major premise was the peculiar multi-cellular character of Indian society that made it both highly resistant to change in its social and cultural aspects and *ipso facto* subject to constant political change and to conquest from without:

> A country not only divided between the Mohammedan and Hindu, but between tribe and tribe, between caste and caste; a society whose framework was based on a sort of equilibrium, resulting from a general repulsion and constitutional exclusiveness between all its members. Such a country and such a society, were they not the predestined prey of conquest?...Indian society has no history at all, at least no known history. What we call its history is but the history of the successive intruders who founded their empires on the passive basis of that unresisting and unchanging society.[1]

One of the most important consequences of this extreme compartmentalism, which Marx described as "the dissolution of society into stereotyped and disconnected atoms", was the discontinuity between the social base and the political superstructure. Parcelled out into a myriad of self-sufficient and self-governing village "republics", each regulated internally by the institutions of caste, society was capable of ordering itself almost independently of superior political authority. The taproot of this self-sufficiency was economic, 'the domestic union of industrial and agricultural pursuits' within the village reinforced by the existence of tied industrial castes. These made otiose rural dependence on urban manufacture and its concomitants, an exchange economy and class differentiation, which had slowly eaten the heart out of Western feudalism.

> The simplicity of the organization for production in these self-sufficing [village] communities that constantly reproduce themselves in the same form and when accidentally destroyed spring up again on the spot with the same name—this simplicity supplies the key to the secret of the unchangeableness of Asiatic societies, an unchangeableness in such striking contrast with the constant dissolution and refounding of Asiatic states, and the never-ceasing changes of dynasty. The structure of the economic elements of society remains untouched by the storm clouds in the political sky.[2]

If compartmentalism was the keynote of the economic and social structure, "oriental despotism" characterised its politics. Whether this arose as Marx believed primarily out of the need for a centralised bureaucratic authority to build and manage irrigation works upon which agriculture depended, or whether it represented simply the systematisation of predatory military rule, is immaterial. But its consequence was the absorption by state taxation of the whole surplus produce of the soil beyond the bare subsistence needs of the cultivator. Hence private rent property in land and a stable allodial aristocracy based upon it never emerged.[3] Whatever magnate or gentry element existed owed its position to revokable state appointments and to stipends consisting of temporary grants or alienations of the public land revenue. In Weber's terminology the Indian nobility was prebendal, and feudal forms could not disguise its original and continuing dependence on state power and its lack of all enduring freestanding rights of its own. The same absence of class autonomy was true of what passed for the bourgeoisie. Given the self-sufficiency of the Indian village, its surplus production was not drawn out by the operations of an exchange economy resting on urban manufacture but had to be forcibly pumped out by the engine of taxation. These tax revenues were expended by the ruler and his satraps on luxury products supplied by the traders and craftsmen who gathered round the military encampments. And Indian towns rarely rose above this level.[4] They remained essentially artificial settlements, without an autonomous life of their own and above all, without a true burgher class possessing jurisdictional and political rights. The differentiation of society into classes did not occur, and the Western *Ständestaat* was not reproduced. Without the counterpoise of feudal 'estates' Asian government was by nature overcentralised and despotic, while its inherent instability prevented the growth of durable territorial states.[5]

The notion of "oriental despotism" may be filled out from other nineteenth-century writers among whom it was a common theme. Sir Alfred Lyall, from whom Maine drew some of his later ideas, used it to explain the break-up of the Mughal empire and the rise of the British power. The Mughals he saw as merely the most recent and most successful of Indian rulers in planing flat the surface of political society and concentrating power in a top-heavy despotism at the centre. Hence when the centre crashed in the eighteenth century there was nothing to cushion its fall. In Lyall's words it was:

An era of chaos unprecedented even in the annals of Asiatic history, such an era as only follows the break up of a wide spreading despotic empire which has so carefully knocked out and cut away all internal or local stays and ties that its fall, when it comes, is a ruinous crash, and leaves a vast territory in a state of complete political dissolution...one important reason why the English so rapidly conquered was this, that the countries which fell into our hands had no nationalities, no long-seated ruling dynasties, or ancient aristocracies, that they had in fact no solid or permanent organisation of the kind, but were politically treasure trove, and at disposal of the first who having found could keep.[6]

Lyall also found the source of political instability and the transience of political structures not in some special Asian propensity to despotism but the Indian social structure. The historical evolution of Indian society had taken a peculiar direction. In Western Europe the tribal unit based on putative kinship had been dissolved into a multitude of nuclear families held together in political groupings based on land and territory, whether in the wide embrace of Roman imperial authority or later in smaller local lordships of feudalism. Out of these had emerged durable territorial states with a sense of nationality, and permanent political institutions capable of resisting the centripetal force of monarchy and hence of surviving the latter's temporary weakness or collapse. In India, however, "religion seems to have stepped in as the tribal institutions dissolved, and to have strung all the kindred groups upon the great circle which we call caste," so that "the trade, or the profession, or the common ritual becomes the bond of union instead of descent or political association." Lyall thus arrives at the same conclusion regarding the discontinuity of the political and social systems.

This emphasis on caste as the prime datum is common to most non-Marxist writers. Marx poured scorn on that tendency to erect the social superstructure represented by caste into the principal causal factor instead of looking to its economic base,[7] and Weber was prepared to accept his explanation of the absence of social change as "due to the peculiar position of the artisan in the Indian village—his dependence upon fixed payment in kind instead of production for the market."[8] But given Weber's notion that major historical change was always the product of the independent convergence of economic forces with an appropriate ideology, he was led to give overriding emphasis to the role of religion in ritualising the hierarchical occupational structure of caste and preventing the institutionalisation of an egalitarian ethic essential to a market economy.

Apart from this difference over the primacy of economic causation, the nineteenth-century attempts to provide a grand sociological framework displayed a broad agreement. Of course they possess the bare starkness of caricature which is their value; specialists in our own time work against the framework they established, modifying, qualifying, sometimes refuting, but never rendering them superfluous. Soviet historians have long since retreated from the notion of the unchanging East and the dogma of the absence of private property in land as the key to its history. They recognise the development of an exchange economy and mercantile capitalism from at least the seventeenth century onwards.[9] Oriental despotism, despite Wittfogel,[10] is too wide and value-loaded a concept to survive as a working tool, but in a sense the view it typifies persists in the school which sees changes in the governmental superstructure rather than in the economic or social base as the key to the emergence of nationalism. The political and social as well as the economic self-sufficiency of the traditional Indian village is recognised as a dubious half-truth, but the village continues to form the unit for study of caste structure and change.

If Marx supplies a useful composite summary of the older sociological analysis, he also provides a convenient starting point for measuring the nature, extent and rate of change producd by colonial rule. He was torn by the desire to vilify it for its wanton destruction of indigenous society, for its crude plundering of Indian wealth, and its parasitic battening on the Indian economy; while at the same time he wished to demonstrate that it was the source of a profound modernising revolution. England has "broken down the entire framework of Indian society, without any symptoms of reconstitution yet appearing", Marx wrote in 1853, within four years of the centenary of Plassey. Previous conquerors had effected no more than political change, but English had struck at the heart of the social system—the Indian village. "English interference... dissolved these small semi-barbarian communities by blowing up their economical basis, and thus produced the greatest, and, to speak the truth, the only *social* revolution ever heard of in Asia." The instruments of the revolution had been English steam and English free trade, flooding India with cheap Lancashire textiles from 1810 onwards, and rupturing the domestic unity of agriculture and industry.

At the same time 'the work of regeneration' was just beginning to transpire 'through a heap of ruins', and its essence was the reversal of those specific characteristics that lay at the root of Asian stagnation. Marx listed its signs: (i) the unprecedented consolidation of the political unity of India, strengthened by the newly laid telegraph; (ii) railways ending village isolation and with the steamship linking India so closely to Europe that "that once fabulous country will thus be actually annexed to the Western World"; (iii) economic development of the country in the interests of the English millocracy, the railway system being the forerunner of modern industry; (iv) modern industry arising to "dissolve the hereditary divisions of labour, upon which rest the Indian power"; (v) the introduction of private property rights in land, instituted since the late eighteenth century; (vi) the emergence of a free press and education bringing into existence a new class of Indians imbued with European science and endowed with the requirements for government. All this led up to the fulfilment of colonialism's historic mission "the laying of the material foundations of Western society in Asia".[11] The interest of this analysis lies in the fact that Marx raises most of the points around which scholarly controversy has turned. At what date can the modernising impact of colonialisation be said to have begun? What was its precise nature? Was economic change primary, bringing in its train social change, or was economic change limited in scope and in its effects on society, and was not government itself through institutional agencies the only begetter of what little change did occur?

For a variety of reasons the older accounts tended to place emphasis on the abrupt transformation worked by the British conquest, whether like James Mill in order to castigate administrative error or like official spokesmen to puff up the British achievement. Marx was not entirely free from inconsistency in this respect. He saw an economic revolution in train from 1810, and an institutional revolution from 1793 following the Bengal Permanent Settlement and the introduction of private property rights in land; he recognised the importance of developments in education and a free press from at least the 1830's. Yet if anything current opinion goes much farther than his general conclusion that the work of modernisation had barely begun by 1857; its tendency is to minimise change of any sort, whether destructive or constructive.

The older accounts of the British conquest viewed the English East India Company as constrained to transform itself into a territorial power because of the insecurity caused by the collapse of the Mughal empire and the emergence of a rival European threat to its trading from the French. Having once stumbled into dominion over the Bengal territories in 1757, so the argument ran, the Company was driven steadily and reluctantly onward in its career of conquest by the military threat posed to its frontiers by the surviving Indian polities which commenced to modernise their armies with the aid of French mercenaries. From a more modern viewpoint such an account gives insufficient weight to the breakaway movement of sub-imperialism on the part of the Company's servants, who like the conquistadors were the real founders of empire. The structure of the Company had always represented an uneasy equipoise between corporate and private interests; and in a situation in which the expansion of the Company's trade with Europe had levelled off, the practice of looking for political profits had commenced early in the eighteenth century. In Bengal, Company officials abused their duty-free import privilege in order to participate in the internal trade of Bengal and to sell the Company's pass or *dastak* to Indian traders. It was this situation that helped bring on the decisive clash of 1756-57 between the Bengal nawab and the British. The Plassey Revolution was the first English essay in private profiteering on a grandiose scale, and it opened the floodgates. The acquiescence of the Home Authorities was purchased on the strength of the argument, first advanced by Dupleix to his masters, that territorial dominion would pay all local establishment costs and yield a surplus tribute that would give the Company its annual shipment of Indian goods *gratis*. In practice the force of local sub-imperialism was such that the Company ran rapidly into the red, for not only were much of the Bengal revenues diverted into private pockets, but the pressure for civil and military posts, supply contracts, and the like, led to constant war and expansion. [12] These conditions soon left the Company a debtor to its own servants, and its annual shipment of goods to Europe became simply a means of remitting interest payments. The Company by the 1780's was little more than a shell for private interests, which themselves derived their wealth primarily from political profits (viz. the perquisites of office, legal or illegal). This reversion to primitive mercantilism, with force itself an economic power, meant that the political frontier between 1757 and 1818 was flung far ahead of the true economic frontier; and it was not until the 1860's that the two began to be brought into closer correspondence. [13]

The consequences of Plassey shaped the form of British overrule and the modes of culture contact. If the trading frontier lagged so far behind the political, it may seem surprising that the British eventually took as much as two-thirds of the subcontinent under their direct administration. Why within fifteen years of Plassey had they abandoned the device of the protectorate in Bengal, and why within thirty years had they so dismantled the traditional Bengal administration, making a clean sweep of not only the old Bengal political elite but of all but the meanest administrative official? Why did not they pursue the Dutch example in Java of effecting a minimal interference with the indigenous society, gearing its traditional tribute system to the production of export products like opium, indigo, and piece goods as tribute, and leaving the people as far as possible under their own chiefs, laws and land tenures? It used to be supposed that the answer lay in the contemporary Industrial Revolution which reversed the economic relationship with India and required the opening up of the country as a market and primary producer for British industry with all that this implied—a market society of legal equals under the rule of law, modern judicial and administrative institutions, private property rights in land, taxes reduced to fixed imposts in cash, and the general monetisation of the economy. J.S. Furnivall attributed the difference between Dutch and British colonial policy in Asia to the absence of an industrial export economy in the one case and its presence in the other,[14] and numerous historians have seen the early British land-revenue settlements in Bengal and Madras as direct responses to Britain's new market requirements.[15]

The evidence of British intentions lends little support to these views. Instead it suggests first and foremost an attempt to bring order and regulation to the decayed indigenous revenue systems. This was the real reason for what appeared to be the exceptionally rapid assumption of direct administrative responsibility and the abandonment of indirect rule through a protectorate system in all the populous regions of the subcontinent. The fact that India unlike Java possessed a tax system yielding huge sums in cash made this the key objective of policy. In order to maximise receipts the Company was driven increasingly to eliminate all intermediaries and, outside the Bengal territories, to undertake direct collection through an official bureaucracy whose subordinate rungs and administrative practice (at the subdistrict level) were taken over from the pre-British rulers. The Company was forced willy-nilly both to intervene in government and yet remain an Asian power. Its purpose remained mercantilist, to wring a surplus from the

Indian revenue sufficient to purchase its annual investment of Indian goods and (through the sale of state-monopolised opium) supply the silver required by the Canton treasury for the China tea trade. Greenberg has noted that not only in this way "the surplus of the Indian revenues were thus sent home in teas from China", but that it was through this payments link with China that India was enabled to purchase the new textile manufactures of Lancashire and become one of the industry's major markets.[16] The situation did not alter fundamentally with the abolition of the Company's trading functions in 1834. Despite the banner of Free Trade it held aloft, Lancashire broke into the new markets of Asia with all the old-fashioned weapons of earlier mercantilism.[17]

If, therefore, the onset of modern economic relations was a much tardier and much less complete process than was at one time assumed, the same may be said to be true of the socio-cultural sphere. Although Cornwallis's attempt to inaugurate a 'regulated imperialism' from the 1780's necessitated the introduction of English administrative and judicial institutions at the superior level, the movement of anglicisation was strictly limited. On grounds of both policy and expediency the East India Company continued to act in many respects as an Indian ruler, striking its coinage with the image of the puppet emperor at Delhi, maintaining the use of Persian in official correspondence and in the law courts, administerting Hindu and Muslim personal law, repressing Christian missionary activity and upholding the religious institutions of the country. Spear has argued that in the age of the nabobs in the later eighteenth century, when the residence of English women was uncommon enough to make liaisons with Indian women a normal practice, the new rulers showed every sign of accommodating themselves to the culture and customs of their subjects, at least away from the seaport presidency towns of Bombay, Calcutta and Madras.[18] But the tendency was rapidly stultified by the psychological need of a conquering minority to preserve social distance; and that potent mixture of suppressed fear and open arrogance, which make up racialism, gained a firm ascendancy from Wellesley's time (1798-1805) as the British extended their power over the entire subcontinent. If 'respectability' made intermarriage socially unacceptable and Indian wives subject to ostracism by European society, cohabitation was practised down to the time that the steamer in the 1860's and 1870's began to redress the sex imbalance of the European population. By the

1880's, despite the occasional tragic *mésalliance* dealt with so idyllically in *Without Benefit of Clergy'*, the 'Unknown Goddess' of Kipling's verses was indubitably white:

> Does the P & O bear you to meward, or, clad in short
> frocks in the West,
> Are you growing the charms that shall capture and
> torture the heart in my breast?

Even so, it must be remembered that, when in 1857 the cannon opened fire at Cawnpore (Kanpur) in the Mutiny, General Wheeler had an Indian Christian wife; and the place in which the European women and children were confined by Nana Sahib, before their massacre and mass burial in the well, was named the Bibigarh, or women's house, where a European had been keeping his Indian mistress.

It is notoriously difficult to fix racial attitudes with precision, or to relate higher cultural and intellectual opinion to the world of everyday expediency. In the early decades of the nineteenth century the onset of the Evangelical-Utilitarian philistinism together with the emergence of a philosophy of economic development and modernisation transformed the Englishmen's admiration of Oriental society into contempt, and the preservationist mentality of men like Warren Hastings gave place to the censorious prophets of Victorian improvement. But how far shifts in formal ideological attitudes run ahead of practice and what is their functional relation to it are problems we are far from resolving. The current tide has set firmly against regarding ideological attitudes as an accurate index of historical change or of allowing them any causal role.[19]

Indeed, it is the undue attention to formal statements of policy aims that, it is now argued, has grossly misled historians about the working practice of British rule. For these both unduly anticipate the introduction of modernising administration and exaggerate its power to alter society. Colonial rule is peculiarly subject to the distortions of bureaucratic structures, which mistake the report for the bullet, the plan for action, and what one clerk says to another for history. On this view the age of modernizing reform which set in reputedly when Lord William Bentinck was appointed Governor-General in 1827 was a grand confidence trick. For all the paper planning at headquarters and the splendid periods of Macaulay's minutes on law reform and education, the British administration, it can be urged, had neither the financial means nor the technical instruments for a development programme. There was neither the requisite British or Indian capital investment nor the communication network of railways and telegraphs that could begin to change the face of the country within the framework of a *laissez faire* economy. It is noticeable in fact that most of the plans for law reform, educational development and scientific revenue systems, were not translated into effective action until the 1860's when the railway system was laid down and India's foreign trade began to leap forward.

Except in the Western enclaves of Calcutta and Bombay, where urban growth stimulated an intelligentsia prepared to employ the new lights of Western learning to attempt syncretist cultural reform movements, and where new literary vernaculars like Bengali sprang to life, the indigenous cultures of India lingered on in the courts of the princes and pensioners. Languages like Urdu and old Marathi survived as the media of lower level administration; and the ostentatious government disavowal of Oriental studies in preference for English in 1835 had little immediate effect.

In keeping with this line of thought some historians in recent years have tended to reverse in their thinking the direction from which initiative and control emanated, and to see the British district officer as a prisoner if not a puppet of local social forces. Dependent on hereditary administrative cadres of Brahmins or Kayasths or Muslims, where hold was not weakened until entry became regulated after 1860 by completion and educational qualification, the British officer was reduced to a game of blind man's buff. That at least is the burden of Frykenberg's account of Guntur district in Madras in the first half of the nineteenth century. Formal decisions as to whether the engagement for the land revenue should be made with large proprietary landholders (zamindars) or with small peasant landowners (ryots) of the dominant castes remained empty of meaning, since under either the zamindari or the ryotwar system the village was subject to the exactions of the same chain of hereditary office-holders and petty revenue collectors.[20] The British administrative systems for all their appearance as products of rival ideologies had to fit themselves to the frame of local society. James Mill and his early school of development economists had believed that, since all social strata above the peasant lived off disbursements of land revenue, the British had it in their power to shape society as they chose according to the type of land-revenue system they adopted. And Indian nationalist writers have strenuously kept alive the notion, first voiced by British administrators, that Indian society suffered in consequence wanton derangement from arbitrary decisions as to what social group should be vested with the novel form of proprietary right in land.[21] But in the intellectual sea-change of our times a number of Indian historians are now coming round to the view to which Baden, Powell lent his authority as long ago as the 1890's when the nationalist attack was first beginning to gather force. So far from being artificial constructions, the land-revenue systems, Baden-Powell maintained, were essentially practical adaptations to local circumstances; they had to be if they were to work at all.[22] Not only were there two sharply differing major types of village, but the village so far from being the unchanging republic of popular myth was an inegalitarian structure subject to constant vicissitudes and strains from within and without. Hence almost everywhere, not merely was the particular type of land controller dominant in a region recognised as the agency of revenue collection and *ipso facto* as landed proprietor—the large landholder in Bengal, the individual peasant landholder in the Madras and Bombay presidencies, the corporate village coparceners in the United Provinces and the Punjab; but also large exceptions were made within each system to allow for local variety. Consequently in the supposedly 'big landlord' settlement of the Bengal presidency the settlement in Midnapur district was made with some 3,000 petty landholders; in the opposing Madras system a third of the presidency was paradoxically left under substantial landlord settlement; outside the Deccan districts of the Bombay presidency the ryotwar system had to be modified to accommodate the joint and superior tenures that prevailed in Gujarat and the Konkan; in the United Provinces large landlord 'estates' were recognised in Oudh and elsewhere. Although in the districts where the ryotwar system was firmly imposed the joint tenure known as *mirasi* might have been dissolved by administrative action, this probably meant that it was already too decayed and exceptional to offer a positive basis upon which to found the revenue system.

The precise degree of interference with indigenous practice is impossible to determine; but what is clear is that irrespective of the legal recognition of tenures the British were scrupulous in avoiding interference with the social structure. For all the romantic notions of the Munro school, the 'peasant' with whom they dealt was of the elite landholding castes, and cultivated his land with the aid of inferior landless castes. In the Madras presidency the agrestic serf class, which amounted in some districts to as much as a fifth of the population, was left unfree under its traditional masters; and for all the formal legislation against slavery which Bentinck and Macaulay promoted, the British district officers were generally cereful to leave this issue to the erosion of time.[23] For here landlord and labourer were rooted in an institution more enduring than political and administrative arrangement, the institution of caste. As in the sphere of race relations the last word appeared to lie with local society irrespective of European intentions and attitudes. In the end the British, it seemed, could only fit into the Indian social structure as yet one more endogamous caste with their freedom of action severely restricted.

Since the Lancashire textile invasion failed to blow up the economic base of village self-sufficiency in any visible manner, as Marx assumed it would, one might suppose that in the sphere of institutional change decisive results would follow. The mere suppression of open violence and the introduction of Western-style law courts seemed in themselves to spell revolution. Attention has naturally fastened on the introduction of freely-alienable proprietary rights in land and the emergence of a land market. The older school spoke freely of the agrarian revolution this had caused, at least among the upper levels of landholding. Nowhere was this more striking than in Bengal where the former zamindar class apparently went to the wall within twenty years of Cornwallis's Permanent Settlement of 1793, and in their place the quick-witted Calcutta banyans and monied men stepped in as the main beneficiaries of British rule. But this simple picture dissolves in the light of modern examination. It is evident that the century before Plassey was as much a period of rapid change in landholding as the period that followed. Not only is there strong evidence of men from commercial and literate castes during the Mughal period making their way into landholding via official office, mortgage and purchase, and of then acquiring ritual *kshatriya* (warrior) status, but it is clear that on their displacement by men of similar origin under British rule the process was in considerable measure repeated. The notion of rigid occupational caste stratification is clearly inapplicable; Bengal at least approximated more closely to contemporary Western Europe, where wealth and official service could in time be translated into landed gentility. Although, therefore, old elites might appear to crumble, they prove on examination to have been far from old, and their successors to have been drawn largely from the same original social base.[24]

The only long-standing hereditary aristocracy were the petty Rajput rajas who were buttressed by their role as clan chiefs and who were scattered broadcast over northern and central India. Most of these suffered slow decay in an age which set a premium on managerial skills rather than fighting prowess. But that did not prevent a significant proportion from making the necessary adjustments and retaining their position as local notables. It is evident that the enormous volume of transfers of proprietary title in the first half of the nineteenth century in northern India represented for the most part circulation within existing dominant landholding castes at the petty proprietary level. The Rajput clans undoubtedly lost ground, mainly to Brahmins, and to a much smaller extent to urban trading castes. But actual eviction was rare, the dispossessed usually remaining as 'tenants' in what was *de facto* a sub-proprietary role. Urban capitalists were more interested in rent-receiving or in controlling the disposal of peasant-grown cash crops than directly engaging in agriculture; so that the introduction of legal private property rights in land tended to lengthen the chain of intermediaries above the actual cultivator and left the peasant *petite culture* intact. Compulsory alienation of land in satisfaction of debt was recognised by the British as a drastic innovation on traditional practice, and official concern was being voiced at the extent of transfers under this head already by the 1850's.[25] Since, however, the peasant was not displaced (and it must be remembered that he himself was a member of the village elite controlling non-elite caste cultivators), it is often argued that he was reduced to the condition of a debt slave to the moneylender. The latter was thus in a position to siphon off the enhanced value of agricultural production brought about by the extension of the market.[26] But any such tendency for caste to turn into class division was frustrated by constant diffusion of roles among the peasantry themselves, one man being able to combine the position of landlord, tenant, and petty moneylender. Before 1857 this degree of complication was only apparent in the overcrowded eastern districts of the present Uttar Pradesh, where fragmentation and parcellation of holdings was already far advanced.[27] For our immediate purpose it can be said that, although rural society must have undergone a profound change by the suppression of open violence and the turning of individual and group struggle into a battle for land rights through the courts, there was no complete structural change. British hopes of the emergence of capitalist agriculture, whether at the peasant or superior level, were disappointed, and the class stratification of rural society b legal revolution into landlord and tenant was never properly consummated.

This conclusion can be given a more general bearing. Of course, there has been and continues to be, a respectable body of historians, Marxist and non-Marxist, who accept the broad argument of nineteenth-century sociology that under colonial rule Indian society moved from status to contract, and from caste to class. Professor Misra has taken it as his principal assumption in his well-known, *The Indian Middle Classes* (1961), while Desai in *The Social Background of Indian Nationalism* and more recently S.N.Mukherjee have accepted the outlines of Marx's historiography as still valid.[28] But they are challenged increasingly by scholars who themselves are drawn equally from opposite ends of the political spectrum. These jointly conclude that the institutional and the economic 'inputs' of modernity were too feeble to blow apart the structure of Indian society and that the elastic, accommodating nature of the latter was adequate to contain them. Anil Seal, while acknowledging that between 1840 and 1886 India's foreign seaborne trade increased more than eightfold and played a vital role in the UK balance of payments, asserts that "these changes were not sufficient to give India social classes based on economic categories. For the most part Indian traders remained as they had always been, men following their hereditary vocations in the traditional way, both unwilling and unable to break down those barriers inside their society which inhibited more active development."[29] Hence nationalism did not come as the older school supposed by the prior emergence of a genuine modern middle-class or bourgeoisie thrown up by economic change. The Western-educated element which took up the modern political struggle against colonialism was an exotic, "more the product of bureaucratic initiative than of economic change." In the struggle among the literate castes, predominantly Muslim, Brahmin and Kayasth, for posts in government service and the related professions of law, education and journalism, one element, usually of aspirants rather than possessors, dropped the traditional Persian and Sanskrit learning and turned to English. From the mid-nineteenth century this element came to man the middle and upper levels of the increasingly technical, legalistic, and bureaucratic machine that was the Raj; and from the 1880's slowly began to secure effective command of the channels of communication between the Raj and the millions of its subjects. The British thus became steadily more dependent on the modernistic section among their collaborators. In consequence, what is usually thought of as the history of the nationalist struggle was little more than the struggle of this section to extort from the British the loaves and fishes of political office and administrative place, followed by an unedifying scramble over the share-out. The ultimate victory of Congress should not be allowed to disguise the fact that what it represented was, on this view, not the victory of a new class but the lateral adjustment of an old elite.

The ineffectualness of the forces of economic change and the limitation of the impact of modernity to a small exotic sector are notions shared by Indian scholars for whom this interpretation of nationalism would appear insultingly cynical. Tapan Raychaudhuri and Bipan Chandra indignantly refute the view advanced recently by Morris D.Morris that the Indian economy experienced significant growth during the nineteenth century. Foreign capital investment merely 'meant the growth of enclaves, their linkage effects being confined to a minimum'.

The most striking feature of colonial economic development is the dichotomy between the traditional and modern—as also between the subsistence and non-subsistence sectors of the economy. The pre-modern subsistence sector accounts for the stagnation of skill, technology, social organization and attitudes. In more extreme cases like Indonesia the colonial market economy grew up in total isolation from the subsistence sector, and at heavy cost to it. In the Indian case the picture was only somewhat different. Recent village studies reveal a marked pattern of socio-economic stagnation in rural India. So far as one can see there was hardly any significant change until after World War I, and very often, until after 1947.[30]

This attack on colonialism as an inhibiting, distorting influence on India's economic growth stems from a nationalist standpoint that views with suspicion Western historians' recent efforts to play down the importance of imperialism as an historical force. It borrows something from latter-day Marxist and Maoist theories which stress the parasitic role of colonialism, its political alliance with 'feudal' landlord elements, and the comprador character of the national bourgeoisie. In this latest Marxist version the reproduction of Western bourgeois society, thought by Marx as colonialism's historic mission, is seen to be necessarily stultified. Whatever the intellectual pedigree of their views, Indian economic historians tend to support Bipan Chandra's argument that the impact of colonialism in the nineteenth century resulted in 'an aborted modernization'. Although after 1860 India began to produce on a significant scale for the world market, this was effected without the mode of peasant agricultural production undergoing any fundamental change; the essentially parasitic structure of ownership, credit, and marketing, on their view, simply "skimmed cash crops off the surface of an immobilized agrarian society."[31]

The concept of a dual economy advanced by Boeke appears to provide a convenient way of acknowledging a measure of development on the one hand and denying its fertilising influence on the greater part of Indian society on the other. In India's case the analogy with Indonesia cannot be pushed too far, yet the concept is valuable in that it recognises that the traditional sector was not totally insulated from the modern but underwent some measure of change. Simply because this change was not progressive but represents an adjustive capacity in traditional society to absorb external forces without structural alteration, it has been christened in suitable paradoxical terms. Boeke spoke of 'static expansion', and more recently Geertz of 'this peculiar pattern of changeless change'. Indeed it is Geertz's refinement of the concept under the term 'argicultural involution' which has produced the most subtle and sophisticated analysis so far developed.

In land tenure, in crop regime, in work organization, and in the less directly economic aspects of social structure.. the village...faced the problems posed by a rising population, increased monetization, greater dependence on the market, mass labour organization, more intimate contact with bureaucratic government and the like, not by a dissolution of the traditional pattern into an individualistic 'rural proletarian' anomie, nor yet by a metamorphosis of it into a modern commercial farming community. Rather by means of a 'special kind of virtuosity', 'a sort if technical hair-splitting', it maintained the over-all outline of that pattern while driving the elements of which it was composed to ever-higher degrees of ornate elaboration and Gothic intricacy ....Perhaps the most trenchant phrase which has been coined to summarize what appears to have been the career of the Inner Indonesian village over the past century and a half is 'the advance towards vagueness'. The peculiarly passive social-change experience which ... rural society has been obliged to endure seems to have induced in it an indeterminateness which did not so much transform traditional patterns as elasticize them. Such flaccid indeterminateness is highly functional to a society which is allowed to evade, absorb, and adapt but not really allowed to change.[32]

Something of this imagery has been carried over into the analysis of the Indian social system. For F.G. Bailey "the more involute is a system of closed social stratification, the more inclined we are to call it a caste system."[33] But involution obtains only in closed small-scale, face-to-face societies; hence it is the village which "provides the boundary at which social relations turn inwards" or involute. Reminiscent of Marx and nineteenth-century sociology, traditional India is regarded as composed of a myriad of self-sufficing village units, each of which was hierarchically stratified into endogamous caste groups whose mutual relations were those of cooperation rather than competition. "The village," wrote Eric Miller, "containing a cross-section of interdependent castes... was more or less self-subsistent," although in Kerala grouped politically in petty chiefdoms or kingdoms. But the cleavages in society were the vertical divisions of politics, not the horizontal divisions of caste. India was a giant Neapolitan ice-cream cut vertically into an infinite number of small portions. "The main structural cleavages were between territorial units—villages chiefdoms, kingdoms—not between castes."[34] It was these vertical divisions that colonial rule eventually destroyed or rendered porous by the enlargement of political and economic scale

> In place of countless small, relatively isolated, traditional political divisions, there are now emerging a few large political arenas which in this context we can take as the States of the Indian Union. Within these States various *jatis* (local sub-castes), which formerly were separated by being in different political systems, are now uniting. What were formerly caste categories are becoming groups.[35]

"Horizontal mobilisation" thus "challenges the vertical solidaritie and structures of traditional societies." The formation of provincial caste associations is seen by the Rudolphs as the key to political mobilisation for the modern democratic system in India, and in this sense demonstrates 'the modernity of tradition'. But the social anthropologists deny any such continuity of structure. Once castes star competing among one another, caste is coming to an end.

The caste society as a whole is, in Durkheim's sense, an organi system with each particular caste and sub-caste filling a distinctive functional role. It is a system of labour division from which the element of competition among the workers has been excluded... Wherever caste groups are seen to be acting as corporations in competition against like groups of *different* caste, then they are acting in defiance of caste principles.[37]

According to the social anthropologists the type of change associated with caste competition is relatively recent, going back in most cases no earlier than 1880 or 1900. But both this assumption and the assumption that such competition did not occur in pre-colonial India (upward mobility of individuals between caste groups being a different matter) are open to question. In southern India, where Christianity made its earliest and most rapid strides among the low caste groups, there was already pressure by the late 1820's among the Travancore Shanars against caste disabilities and in Pondicherry in 1833 from the Pallis. Yet other types of social conflict between right and left hand castes, which had occasioned quarrels in the eighteenth century died mysteriously away from the early nineteenth century. Here the action of the British administration in throwing open the acquisition of land ownership rights enabled merchant and artisan communities to translate wealth much more readily into social status and muted rivalry with those castes with hereditary rights to land.[38]

There are also grounds for questioning the typicality of the areas from which Bailey and Miller drew their material for the concept of the tightly insulated village or chiefdom unit. Both highland Orissa and Kerala were outside the great agricultural plain areas that for centuries before the British had experienced large-scale political organisation. Bailey has argued that it was only on the encapsulation of the village society in the larger administrative unit that the need for middlemen or political brokers arose, and that this is the stuff of modern politics.[39] But in areas that had long lived under the hand of centralised power there was no such sharp discontinuity between the local social structure and the larger political superstructure. The role of political middlemen was traditionally performed by those local notables termed *taluqdars*, *zamindars* and *chaudhuris* (in the north), *deshmukhs* and *despandes* (in the west) or *nayakas* and *poligars* (in the south). It was a role contested by the officials of central power whether *amils, mamlatdars,* or *tahsildars*, who struggled to assert their own undivided authority but in the end struck up a *modus vivendi* with them. It is also evident that outside northern India, famous for its coparcenary village 'republics', the typical Indian village was a body of discrete families held together by the headman, a semi-hereditary political appointment but necessarily dependent for his tenure on the favour of the ruling power. Hence political isolation and self-sufficiency were an impossibility. Likewise the notion of the economic self-sufficiency of the village and its physical isolation have always been recognised as relative truths, but the very notions tend to belie the close web of communication which plain villages maintained with surrounding areas, and the degree of movement and travel carried on by means of trade, pilgrimages and fairs.

If simple models based on atypical regions have too often coloured the thinking of social anthropologists, and continuities were more dominant than abrupt caesuras, has there been no significant alteration in the institution of caste? Has there been merely that elastic adaptation so noticeable in other spheres of life? Certainly it would be wrong to suppose that caste conflict constitutes the essential feature of modern politics any more than it did in the past. The reverse is the case. For the most part elite castes sustain the tradition Miller has postulated of the petty Nayar chiefdoms in what is now Kerala State: they compete among themselves and build up multi-caste factions vertically, drawing their followers from economic inferiors belonging mainly to the non-elite castes. To put the matter briefly and therefore crudely, caste competition as such is usually only to be found among middle and lower castes among which a prospering element has been denied political authority and social prestige commensurate with its economic success. This element then seeks to advance itself through the mobilisation of its poorer caste fellows, but once it has achieved its objective it identifies itself with the elite circle into which it has broken, and politics resume their traditionally factional character.[40] Doubtless in the modern setting this means that the social composition of the elite is being steadily widened, but the overwhelming preponderance of the old elite castes in the modern elite has not been seriously affected.

But how far was the caste structure among the dominant landed elites weakened as a result of the dismantling of the subordinate local political organisations of the clan group? These were, of course, strongest among the coparcenary communities of Rajputs, Brahmins, Jats, Ahirs, and so forth that characterised North Indian land tenures, but they also had analogies elsewhere. It has recently been argued that the effect of a powerful centralised bureaucratic structure was to atomise relationships within society, particularly as a result of the extension of state-revenue collection and rental control to the individual peasant landholder. The local political substructures of *tappas*, at which level the state had traditionally come to terms with the dominant local structure, were gradually obliterated. The local clan, under its traditional heads (*rajas, rawats, raos,* or *chaudhuris*) was drained of all political authority, a process that seems to have advanced quite far within the first century of British rule.[41] Why then has the institution of caste survived? Why was the kinship group not narrowed to the immediate family and swallowed up within the homogeneity of the territorial state as in Europe? The usual answer is that endogamy has proved too strong a social practice, reinforced as Louis Dumont and his school would argue by the subjective notion underlying caste of ritual inequality between the 'clean' and the 'unclean'.[42] Yet without denying the force of religious and ideological sanctions, one can reasonably argue that social anthropologists working on India (as distinct from Ceylon) have curiously neglected the economic factor. True they have noted that the decline of the local kinship group has been compensated for by the strengthening of caste as an attributional category conferring upon an individual valuable status advantages, and so employment opportunities, in a society of enlarged scale. But almost no attention has been paid to the role of landed property. Now the constant fractionalisation of land rights through joint partition among heirs has traditionally forced out the less prosperous members of dominant landed castes into military and other services. The East India Company drew its high-caste Brahmin and Rajput sepoys precisely from those regions—southern Oudh, Benares, Shahabad—where through the proliferation of numbers the land-controlling lineages had been reduced to swollen bodies of co-sharers on petty holdings. But the pressure on land also had important internal effects. One has no need to go as far as Leach in asserting that "the kinship system is just a way of talking about property relations" in order to recognise how vital the struggle to retain possession of the land has been in the maintenance of the corporate character of local caste systems.[43] A sample survey of 1951 showed that in Bihar Brahmins and Rajputs together, although comprising only 9.6 per cent of the families surveyed, still made up 78.6 per cent of landowners.[44] It is the tenacious hold of the dominant castes over the land, despite the numerous internal transfers and changes, that constitutes the great element of continuity. In 1886 D.T. Roberts, the settlement officer of Ballia district in the Benaras region, summed up judiciously the effects of British rule:

> The dominion which these Rajputs and their attendant Brahmins then acquired (at the time of their original conquest) has been retained by them up to the present day, and an inquiry into the tenures of this district is mainly an enquiry into the legal forms under which this dominion is now exercised. Changes of government, changes of law, the progress of civilization, and the development of individual rights have affected more or less the distribution of the produce and the modes and extent of authority exercised over the land by the descendants of these colonists, but they still possess it. At once supple and tenacious, their connection with the soil has been indeed, regulated and defined, but neither weakened so much nor strengthened so much under British administration as it is usual to suppose.[45]

It has been said that the stark dichotomies of nineteenth-century sociological thought continue to haunt the recesses of our own thinking. Sociologists and economists are perhaps the most susceptible, unable to rid themselves in their search for precision of their proclivity to define change as necessarily absolute. Confronted by the economic and social transformation of Russia or Japan it is easy to designate as stagnation in India what the Victorians saw as revolution. From the historian's viewpoint, the period that ran from Plassey in 1757 to the 'Mutiny' in 1857, and spanned the lifetime of the East India Company as an administrative power, is a relatively intelligible entity. It is possible to define within it the effect of the colonial impact by regarding change as occurring differentially—affecting the different regions, levels of society, and levels of administration at an uneven rate. Conquest decapitated the superior political elite, totally in the case of British India, and with more gradual effect in the protected states. The intermediate political elite, the local notables mentioned above, suffered less drastically and a minority were able to adjust to the new role of landowners. The administrative elite before 1857 suffered least, in many cases enriching themselves from office under the British and constituting a new landlord class. But by the 1850's the enlargement of political and economic scale effected by the British district and provincial administration, by institutional changes in landholding and by the expansion of cash-cropping, were (in northern India at least) beginning to produce novel strains. The British had reached the stage when, in the interests of a more advanced technical administration commensurate with a sophisticated property market in land, the subdistrict level of administration commanded by the old tahsildar class had to be invaded. A public service based on competitive entry by educational qualification was about to edge out the old system of subcontracting lower-level administration to traditional hereditary groups.[46] In similar fashion the British with their General Service Enlistment Act of 1856 and the use of greased cartridges for their new rifle threatened the monopoly of the traditional high-caste Rajput and Brahmin warrior castes in recruitment to the army, and resentment boiled over in the Mutiny of 1857. By the 1880's the dominance of the local notable, in town and more slowly in the country, was being effectively challenged by a new political broker, operating on the new enlarged scale. The 'modern' political had arrived.

Under this notion of the slow, uneven, but progressive intensification of administrative and economic pressures, the village would be the last level to be directly invaded. That is not to say that through its external links it had not always been constantly subjected to change imposed from above, but until directly invaded it was the level most capable of absorbing it. In the first century of British rule the village was given external peace and high, unremitting taxation, conditions which created a major problem of adjustment for the village elite. The period saw the slow decline of warrior castes and the enhanced prosperity of thrifty, agricultural castes, the gradual fragmentation and fractionalisation of landholdings, and a tighter dependence on the moneylender-graintrader. But none of these processes went far. It was the upper levels of society that took the full shock of conquest.[47]

In similar fashion, one may resolve some of the apparent contradictions concerning the character and purpose of British rule. The modernising impulse, so triumphantly proclaimed in the Bentinck-Macaulay period from Calcutta, was not the less real or significant because society in the Guntur district still appeared to be quite untouched by the transfer of power to British hands. And in this sense the study of British policy and its ideological background still retains its validity. But the differential rate of the colonial impact, and the uneven development of its own internal structure, gave it that air of paradox that Marx noted, at once free-trader and mercantilist, the fugleman of modernity and the latest of the predatory conquerors of Asia.

Notes and References

1. K. Marx, *New York Daily Tribune*, 8 Aug. 1853, cited in S. Avineri (ed.), *Karl Marx on Colonialism and Modernization*, New York, 1969, p. 132.

2. K. Marx, *Capital* (1867), i, ch. 14, sect. 4, cited Avineri, op. cit., pp. 40-1

3. Marx merely shared the common assumption of his time in this respect. Cf. H.S. Maine, *Village Communities in the East and West*, 3rd edn., London, 1979, p. 179.

4. It is noticeable that Maine held the same theory of Indian towns without the benefit of Marx; Maine, op. cit., p. 179.

5. This is a simplified thumb-nail sketch of Marx's ideas. For detailed critical treatment, see E.J. Hobsbawm's introduction to Karl Marx, *Pre-Capitalist Formations*, ed., E.J. Hobsbawm, London, 1964, and D. Thorner, 'Marx on India and the Asiatic Mode of Production', *Contributions to Indian Sociology*, ix, 1966.

6. A.C. Lyall; *Asiatic Studies*, 2nd edn., London, 1899, i, p. 204.

7. K. Marx, *The German Ideology*, ed., R. Pascal, London, 1963, p. 30.

8. Max Weber, *The Religion of India*, Glencoe, 1958, p. 111.

9. Cf. V.I. Pavlov, *The Indian Capitalist Class*, New Delhi, 1964. Indian Marxist historians have naturally been quicker to reject Marx's primitive image of India before colonial rule. Irfan Habib has laboured to show that a modified form of private property rights in land was fully established in Mughal India; I. Habib, *The Agrarian System of Mughal India* , London, 1963. On merchant capitalism in Mughal India, see I. Habib, 'Potentialities of Capitalist Development in the Economy of Mughal India', *Jl. Eco. Hist.*, xxix, no. i (1969). His more recent work has sought to demonstrate that so far from testifying to 'the unchangeableness of Asiatic Societies' (Marx), Indian medieval history was characterised by significant technological innovation; I. Habib, Presidential Address to Medieval Section, *Indian History Congress Proceedings, 31st Session*, Varanasi, 1969, Patna, 1970.

10. K. Wittfogel, *Oriental Despotism*, New Haven, 1957.

11. *New York Daily Tribune*, 25 June and 8 Aug. 1853 in Avineri, *Karl Marx*, pp. 93, 132 ff. It is interesting that Marx is still used by modern political scientists and social anthropologists to supply them with some of their critical assumptions. Cf. L. I. and S.H. Rudolph, *The Modernity of Tradition*, Chicago, 1967, pp. 17 ff.; Louis Dumont, *Homo Hierarchicus*, Paris, 1966, p. 275, Paladin edn., London, 1972, p. 265.

12. The best analysis of this process remains H. Furber, *John Company at Work,* 2nd edn., Cambridge, Mass., 1951.

13. On the economic background, see P.J. Marshall, *Problems of Empire: Britain and India 1757-1813*, London, 1968, pp.78 ff.

14. Cf. J.S. Furnivall, *Colonial Policy and Practice*, Cambridge, 1948, and *Netherlands India*, Cambridge, 1939.

15. Cf. Ramkrishna Mukherjee, *The Rise and Fall of the East India Company*, Berlin, 1958.

16. M. Greenberg, *British Trade and the Opening of China*, Cambridge, 1951, p. 15. Also cf. K.N. Chaudhuri, 'India's Foreign Trade and the Cessation of the East India Company's Trading Activities, 1828-40', *Econ. Hist. Rev.*, 2nd ser., xix (1966).

17. Cf. K.N. Chaudhuri, *The Economic Development of India under the East India Company, 1814-58*, Cambridge, 1971. See also Peter Harnetty, *Imperialism and Free Trade: India and Lancashire in the Mid-Nineteenth Century*, Manchester, 1972.

18. Percival Spear, *The Nabobs*, Oxford, 1932.

19. There is a large literature on the ideology of British colonialism in India. Cf. E. Stokes, *The English Utilitarians and India*, Oxford, 1959; G.D. Bearer, *British Attitudes Towards India 1784-1858*, Oxford 1961; R. Guha, *A Rule of Property for Bengal*, La Haye, 1963; F.G. Hutchins, *The Illusion of Permanence: British Imperialism in India*, Princeton, 1967; R. Kumar, *Western India in the Nineteenth Century*, London, 1968; Clive Dewey, "Images of the Village Community; a Study in Anglo Indian Ideology', *Modern Asian Studies,* vi (1972).

20. R.E. Frykenberg, *Guntur District 1788-1848*, Oxford, 1965, pp. 67-8.

21. The nationalist view of the effects of colonial rule on Indian society has a long historical pedigree and borrows heavily from arguments used in controversial policy debates by British administrators themselves. R.C. Dutt, *Economic History of India in the Victorian Age*, London, 1906; Radhakamal Mukerjee, *Land Problems of India*, London, 1933, and M.B. Nanavati and J.J. Anjaria, *The Indian Rural Problem*, Bombay, 1944, are among the more sober authorities on which much wilder generalisation has frequently been based. For a valuable summary and critique of orthodox nationalist view, see Dharma Kumar, *Land and Caste in South India*, Cambridge, 1965, pp. 186 ff.

22. B.H. Baden-Powell, *The Land Systems of British India*, Oxford, 1892, i, p. 244. Also B.H.Baden-Powell, *A Short Account of the Land Revenue... in British India*, 2nd edn., London, 1907, pp. 46-7; B.H.Baden-Powell, *The Indian Village Community*, London, 1896, pp. 430 ff.

23. Dharma Kumar, *Land and Caste*, pp. 72ff., Cf. N.E. Mukherjee and R.E. Frykenberg, ch. 9 in R.E. Frykenberg (ed.) *Land Control and Social Structure in Indian History* , Madison and London, 1969.

24. See the contributions of B.S.Cohn and T.Raychaudhuri in Frykenberg (ed.), op. cit. Also N.K. Sinha, *Economic History of Bengal*, ii Calcutta, 1962, pp. 179-80.

25. P.H.M. van den Dungen, *The Punjab Tradition*, London, 1972, pp. 42ff.

26. This notion, which has been used *ad nauseam*, was first voiced by British administrators themselves, notably Sir George Wingate in 1852.

27. Cf. Elizabeth Whitcombe, *Agrarian Conditions in Northern India*, Berkeley, 1972, pp. 143-4.

28. B.B. Misra, *The Indian Middle Classes*, Oxford, 1961; A.R. Desai, *The Social Background of Indian Nationalism*, Bombay, 1948; S.N. Mukherjee, 'Class, Caste and Politics in Calcutta, 1815-50' in E.R. Leach and S.N. Mukherjee (eds.), *Elites in South Asia* , Cambridge, 1970.

29. A. Seal, *The Emergence of Indian Nationalism*, Cambridge, 1968, p. 34.

30. T.Raychaudhuri, 'A Reinterpretation of Nineteenth Century Economic History', *Indian Soc. and Econ. Hist. Rev.*, v (1968), pp. 98-9; M.D. Morris, 'Towards a Reinterpretation of Nineteenth Century Economic History', ibid., pp. 1-15. Also Morris, 'Trends and Tendencies in Indian Economic History', ibid., pp. 319-88; Bipan Chandra, 'Reinterpretation of Nineteenth Century Economic History'. ibid., pp. 35-75. This important debate has been collected in M.D. Morris *et al.* (eds.), *Indian Economy in the Nineteenth Century; A Symposium*, Delhi: Indian Economic and Social History Association, Delhi School of Economics, 1969.

31. Cited by D. Rothermund, *Phases of Indian Nationalism*, Bombay, 1970, p. 264, n. 19.

32. C. Geertz, *Agricultural Involution*, Berkeley, 1963, pp. 90, 102-3. For Boeke's concept of economic dualism, see J.H. Boeke, *The Structure of the Netherlands Indian Economy*, New York, 1942, and *Economics and Economic Policy of Dual Societies*, Haarlem, 1953.

33.   F.G. Bailey, 'Closed Social Stratification in India', *Archiv., Europ. Sociol.,* iv (1963), pp. 107-24.

34.   E. Miller, 'Village Structure in North Kerala', in M.N.Srinivas (ed.), *India's Villages*, Bombay, London, 1960, pp. 45-6.

35.   Bailey, op. cit.

36.   L.I. and S.H. Rudolph, *The Modernity of Tradition*, Chicago, 1975.

37.   E.R. Leach in E.R. Leach (ed), *Aspects of Caste in South India, Ceylon and N.W. Pakistan* , Cambridge, 1962, pp. 5,7.

38.   Brenda E.F. Beck, 'The Right-Left Division of South Indian Society', *Jl. of Asian Studies,* xxix (1970).

39.   F.G. Bailey, *Stratagems and Spoils*, Oxford, 1969, esp. ch. 8.

40.   The best recent study is R. Kothari (ed.), *Caste in Indian Politics*, New Delhi, 1971.

41.   Richard G. Fox, *Kin, Clan, Raja, and Rule*, Berkeley, 1971.

42.   Louis Dumont, *Homo Hierarchicus.*

43.   For this important controversy over the economic *raison d'etre* of the kinship system, see the account in Meyer Fortes, *Kinship and the Social Order*, Chicago, 1969, pp. 294-302. Also E.R. Leach, *Pul Eliya: Village in Ceylon*, Cambridge, 1961. and G, Obeyesekere, *Land Tenure in Village Ceylon* , Cambridge, 1967.

44.   Cited by Ramashray Roy in Kothari, *Caste in Indian Politic,* pp. 231-2.

45.   D.T. Roberts, *Report on the Revision of Records... of Ballia District* , Allahabad, 1886.

46.   I am indebted to my colleague, Christopher Bayly of St Catharine's, Cambridge, for this idea; cf. C.A. Bayly, 'The Development of Political Organization in the Allahabad Locality, 1880-1925', University of Oxford D. Phil, thesis, 1970; and *The Local Roots of Indian Politics: Allahabad 1880-1920*, Oxford, 1975.

47.   Cf. K.A. Ballhatchet, *Social Policy and Social Change in Western India 1817-1830*, Oxford, 1957; Burton Stein, 'Integration of the Agrarian System in South India' in Frykenberg (ed.), *Land Control and Social Structure*, pp. 201-21 Imtiaz Husain, *Land Revenue Policy in North India*, Calcutta, New Delhi, 1967, pp. 170ff.

11

In this challenging assault on conventional historiography, Washbrook insists that the pre-colonial India of the eighteenth century, far from being stagnant, had a far greater potential for capitalist development than is usually assumed. In the end, however, this openness to the world economy, by providing the British with a foothold in India, only facilitated its conquest. Subsequently this process of indigenous modernization was brought to an end as the British in the nineteenth century created the "traditional" India their imperial system required.

Progress and Problems:
South Asian Economic and Social
History c. 1720-1860
D.A. WASHBROOK

Over the last fifteen to twenty years, interest in the history of early modern and modern South Asia has grown enormously and has engaged the attention of an increasingly international audience.[1] Whereas, at the end of the 1960's, research in the subject was largely confined to universities in South Asia itself and the rest of the British Commonwealth, today a variety of projects, conferences and regular workshops link together scholars from South Asia and the Commonwealth, with those in Japan, Indonesia, France, the Netherlands, Denmark, Sweden, Germany, Italy, Eastern Europe and the United States. Equally, whereas twenty years ago the publication of South Asia-related research was restricted to a few specialist journals, today this research provides the staple of at least four quarterlies with major international circulations and appears regularly in most of the leading historical periodicals. In the last five years, monographs on South Asia-related historical subjects have been published by presses in Germany, the Netherlands, Sweden, France, the Soviet Union and Japan as well as, of course, India and Pakistan, the rest of the Commonwealth and the United States.[2]

© 1988, Cambridge University Press. Reprinted by permission from *Modern Asain Studies*, Vol. 22 (1988), pp. 57-96.

Behind this growth of international interest, it is possible to see the history of South Asia coming to play an extremely important role in at least two of the principal developments transforming approaches to historical scholarship in recent times. The first of these is the attempt to transcend the traditions of 'national' history, bequeathed by the nineteenth century, and to investigate the transnational relationships and forces shaping world history over the last few centuries. South Asia, with its pivotal position in the international trade of the early modern era and subsequent central place in the nineteenth-century British Empire, necessarily figures large in this attempt and historians with perspectives as diverse as those of Braudel, Wallerstein, Anderson and Roberts have all been obliged to consider its experience.[3] The second significant development is the attempt to deepen the relationship between history and the social or cultural sciences in order both to make historical interpretation more conceptually adequate and social/ cultural science more historically aware. For 'historical sociology', too, South Asia's experience has become important. On the one hand, it throws into sharp relief the facile unilinear theories of social evolution and the ethnocentric conceptual schema inherited by Western social science from nineteenth-century positivism and still informing a surprisingly wide range of its assumptions. On the other hand, it also provides extensive empirical data and a vast literature of case study, which cannot easily be ignored when attempting to develop general theories of, for example, peasant economy and society, the relationship between European and non-European cultures, transitions in the nature of the state and the development of capitalism.

The twin spotlights of 'world' and 'sociological' history have done much to change the appearance of the South Asian past, which previously had been seen mainly in the shadows of the colonial relationship. The original traditions of historical scholarship, pioneered in South Asia and the Commonwealth, were dominated by the questions of imperialism and the ultimate emergence of nation states. Even into the 1960's, South Asian economic and social history revolved around assessments of the impact of British governing structures and policies on the well-being and development of the immanent national economies and societies of the subcontinent.[4] Such a focus had an important point in the context of its times and promoted some very valuable and lasting research. But it was an extremely narrow focus which was blind to many wider issues concerning theories of economic development and social change and the place of South Asia in world history. Moreover, it was informed by questionable values, which assumed capitalism to be synonymous with development and the growth of nation states to be the end of history, and it was inclined towards teleology as all phases of the South Asian past were folded into the events of 1947. The new spotlights have revealed dimensions of South Asian history not noticed before and have posed new and crucial issues for historical debate.

A first area of world history to which the contribution of recent research on South Asia has been marked is that concerned to recover the historical and economic geography of the pre-modern era from the influence of modern nationalist ideology. Here, a major problem has been to avoid treating the economic systems of the seventeenth and eighteenth centuries in terms of the national economies which emerged in most parts of the world only in the nineteenth and twentieth centuries. In the South Asian context, growing interests in 'maritime' history and in the social history of Islam have helped to redraw the map of the Indian Ocean, while research on internal economic and cultural networks has helped to redraw that of the subcontinent itself.[5] Following lines of sea-borne trade in goods, specie and people, for example, there is much to suggest that South-east India should be understood as part of an economic system embracing substantial parts of South-east Asia. Similarly, South-west India was strongly drawn into the orbit of Arabia and Northern India into that of Iran and West Asia. These 'external' linkages carried wide ramifications 'internally': giving South-east India a completely different (gold) currency base to the rest of the subcontinent and tying the expansion and contraction of production and trade in the North and the West to developments hundreds of miles beyond the Mughal frontiers.

Besides helping to clarify discrete features in the economic and social history of South Asia itself, however, this research is important for what it begins to suggest about the early modern 'world' economy. It establishes the existence of networks of exchange and production of great size and complexity focussed on Asian centres and commanded predominantly by Asian merchants, manufacturers and bankers. What once appeared to be a series of tiny and isolated enclaves of commercialism at the extremities of a vast and inert continent look different when they are linked up into circuits through which a huge volume of transactions passed. South Asia was the hub of several of these circuits, was responsible for a much larger share of world trade than any comparable zone and, between the sixteenth and eighteenth centuries, may have possessed upwards of one-quarter of the world's total manufacturing capacity. The weight of its economic power even reached Mexico where, in the early eighteenth century, textile manufacture suffered a crisis of 'de-industrialization' due to South Asian cloth imports.[6]

These findings begin to question interpretations of the growth of the world economy, or of 'The Modern World System', which would place its origins in European history and understand it, in the end, as little more than the expansion of the European economy. Prior to the eighteenth century, there would seem to have been a number of different 'mini-world' or regional systems, bearing many of the characteristics (such as core-periphery relations) which Wallerstein attributes to the European-centred system but either having little to do with Europe or else treating Europe as an essentially peripheral zone. Indeed, in looking at the effects of the cloth trade between Europe and South Asia in the seventeenth century, it would be difficult to decide which was 'core' and which 'periphery'. South Asian exports threatened to 'de-industrialize' European textile industries to the point at which state action, in the form of tariff barriers, had to be taken against them; European demand, backed by Mexican silver, promoted economic growth and the expansion of manufacturing in several South Asian regions, most notably Bengal. But, at least before the eighteenth century, Europe represented no more than one of several trading systems feeding into various South Asian regional economies and, except perhaps in Bengal, was never the largest. The volume of trade with West Asia, Arabia and South-east Asia would seem to have dwarfed that with Europe and, importantly, to have been of a kind designed once more to benefit South Asian economies most. South Asia was a major manufacturer of goods, even those for popular rather than luxury consumption, in all these markets.[7]

In addition to recovering much more of the world's economic past, however, research into 'the trading world' of South Asia can also be seen to have raised two important problems for historical interpretation. Whatever may have been the position in the sixteenth and seventeenth centuries, there can be no doubt that, during the later eighteenth and early nineteenth centuries, Europe did come to dominate the world economy and to create a 'world system' centring upon itself. The question of how it achieved this pre-eminence no longer looks as easy to answer as once it did. If the world economy did not have its origins in Europe then dominance cannot be reduced to a simple function of expansion and to the progressive 'incorporation' of more and more areas of the world, themselves previously inert, into Europe's system. Equally, appeals to the latent power of industrialization would seem anachronistic. To a considerable extent Europe's, especially Britain's, hegemony over the East was established *before* the products of the industrial revolution began to transform world trade. South Asia, for example, did not seriously feel the pressures of competition with Lancashire until the late 1820's when the East India Company was already long established as the dominant power over the South Asian economy. Indeed, the ability of the British industrial revolution to transform world trade may be seen as due, in no small part, to the prior dominance of Britain, which permitted 'obstructions' to be cleared out of its path. Where, then did lie the sources of European supremacy?

The second problem is a corollary of the first and, arguably, represents the central question of early modern history. Wallerstein, following Braudel and a long tradition of European sociological theory, linked the expansion of the world system to the development of capitalism, which he took to have its roots in European history going back to the later middle ages. Until relatively recently, the history of South Asia, as indeed of the rest of Asia, seemed to confirm this position. Few of the social and cultural qualities associated with the growth of capitalism in Europe—the political independence of urban merchant groups, the growth of private property rights and of markets in labour, the development of accountancy and banking skills, etc.—looked to have parallels elsewhere. But, increasingly, historians of Asia have come to wonder whether this was really so. The difficulty is that much of the economic and social history of Asia was written in the light of concepts drawn from precisely the same sociological tradition as that of Braudel and Wallerstein, which presumed European capitalism to be original and unique. As a result, historians of Asia set out to look for differences, which would explain the apparently different development of their regions, at the expense of considering similarities. In retrospect, this can be seen to have cast a very negative or counterfactual slant to interpretation. South Asian economic and social history was written more to explain why the region did not develop like Europe, or perhaps did not develop at all, rather than to account for the changes and developments which did actually take place. In recent years, this history has come to adopt a much more positive approach to conceptualization and to try to throw off the shadow of European epistemological hegemony. One consequence has been the discovery of many more parallels with early modern European 'capitalism' than had originally been supposed. A second has been the questioning of the concepts of 'capitalism' and 'development' previously applied.

It would now be very difficult to specify the structural features of the South Asian economy which necessarily precluded it from undergoing a European-style development of capitalism between the sixteenth and eighteenth centuries. It is not, of course, that the institutions and cultural norms of the two were identical but rather that, the differences notwithstanding, both seem capable of supplying broadly similar economic functions. Marketing systems, which once were deemed disorganized and pedlar-based, have now been shown to have been highly organised and price responsive. Merchant groups, once thought to have been powerless before military authority and incapable of organizing themselves beyond the limits of caste, have now been shown to have possessed in the institution of 'mahajan' a means of both collective defence and extensive organization. Accountancy skills, once considered far beyond the capacities of South Asian culture, have been shown to have been developing rapidly, especially in Western India, from the sixteenth century. Discrete and alienable property rights, once assumed barely to have existed in South Asia, have been traced back (albeit through the mediated form of claims to shares in 'communal' or prebendal properties) to the early middle ages and a brisk market in such rights would seem to have existed in the late seventeenth and eighteenth centuries. The division of labour and the organization of manufacture, once analysed largely in terms of the functions of the caste and jajmani systems, have been shown to have passed increasingly under the logic of mercantile capital from the sixteenth century. The ability of the textile industry in various regions rapidly to expand in order to accommodate new forces of demand and of agriculture to expand and contract on a seasonal basis, depending on climate and market opportunity, also indicate a higher degree of labour mobility, and hence more of a labour market, than once was conceived possible.[8]

These reassessments of South Asia's 'potential for capitalism' have come about in the course of research which has profoundly altered understandings of how South Asian economies were organized and functioned. Few of the conceptions of twenty years ago would seem tenable today. The notion, derived from Moreland and Marx, of a productive base structured around the self-sufficient village community and operating on the principles of the jajmani system looks less and less plausible as evidence increases. In Bengal, there never was a jajmani system; in Tamilnadu and Andhra Pradesh, the specialization of production was so advanced that it precluded village self-sufficiency in most places; in Maharashtra and Gujarat, most of the contemporary evidence on village community and jajmani treats them as being in a state of collapse and transition by the seventeenth century. Similarly, the idea, also derived from Moreland and Marx, of production being sucked dry by the revenue and consumption demands of the state and its ruling elites, has come to be questioned. On the one hand, it is unclear how much the surplus nationally claimed by the state was actually extracted from local society or was ever meant to be. Systems of bureaucracy were weakly articulated and difficult to control; the primary collection of revenue lay with members of the local communities actually being taxed; state theory in the Mughal period would seem to have recognized a far higher degree of autonomy in local community organisations than once was supposed. In effect, high claims to revenue may have served more as symbols of sovereignty, meant to dazzle local community groups and bind them loyally to the throne, than as the bases of a centralized fiscal administration.[9] On the other hand, what is becoming clear is that some , at least of the surplus that was extracted by elites, percolated back into agricultural production and that 'the towns', or rather their ruling elites, were not simply parasites on the countryside. Particularly important here would seem to economic functions of 'religious' and cultural patronage, which promoted the investment of resources, notionally taken by 'the state' as revenue, in the development of production. Inams, waqfs and temple endowments served as mechanisms whereby capital was invested in garden land, irrigation and artisan crafts behind the walls of taxation immunity. No less important would seem the semi-regular system of leakages created by the degree to which 'zamindars' were embedded in local community structures whose reproduction and development they had to support in order to maintain their own authority. Again, what might appear to be 'extracted' revenue was recycled back into production as famine relief, taccavi, well and tank inam and lowered taxation rates for the cultivation of virgin land. Theories of South Asia's economic stagnation, which rest upon the implications of 'Asiatic Despotism', are progressively losing their credibility.[10]

Research on three specific areas of economic and social history has perhaps done most to promote an alternative understanding of South Asia in the early modern period. The first concerns the 'indigenous' dimension of social structure and cultural order. Nearly thirty years ago, calls for an 'ethno-history' of South Asia came out of a standpoint in American cultural anthropology, which perceived the conventions of existing historical analysis to be dominated by colonial sociology and by the concepts of ruling elites. Ethno-history set out to deconstruct South Asian tradition and to reconstruct a past more in keeping with the values and understandings of the historical agents who lived it. Ethno-history's subsequent achievements, not least in broadening the recognized base of source materials to include 'indigenous' forms of evidence previously overlooked, have been very considerable and have reshaped South Asian sociology. While few ethno-historians have addressed the issue under consideration here, much of their work can be seen as having implications for it. In place of a society apparently organized 'from time immemorial' around the principles of caste, village community and jajmani system, ethno-history has suggested one whose key institutions were more 'little kingdom', 'kaniachi', 'watan', 'lineage group', 'temple sect', 'gift' and 'honour'.[11] The significance of this is that, if the relationships governed by these institutions are explored, it becomes clear that we are dealing with a society whose articulations were much more complex and potentially dynamic than the concept of 'tradition' presupposes. Rather than standing against and precluding many of the developments associated with early modern types of capitalism, some of these institutions can be seen to have accommodated and even encouraged them. The relations of temple sects, for example, involved extended exchanges of goods, services and investment capital, which, from at least the eleventh century, were mediated by money forms and which both facilitated the accumulation of wealth and legitimated the privileged appropriation of it. It would be hard indeed to conceive of an 'economic' institution better adapted to the functions of commercial production and a 'religious' institution more sensitive to the divine status conferred by wealth than the South Indian temple. Equally, as ethno-history has come (albeit somewhat belatedly) to confront the problem of social change, it has drawn attention to the close relationship between community forms and structures and the imperatives of the material context in which they were situated. Changing political and economic conditions produced changing organizations of lineage, sect and caste.[12] Viewed this way, the meaning of Louis Dumont's remark, that traditional India had no concept of economy, becomes increasingly obscure and a materialist dynamic appears beneath South Asian history, albeit one whose specific outcomes were mediated through specific cultural forms. There would seem, however, very little in those specific forms to deter the principles of production for exchange, privileged appropriation of surplus and social differentiation based upon the possession and accumulation of wealth.

The second focus of research, which has done much to alter our perceptions of South Asian economic history, is that on internal or trans-regional trade. That trade in luxury items took place across long distances between court and religious centres, and that trade in some bulk items of common consumption took place along the coasts and up the navigable rivers, was long known. What has come to be appreciated much more now, however, is the extremely large trade in basic foodstuffs, raw materials and capital goods carried through the interior by banjara caravans. Exactly how many bullocks were involved in this trade at any one time will never be known. But some idea of scale may be provided by the fact that, in a single 'salt season', between 70,000 and 120,000 bullocks were expected to visit each of eight major salt-trading centres along the South-east coast. When harnessed to military purposes, banjara trains were said to stretch for twenty miles and more behind marching armies. Banjara networks facilitated an exchange economy of surprising depth stretched over great distances. Much of the cotton woven by the large textile industry on the South-east coast came from Maharashtra and Berar; the whole interior of the southern peninsula was dependent for salt on supplies brought from the sea; the 'lower orders' of the rice-growing riverine systems of the South-east ate, not the expensive paddy crops which they produced, but millets and dry grains carried from the interior. Recognition of the vital economic functions performed by the once-despised 'gypsies' of South Aisa has changed understanding of the relationship between exchange and self-sufficiency in the reproduction of the economy. Large sections of even agrarian society were involved in extended relations of exchange, not merely to earn cash to pay revenue, but to survive and to obtain goods vital to the continuaton of production. Indeed, surveys from the eighteenth century suggest that 'market dependence' reached down to the very bottom of 'peasant' society and included the landless labouring poor, many of whom, paid in shares of crops which they would not or could not consume, had responsibility for encashing their own wages in order to buy food.[13]

The third focus, albeit the one most blurred and most in need of further attention, is that on the relations of production. Recent impressions are that, certainly in comparison to the nineteenth century, the role of agricultural cultivation in the economy was very much smaller. To some degree this was because, as has long been known, early modern South Asia contained large cities with vast contingents of soldiers, courtiers, priests, merchants and artisans. But a second reason, whose full significance has not been appreciated until recently, is that a substantial section of the rural workforce was engaged in pastoralism and / or in the exploitation of forests and jungles. This high degree of specialization can be seen to have had several implications. First, and most obviously, it further promoted the exchange economy: in most parts of South Asia, 'self-sufficient' village communities acquired their most vital and most expensive capital good, cattle, from outside themselves. A second implication, well documented in source materials from the eighteenth and early nineteenth centuries, is that cultivation tended to be concentrated on high quality lands, to be extensive and soil-replenishing in its techniques and to be extremely strongly supported by 'animal' inputs. As a result, there is every reason to believe that per acre yields were substantially higher than those generally achieved in the later nineteenth century. The pastoralist economy also added a further dimension of physical mobility to rural society. But then evidence for regions as diverse as Maharashtra, Bengal, Bihar and the South suggests that 'cultivating' or 'peasant' society itself may have been highly mobile and by no means tied to its village communities from time out of mind. Substantial sections of the peasantry were armed and spent part of their year as mercenaries serving in distant locations. Not infrequently, they moved their family and agricultural 'bases' to take advantage of opportunities for military earnings. Attempts to offset the regular instabilities of climate and market provided another cause of movement: most land tenure systems recognized and welcomed the 'pykari' cultivator who moved with his family labour and small capital to escape poor conditions and / or take advantage of better ones. In relatively underpopulated and scarcity-prone regions (i.e. most of the pre-nineteenth-century subcontinent) such peregrinations were common and large-scale.[14]

Seen in the context of an extended and penetrative exchange economy, high degrees of mobility in capital and labour, mechanisms designed to reinvest surplus in production and institutions sustaining and recognizing as alienable privileged rights to appropriate and accumulate wealth, it becomes progressively less clear why the developments traced by Braudel in the European economy from the thirteenth century, and dubbed by him 'the development of capitalism', should not be seen to have had direct parallels in the history of South Asia (and, judging by the work of historians on other parts of Asia, quite broadly across large parts of the continent). Moreover, certain other developments, frequently seen as taking capitalism towards its higher stages in Europe, would also seem to have been part of South Asia's experience, at least from the later Seventeenth century. These developments were the growth of 'state fiscalism', its penetration and takeover by the merchant and banking capital and the subsequent promotion of processes of class formation.

Much recent research has concentrated on the eighteenth century and has sought to rescue its reputaton from the caricatures of historians of both Mughal and British India. Familiarly, the epoch was seen as one of collapse and chaos, which marked an interregnum between Pax Mughalia and Pax Britannica. A strong trend in the current historiography, however, is to reinterpret the period in a much more positive light and with considerable implications for conventional understandings of both Mughal and British Indian history. Rather than falling in ruins, the Mughal empire might now be seen as having been superseded from below by regional states more 'modern' in many of their functions. And rather than representing a set of governing principles imported from a foreign and 'more advanced' culture, the early East India Company state might be seen as a logical extension of processes with distinctively 'indigenous' origins. The key here would seem to be (as indeed it was in 'Absolutist' Europe) the imperatives generated by the rise of new forms of military technology and organization. Armies became increasingly professional and expensive; to pay them, new relationships were developed between rulers and the economy; to articulate those new relations, new state instruments of bureaucracy and fiscal control were forged; through the manipulation of those instruments, classes were formed based upon new types of dominance over commerce and production and new forms of privilege and 'right' to appropriate and accumulate surplus.[15]

These processes of 'military fiscalism' can be traced back through Mughal history. Where the issue may have become critical, however, was in the way that commercial and economic development favoured the peripheral, especially maritime, fringes of the Empire over its heartland. Attempts at incorporating these fringes eventually broke down and gave rise to new regimes based more directly in them, which adapted an advanced Mughal fiscal techniques but to much greater purpose. In Hyderabad, Bengal, Maharashtra, Awadh and Mysore, the successor states exercised, or attempted to exercise, a much deeper control over commerce and production than any of the regimes they replaced. By so doing, they began also to change the nature of 'the state' and the relationship between rulership and society. There is much to suggest that, before the late seventeenth century, 'the state' in South Asia should be understood as based upon two distinct, although interrelated, sources of authority of 'the ruler' and that of 'community' institutions and groups of various sorts and sizes. Such institutions and groups possessed a high degree of autonomy and performed many of the functions of the state. During the course of the eighteenth century, the new pressures to extend rulership tended to bring collisions with community institutions, which, besides exacerbating conditions of internal conflict already intensified by the rivalry between new states, weakened and undermined the latter. In Maharashtra, for example, the *gota* assemblies of local landed groups, which had adjudicated disputes and settled 'custom' in earlier periods, ceased progressively to meet. In Mysore and Hyderabad, rulers sought to reduce or eradicate entirely the 'privileges' of poligars, the clan-based 'little kings' of the peninsula, and eventually even to threaten the 'immunities' enjoyed by temple sects, inamdars and mirasidars.[16]

But who controlled and benefited from the attempted certralization of rulers' authority? The problem here would seem to have been that, neither in their ability to impose a bureaucratic discipline nor in their ability to establish fiscal administration, did the new regional states live up to the ideal reflected in their claims to authority. As their fiscal administrations developed, so they were increasingly 'farmed out' (or privatized?) to merchant and banking groups who utilized them as much, or more, for their own advantage than for that of their rulers. As the oretensions of their government developed, so they were adopted by the scribal groups who carried out bureaucratic functions and who utilized them to the advantage of their own kith and kin. The process has been described as 'the commercialization' and 'scribalization' of royal power. Its corollary, with considerable implications for both 'capitalism' and class formation, however, was the 'royalization' of commercial and scribal power.[17]

In the name of the state, and often using the threat of its coercive capacity, commercial and scribal groups were able to lay claim to resources previously held within 'community' institutions. But, because simultaneously they enjoyed an independence from their rulers, they were able to keep these resources under their own *de facto* control and, indeed, to draw in further resources from the ruler's side of the state. Studies of Maharashtra, North India, Bengal, Hyderabad and the South-east have noted, during the late seventeenth and eighteenth centuries, the rise of 'great households', 'vakil / dubashi / mirasidari elites', 'new gentries' and 'commercial zamindars' whose growing fortunes were based upon the accumulation of wealth drawn from privileged rights previously held under ruler's and / or community prerogative. Indeed, the developments of the period can be seen to have put under severe strain South Asia's previous conventions regarding property rights and to have promoted new ones. Broadly speaking, before the seventeenth century, property rights, (i.e claims to privileged entitlement) had been sustained by three different sources of authority. Prebendal rights dervied from the prerogatives of the ruler. What might be termed 'communal' rights (watan, mirasi, some types of inam) derived from the prerogatives of corporate groups. Personal rights, which inhered in the person of the holder, were derived mainly from religious authority and were the least developed of the three, pertaining almost exclusively to Brahmins. Over the course of the eighteenth century, however, there appears to have been a considerable growth of both *de facto* and *de jure* claims to personal property right. *De facto*, this occurred as a natural corollary to the weakness of both community institutions and ruler's power before 'royalized' commercial and scribal groups. In Maharashtra, the 'great households' built up their 'estates' out of parcels of prebendal (swaranjam) and communal (watan) rights. But with, on the one side, rulers becoming increasingly dependent on the support of 'great households' and, on the other, *gota* assemblies and other institutions defending community prerogative falling into disarray, the sources of authority defining and circumscribing swaranjam and watan right were both becoming ineffective. For practical purposes, great households held their estates as personal properties and would seem increasingly to have developed an ideology of 'ownership' over them. *De jure*, the development was marked in some regions by the growth of Brahmin-type inams over very large quantities of resources—a fact scarcely to be disconnected from the extensive representation of Brahmins among the royalized commercial and scribal elites. In various ways, then, claims to privileged entitlement were changing, and changing in the direction of personal— or perhaps even 'private'—forms of property right.[18]

For both capitalism and class relations, these developments can be seen as highly significant. Increased control over both state revenue and local community systems gave emergent 'great households' (gentry, commercial zamindars, etc.) increased security to invest capital in production, especially for commercial purposes, and increased command over producers and methods of production. Evidence of the growth of investments in wells, market centres, taccavi and new crops during the eighteenth century comes from regions as diverse as North India, Maharashtra and Mysore. Evidence of the other side of capitalist development, namely the subordination of labour and control of its production practices, can be seen in the growth of conflicts between merchants and artisans, zamindars/revenue farmers and peasants, dominant and inferior agrarian groups, which have been documented for most regions. Between merchant capitalists and artisans the central issue concerned the freedom of contract previously enjoyed by craftsmen; between zamindars and peasants, the right to move in search of subsistence without clearing revenue and loan debts; between dominant and inferior agrarian groups, the size of 'shares' in the community product to be allotted to each.[19] In looking at some of the principal cultural developments of the period, it is possible to see them in terms of various manifestations of class formation albeit 'disguised' by the unique and 'exotic' symbols of Oriental tradition. The phenomenon of 'Marathaization', of the development of an identity expressing the collective dominance of Maratha groups over Western Indian society, may well be traced back to the attempts of the 'great households' to find a social legitimation for their rising influence. 'Rajputization', 'Gounderization' and 'Brahminization' (the latter, in Southeast India, linked to a new awareness of and attempt to enforce the prerogatives of *varnashramadharma*) were perhaps parallel manifestations of the same processes in other regions.

Much recent research, then, would suggest that, in a great many ways, South Asia was involved in 'the social history of capitalism' from a very early period and underwent many of the same types of social development as those taking place in Western Europe. In this it was not alone. Studies of the Ottoman, Iranian and Ch'ing Empire have started to show many parallel patterns in their histories. Once more, commercial expansion and 'military fiscalism' from at least the seventeenth century appear to have undermined their old imperial systems, to have created tighter, more regionally-based, 'para-state' systems and to have 'royalized' commercial power or given it a more clearly defined class character and base. Indeed, one of South Asian history's main claims to importance now is the extent to which it fits into and supports those trends in world history, which seek to recover the subject from European history, to restore the status of Asian history and to put historical theory on a rather more objective, or at least less ethno-centric, footing.[20]

But two crucial problems remain: if the dynamics of Asian history were so strong, how was it that the Europeans came eventually to dominate them; and, relatedly, what was it about European theories of 'capitalism' (and 'modern' history-which are the same) which made it seem for so long that Asian 'tradition' lay outside them? Recent research on South Asia may have helped to bring both questions into focus. With regard to the rise of European dominance, for example, the specific logic of the 'indigenous' processes of change noted above may be seen both to have drawn the Europeans into the South Asian 'interior' and to have promoted the status of certain features of their historical character. Briefly, the processes enhanced the importance of cash, guns and the security of 'property' in ways which gave the Europeans and particularly the British, strategic advantages over Asians as a result of their own very peculiar history.

In the first place, the imperatives generated by the expansion of commerce and the growth of 'military fiscalism' pointed to the significance of the sea. Both required increased flows of specie, which as South Asia produced very little bullion metal, could only be acquired, in adequate quanities, from overseas trade. The significant roads of commerce led increasingly to the coasts and down them began to come the Europeans, ready to foster and support the trading and banking systems on which the new regimes depended in return for a piece of the action. Many of the monopolies, privileged rights and revenue concessions, being created and / or newly enforced by military fiscalism, found their way into the hands of the Europeans (as often acting in a 'private' as a 'Company' capacity). Of course, they did not only find their way into the hands of Europeans nor, directly, were Europeans the principal beneficiaries of this fiscalism. Inside South Asia, indigenous capital was dominant and most of the European Companies traded with and through indigenous commercial and banking networks. But what was happening outside South Asia during the course of the eighteenth century may be seen to have altered the previous balance in this relationship. On the one hand, a European mercantile marine seems to have been progressively displacing South Asian shipping in the carrying trade, even the carrying trade with other parts of Asia. This gave the Europeans increasing control over the arteries of specie flowing into South Asia. The point was not lost on those regimes which, by the later years of the century, saw the English East India Company as the real threat it had become and recognized the importance of the seas if they were to compete against it: Hyder Ali and Tipu Sultan of Mysore struck out of Karnataka to the West Coast in a desperate effort to develop and protect their own overseas trading empire. But they were at least forty years too late: even with French help, English control of the seas could not be broken. On the other hand, by virtue of their extensive international commercial networks, the English were able, at certain crucial moments, to organize and inject into South Asia specie in such large quantities that they could flood its economic system and virtually buy their way to dominion. This last was very much the tactic employed during the final phase of conquest, around the turn of the ninteenth century, when the Company's policy of restricting the import of treasure, followed since the acquisition of Bengal revenues, was temporarily abandoned. Wellesley's war machine was primed with many more than thirty pieces of silver, enabling the Company to take a firm grip on the internal commercial system and to 'buy out' the underpinnings of most of the regimes with which it was in conflict. One visible result of this policy was the huge increase in the Company's debt—which rose from £8 million in 1786 to £32 million by 1832—and for which South Asia was later to pay dearly. Strategic control of 'cash and carriage', then, may have represented one of the Europeans' most important advantages. But, of course, and like any 'cash and carriage' trade, it became important only because somebody wanted or needed to buy. The indigenous logic of military fiscalism and commercial expansion led on to the conjuncture which produced colonialism as much as did that logic of European history, which pushed its sailors out into the sea.[21]

Europe's second strategic advantage would seem to have lain in military affairs although the debate is still open about precisely where. Until the middle of the eighteenth century, the Europeans possessed scarcely any advantage at all: South Asian battlefields were still dominated by cavalry and siege artillery where indigenous tradition was stronger. From the 1740s, however, the introduction of disciplined musketry and field artillery temporarily altered this situation, giving the Europeans their first major military successes. Yet South Asian regimes were exceptionally quick to learn and adapt and by the 1760s, as the first two Mysore Wars showed, indigenous armies were back on level terms (and more) with East India Company forces. Indeed, it was the pressure to 'modernize' their military that pushed many regimes towards the intensified fiscalism noted above. Two explanations are currently available to account for the ultimate collapse of South Asian military opposition to the Company and both, in a sense, emphasize more internal 'subversion' than external technical superiority. On the one hand, it has been suggested that the Company's strong financial position enabled it to buy out the best cavalry from under indigenous regimes. On the other hand, and perhaps more plausibly, a key feature has been noticed in the longer tradition of disciplined infantry warfare possessed by the Europeans. What it meant was that the increasingly crucial infantry sections of indigenous armies were almost universally officered by European mercenaries who, whether from threats, divided loyalties or simple bribery, proved themselves prone to desert to European opponents at crucial moments. If the latter explanation is given more force, it points yet again to the significance of those processes leading to changes in indigenous military organization, which drew the European into the central institutions of South Asian regimes and precipitated the fatal conjuncture with European history.[22]

The third strategic advantage of the Europeans, or in this case very much of the English, to which recent research has drawn attention, concerns the ideology and institutions of their state and legal systems. From the sixteenth century but, more emphatically, during the seventeenth and eighteenth centuries, the protection and reproduction of private capital became increasingly the principal, and at times it would seem the only, function of the English state and legal systems.[23] Nowhere else in Western Europe (with the possible exception of the

Netherlands) were 'private' rights to property so deeply entrenched and the privileges of wealth seen to carry so very few social obligations. In the context of the social developments taking place in South Asia, this gave the English an overwhelming advantage in principles of state building. They could attract the support and flatter the ambitions of the newly dominant classes, rising in most regions through the expansion of commerce and the pressures of military fiscalism, by offering them property rights more secure and forms of privilege less socially circumscribed than any they could hope to achieve elsewhere. Although, as noted above, there is much to suggest the development of more 'personal' forms of property right, in the estates of 'the great households' etc., these forms were more usually of a *de facto* than *de jure* character and were not wholly uncontested. Part of the development of 'military fiscalism' involved rulers laying 'Sultanist' claims to the possession of all resources in their domains and, while they could rarely realize an administrative control over the resources held in their name by scions of the new classes, they could occasionally resume or confiscate them. Particularly in the context of military crises, merchant capital and ertswhile 'personal' wealth not infrequently found itself at risk of confiscation. On the other side, as the conflicts noted above concerning the destruction of 'community' rights and the greater subordination of labour and production to the imperatives of commerce indicate, the pretensions of 'property' and 'capital' were capable of being resisted. In the critical period of its rise (if somewhat problematically later), the Company can be seen to have gone out of its way to offer security from both Confiscatory Sultanism above and class and community resistance below to the wealth accumulations of the newly 'propertied' classes. The principles (if not, as things worked out later, necessarily the practices) of the Permanent Settlement and its attendant court system could hardly have been better designed to suit the interests of the rising groups of the period. And, painful though it has long been for a historiography heavily influenced by twentieth-century nationalism to accept, there seems now preponderant evidence that the Company's achievement of state power in most parts of South Asia was accomplished through, and on the back of, these groups, who no infrequently 'subverted' the regimes of their sometime rulers in order to precipitate the establishment of that of their new one.[24]

What, then, might South Asian history have to say about the causes of European world domination? Obviously, these did to some degree lie in certain 'superiorities' achieved by European historical development. But, in and of themselves, they seem rather narrow superiorities. What gave them their full significance was the way that they came into conjuncture with specific dynamics in South Asian historical development. Colonialism in South Asia had a set of 'indigenous' origins as well—and origins which were no less part of the social history of capitalism than those deriving from Europe. In a certain sense, colonialism was the logical outcome of South Asia's history of capitalist development.

All of which points to the importance of the second question raised above: why is it that, until relatively recently, South Asia (and the non-European world at large) failed to be recognized as active agents in the history of capitalism but were treated either as inert repositories of 'tradition' or as passive receptacles of 'modernization'? The answer perhaps lies in the extent to which all the classical European sociological traditions, orginating in the nineteenth century, presupposed that the telos of 'capitalist' development was 'industrialization' and 'modernization'. Put bluntly, as South Asian history clearly did not terminate in the development of modern industrial society, it could not have been part of the history of capitalism. Indeed, it could not have been part of history at all for in these theories 'history' meant modernization and capitalism: their category for the past was static and changeless 'tradition'. In many ways, the most important item on the agenda of historical scholoarship over the last twenty years can be seen as the attempt to disentangle the concepts of 'capitalism', 'industrialization' and 'modernization' from one another and to rescue 'modern' history from a teleology which increasing empirical knowledge of the pre-nineteenth century and non-European pasts has made absurd. The task, at the very least, is to specify the relationship between the emergent social order of capitalism and the logic of technological development and modernizing social change. It is not as yet a task which even historians of Western Europe have been able to meet. None of the various formulae—from Weber's manic concept of rationality to Rostow's stages and preconditions of growth to Mendel's proto-industrialization to even Hagen's methods of Methodist potty-training—do very much to convince. Indeed, the struggle to find a plausible link has now reached a stage where it threatens to explode much that was thought to be 'knowed' about the history of industrialization. Debates on the British industrial revolution, having already undermined simple notions as to its dating and description, appear to have got to the position of questioning whether it ever happened—or at least to noting that France, where it was supposed not to have happened 'properly', may have had a more successful economic history than Britain.[25] The doubts and confusions are, of course, critical to the general theory of industrial capitalism because Britain represents the only possible 'pure' case in which the 'evolution' of capitalism to industrialism can be studied. All sub-sequent cases were 'artificially' mimetic or politically forced. Added to the problem, then, of having to develop general theories from single cases, there is the difficulty here that the nature of the single case is becoming increasingly obscure.

It would be pretending too much to claim that the history of South Asia can go far in resolving these major conceptual problems. But recent research into it may have helped us reconsider and re-formulate some of the questions. In particular, this research suggests that the evolutionary link between capitalist development and industrialization, if there is one, may be better seen as a unique historical deformity than a universal historical model; that the imperatives of capitalist development and those of technological and social modernization may be at best tangentially related; and that the 'success' of capitalism is, in its own terms, poorly judged against standards of industrialization and modernization.

In the first place, there is the question of technological development during the seventeenth and eighteenth centuries, during the indigenous phases of South Asia's history of capitalism. Conventionally, the epoch has been regarded as one of technological 'stagnation' and, if one is looking for 'breakthroughs' of a major order then it may deserve the term, although there is copious evidence of 'the diffusion of best techniques' and of minor adaptations in various methods of production. But why should one look for or anticipate a constant series of 'breakthroughs'? If the logic of technological development is related to one of social need, rather than being seen as a wholly independent dynamic drawn forward teleologically by its own drive to unfold, then major transformations are likely to occur only when expanding social needs can no longer be met out of existing technological means. It is unclear that the South Asian economy had reached this state in any important regard before the second quarter of the nineteenth century. In many regions, agricultural techniques, so far from earning the mockery of Western 'experts', were regarded as being at least as, if not more, advanced than those found in comparable 'Western' situations: the rice yields of the Kaveri delta, for example, were compared more than favourably with those of the Carolinas; the cotton yields of the 'black soil' areas of the peninsula were frequently higher than those of Georgia. Handicraft manufacture, too, was scarcely in need of an industrial revolution: the market for cloth exports out of Calcutta continued to expand until the 1820's and drew supplies from an ever deeper hinterland in North India. Indeed, not only was the quality of production high but the means for expanding its quantity were relatively elastic. Increased demand for cloth was met by drawing into the textile industry new workers (there was a noticeable growth of 'pariah' weavers in South India in the eighteenth century); new lands were being opened up in various regions throughout the period. So what was the need for technological transformation? Economic historians of South Asia (as indeed of China) have been inclined to describe the situation as one of an 'equilibrium trap'. But it is hard to see what precisely was trapped when production so clearly was capable of expansion. It might as well be said that the motor industy in the West has been in an equilibrium trap for the last one hundred and twenty years since no major breakthrough has followed the invention of the internal combustion engine.[26]

Obviously, the ghost of Europe haunts these concepts and what is really being asked is why did South Asia not undergo the particular types of change then transforming European technology. But if historical change is the result of specific causation, it is difficult to think why South Asia (and the rest of human society) should be expected to have undergone precisely the same history as Europe. The relevance of Europe's technology and modernity for South Asia would seem better dated from the time when they made their actual impact and demonstrated, through the forces of competition, the obsolescence of the latter's inheritances. In effect, the 'problem' of technological development in South Asia may be one which belongs to the nineteenth, rather than seventeenth or eighteenth, century and which turns on the question of the weakness of South Asia's response to European industrialization after the latter had happened (for whatever specific reasons, which presently remain obscure).

If attempts to deal with this question in terms of the supposed innate 'irrationalities' of South Asian cultural values and social institutions are discounted as unhistorical, the most obvious answers would seem to lie in the implications of colonialism and underdevelopment. And a very strong *prima facie* case can be made that, especially between the 1820's and 1850's, British rule restructured South Asian society and economy in ways meant to serve its own interests and which had the consequence of all but permanently precluding the transformation to modern industrialization. It was in this era that many of the social and economic features, understood by later generations to be the products of changeless tradition and taken to constitute the barriers of 'backwardness' to development, can be seen to have crystallized. Recent research has given particular attention to the nature and implications of the long-term price depression which descended on the South Asian economy towards the end of the 1820 's and did not lift, in some areas, until the early 1850's. In part, the depression reflected worldwide trading conditions. But in South Asia, it was exacerbated by three factors which can be directly associated with colonial rule: the export of large quantities of specie to service the China trade; the dismantling of many indigenous court, military and religious centres, which had provided the main foci of internal demand, in the wake of the establishment of Pax Britannica; and the impact of Lancashire on South Asia's previous overseas and luxury textile markets. The depression, and these particular causes of it, can be seen as having knocked the stuffing out of a large part of South Asia's 'ancien regime' mercantile capitalist economy. Moreover, much of what was left was now taken out of the hands of indigenous capitalists and passed, via the monopoly powers of the state, to British ones. The period was marked by swingeing revenue demands and attempts to monopolize the most valuable areas of commerce, which, backed now by greater coercive force than under pervious regimes, were made the more effective. The 'bureaucratization' of government in these years had its corollary in the attempt to separate indigenous capital from the institutions of state fiscalism around which it had become organised over the previous two centuries. The consequences were serious in several ways. Stripped of state banking and revenue functions, indigenous capital lost much of the framework sustaining its previous structure and was reduced to petty roles in local moneylending and commodity peddling. Stripped of the security given by control over revenue collection and remittance, its propensity to invest in production declined. The functions which once it had performed were now held to be the duties of 'the state' behind which hid the interest of private British capitalists—shareholders in the Company which owned 'the state' or, more usually, agency houses using state powers and liens on the revenue to their own advantage. The extent to which the new state fulfilled the functions which it had arrogated to itself may be seen in the declining availability of specie and in the several reports of the 1840's and 1850's, which noted the collapse of investment in credit and irrigation and called, somewhat belatedly, for radical reform in revenue and fiscal policies.[27]

The principal process of economic change during these years has been described as 'peasantization'. Displaced soldiers, courtiers, priests and artisans found their way onto the land, which was fast becoming the only available base of subsistence. They were joined, too, by increasing numbers of pastoralists and forest peoples. Road building programmes, undertaken as much for military as for economic reasons, undermined the banjara economy, while policies of rapid forest clearance and the enforced settlement of mobile peoples reduced the peripatetic elements in the economy. The many and diverse paths along which the peoples of the eighteenth century had earned their livings tended to converge on generalized 'peasant' petty commodity production in the nineteenth. Viewed from certain vantage points in economic theory, these developments might be seen as positive for growth. They undoubtedly led to a great expansion in agricultural production and to the redeployment of much erstwhile 'unproductive' labour. Moreover, they were attended by the opening out of new markets for South Asian primary products in Ceylon, China and Europe. Yet seen in wider structural perspective, 'economic development through progressive peasantization' may be judged problematic and to have stored up many difficulties for future development in the later nineteenth and twentieth centuries. While the agricultural sector grew, all other sectors declined. State intervention broke connections between the commodity market and markets in investment capital, freely mobile labour and land. Depressed market prices and confiscatory revenue demands limited the possibilities of building up capital in agriculture. Cultivation expanded, under the pressure of sheer numbers, towards poorer soil margins and lower animal input/acreage ratios. In effect, the South Asian economy was set upon a course which, as the availability of new land began to decrease and as overcropping brought on soil exhaustion, would reach crisis points of stagnation and involution later on and which, with fractured linkages between agriculture and other economic sectors and a proliferating mass of starveling subsistence peasants and labourers, would prove highly unresponsive to the needs of industrialization.[28]

The social processes attendings this 'peasantization' might be termed 'traditionalization'. Of course, what exactly is meant by 'modernization', and how far it exists in or is necessary to capitalist industrialization remain bitterly disputed questions. But if the standard indices of 'modernization' were applied to South Asian society in this era, there is much to suggest a backwards regression to 'tradition'. Literacy rates may well have declined as a result of the dismantling of court and religious centres. De-urbanization was a pronounced trend in some regions. Physical mobility was reduced as opportunities declined, the land filled up and the state set out to fix groups more firmly in their locations so that they might be taxed and controlled better. With the development of the Anglo-Indian personal law, possibilities of social mobility, and of structural change in many social institutions, were reduced for the best part of a century. The courts administered a rigid conception of 'custom' and 'tradition', presupposing them to represent social forms given 'from time immemorial' and incapable of undergoing 'legitimate' historical change. Thus they froze them as they found them—or thought they found them. In fact, legal notions of South Asian 'tradition' frequently owed more to the scriptures than to current conditions and their implementation represented a 'Brahminization' of society, pushing its norms back into deep antiquity or, rather, making the values of one section of present society (Brahmins) artificially dominant over those of others. The principles of caste became more deeply entrenched and displaced many of the social functions of lineage, temple sect and little king, which the law refused to recognize.

The traditionalization of social relations can be seen as having had wide ramifications for economic relations, making 'market economy' and 'entrepreneurship' extremely difficult. As argued above religious institutions had played very important roles in commerce and economic development in the past. The Anglo-Indian law, however, insisted on a separation between the domains of the material and moral, placing the latter under the rubric of undynamic tradition and the former, in this period, in the coffers of the state. The economic functions once supplied by the South Indian temples suffered as their assets were confiscated by Collectors and their trustees, who sought to profit from commerce, were prosecuted for corruption. Similarly, the law tended to draw now-rigid lines of prescriptive social obligation so broadly that they began to interfere with the residual functions of the market. What became the definition of 'ancestral property right' questioned the possibility of a market in rights over land since it was extremely unclear whether inherited family property could be alienated or at least who had the right to alienate it. Certain types of mirasi rights were defined in a similarly restrictive way, making the vendor go through the (extremely expensive) practice of gaining the formal written permission of all other members of the mirasi group to the sale. The definition of 'individual' in relation to 'family' right became so narrow that if family members had contributed at all to the costs of educating or 'skilling' one of their number, all of his subsequent earnings belonged to them. The enforcement of social conventions such as these threatened the bases of any kind of economy founded on commerce and relations of market exchange. But then, of course, most of what might be thought of as the commercial economy was no longer in the market place but had been engorged by the state. In relation to the claims of the state for revenue payments and debts (the dominant mechanisms of exchange), none of these 'traditional' family and community institutions was permitted privilege. Indeed, by defining the bases of family and community responsibility so widely, the state was always able to find somebody who was 'obliged' to meet its demands for revenue and debt payment.[29]

Much of India's ancient past, then, may have been made during the second quarter of the nineteenth century and, not least, the past of Asiatic Despotism. For the structure of society and economy then taking shape would seem nearer to the ideal-type of Asiatic Despotism than anything South Asia had seen before: a sovereign affecting the claim to possess all resources in his domain, running the economy through his bureaucracy and presiding over a society of self-reproducing village communities, themselves organized around the principles of caste and jajmani. The parallels, of course, are not coincidental for an important part of the British Indian state's claim to legitimacy was that it inherited and followed South Asian tradition. Hence it had to distort a tradition suitable to its purposes and bequeath this to South Asian history. It has taken an unconscionably long time for history to begin to question the legacy.

Viewed in these terms, colonialism would seem to have prime responsibility for India's 'underdevelopment' and inability to adopt, imitate or respond to European industrialization. Indeed, as the supplier of raw materials to and the consumer of manufactures from Europe, India promoted the latter's industrial advance. And yet there remain problems with this otherwise self-evident formulation. In the first place, it still rests on the implication that had South Asia's capitalist development not been captured and diverted by Europe, its dynamic would, could or should have produced industrialization. But this merely returns us to the teleology whence we came and throws little light on the question of how it is that capitalist development ever produces industrialization to start with. Moreover, it overlooks the significance of the conjuncture with Europe in the seventeenth and eighteenth centuries, which, as we have suggested, led to the picking up and strengthening of indigeous tendencies towards capitalist development and to their consolidation in social classes and 'private' property rights. Europe 'developed' the social relations of South Asian capitalism even if, and simultanteously, it prevented their 'normal' economic consequence in industrialization. Second, the formulation also makes difficult an explanation of much that happened in South Asia in the nineteenth century. In spite, for example, of the awesome pretensions which the Company state and British capital had assumed by the 1820—to enjoy the privileges previously possessed by indigenous capital, to suck out surplus through penal revenue demands, to confiscate the fiscal system around which indigenous capital had organized, to freeze indigenes out of the market economy by 'traditionalizing' their social relaions, etc.—there appears to have been remarkably little political resistance. After a few early misunderstandings, South Asia's capitalist social classes became the most loyal supporters of the British Raj and sustained it throughout the middle and later decades of the nineteenth century. Theirs was not the Mutiny of 1857: according to Stokes, the 'magnates' remained firm against a wave of insurgency set up more by declining aristocracies and military groups and dispossessed forest and pastoralist peoples. If, as recent research strongly suggests, captialism in South Asia had indigenous roots and if its own developmental logic was brutally disrupted by mid-nineteenth century colonialism, this quiescence needs to be explained.[30]

One point of explanation may lie in the extent to which, in spite of all that was being done to them and to the shape of the South Asian economy, 'magnate' groups quite clearly continued to enrich themselves. Indeed, few of them can have 'had it so good'. Subordination to the dominance of British capital and loss of control over the central institutions of the commercial and fiscal systems meant the reverse of any inability to make and accumulate 'private' wealth.

The new colonial cities thrived; 'great households' extended their estates or congeries of property rights; new magnates—Marwaris, Nadars, Chettiars—appeared to join the more established commercial elites. Of course, there were some casualties too, especially among those whose wealth lay in land where it was most vulnerable to state confiscation. But they may better be seen as particular 'hard luck' cases rather than as representatives of the broader trend whose character was reflected in the proliferation of luxury houses, urban villas and zamindari palaces/country-houses in many regions during this period. If the appearance of so much prosperity in the context of an economy undergoing processes of 'depression', 'peasantization' and 'traditionalization' is paradoxical, it may be resolved by examining the relationships between the market and production, and between those of capital and labour, which these processes implied. Price depression cheapened the cost at which commodities could be acquired; desperate demands from producers for cash to meet higher revenue payments raised the returns of usury; the flood of labour out of armies, courts and religious centres and out of decaying artisan industries lowered its price in agriculture, the one area of production to retain some viability. These processes put the possessors of capital, whatever their ethnic origins, into an increasingly dominant and privileged position over producers and labourers. They were advanced and consolidated, too, by the development of the law. The Anglo-Indian courts took a highly eclectic view of 'custom' and 'tradition', limiting their prerogatives essentially to the relations of 'real' property. 'Non-real' property relations, such as the subsistence and share claims of labourers and of many types of tenant, were deemed to have no status in custom and tradition (perhaps because they reflected market relationships which, legally, could not have existed in the 'traditional' past) and were afforded no protection. Thrown open to the 'healthy' forces of competition, in the context of declining prices, employment opportunities and land availability, it is not difficult to conceive the consequences of labour's 'modernization'. Indeed, its position as the one 'modern' element in the colonial economy was rendered the more anomalous for 'traditionalization' of everything else now made it more difficult for the rewards of labour and skill, if there were any, ever to gain the privileges of property and capital. The freezing of the latter into traditional forms, and their taking out of the market place, reduced the degrees of competition for their possession. Revenue rights, which 'military fiscal' regimes had once auctioned to the highest bidders and whose holding as 'property' had implied at least some ability to meet revenue, commercial and debt demands, now became the economic supports of 'an ancient aristocrat' whom market pressures could not remove. Mirasi and inam rights, once bought and sold as 'property' in response to the gains and losses of commercial fortune, now became fixed rigid in the 'ancient' possession of those then holding them. With the strengthening of caste tradition, through the force of Anglo-Indian Brahmin law, varna status ascription intruded into relationships where it had had little influence before (such as the South Indian temple) to reduce possibilities of social mobility and, where 'caste' privilege implied claims to economic resources, of economic mobility as well.[31]

'Peasantization' and 'Traditionalization', then, were not only of advantage to British capital but also to capital-in-general, in terms of its relationships with labour and production, and to all possessors of capital and 'real' property rights, in terms of their competitive relationships with one another. Indigenous capital shared no less in these benefits which, in comparison to the residual problems which it had with colonial rule, would seem of much greater structural significance. Those problems concerned the realization of surplus value and the confiscatory claims of the new state but both were clearly manageable. Deepressed markets in South Asia itself temporarily made it difficult to encash the surpluses squeezed from peasants and labourers. However, even by the 1820's, markets for South Asian primary products were opening up in China, Ceylon and Europe. Company fiscal policies, which pretended a state revenue right to virtually all surplus, threatened the confiscation of indigenous private wealth, the very existence of which, in the eyes of some Company officials, was a sure sign of the 'corruption' of the state's administration. But the cultural blindness, internal contradictions and more meaningful 'corruptions' of the regime made successful 'concealment' of wealth not only possible but more the rule than the exception. The formal illegality of their transaction does not seem to have overly inconvenienced the celebrated Brahmin bureaucrats (more properly bankers, commercial agents and landowners) of Guntur who ran the district under the British; nor does it the six leading mirasidari families of Tanjavur who ran the Collectorate office and, between 1819 and 1835, 'acquired' land rights in about one-third of all the villages in the district. Indeed, to rub salt into the wounds of the Company as well as to illustrate which was dominant in the relation between capitalism and colonialism, these families, when tried and imprisoned by the criminal courts for 'corruption', turned to the civil courts and invoked the sacred rights of private property in order to hang on to their 'ill-gotten' gains.[32]

In comparison to the structural advantage of security of property, dominance over labour and restriction of internal competition gained by South Asian capitalists from the coming of colonial 'underdevelopment', the disadvantages of subordination to British capital and the Company state look extremely minor—and clearly looked extremely minor to 'the magnates' of 1857. In fact, those advantages look so substantial that they begin to raise questions about how they were achieved and why 'the development of capitalism' is not, or at least should not, be seen, following the social passage of 'peasantization', 'traditionalization' and 'underdevelopment', as its normal, rather than deviant, form. If, from the perspective of capital, the purposes of a capitalist system are to facilitate accumulation, secure property and extend the range of social privilege associated with it, India, by the middle of the nineteenth century, must be regarded as one of the most successful of all contemporary capitalist societies. The rate of profit inside the economy was extremely high; far higher than in the 'developed' economies of the West where the colonial state had to go for 'cheap' loans. Apart from the short-term effects of confiscatory 'revenue' policies, property rights in the major component of the productive base were extremely secure: so secure that displacement due to land sales was lower than in the 'developed' economies and much lower than it would seem to have been in the more commercialized sectors of the eighteenth-century economy. Able to call on the new ideologies of Western racism and aristocracy and on the Anglo-Indianized version of caste privilege, propertied groups affected cultures of social dominance and exclusivity unavailable to them before.[33]

The secret of this amazingly successful development of capitalism may be seen to lie in the extent to which it built up capital almost exclusively by expropriating an ever larger share of resources from labour and the production system without having to take the risk of reinvesting more than a tiny fraction of profit. The dynamic of expansion came not from the 'dangerous' entrepreneurship of capital but from the pressure of social necessity which forced previously 'unproductive' groups and groups productive in now unviable sectors on to the land to work. This pressure, by increasing the competition of labour for land and subsistence, also increased the dominance of capital and enabled it both to claim a progressively higher share of the social product and to cast off more and more of its responsibilities for the social reproduction of the labour force. The contrast between the mid-eighteenth and mid-nineteenth centuries is most instructive: then, faced with the problem of relative labour scarcity due to multiple opportunities and mobility, emergent capitalists had frequently to risk substantial investments in irrigation and taccavi in order to attract cultivators and to take risks with their revenue obligations by offering low rates for new settlements; faced also with competition from rival banking and commercial groups, who might take over the rights they held from 'military fiscal' regimes, themselves in open rivalry, there were pressures to drive down their retained rates of profit. By the mid-nineteenth century, many of these pressures were gone. In most areas, rising peasant densities were making it possible to charge competitive rents and to enforce subsistence-debt contracts in relation to minimal expenditures systems but not, itself, interested in the formal possession of property rights, and with property rights themselves tied up in traditional social forms, competition through the market place dwindled and potential rates of profit rose. With social hierarchies fixed rigid by the legal forms of caste deference, rather than being the product of competitive interaction in search of royal and divine 'honours', the need for elites to justify their privileges by spending on causes of cultural and social value (education and literature, temples and charities) was also diminishing. Rarely in history can capital and property have secured such rewards and such prestige for so little risk and so little responsibility as in the society crystallizing in South Asia in the Victorian Age.[34]

Many of the forces lying behind this shift doubtless came from Britain's conquest of India. But, in a number of institutional ways, the momentum can be seen to have been set up by the logic of indigenous capitalist development, especially in its later stages from the seventeenth century, when social classes began to form. As suggested above, an important dynamic behind development in this era was 'military fiscalism', which led rulers to question the relationship of duality with 'community' institutions, which previously had characterized their states. They advanced the pretensions of 'Sultanism', as Weber termed it, to claim the possession of all resources in their domains, particularly those previously held under 'community' institutions. Inside community institutions—temple sects, lineage-based 'little kingdoms', mirasi villages—relationships between privilege and responsibility and between the appropriation of surplus and its reinvestment in production can be seen to have been close. The power of the 'little king' was in many ways transmitted and legitimated through the 'gifts' he bestowed on his favoured subjects. Mirasidars not only enjoyed entitlement to a fixed share of communally-produced surplus but also possessed an obligation to invest, according to their share, in the production of that surplus. Many inams were granted in return for implied economic and social services, such as investing in gardens, tanks and wells.[35] At the level of formal rights, the claims made by Sultanist rulers over community resources involved no such concessions to mutuality and obligation. Although, under the contingent pressures of the times, rulers might, indeed, invest in irrigation works and taccavi, in order to attract cultivators, labourers and artisans, their claims to sovereignty in no way formally depended on their doing so. And should contingent conditions dictate otherwise, they could advance their power and interests by quite other means involving force, expropriation and destruction. The most 'Sultanist' of all late ancien regimes, that of Hyder and Tipu in Mysore, balanced its substantial investments in irrigation, taccavi and textile production with savage displays of force involving the destruction of rival economic bases and the compulsory mobilization of labour as well as the threat to confiscate temple, inam, little king and mirasi rights. Reinterpretations of the eighteenth century may have been inclined to play down the real escalation of violence which the period saw—not just, and perhaps not mainly, between organized armies but at points of conflict between 'ruler's' and 'community' rights and between state demands and labour's needs for consumption.[36]

Theoretically, if perhaps never much more than that, the society envisaged by 'Sultanism' was in many ways that which did begin to take shape in the second quarter of the nineteenth century. The sovereign held all power over material resources and society existed as a function of his needs. Commerce should be monopolized by the state and organized by it down to the level of production; producers should be stripped of all supra-subsistence surplus and their society reduced to that of labour 'atoms'. The ryotwari revenue system, penal taxation, resumption of community assets and ruler's monopolies over commerce and manufacture were all developed by Tipu, at the level of concept, before the East India Company got around to realizing them more vigorously and more completely than he could have dreamed possible. Once British supremacy had been achieved and the pressures of internal warfare had decreased, the Company turned its military force on to 'civil' society to realize formal claims over commerce and community assets as never before; and utilized the increasing desperation of the displaced and disemployed to raise the share of the social product which it could appropriate. In these circumstances, where military coercion and a distorted labour market sustained the rates of profit and accumulation, what need was there to risk capital and expend resources in investment ?

The similarities between Sultanist ideals and Company Raj realities were, of course, no coincidence. Once the Company had ceased trying to undermine rival regimes and had become itself the supreme sovereign in South Asia, its ideology was transformed as if by magic and it found much to admire in the traditions of the South Asian state, especially those of Sultanist pretension, which once it had excoriated. The version of Asiatic Despotism by which it now legitimated its rule was little more than an extension of the Sultanist 'distortion': distorting because it wholly ignored the rights and prerogatives of community institutions. But this extension was significant not only, and perhaps not primarily, for the abstract theorization of the colonial state. Much more it was significant because, as we have argued above, it was principally by penetrating and taking over the dynamics of the military fiscalist Sultanist state, through revenue and monopoly farming, that capital and commercial power 'royalized' themselves and established a base in social class. In the name of the Sultan, commercial and scribal groups interrupted community circuits of material production and social reproduction to expropriate surplus and hold it under a socially irresponsible and personal form of privilege. Again, in the context of the eighteenth century, the full implications of this might be obscured by the temporary need to invest in production in order to attract scarce labour and to meet the competition of rivals. But the underlying meaning sometimes emerged as and when some revenue renters found it more 'economically rational' simply to asset-strip and destroy by force the resources and labour supplies of their rivals, as sometimes they did. Early forms of capital accumulation in South Asia, no less than elsewhere in the world, could be attended by violence. Moreover, once Company Raj brought the interpenetration of Sultanism and Capitalism to orgiastic climax with the Sultan as Capital and 'the state' owned by a firm (or rather by a series of British and Indian 'firms') and, once peasantization and traditionalization had begun to do their work in reducing the force of competition and in undermining the resistance of labour and community institutions, it became progressively more 'economically rational' to sustain accumulation through coercion and the 'natural' decline in the share of the social product accorded to labour rather than to put valuable capital at risk by investment. The logic of South Asia's own process of 'indigenous' capitalist development, as much as that of colonial rule, guided the economy towards systemic 'underdevelopment'.

Where South Asia's experience may help towards an understanding of the nexus between the social relations of capitalism, industrialization and social modernization is in pointing towards the dual importance of competition and the struggle with labour and 'community' in forcing capital to invest and to spend on social welfare. By its nature, capital must accumulate continuously and thus must cheapen the relative costs of labour: but, as Robert Brenner (following Marx) has argued, there are two ways in which this can be accomplished: either by raising productivity through investments in technology and human capital (modernization) or though reducing the share of a more restricted social product accorded to labour. In South Asia (and most of the world), 'development' followed the latter course which, on the face of it, seems the more desirable of the two options for capital since it involves so little economic risk. Political control over the forces of market competition and increasing dominance over labour and its processes of reproduction gave capital a comfortable history in colonial South Asia. This, however, throws the ball back into the court of European history to explain what was peculiar about the social relations of capitalism there—particularly the less restrained forces of competition and the greater rights and freedoms of community institutions and of labour—which forced capitalism along the riskier paths of investment in technology and the improvement of human capital in order to sustain itself. Brenner's work apart, we remain a long way from being able to answer the question.

South Asia's contribution to such an answer may be to draw attention counterfactually to those factors which weaken labour's ability to resist capitalism and the ability of community institutions to resist the encroachments of an expropriatory form of state. Why were the interests of labour and of 'community' in South Asia so feeble before the rising powers of Sultanism and capitalism? The research necessary to answering this question is still in its early stages: as elsewhere in the historical universe, a discipline whose original function was to flatter the vanity and express the ideology of social elites and dominant classes has had little to say about the pasts of their victims. Indeed, in the 'Orientalist' context, those pasts were even stripped of an historical status and rendered vacuous by the concept of 'tradition'. The research that is beginning to emerge, however, points to several structural problems in the position of labour and the integrity of community institutions. A first concerns the very high degree of social differentiation permitted by and built up within many forms of community institution from the later middle ages. Although, for example, South Indian mirasi rights were conceptually shared equally between all mirasidars (thus villages were divided into a notionally fixed and unchanging numbers of shares), conventions developed from at least the eleventh century that individual families might hold more that one 'share'. Wealth became increasingly differentiated—a process further enouraged by the growth of the exchange economy from the sixteenth century, by the incorporation of new labouring groups from the poorer uplands into the developing economies of the river valleys, etc. Such substantial differentiation may be seen to have put strains on the maintenance of original communal reciprocities and obligations, not least because of the availability in South Asian culture of at least two alternative theories of privilege which secured it with less commitment to social responsibility. Brahminism took privilege to inhere in the person of its possessor by virtue of his spiritual (and bodily) mystique; Sultanism took it to inhere in the person of 'the king' by virtue of his armed power. Hardly suprisingly, many of the groups achieving greater wealth through the growth of the later medieval and early modern economies attempted the Brahminization or Sultanization (Mughalization) of their customs and values. Until military fiscalism and its final expression in Compan Raj provided an alternative political order, however, these pretensions to personal privilege could never be adequately realized. Community pressures on lineage heads and rajas, on mirasidars and inamdars, forced them to meet their obligations in order to preserve their positions in society. But as, during the eighteenth century, this alternative political order came gradually into existence, the case was progressively altered. The significance of this, from the perspective of the ability of community institutions to protect themselves, is that they were, to a considerable degree, subverted from inside. The new 'propertied' classes grew outwards from inside them as the wealthier mirasidars, merchants and zamindars latched on to royalized commercial power, through rented revenue and monopoly rights, in order to emancipate themselves from previous obligations and restrictions on their privileges. In the name of 'the state' and with its usurped powers they broke free. With subversion coming from inside, however, the collapse of community institutions was all the more complete and subtle: their own erstwhile most privileged members and leaders deserted them first, leaving resistance without authority, and then proceeded to deny the force of their claims, leaving resistance without coherent ideology. Indeed, so complete and subtle was their collapse that apologists for colonialism in South Asia were soon able to wipe broader communitarian principles of social organization, beyond the useful caste and village, off the map of South Asian history and pretend that they never had existed.[37] Those component parts of community institutions whose rights were stripped and who fell into the category of simple labour were left without a history and an identity through which they could assert themselves in anything but frustration.

With regard to the place of labour in production, even less can be surmised for even less has been researched. But two features of note have emerged from recent studies. A first concerns the implications of the hostility and instability of production conditions in many regions. Water is the key to life in South Asia and, if enough of it can be found and controlled, very high levels of production are possible. But inconstant monsoons and primitive irrigation technology long made its full potential difficult to harness. The patterns of peripatetic mobility and of extended exchange relations, which we have noted, can be understood in many ways as attempts to cope with this problem. Small-scale capital and labour were constantly on the move, looking to make the best of variations in production conditions, and extended exchange relations acted as mechanisms of insurance against localized failures. Viewed this way, and importantly, the growth of the market and the appearance of economic 'opportunity taking' in South Asia from the later middle ages may have had at least much to do with the logic of social reproduction as with that of 'the development of capitalism'.[38] Indeed, the stronger relationship between the growth of labour and commodity markets and the needs of social reproduction, rather than the accumulation of private wealth, may be gauged from the extent to which this growth was regulated by 'community institutions' enforcing mutualities between surplus appropriation and surplus production and between privilege and social responsibility.[39] But that community was reproduced through such complex machanisms of exchange and mobility made it highly vulnerable. It generated within itself both structures of wealth differentiation and, by the early modern period, attractions towards systems of exchange predicated on other social principles. Artisans were doubtless eager to take the cash of merchants connected to political rulers and foreign companies, and farmers to sell to new armies and courts, for, by extending their networks of exchange, they improved their own chances of survival. But as they became more dependent on those exchanges so they gave hostages to fortune and slowly passed under the potential control of capital and the ruler's state: their own reproduction becoming progressively more impossible without reference to the latter who, thereby, could penetrate and overturn the previous conventions of 'community' governing resource distribution. In a sense, the development of capitalism in South Asia saw labour exchanging the political rights and mutualities which it had possessed in community institutions, for a greater material stability and ability to safeguard its economic reproduction. Population increased from second quarter of the nineteenth century, sustained by an increased social product as much 'unproductive' labour was obliged to work. Much later, technological improvements in agriculture further improved prospects of survival. But, of course, the price was heavy in terms of the share of the social product which labour could command and the freedom it lost over the methods by which it socially reproduced itself.[40]

A second feature throwing light on the destiny of labour is related to the first and concerns the problem of territoriality and the state. The high degree of mobility and of exchange through which they sustained themselves meant that the institutions of community tended to be very unspecifically related to territory. They depended on exchange relations ramifying much beyond the extent of their political control and their component elements were in constant motion. This, too, made them vulnerable. The processes of military fiscalism opened out deep fissures in the political geography of South Asia as regimes sought to maximize the resources of labour, production and commerce contained in their domains and to destroy those held in the domains of their rivals. Lacking discrete territorial bases to defend and the means to defend them, many types of community institution fell prey to the pressures of the period. Disruption to the networks of commercial exchange and labour mobility, through which they secured and reproduce themselves, left them eviscerated and unable to sustain their basic material functions. Once more, in order to survive, those of their component elements who could not claim the privileges of 'private' wealth were left with few alternatives but to accept incorporation as rightless units of labour power in the structures devised by Sultanism but activated by capitalism. In the end, weaknesses and internal contradictions of the community institutions, through which it had protected its rights, may be held to account for labour's pitiful social history in South Asia—weaknesses and contradictions which, in comparison to Europe's experiences, made it less able to resist the rising forces of capitalism and the modern state and thus less able to force 'development'.

The growing interest of scholars from many different national backgrounds in the early modern and modern history of South Asia, then, can be seen to reflect the extent to which research in the latter has been coming to inform many of the wider issues currently concerning historical scholarship. Europe's rise to world dominion, the social and economic origins of capitalism, the underlying processes of industrialization and modernization, on the one side, and of underdevelopment and peasantization, on the other, all form part of its subject matter and all may gain, in the conceptualization of their problematics, from its experiences. Important, too, is South Asia's contribution to the major item on the agenda of the Western social sciences: the need to emancipate theory from its historical origins in the self-regarding and self-justifying ideology of the nineteenth-century European bourgeoisie. Indeed, it is perhaps only in the light of reflections from South Asia, Africa and other parts of the non-European world that Europe itself can come to appreciate the nature and significance of its own history.

Given the role which South Asia is capable of playing in the development of the historical discipline on many fronts, a strong case can be made for its continued support through reasearch funding. It is a case which has been made, and answered favourably, in a great many different countries of late. In Britain, however, the case is substantially stronger than anywhere else outside South Asia. Due to the accidents of history and the British Empire, some of the most important source materials for the study of South Asian history are located here in the

National Library, the India Office Library and the libraries of the University of Oxford, Cambridge and Edinburgh. Moreover, established traditions of scholarship and expertise exist in many specific fields. These source materials and traditions attract annually a large flow of scholars, research students and archivists from all over the world. It would indeed be a strange paradox if, due to denial of reasearch funding, not only were British scholars prevented from contributing to the understanding of history through work on South Asia but, even more, if they, in the context of increasing international interest, came to have less practical access to the expertise and source materials on their own doorsteps than the rest of the scholarly community.

Notes and References

1. The extremely voluminous literature published over recent years on South Asian history c. 1720-1860 makes it impossible, within the space available, either to provide a comprehensive survey or to review and critique with adequacy and justice the specific contributions of individual historians. This paper is meant merely to promote the discussion of some general issues. Consequently, I have taken the liberty to keep the references to a minimum and to use them as a general pointer towards large bodies of literature within which the general questions under discussion are raised.

2. The four major journals publishing a large amount of South Asain hisotry are: The *Indian Economic and Social History Review (IESHR); Modern Asian Studies (MAS); The Journal of Asian Studies (JAS); The Journal of Peasant Studies (JPS).* Over the last five years, South Asia-related research has also appeared in: *The Economic History Review; The Journal of Economic History; Comparative Studies in Society and History; Past and Present; the Historical Journal; Itinerario; Review; Daedalus;* etc.

3. F. Braudel, *Copitalism and Material Life,* 3 vols, London, 1973; and *Afterthoughts on Material Civilization and Capitalism,* Maryland, 1977; P.Anderson, *Passages from Antiquity to Feudalism and Lineages of the Absolutist State,* London, 1974; I. Wallerstein, *The Modern World System* 1 and 11, New York, 1974, 1980; J. Roberts, *History of the World* , London, 1976.

4. See the classic debate in M.D. Morris, *et al., The Indian Economy in the Nineteenth Century: A Symposium,* New Delhi, 1969.

5. K.N. Chaudhuri, *Trade and Civilization in the Indian Ocean,* Cambridge, 1985; A. Das Gupta, 'Indian Merchants and the Western Indian Ocean,', *MAS* 19,3 (1985); K. McPherson, 'The History of the Indian Ocean Region', *The Great Circle* 3, 1 (1981); 1. Habib and T. Raychaudhuri (eds.), *The Cambridge Economic History of India,* I, Cambridge, 1982, chs XIII (1,2); C.A. Bayly, 'South Asia in the 18th century', paper read at conference on South Asia in 18th century, University of Warwick, 1985.

6. P. Bairoch, 'International Industrialization Levels from 1750-1980', *Journal of European Economic History* 11,2 (1982); K.N. Chaudhuri, *Trade and Civilization* and *The Trading World of Asia and the English East India Company 1660-1760,* Cambridge, 1978; F. Perlin, 'Proto-industrialization and Pre-colonial South Asia', *Past and Present* 98(1983).

7. Chaudhuri, *Trade and Civilization;* Perlin, 'Proto-industrialization'; P.J. Marshall, *East India Fortunes,* Oxford, 1976; O. Prakash, 'Bullion for Goods', *IESHR* 12 (1976).

8. K.N. Chaudhuri, 'Markets and Traders in India during the Seventeenth and Eighteenth Centuries' in K.N. Chaudhuri and C. Dewey (eds), *Economy and Society,* New Delhi, 1978; C.A. Bayly, 'Indian Merchants in a Traditional Setting' in A. Hopkins and C. Dewey (eds.), *The Imperial Impact,* London, 1978; F.Perlin, 'Protoindustrialization' and 'State Formation Reconsidered', *MAS* 19, 3, 1985; K. Hall, *Trade and Society and Statecraft in the Age of the Colas,* New Delhi, 1980; B. Stein, *Peasant State and Society in Medieval South India,* New Delhi, 1980; D. Ludden, *Peasant History in South India,* Princeton, 1985; See also essays by Perlin, Stein, Mukhia, Sharma and Habib in Special Issue on 'Feudalism', *JPS* 12, 2-3 (1984-85); I. Habib, 'Potentialities of Capitalistic Development...'*Journal of Economic History* 29, I (1969).

9. A. Wink, *Land and Sovereignty in India,* Cambridge, 1986; H. Mukhia, 'Illegal Extractions from Peasants', *IESHR* 14 (1977); S. Moosvi, 'The Zamindar's Share in the Present Surplus of the Mughal Empire', *IESHR* 15 (1978); N. Dirks, 'The Structure and Meaning of Political Relations in a South Indian Little Kingdom', *Contributions to Indian Sociology* 13 (1979); Perlin, 'State Formation Reconsidered'; N. Ziegler, 'Some Notes on Rajput Loyalites during the Mughal Period' in J. Richards (ed.), *Kingship and Authority in South Asia,* Madison, 1978.

10. Moosvi, 'The Zamindar's Share'; M. Alam, 'The Zamindars and Mughal Power in the Deccan', *IESHR* 10 (1974); F. Perlin, 'Of White Whales and Countrymen', *JPS* 5 (1978); B. Stein, 'Politics, Peasants and the Deconstruction of Feudalism in Medieval India', *JPS* 12,2/3 (1985); Wink, *Land and Sovereignty;* D.Singh, 'Ijarah System in Eastern Rajasthan 1750-1800', *Proceedings of Rajasthan History Congress VI* (1973).

11. B.S. Cohan, 'Political System in 18th Century India', *Journal of the American Oriental Society* 83 (1962) and 'Structural Change in Indian Rural Society 1596-1885' in R. Frykenberg (ed.), *Land Control and Social Structure in India History,* Madison, 1969; Stein, *Peasant State;* A. Appadurai and C. Breckenridge, 'The South Indian Temple: Authority, Honour and Redistribution', *Contributions to Indian Society* 10, 2 (1976); Dirks, 'Political Authority' and 'The Pasts of a Palaiyakarrar', *JAS* 41 (1982); A. Appadurai, *Worship and Conflict,* Cambridge, 1981; K. Leonard, *The Social History of an Indian Caste,* Berkeley, 1979.

12. Leonard, *Social History;* N. Dirks, *The Hollow Crown,* Cambridge, forthcoming.

13. C.A. Bayly, *Rulers, Townsmen and Bazaars,* Cambridge, 1983; *CEHI I* (ch.11); D.Washbrook, 'Some Notes on Market Relations in South India c. 1750-1850', paper presented to workshop on Comparative Colonial History, University of Leiden, 1981.

14. S. Moosvi, 'Production, Consumption and Population in Akbar's Time', *IESHR* 10,2 (1973); I. Habib, 'Aspects of Agrarian Relations and Economy', *IESHR* 4 (1967); Bayly, *Rulers;* C.J. Baker, *An Indian Rural Economy,* Oxford, 1984; *CEHI I* IX (ch. 2); Perlin, 'Of White Whales'; Washbrook, 'Some Notes'; R.Ray, *Change in Bengal Agrarian Society 1760-1850,* New Delhi, 1979; A. Chowdhury-Lilly, *The Vagrant Peasant,* Wiesbaden, 1982.

15. B. Stein, 'State Formation and Economy Reconsidered', *MAS* 19, (1985); Bayly, *Rulers;* Athar Ali, 'The Passing of Empire', *MAS* 9, 3 (1975).

16. P. Calkins, 'The Formation of a Regionally Oriented Ruling Group in Bengal 1700-1740', *JAS* 29,4 (1970); K. Leonard, 'The Hyderabad Political System and its Participants', *JAS* 30, 3 (1971); R. Barnett, *North India Between Two Empires,*

Berkeley, 1980; Perlin, 'State Formation Reconsidered'; A. Sen, 'A Pre-British Economic Formation, in B. De (ed.), *Perspectives in the Social Science* 1, Calcutta, 1977.

17. Bayly, *Rulers;* 'Stein, State Formation'; Perlin 'Of white Whales'.

18. Perlin, 'State Formation Reconsidered'; Wink, *Land and Sovereignty;* Bayly, *Rulers;* E. Stokes, *The Peasant and the Raj,* Cambridge, 1978, ch. 2; Ludden, *Peasant History.*

19. Mukhia, 'Illegal Extortions'; R.P. Rana, 'Agrarian Revolts in North India during the Late 17th and Early 18th Centuries', *IESHR* 18 (1981); K.Rajayyan, *Administration and Society in the Carnatic 1701-1801,* Tirupati, 1966, and *The Rise and Fall of the Poligars,* Madras, 1974; Bayly, *Rulers;* Ziegler, 'Some Notes'; S. Arasaratnam, 'Weavers, Merchants and the Company', *IESHR* 17 (1980); H. Hossain, 'The Alienation of Weavers', *IESHR* 16 (1979); Ludden, *Peasant History.*

20. See M. Elvin, *The Pattern of the Chinese Past,* London, 1973, and J.Spence 'Turbulent Empire', *New York Review of Book* 16/1/86; also R.Owen, *The Middle East in the World Economy 1800-1914,* London, 1981, intro.; Athar Ali, 'The Passing'.

21. Marshall, *East India Fortunes;* Stein, 'State Fromation and Economy Reconsidered'; Barnett, *India between Two Empires; CEHI I* (ch. XIII:2); Bayly, *Rulers;* I.B.Watson, *Foundations for Empire,* New Delhi, 1980.

22. J. Pemble (intro), H. Compton, *A Particular Account of the European Military Adventurers of Hindustan from 1784 to 1803,* Karachi, 1976 reprint; D.Kolff, 'The End of an Ancien Regime: Imperialism in India 1798-1818', mimeo.

23. See E.P.Thompson, *Whigs and Hunters,* London, 1975.

24. Ludden, *Peasant History;* A.M.Khan, *The Transition in Bengal,* Cambridge, 1970. R. Guha, *A Rule of Property for Bengal,* The Hague, 1963; Stokes, *The Peasant;* Ray, *Agrarian Relations;* R. Frykenberg, 'The Silent Settlement' in R.Frykenberg (ed.), *Lond Tenure and Peasant in South Asia,* New Delhi, 1977.

25. For a penetrating discussion of the problem of 'industrialization', see R. Chandavarkar, 'Industrialization in India before 1947', *MAS* 19, 3 (1985).

26. Elvin, *The Pattern;* K.N. Chaudhuri, 'The Structure of the Indian Textile Industry in the 17th and 18th Centuries', *IESHR* 11 (1974) and *The Trading World of Asia;* Perlin, 'Proto-industialization'; I. Habib, 'Technology and Economy in Mughal India', *IESHR* 17 (1980); V. Ramaswami, 'Notes on the Textile Technology of Medieval South India', *IESHR 17 (1980);* Ludden, *Peasant History;* Bayly, *Rulers.*

27. Bayly, *Rulers;* A. Siddiqi, *Agrarian Change in a Northern Indian State,* Oxford, 1973, and 'Money and Prices in the Earlier States of Empire', *IESHR* 18(1981); A. Guha, 'Raw Cotton in Western India', *IESHR* 9(1972); D. Kumar and M. Desai (eds.), *CEHI II* (chs III:1, 3, 4);Stokes, *The Peasant.*

28. C.A. Bayly, 'Peasantisation', paper read at workshop on comparative colonial history, University of Leiden, 1985; R. Ray, 'The Crisis of Bengal Agriculture', *IESHR* 10 (1973); Guha, 'Raw Cotton'; *CHEI II* (ch. III); Baker, *A Rural Economy.*

29. *CEHI II* (chs II, III); Bayly, *Rulers;* D. Washbrook, 'Law, State and Agrarian Society in Colonial India', *MAS* 15,3 (1981); Appadurai, *Worship and Confict;* N. Dirks, 'From Little King to Landlord', *Comparative Studies in Society and History* 28, 2(1986).

30. Stokes, *The Peasant,* chs. 5-8.

31. T. Metcalf, *Land, Landlords and the British Raj*, Berkeley, 1979; B. Kling, 'Economic Foundations of the Bengal Renaissance' in R. van Baumer (ed.) *Aspects of Bengali History and Society*, Hawaii, 1975; Ludden, *Peasant History;* Washbrook, 'Law'; Appadurai, *Worship*.

32. R. Frykenberg, *Guntur District 1788-1848*, Oxford, 1965; Ludden, *Peasant History;* Stokes, *The Peasant;* Cohn, 'Structural Change'.

33. T. Metcalf, *Land;* Appadurai, *Worship;* R. Frykenberg. 'On Road and Riots in Tinnevelly', *South Asia* 4, 2 (1982); D. Washbrook, 'Ethnicity and Racism in Colonial India', in R. Ross (ed.) *Race and Colonialism*, The Hague, 1982.

34. Appadurai, *Worship;* Dirks, 'From Little King'; Baker, *Rural Economy*.

35. Dirks, 'Structure and Meaning'; B Stein, *Peasant State* and *All the King's Mana*, Madras, 1984; Perlin, 'State Formation Reconsidered'.

36. Ludden, *Peasant History;* Mukhia, 'Illegal Extortions'; Sen, 'A Pre-British Economic Formation'; Stein, 'State Formation and Economy Reconsidered'.

37. Ludden, *Peasant History;* Dirks, 'From Little King'; T. Kessinger, *Vilyatpur 1848-1968*, Berkeley, 1974; C. Dewey, 'Images of the Village Community', *MAS* 6, 3 (1972).

38. It need hardly be said that this point opens up a huge question concerning the relationship between exchange and capitalism. Braudel's conventions, by subsuming virtually all relations of exchange (or at least those mediated by money) under the label 'capitalism' may be judged teleological and certainly seem to miss the extent to which extended relations of exchange can have their roots and logic in attempts to safeguard subsistence under specific conditions. But space does not permit the pursuing of that line of inquiry here.

39. Stein, 'Peasants, Politics'.

40. The decline in the relative share of the social product going to agricultural labour is well documented for the late nineteenth century onwards: see *CEHI II* (ch.III: 4); Baker. *Rural Economy*. My own researches would suggest a decline, too, from the late 18th century.

12

Central to the policy of reform was the provision of education in Western knowledge. For the Victorian liberal nothing else, with the possible exception of the rule of law, offered such promise of success in the effort to eradicate depravity and vice from the heart of Indian culture. But when the reformers arrived upon the scene, they found already flourishing an indigenous vernacular school system and institutions of classical Arabic and Sanskrit learning patronized by a British government sympathetic to tradition. The struggle that ensued has become famed as the Anglicist-Orientalist controversy. Its resolution in 1835 set Indian education on a path it maintained to the end of British rule. In this article the British historian Percival Spear sets the controversy in the broader perspective of the social history of the time and shows how the issues have been oversimplified by an excessive preoccupation with Macaulay's Minute on Education.

Bentinck and Education
PERCIVAL SPEAR

I. MACAULAY'S "MINUTE"

The popular mind loves the dramatic and the macabre, and so it has come about that the two events of British Indian History which the man in the street is aware of are the Black Hole of Calcutta and the Great Mutiny. When there were no Mutiny horrors to contemplate, their place was taken by the legend of Tipu Sultan; even in 1831 Ram Mohan Roy was followed by crowds in London crying Tipu Tipu. It had been a misfortune for British Indian understanding that these two events seemed discreditable to India; for though Seraja-Daula is now acquitted of responsibility for the Black Hole, and the military revolt theory of the Mutiny generally prevails, the popular legend continues. The well of Cawnpore is remembered where the well of Ujnalla is forgotten.

The same misfortune has dogged the cultural understanding of India with the West. Whenever Indian education is under review, the Minute of Macaulay jumps into the mind, with its sweeping

Reprinted by permission from *The Cambridge Historical Journal,* Vol. VI, No. I (1938), pp. 78-100, with omissions.

condemnation of Oriental learning, and its disregard for Indian tradition and culture. Macaulay's estimates of Clive and Warren Hastings have been revised by later historians, but the Minute is still generally considered a landmark of English educational policy in India. It is held to have heralded, and even to have caused, the necessary victory of Western over Eastern knowledge. It is the purpose of this article not so much to praise or blame Caesar, as to bury him or rather to place his ideas in their proper perspective, first in relation to the formation of Indian Education policy, and then in relation to the social circumstances of the time.

From the moment of its composition the Minute was a Secretarial sensation; within four years large portions were made public by the zeal of Macaulay's brother-in-law Charles Trevelyan, and within thirty years it had been published in full four times. The already great reputation of Macaulay assured the Minute's notoriety in India, and later his meridian fame secured its cordial reception in England. His genius for simplifying issues, for setting the field between right and wrong, between reason and absurdity, darkness and light, was never better exhibited. But just what was its place in the educational controversy, what was its significance and what did it accomplish?

The circumstance which gave birth to Macaulay's Minute was a controversy over the proper interpretation of a clause in the Charter Act of 1813. This clause in itself was born in a controversy between the Evangelical group of Wilberforce (whose adviser on Indian matters was Charles Grant) and the advocates of non-interference in Indian customs, which began with the Charter discussions of 1793. The clause of the 1813 Act was itself a compromise, inspired partly by the Evangelical zeal for improvement and partly by the Company's knowledge that a purely negative attitude had no longer any hope of success. A via media had been suggested by Lord Minto's Minute of 6 March 1811, in which he had stressed the Indian tradition of governmental patronage of learning, and suggested that in some such patronage a hope of revival might lie. So the Charter Act of 1813 laid down that a lakh of rupees a year (or ten thousand pounds at the then rate of exchange) should be devoted to educational purposes out of any surplus of Government funds. The clause in question runs as follows:

And be it further enacted that it shall be lawful for the Governor-General-in Council to direct that out of any surplus revenue that may remain a sum of not less than one lac of rupees in each year shall be set apart and applied to the revival and improvement of literature and the encouragement of the learned Natives of India and for the introduction and promotion of a knowledge of the sciences among the inhabitants of the British Territories in India.

There are three points of notice in this clause. First, the grant of money was dependent on their being a surplus in the Company's funds; second, that the money so used was to be devoted "to the revival and improvement of literature and the encouragement of the learned Natives of India"; and third, that the promotion of European science was specially provided for. The first of these considerations provided a loophole of which Lord Hastings availed himself to escape altogether from the obligation of diverting funds to education. As his Minute of 2 October 1815 shows, Lord Hastings agreed with Minto as to the existing degradation of Indian learning, but he struck a new note (outside missionary circles) in considering that learning not to be worth reviving. But at that point the successive entanglements of the Gurkha, Pindari and Maratha wars unbalanced his budget and made it unnecessary to take any practical steps at all. Peace came and surpluses returned, but when the stately Hastings left in January 1823 the lakh of rupees was still unspent. The first positive move was made during the acting Governorship of John Adam. He set up a General Committee of Public Instruction to administer the lakh of rupees for educational purposes, and to give them a start he ordered the payment of two years arrears from 1821. To this Committee was further transferred the control of the Calcutta Madrasa, or Arabic College, founded by Warren Hastings in 1781, and of the Sanskrit College of Benaras, founded by Jonathan Duncan in 1794. Till 1823 these two colleges represented the sole contribution of the Government towards the encouragement of Indian culture.

The Committee was charged to work under the terms of the Act of 1813, and for some years they proceeded according to its spirit. New oriental colleges were opened, translations and printing were undertaken on the one hand, while English schools were encouraged, English classes opened in existing colleges, and steps towards the introduction of Western science and medicine were taken on the other. The Hindu School and College, a private institution where English was taught, was taken under its control. The general idea was to meet the demands which existed according to the means at their disposal. But by 1830 a rift had appeared among the builders of Jerusalem. Were they repairing the walls of the old, or laying the foundation of the new city? Into the ranks of the Committee was gradually introduced a younger element which thought that the old learning was mere superstition and its support the throwing of good money after bad. The older men, like H.H. Wilson, the two Prinseps and Sir W.H. Macnaghten, were mostly oriental scholars of distinction, and they maintained that the two learnings should be encouraged side by side. The division of opinion was by no means so clear cut as Macaulay's Minute would suggest. The Orientalists admitted and welcomed the demand for English teaching and the superiority of Western science over Eastern; they even rather spiritlessly admitted a superiority of Western literature over Eastern, and very curiously failed to emphasize the worth of Sanskrit philosophy or the Aristotelian element in Arabic. Some of the new school, too, admitted that Western learning could not be imposed overnight on an unwilling people. They based their case on the belief that the people wanted it, and predicted that Western education would swiftly disintegrate the whole Hindu and Muslim systems as confidently as the French philosophers of the eighteenth century predicted the fall of Christianity before the march of reason within thirty years. The point where the division became acute was not as to the *teaching* of English, but as to the educational value to be attached to it. To the new school, English was the open sesame of Western civilization, the charm to admit India to the cloud-capp'd towers and gorgeous palaces of the new science; to the older men it was mainly a utilitarian convenience for the purpose of a career. H.T. Prinsep insists again and again in his Minutes that English education was confined to the tracing of alphabets and the lisping of grammars by people who should be studying philosophy. Though this contained a grain of truth, it went against much obvious evidence and nothing annoyed the Westerners more.

A minor question, as is often the case, that of making English a compulsory subject in the Arabic College of Calcutta, finally put the match to the train of the major controversy of 1834. H.T. Prinsep in an angry Minute threatened resignation and the battle was joined. It was then found that both sides were equal in number on the Committee, while the President was the newly arrived Macaulay, who stood aloof until the controversy should be decided. Both sides therefore appealed to the Government-General-in-Council in January 1835. The Westerners stressed the value of English as a guide to the new learning, and the popular demand for it, as against the superstitions and absurdities of Sanskrit and Arabic literature. The Orientalists maintained the public demand for the old learning, and asserted (with qualifications) its value. But their main plank was the Charter Act of 1813, which enjoined the encouragement of Eastern learning as a statutory obligation.

It was at this point that Macaulay came into the picture. He had arrived in India the previous July, with an already great reputation in literature and politics, and had proceeded immediately to Ootacamund in the Nilgiri Hills, where he lived for some months with Lord William Bentinck. Here a friendship sprang up which stood him in good stead. On the strength of it Macaulay is often credited with being the driving mental force behind Bentinck's educational policy. But before accepting that conclusion there are other factors also to consider. It is true that both were men of liberal ideas, both of reforming zeal, that both disliked abstract subtlety and that both were thoroughly English. But here the resemblance ended. Lord William was a soldier and a man of action as well as a humanitarian reformer. He was a man of impluse, which in youth sometimes led to indiscretion, but in age seems to have given him just that extra tinge of resolution which enabled him to reform where others had only deplored and pitied. He was no man of letters, and once confessed that it was only with effort that he read anything. He took liberal principles as it were on trust or by instinct, and in India liberal principles meant to him humanitarianism and the preference of English methods to Indian if the two were called in question. His impluse to action, his desire to do right in the time allotted to him, sometimes cut across his respect for ancient and complicated institutions and his desire to understand their spirit. So when confronted with the educational tangle his natural impulse was to take the "common sense" view that Western knowledge was naturally desirable and that English was the obvious language in which it must be imparted.

But that was not his only consideration. One of his main labours was to economize the administration, and one of the main items of expense was the high pay of the English officials. To remedy this Bentinck introduced a higher class of Indian subordinates in both judicial and revenue branches. It was desirable that they should know English, and this provided another strong motive for the introduction of English teaching. A third motive was provided by his desire to replace Persian as the official language—a language, as was often repeated, dead to European and Indian alike. This change was effected in 1835.

Then we must note other personal influences tending in the same direction. For years Bentinck had worked with Sir Charles Metcalfe, as convinced a liberal as himself, and one who looked forward to the possibility of Indian independence as the result of Western influence. In the Calcutta Secretariat was the rising young civilian Charles Trevelyan, who had already won notice by his report on the abolition of Transit duties, and for his educational zeal. Though only a secretary, it is known that Bentinck valued his opinion in these matters. Outside the official ranks was Dr Duff, the Scotch missionary, who is also known to have influenced him.

For these reasons it must not be assumed, as has often been the case, that Bentinck was influenced by Macaulay alone, that his mind was a *tabula rasa* upon which the moving finger wrote as Macaulay willed. Advocates of this radical view should remember that Bentinck drew back from Macaulay's full programme even at the moment of passing his famous resolution of 9 March. Nor can it be maintained, I think, that Macaulay's was the *decisive* influence in an otherwise equal contest. For this to have been the case, it must be assumed that without his intervention the result might have been otherwise. Macaulay has been too much praised and too much blamed; his contribution was like the lightning flash which vividly illumines the storm and reveals the landscape, albeit in fantastic proportions and bewildering lights, but which neither directs its course nor ordains its conclusion.

It is to England rather that to India that we must look for the decisive change over in Indian educational policy. The change in the attitude to Indian education was only part of a general change in English ideas about India which took place in the first thirty years of the nineteenth century. The process of this change will be more fully considered in a later section of this paper, and here it may suffice to point out that it is in changes in England rather that in India that the cluse of this change of policy must be sought. The two sources of these ideas were, briefly, the Evangelical and the Utilitarian. Both had been influential with the Company for many years, and in Lord Grey's administration both were influential with the Government. The Utilitarian influence in India House was exercised from 1820 by James Mill, who had the preparation of many dispatches to India. His was the pen which wrote: "The great end of Government should not be to teach Hindu or Mahommedan learning, but useful learning."

By 1830 the Directors had quite lost their old respect for Indian learning and culture. They were already pressing the Government towards the use of the English language and the concept of education as the acquisition of useful knowledge. All that was needed by 1834 was an educational expert to sanction and a reformer to implement the new ideas. Macaulay and Bentinck filled the respective parts, and they were, therefore, more in the position of accessories after the fact than of the instigators of a new policy. The Evangelical influence was exercised through the Grants, the younger of whom was President of the Board of Control under Grey. Macaulay's father,too, was one of the Clapham sect.

With these considerations in mind the true significance of the Minute can be explained. It was called for by the Governor-General from Macaulay, not only as an educational expert, but quite as much as the new Law member of the Government. For the strongest argument of the Orientalists was the legal one, that the Committee was bound by the Act of 1813 to encourage Oriental learning as well as Western learning. One member of Council suggested a reference to the Directors on the interpretation of the Act—a course which would have postponed the question until after Bentinck had left India. This accounts for the form of the Minute—a preliminary and rather perfunctory consideration of the legal aspect, and a full and slashing attack upon Oriental learning. The former was the important question for the Council. The consideration was perfunctory because Macaulay knew that legally there was no case for the course he was advocating. No argument is to be found there, but merely an olympian statement of opinion that the Act of 1813 intended the exact opposite of what its words implied. Then comes the attack on Oriental learning to cover up the nakedness of the legal hand. That he himself felt this is shown by his marginal comment to the legal argument in H.T.Prinsep's "Note". He again gives no argument but merely quotes the opinion of a judge who happened to agree with the new policy. The main body of the Minute was thus in the nature of an intellectual red herring drawn across the legal track to distract attention from the absence of a legal case. He brought in the new learning to redress the balance of bad law; and he succeeded so perfectly that from that moment the legal issue was forgotten in discussion of the rights and wrongs of Arabic, Sanskrit and English.

What then was the precise result of the Minute? Tactically, it was clearly a brilliant success. It gave to Bentinck the cue for which he had been waiting, the confidence to go forward on a subject upon which he lacked the necessary intellectual though not the moral conviction. But the fact remains that it neither instigated nor dictated a new policy, nor even decided a doubtful issue. It was the shot that signalled the advance, but not the shot that decided it. It provided an ideological banner for the new policy, but it was not that new policy itself. It was the highest wave of an advancing tide which broke with the most reverberating roar; but the tide itself had its sources in the intellectual deeps of England and would in any case have submerged the sand castles of the Orientalists...

II. THE NATURE OF THE PROBLEM

Before judging the new educational policy of Bentinck it is important to understand the social, intellectual and cultural conditions upon which it was imposed. Much harm has been done by the discussion of this question as it were *in vacuo,* as if no account need to be taken of what had gone before, of the mental traditions and habits of the people. Even writers sympathetic to the Indian side of modern Indian history have tended to dismiss the Indian educational past as something not worth consideration, an affair of dust grubbing, of vain repetitions, and of learning by rote. They have, I believe, been misled by the utter simplicity of many of the arrangements of the indigenous system, which have been dismissed as beneath consideration in consequence. The West loves a sign, and when it finds no large buildings labelled "the Smith College" or "the Jones High School" it is apt to assume that there is no such thing as education in the land. Herein lies one of the most fruitful sources of misunderstanding of things Indian. The Western genius in material things may be described as constructive ingenuity, which leads to ceaseless elaboration and creates new wants by supplying them. The Indian genius in material things, on the other hand, consists in a constructive simplicity, which supplies the main wants of man in a way at once so simple and so effective that its existence is not even realized by those who are looking for the great and the mighty: it is only when compared with their Western equivalents that the extent of the achievement is clear, and those who complain that India has no material genius find nothing because they are looking for complexity when they should be looking for simplicity. The same law holds good of some of the features of Indian education.

We must beware, then, of despising the traditional content of education (as Duff and Macaulay did) because it was different from ours, or the instruments of education (as nearly everyone has done since) because they seem scanty or non-existent. We must remember that education was made for man, and that it must fit into his social and intellectual environment as well as inspire him to rise beyond it.

What then was the system as it existed up to 1830? There were the two great communities, the Hindu and the Mohammedan. Between them they had many vernaculars and three classical languages, Sanskrit, Arabic and Persian. Sanskrit and Arabic were both sanctified by religion, and contained the sacred literature of each community. Both also contained much more—in Arabic Aristotle and Plato were studied, and in Sanskrit the whole range of Hindu philosophy. Persian was the official and polite language of the upper classes, and occupied much the same position in India as French did in medieval England. It, also, possessed a large literature, from the epic of Firdausi to the wisdom of Saadi and the mysticism of Hafiz, and in prose it was rich in history from the works of Abu'l Fazl downwards. Hindu and Mohammedan culture was unprogressive and static in outlook; its purpose was to hand on the traditions of the elders rather than to develop anything new. So on one side Indian education consisted in training the repositories of the tradition, the *maulvies* and the *pundits*. On the more mundane side it had to provide the intellectual needs of the various classes of society. Standards of conduct and deportment, of elegance and taste, were provided by Persian literature, and this was the study of every gentleman in northern India at least. The learned or the devout studied Arabic and Sanskrit as well, but Persian was spoken and written in all the Durbars from Lahore to Tanjore.

The professional classes were, besides the *maulvies* and *pundits*, doctors, lawyers, clerks and the literati in general. These professions were largely, though not entirely, hereditary, and they all required a knowledge of one or other of the three classical languages. Of the three, Persian was by far the most used, and this fact was reflected in the numbers studying it. It is only when we come to the commercial classes that we reach the level of vernacular education. Here reading and writing and accounts in the local vernacular were learnt, and often a knowledge of Persian was added to give an understanding of local public business. In the rural districts the same course was followed. The landless man and the man of low caste did not aspire to any education, but the farmer or man of some substance would learn his vernacular and his smattering of Persian in order to deal with the local revenue officials.

The methods of education in all its stages were two-fold—public and domestic. The great principle of education was patronage. It was the wealthy man's religious duty to foster learning, and his privilege to cultivate it himself. So public institutions were regarded as concessions to the poor, and everyone who could, studied at home. This simple fact is of the utmost importance in estimating the extent of Indian education, and radically modifies the conclusions based on the early reports. The elementary village school often met in the house of a rich man, who engaged a teacher for his children, and allowed others to come in as well. The Mohammedan schools of learning or *Madrasas* were on so definite a basis of charity that the pupils were paid to attend; any man of position got his learning from the *maulvi* in his own home. This was substantially though not quite equally true of the Sanskrit *tols*. In general those who went to any sort of institution were those who could not afford private tuition, and all institutions of higher learning were supported either by grants of land or by private munificence. Patronage and religious duty were the keynotes of the whole system. To support learning was an act of piety, and where religion governed the whole of life it became a matter of social obligation.

This system depended upon the security which would endow the patrons with the necessary means, and upon religious belief which would supply the necessary motive. It therefore declined when the Moghul framework of government collapsed in the eighteenth century, and it failed to revive when the British took their place because they lacked the necessary motive to patronage. Government example had always been the mainspring of private patronage, and its absence hindered, though it did not entirely prevent, a revival. Much was lost through the resumption of rent-free tenures formerly devoted to the support of learning, but which during the troubles had been diverted by the incumbents for their private use. In this way a most important traditional source of governmental patronage of learning was silently cut off in the name of reform and economy. The officials of the time often mistook for immemorial custom the special conditions created by the collapse of the empire.

All authorities are agreed as to the depressed condition of the indigenous system in the early years of the century. Yet the surprising thing in the circumstances was not so much that the system was depressed, but that so much learning and general education existed in spite of lack of funds and the chill atmosphere of Government disdain.

The various reports are nearly all hostile to the classical learning, yet Adam recounts the existence of real scholars in rural Bengal, whose works he enumerates, and we have similar evidence with regard to Delhi. The greatest scholar of them all, Ram Mohan Roy, was himself a product of this system, and so was Raja Radha Kant Dev, his learned orthodox opponent. And the reports omit both the Indian states, where learning was still actively patronized, and the products of the domestic system of instruction. The underestimate was perhaps natural, for where the content of learning is despised, its quality is not likely to be fairly adjudged. The intimate friends of Warren Hastings, the intellectual circle in Calcutta, and all the assistants of the English officials, were the products of the classical system even in its depressed condition.

Elementary vernacular education was equally at a low ebb and for the same fundamental reason—lack of patronage. Yet Adam's investigation showed that without any Government support whatever, in Bengal, approximately 9 per cent of the boys between five and fifteen were at school. In Delhi territory, Metcalfe's report shows a percentage of about 10, and in the Bareilly district there was evidence showing an increase in the range of castes attending schools. When this percentage is compared with those of the present day, after a century's expenditure of energy and treasure, there is the less cause to belittle the voluntary effort of an impoverished community. Many schools and some methods were rightly condemned, as where the Koran was learnt by rote by boys who knew no Arabic, and in the Persian schools where the same method was sometimes used. But there were two directions in which criticism overshot the mark—as to method and moral content. With singular inconsistency the methods were often condemned at the very time when one of the most prevalent, under the name of Dr Bell's system, had been introduced and become popular in England. There is a constant refrain of the lack of any moral training, while at the same time it is made clear that the *Ramayana,* "The Hindu Bible of Northern india", and the *Hitopadesa* in the various vernaculars, and *Saadi* in Persian, were very general books of reading. The criticism was only justified if all Hinduism was superstitious and immoral, and that, as we shall see, was then a common view. When only the morality of Dr Smiles was looked for, its absence was identified with moral turpitude.

It was this system, anaemic from the loss of its lifeblood of partronage, which had to meet the new conditions of the British supremacy. The policy of non-interference involved no drastic change, but though indirect, the British influence was inevitably very considerable. Until the 'twenties the Western ideas and philosophy of life made little impact upon the Indian mind. Indian and European lived side by side in two mentally different worlds. But from the time of Warren Hastings the English influence increasingly modified the body of useful knowledge required by the educated Indian. Though Persian remained the official language, and its study an opening to a career, English came more and more to be a *desideratum* for an educated man. It was needed by the "banians" and "dubashes" or stewards of the English gentlemen, who often made fourtunes and purchased estates; for official assistants or "dewans" who were often men of great influence; and for all those who had made contact with Europeans. It was desirable for Bengal zamindars and for all gentry in contact with centres of administration, and it was essential for all those connected with the commercial houses of Calcutta and Madras. The Cornwallis Criminal Code made it also desirable for legal assistants and lawyers in the courts. The English dislike of foreign languages strengthened all these influences, for it is quite clear that at least from the time of Warren Hastings only a minority of Englishmen understood any Indian language thoroughly. Hence arose a demand for the teaching of English, and it was this demand (rather than a passion for western ideas) which made possible the successful launching of the Hindu College or Vidyalaya by a group of Calcutta citizens in 1817. Out of this undoubted popular demand arose a small group of whom Ram Mohan Roy was the leader, who demanded not only the teaching of English as a language, but the *content* of English education—English literature and Western science.

It now remains to complete the picture by noting the changing attitude of the English governors to things Indian, and so to the problem of Indian education, and, as its complement, the attitude of Indians to Western ideas.

It is usual to explain the English attitude on the ground that whereas they originally regarded themselves as only traders, policemen and revenue collectors, from Bentinck's time they added the idea of the public welfare to their political concepts. But this is too narrow a ground on which to explain the change. It was not merely a change of policy or a stirring of conscience, but a change in fundamental ideas, and, in consequence, of their whole attitude to India. To understand the process, the changing policy must be related to changing ideas in contemporary England.

The English attitude to India passed successively through the phases of wonder in the time of the Great Moghuls, greed, when Clive marvelled at his own moderation, to that of interest and appreciation under Warren Hastings. Himself a Persian scholar, Hastings in this aspect embodied an attitude and a school of thought which was predominant till after 1800. The attitude of these men was a reflection of the Age of Reason, brightened by a Rousseauite enthusiasm for the child of nature, with its tendency to discover that person in any civilization but the European. The Abbe Raynal, in his *Histoire des Indes,* directed attention to India, and interested people soon found evidence of what they thought ought to be there. So for a generation there was a current of genuine interest in and appreciation of things Indian with no more than philosophic disapproval of superstition and offences against natural morality. At its best it blossomed into the learned enthusiasm of Sir William Jones and the Sanskritist Colebrooke. A typical example of it is to be found in the *Memoirs* of James Forbes. At its worst it descended to an easy tolerance and justification of every abuse, as is exposed in the writings of Scott Waring.

The reforms of Cornwallis gave the first sign of change. By vigorously attacking Indian corruption and eliminating Indians from the higher official ranks, he created a gulf between the two races and a spirit of disparagement which went far to encourage already latent feelings of racial superiority. "Every native of Hindustan I verily believe," he wrote, "is corrupt." Social forces, such as the influx of English women and men of mature mind, encouraged this process, so that by 1810 we find that an attitude of criticism and disdain has replaced the former attitude of appreciation and interest. The note of disapproval was more strident, and understanding was left to lonely settlement officers like Munro or politicals like Metcalfe, Elphinstone and Palmer, who still mixed much with the Indian gentry. This attitude is reflected in the Journals of Lord Hastings and Lady Amherst, but in itself it would never have led to positive action. In England a critical attitude was fostered by the prolonged proceedings of Warren Hastings' impeachment. But the spur to action was provided, as has already been suggested, by the Evangelical and Utilitarian movements.

The influence of the former was felt first, through the Evangelical group of chaplains headed by David Brown and Henry Martyn, and the laymen Charles Grant, George Udney and Sir John Shore. India was well represented in the Clapham sect, and through Grant and Wilberforce their influence was strong both in the India House and the House of Commons. Their programme was twofold—the Government support of missions (on which they were defeated in 1793), and the suppression of inhuman practices like infanticide and suttee. The Evangelical horror of sin and idolatry was the basis of these demands, and it had two results—the honourable Evangelical record of social reform, and an unfortunate condemnation of everything Indian. Hinduism was superstitious and idolatrous, Islam was profligate, the classical literatures were immoral, and both systems were the work of the Evil One. Henry Martyn, on visiting a temple, "shivered at being in the neighbourhood of hell" and his heart "was ready to burst at the dreadful state to which the Devil had brought my poor fellow creatures." William Carey wrote that the Hindus "were literally sunk into the dregs of vice," and Dr Duff, the missionaries' leading representative in Bentinck's time, called the two religions "two of the mightiest anti-Christian systems that ever scourged the earth or shed a baleful influence upon the immortal destinies of man."

It is this condemnation of things Indian because they were "heathenish" that here concerns us. For it involved a condemnation of Indian culture, and with it, of course, its classical education. It was vigorously expressed in Grant's *Observations on India,* where he proposed a general scheme of English education which was to be a prelude to a general conversion to Christianity. Hinduism was a "fabric of error". "The true cure of darkness is the introduction of light. The Hindoos err, because they are ignorant, and their errors have never been laid before them." Dr Duff believed the same thing. English education would let in the light of reason; this would aotomatically dissolve the structures of Hinduism and Islam (both based on superstition) and so pave the way for Christianity. The Abbé Dubois, in his *Manners and Customs of the Hindus,* evinces the same severity towards Hinduism, but lacks the Evangelical optimism about conversion and improvement.

The Utilitarians reached the same practical conclusions by a different route. Hinduism and Islam were also for them superstitious structures which would collapse at the touch of reason. They also had a horror of moral abuses, being to them offences against natural religion. Bentham taught that people could be transformed by legislation, and his influence was then in its robust youth. His disciple, James Mill, has given the Utilitarian view of Indian culture in Book II of his *History of*

India. Static, degraded and unenterprising, there was no hope for India but by an infusion of Western ideas and knowledge. Mill was strategically placed in the India House, and where the fervour of Grant evoked no response, the dry light of his logic prevailed. Utilitarians and Evangelicals were thus both enthusiastic Anglicists; both saw no good in Indian culture, and both shared Macaulay's vision of "a class of person, Indian in blood and colour, but English in taste, in opinions, in morals, and in intellect."

These prevalent ideas were carried to India by the younger generation of civil servants. While the Evangelical cause found a new champion in Duff, Utilitarian influence was plainly discernible in young civilians like Charles Trevelyan. More and more emphasis was laid upon "useful knowledge" and the necessity of moral uplift. They appeared in unlikely places. William Fraser of Delhi wrote of the "ignorance and immorality" of the peasants whom Metcalfe had praised for their "manliness of character". A tone of moral reprobation, almost missionary in its severity crept into official correspondence.

It now remains to consider the Indian reaction to this English influence. At first it seemed disappointingly meagre; a Hyder, a Tipu and a Scindia thought only of battalions and European discipline, and even the Socratic curiosity of Ranjit Singh led in practice no further than to guns and horses. It was in Calcutta after 1810 that there appeared the first stirrings of an Indian response, and it is rightly associated with the Baconian intellect of Raja Ram Mohan Roy. The belief that India much assimilate Western knowledge and science in order to revive her own culture was derived from him, although it is not clear from his writings exactly how far he was prepared to go in the pruning process. There were so many obvious targets for the reformer's shafts that there was no need for him to distinguish nicely between ultimate objectives. In practice he was a convinced Anglicist, and a reformer only less drastic than Bentinck himself.

So much is common ground with all students of the period. But here a respectful caveat must be entered against the belief that there was anything like a united demand for Western culture, even in Calcutta, or even that Ram Mohan Roy's was the dominant intellectual group. Against these assertions must be set the following facts. All the contemporary authorities agree that there was a rapidly growing demand for English teaching, but they equally emphasize that this was mainly desired for its worldly advantages. Boys in the S.P.G. schools professed a great desire for English, "chiefly, however, it is to be feared, with a view to their better qualification for employment in the mercantile offices." The Reports of the General and local Committees of Education up to 1834 emphasize the demand for English teaching for its utilitarian rather than for its cultural value, and the records of the Indian-managed Hindu College, the supposed citadel of the new ideas, make this clearer still. The orthodox party were strong on the Managing Committee from the beginning, and its leader, Rajah Radha Kant Dev, was a prominent member. In 1831 Derozio, the young apostle of the new ideas, was turned out of the College on the ground of his subversive activities, which in fact were very mild. In a memorial to the Government in 1834 the managers pleaded for support on the ground of the growing demand for English in anticipation of its speedy replacement of Persian as the official language. The College was, in fact, the battleground of new and old rather than the citadel of the new: that was to be found in Ram Mohan's mansion. Even in his newly founded Brahmo Samaj the two attitudes to the West existed, which years later led to its split.

The ideas of the group were no doubt a leaven working in the lump of Bengal Hinduism, but even so their cooperation with the Westerners a was matter of policy rather than of ultimate principle. For ultimately they believed in rejuvenation rather than in replacement. Ram Mohan Roy was the most radical of them all, but the limits of his radicalism are defined both by his attitude to the *Upanishads* and in his controversies with the Serampore missionaries. The Indian Westernizing movement in Macaulay's sense sprang up later, and was a by-product of the new policy rather than a cause of it. The weight of the popular demand was for English teaching as an aid to a career, and this was the force of opinion which provided the effective support for the new educational policy.

III. THE SOLUTION OF THE PROBLEM

The decisive point of the controversy was the Resolution of 7 March 1835, which in its essential passages declared:

> His Lordship-in-Council is of opinion that the great object of the British Government ought to be the promotion of European literature and science among the natives of India, and that all funds appropriated for the purpose of education would be best employed on English education alone...

His Lordship-in-Council directs that all the funds which these reforms will leave at the disposal of the Committee, be henceforth employed in imparting to the Native population knowledge of English literature and science through the medium of the English language...

This resolution covered, of course, only the matters immediately under dispute, namely the proper use of the money allocated to education from the public funds. That money was to be used for the spread of Western knowledge taught through the medium of the English language. The new policy of the Government as a whole, which is to be found in the proceedings of the General Committee of Public Instruction, and in the Regulations of the Government, may be summarized as follows. First, the proper content of higher education was Western literature and science and to this object alone should any available funds be devoted. The classical learning of India, described in the Resolution as "a branch of learning which in the natural course of things would be superseded by more useful studies," was rejected in favour of the learning of the West, and therefore if Indians still desired to cultivate it, they must do so at their own expense. Vested interests, however, in the shape of moneys earmarked for the encouragement of Oriental learning, were respected. Next, Western literature and science were to be taught through the medium of the English language, because the classical languages were too remote from the mass of the people, and the vernaculars were too crude to be suitable vehicles for the new knowledge. Third, for administrative convenience English was to become the official language in place of Persian, and the language of record in the courts of law. Fourth, the principle of the percolation of knowledge from above to the masses was adopted, and it was therefore determined to use the available funds to encourage higher and English education rather than elementary. By these means it was anticipated that a knowledge of the English language, and of "useful knowledge" in the Western sense, would percolate from the upper to the lower classes, and that the Hindu and Mohammedan systems would be steadily undermined by the force of pure reason.

The great implication of the policy was that Indian civilization was of no value, and ripe, not for enrichment by Western knowledge, but for replacement by Western civilization. Existing institutions and ideas were respected as vested interests only and not as things of intrinsic value. Herein lay the radical departure of the new policy, for this view contrasted with that prevalent up to 1800, that Indian culture had a value of its won, worth respect, though of course it could not compare with the enlightenment of Europe. The confident expectation of the collapse of Hinduism and Islam existed not only in the minds of missionaries like Martyn and Duff, or of a newcomer like Macaulay, but was generally diffused among the younger civil servants. Thus Trevelyan wrote, "a mere acquaintance with English Literature and Science, independently of any deep theological research, is subversive of Mohammedanism and still more of Hinduism—these false religions."

A second implication was that the only possible medium for the new learning was the English language. This meant that not only the classical languages were set aside, but that the claims of the vernacular, ably championed by Brian Hodgson, were also neglected. It is true that they were not altogether ignored. Macaulay, at the end of his Minute, contemplated their later use, and indeed their enrichment by English, but the prevalent view was that they were not yet sufficiently developed to be suitable vehicles. Hodgson's argument that development *comes* from use was disregarded. A further implication was the uselessness of Persian. It was assumed that its study was entirely pragmatic, and that it would disappear when the official use of Persian was abandoned. It was nobody's interest to defend it and its case went by default....The precise way in which the new policy diverged from the Orientalists' views may now be noted. The difference with regard to the value of Indian culture was of course fundamental. With views that held Eastern learning to be compounded of falsehood, gross superstition and immorality, they were naturally indignant. But apart from this, the difference was one of degree rather than of principle. They did not oppose the introduction of Western knowledge, or the teaching of the English language. Prinsep thus defines his policy:

> the *true principle* in my opinion is that of leaving the Natives to choose their own courses of education and to encourage all equally on the part of Government, making it our business to give to them the direction to true science and good taste which the superior lights of Europe ought to enable us to bestow.

What they wanted was for the two systems to exist side by side and for the old gradually to assimilate the new by means of translations and mutual intercourse. In this they were following Burke's teaching of the paramount importance of tradition as against the new Benthamite doctrine of improving legislation....

To trace all the results of the new policy would be to follow Indian education throughout the nineteenth century. But some of its more immediate efforts may be mentioned as the basis of an assessment of its value. The first result was the depression but not the destruction of Oriental learning. It was soon evident that there was more behind Oriental studies than mere habit, superstition and material prospects, and Lord Auckland in 1839 by a characteristically English compromise gave a limited countenance to these subjects without renouncing the implications of the new policy. A corollary to this was the impression created upon the Indian mind, vague and undefined though it may have been, that the Government intended the disruption of Hinduism and Islam. This was the beginning of that mood which later innovations strengthened and crystallized into that feeling of alarm for Hindu institutions which provided the mental electricity for the pre-Mutiny atmosphere. It must be recognized that while the Government certainly intended no overt action against Hinduism, many of its officials as certainly anticipated its speedy demise, and looked forward to it with considerable complacency.

A second result was the failure of the infiltration theory. The sieve through which Western ideas were to percolate had no vernacular holes in it, with the result that the new "English-knowing" class was divided by a wall of literary pride and supposedly useful knowledge from the rest of the people. This understanding of the spirit of the West often went no further than the adoption of certain external customs, and these Western habits in turn prejudiced the mass of the population against foreign innovations. Beef-eating clubs and dreaming in English were the natural consequences of shallow imitation of an alien culture. India in general regarded the learning as a strange new letter and not a new spirit, and in consequence has not even yet absorbed the real intellectual gift of the West—the scientific spirit. English education to the great mass of students still appears to this day like a Sanskrit *mantra*— something which confers power and "success in life", but which has no relation to real enlightenment or ultimate truth.

A third result was the growth of a large English-speaking secretarial and professional class. The legal, the medical and the secretarial classes as they exist today are the result of these changes. As is well known, they imbibed English political principles even more readily than they learnt English, and it has been this class which has provided the core of the great nationalist movement. But these people belonged either to classes outside the range of Government, or to positions subordinate to Government. Ideas of independence grew up in the minds of people in dependent positions. The movement found the only leaders available—the lawyers—and so grew up that mixture of argumentativeness and lack of practicality which has both hampered and warped its natural growth. Political leaders were too often doctrinaire in their ideas and intractable in their conduct. A cloud of cross purposes and misunderstanding in consequence clouded Anglo-Indian understanding, which has not been dissipated yet. For in Indian political evolution there has been a missing link—the upper classes. Apart from a few leading families, the zamindars of Bengal, later the taluqdars of Oudh, and all the old landed aristocracy with traditions of Government service, held aloof from the new Colleges. The new education had for them neither the sanction of the old religions (as the old education had) nor the prospect of honourable Government service, since the higher posts of the Government were still monopolized by Europeans. If the language barrier prevented the new learning from filtering down from the middle to the lower classes, the barrier of pride prevented it from being drawn up from the middle to the upper classes. Apart from a small circle in Calcutta, the new learning became the clerk's "vade mecum", and as such was not good enough for the upper classes....

But, it may be said, the criticism of a hundred years after without any alternative suggestion is no more than a mournful analysis. This alternative turns on the question as to how the new policy could have been fitted into the social structure of Indian life. Assuming, as we are bound to, that there was a genuine desire to introduce the knowledge of the West into India, we may suggest that the new education policy should have been but one part of a long-term policy for placing India on a self-governing basis. This is not so fantastic as it sounds, for the idea of Indian independence as the fruit of Westernization was present to many minds at the time. Elphinstone wrote in 1823:

If care were taken to qualify the natives for the public service, and afterwards to encourage their employment, the picture would soon be reversed... it may not be too visionary to suppose a period at which they might bear to the English nearly the relation which the Chinese do to the Tartars, the Europeans retaining the government and the military power, while the natives filled a large portion of the civil stations, and many of the subordinate employments in the army.

If the country was ever to be self-governing, and Western education would certainly implant the desire even if it had existed before a self-governing class would have to be trained. The old governing class, then living in retirement and dreaming of a mythical or Moghul past, were unfit in their then condition for the task. Their outlook is revealed by their Governments in 1857. The only way to prepare them was to associate Indians with the higher rather than the lower branches of the administration, and by education to give them the outlook and standards which would make cooperation with the British possible. As Cornwallis bound the tax-gatherers by ties of self-interest to the British connexion, the whole governing class could have been bound by common ideas and the prospect of honourable Government service. If some such plan as this had been possible, India might have been self-governing fifty years ago. But there would have been this difference—that then the spirit of cooperation would have been enthusiastic, instead of, as it is today, halting and doubtful and tinged with suspicion.

13

Western education did not arouse in Indians only a desire to reform their society on a Western model. Many among them, most notably Ram Mohan Roy and his followers in the Brahmo Samaj, were attracted by the liberalism and rationalism of contemporary Europe, although even they renounced much less of their traditional heritage than has often been assumed. However, seductive as the West was, it was also harsh, aggressive, and, with schoolmasters who were often Christian missionaries as well, deeply threatening. The Hindu religion itself, with all the cultural values it enshrined, was seen to be in danger. There was an urgency, in other words, not only for reform but for defence. Yet the powerful lure of modernization remained. A Hinduism resurgent had to be a Hindusim reformed. The new values, whose Western origin could not be acknowledged, appeared under the guise of a call to return to a purer past, while the new tactics of militancy were openly drawn from the Christian armoury. This essay analyses the growth of one successful communal movement—the Arya Samaj—and shows how the Punjab provided exceptionally fertile soil for religious controversy.

Communalism in the Punjab: The Arya Samaj Contribution
KENNETH W. JONES

Few features of modern South Asian history have received more comment than communalism, its impact on the development of nationalism and its threat to the continued existence of a secular Indian state. For many supporters of Indian nationalism, communalism was the result of British machinations, of a "divide and rule" policy used to impede and, finally, to frustrate the ambitions of those who desired a free, united India. For the proponents of Pakistan, communalism was not an issue, since they premised their actions on the concept of "two nations", one Hindu and one Islamic, which both sought to establish themselves as political entities. Their world was defined by religion and

Reprinted by permission from *The Journal of Asian Studies*, Vol. XXVIII, No. I (Nov. 1968), pp. 39-54, footnotes omitted.

what others called communalism was nationalism in such a world. Communalism exists as a historic reality and a common though ambiguous and increasingly pejorative analytic concept.

In this study communalism is defined as a consciously-shared religious heritage which becomes the dominant form of identity for a given segment of society. In the South Asian experience, this identity has generally been expressed through a specific language with its own unique script. Religion, language, and script are the basic triad of self-awareness to which are fused a reinterpreted history, coupled with a new conceptualization of the world and the position of the identity group in that world. Expression of this consciousness in demands for a state, a nation which would embody the unique qualities of the religious group, mark the transition from communalism to religious nationalism.

Religious identity has persisted into the post-independence world, a world now dominated by nation states. Present forms of communalism are opposed not only to the formal governmental structure under which they exist but also to the nationalism supporting that structure. Communalism possesses the potentiality of a new nationalism, a rival ideology that may divide or destroy the state. The recently successful drive for a Punjabi Subha in India and the continual tension between Singhalese and Tamils in Ceylon attest to the vitality of contemporary communalism.

Communalism is not new, but is part of traditional South Asian civilization, modified during the nineteenth century by the dual influences of modernization and Westernization. The self-conscious aspect of communalism was heightened by new modes of communication, by the attitudes, institutions and methodology of Christian missionaries and, in part, by the dynamics of British administrative policies. The degree to which the British are responsible for the creation of a modernized communalism, the question of whether or not they practised a policy of "divide and rule" is not at issue here. Instead, we focus on the contribution of the Arya Samaj to the worsening of communal relations within a single British province, the Punjab, during the latter part of the nineteenth century. As a modernising Hindu movement the Arya Samaj exemplifies non-British forces which affected the previous structure of inter-communal relations and established patterns of religious identity.

Traditionally the Punjab has been an area of diversity unsurpassed in the remainder of the subcontinent. Three religious groups, Hindus, Muslims, and Sikhs, three languages, Hindi, Urdu and Punjabi, each with its own script, coexisted in an uneasy balance. Muslims were most prevalent in the west, Hindus in the east, and Sikhs grouped roughly in the centre, while a near balance existed with the number of Hindus and Sikhs almost equalling the number of Muslims. This population distribution, with its east-west division, gave no community a controlling position by weight of numbers or by advantageous distribution. No single group dominated politically, economically or socially, nor was there a single overriding social system. There were, instead, three separate but interconnected systems, one in each religious community. Each group possessed a complete social hierarchy, ranging from outcastes to religious and aristocratic elites. Added to this diversity were past migrations and invasions which gave the province a history of continual change unparalleled in South Asia.

The traditional varieties of religious competition and conflict in the Punjab were several: a struggle for converts introduced by the two proselytizing religions, Islam and Sikhism; political rivalry between the aristocratic elites in each community; economic tensions where class and religious differences overlapped; and periodic mob violence arising from points of tension inherent in the communal structure. The British annexation in 1849 ended one form of competition—that between the ruling aristocracies. No longer could a Nawab or Raja hope to make himself the paramount power of the province through war or intrigue; the only sphere of competition left for those who once ruled was the sterile quibbling over honours and precedence granted to each by the new political power, the British. Competition was limited to other, apparently less dangerous, spheres of activity.

Religious movements continued to develop freely and only felt the restricting hand of the government when they threatened or appeared to threaten the stability of the state. One such religious movement that directly challenged British rule was a *Jihad,* or holy war, led by Saiyad Ahmad Shahid. Originally begun as an attempt to wrest the Punjab from Sikh rule, the war continued into the eighteen sixties against the newly organized British administration. While the fighting took place on the north-western border of the Punjab, the *jihad* did not receive significant support from Punjabi Muslims but gained most of its strength from the hill tribesmen of the frontier with leadership and support from the Islamic communities of the Gangetic Plain and Bengal.

The only Punjabi religious movement suppressed by the British during the nineteenth century was the Sikh revivalist and reform sect, the Namdharis. Founded in the eighteen fifties by Balak Singh as a social reforming sect, it was not until Ram Singh assumed leadership in 1862 that it turned toward a course of potential conflict with the government. In that year Ram Singh prophesied the rebirth of Guru Gobind Singh and the establishment of a new Sikh dynasty to replace the British. Surprisingly enough, it was not this clearly political challenge of the Namdharis that produced government reaction but the results of their intense desire to protect cattle from slaughter. Veneration of the cow was characteristically a Hindu attitude and a long standing point of tension between Hindus and Muslims, who ate beef and sacrificed cows in certain religious ceremonies. The defence of kine became a major element in Namdhari ideology, and so strong was their belief that in 1871 Namdhari extremists murdered several Muslim butchers in the Amritsar and Ludhiana districts. This violent outbreak was followed in 1872 by an attempt to seize arms in the state of Malerkotla. The British responded to these acts with their own form of violence. Following the Malerkotla affair, 66 Namdharis were arrested and summarily blown from guns by the Deputy Commissioner of Ludhiana. Ram Singh was arrested and deported to Burma. Following this decisive action by the British the Namdhari movement subsided continuing to exist only as a shadow of its earlier self.

The effective suppression of both the followers of Saiyad Ahmad and those of Ram Singh, as well as the re-establishment of British power after the 1857 uprising, clearly demonstrated that direct challenges to existing authority were impossible. No religious movement commanded sufficient popular support to openly oppose the British and by the eighteen seventies religious nationalism was no longer a feasible goal. Competition between the religious communities could only proceed under the umbrella of British power and could not hope to challenge that power. Communal competition continued, as did communal violence but under new rules and an altered set of conditions.

Another feature of Punjab society was exemplified by the Namdhari movement, the pattern of casual and accidental violence arising from points of tension between the Muslim community on the one side and the Sikhs and Hindus on the other. Various forms of activity caused sporadic communal rioting. The greatest cause of such riots was the same as that which triggered the Namdhari clash with the

British government, the issue of cow-killing. The sacrifice of cows at Id, a major Muslim celebration, created periodic outbursts and, on occasion, the public sale or carrying of meat through a Hindu or Sikh section of town would produce violence. Religious festivals, particularly Holi or Muharram, were often marked by disorders and on those unlucky days when two festivals—one Muslim and one either Sikh or Hindu—would be celebrated, then rioting was almost inevitable. Hindu processions, playing music in front of a mosque, pipal trees cut to allow the passing of *tazias* on Muharram, a Brahman bull wandering into a Muslim procession, these and numerous other events created outbursts. Such occurrences, however, were accidental. They happened sporadically and seemed implicit in the nature of Punjab society.

Into this diverse province the British introduced a new element of communal conflict and competition—the Christian missionaries. In 1834 the missionaries established their first headquarters in the Punjab at Ludhiana. The Christian missionaries moved forward with each new British annexation. In 1846 mission stations were opened in Jullundur and in 1849 in Lahore. By the eighteen eighties a network of missions covered the Punjab, from Delhi north to Simla, from Ambala west to Peshawar, from Lahore south to Multan, and from Peshawar south along the border to Dera Ghazi Khan. The number of Christian converts rose rapidly from 3,912 in 1881 to over 19,000 a decade later, and by 1901 had reached nearly 38,000. While numerically conversions were insignificant, they struck at two segments of the Hindu social structure—outcastes and upper caste students attending the newly established Christian schools. The former threatened Hindu society at its weakest point. Already lost were masses of outcastes who had converted to Islam and Sikhism. The latter caused the greatest public and private concern, as it threatened the integrity of the rising Hindu elite. Western education was necessary for economic success, but carried with it the nightmare of potential conversion.

The missionaries brought both a new aggressiveness and new methods of action. They introduced the first printing press in the Punjab and along with it, the tract, the pamphlet, and the religious newspaper. Missionaries began preaching in the streets and bazaars and even took part in *shastrarths*, a form of traditional religious debate. They developed and maintained a widespread network of schools, orphanages, medical missions, and introduced the zenana mission designed to reach women and girls in the seclusion of their homes. The missionary, himself a disciplined, paid professional preacher, added a new dimension to religious propagation. In short, the Christian missionaries introduced Western institution and methods of religious competitiveness. The success of these methods in converting Indians to Christianity, plus the close ties between missionaries and the government, created in the minds of many Indian religious leaders a deep fear of the "Christian threat", a fear which became one of the major motivating forces for religious revivalism throughout the Punjab.

It is into this province, traditionally the home of conflicting communities—communities which were just beginning to adjust to the new world created by British rule, by Christian missions, and by the impact of Western concepts—that the ideology of the Arya Samaj was introduced. Swami Dayanand, a wandering ascetic from central Kathiawar in western India, proclaimed a purified and revived form of traditional Hinduism. After various attempts to achieve reform by persuading other Brahmans to accept his ideas, he turned to the literate, semi-Westernized segment of the Hindu community, and here he found significant support. In 1875 he founded the Arya Samaj (Aryan Society) in Rajkot, Gujarat, as an organizational vehicle to promote his new Hinduism. The Arya Samaj met with limited success in Gujarat and Maharashtra—widespread support came only in the north, from the Punjab and the United Provinces. Swami Dayanand arrived in Lahore on April 19, 1877, and left the province 15 months later in July, 1878. During this one trip he simplified and reorganized the basic tenets of the Samaj and founded nine local Samajes. He held public meetings, private discussions, and entered several *shastraths* (public debates) with orthodox pandits and Christian missionaries. While he met with strong and, at times, violent opposition, it was almost solely from the forces of Hindu orthodoxy. Seldom did he criticize Islam or Sikhism, as his main targets, outside of Hinduism, were the Christian missionaries. Following this trip and up to his death in 1883 there was only the beginnings of organizational and proselytizing activity by the various Arya Samaj branches.

The years immediately following the death of Dayanand saw two major changes in the Samaj: one the attraction to the movement of young Punjabis who were to lead and dominate it for the next three decades and, secondly, the development of a new interpretation of Dayanand. There men played determinant roles in creating these new trends: Pandit Guru Datt, Pandit Lekh Ram, and Lala Munshi Ram (later known as Swami Shraddhanand). Pandit Guru Datt joined the Samaj in his native Multan on June 20, 1880. A brilliant student and writer, he dominated the small group of students at the Government College, Lahore, a group which included two future Samaj leaders, Lala Lajpat Rai and Lala Hans Raj. Between 1885 when he received his M.A. and his death in 1890, Guru Datt played an increasing role in the reinterpretation of Dayanand that began after his death. In his writings and public speeches Guru Datt stressed the religious nature of Dayanand's work: for him, Dayanand was not merely a reformer but a *rishi*, or saint, on par with the sages of ancient India, while the *Satyarth Prakash (The Light of Truth)*, Dayanand's main polemical and ideological work, became a sacred text to be followed without question. In Guru Datt there was a growing emotionalism and an intense religious fervour. He turned his attention increasingly to the propagation of Aryan Samaj tenets. In 1888, he founded an *Updeshak* class to train ministers and the following year began the *Vedic Magazine* as a vehicle for publicizing his views. Guru Datt's main contribution to the Samaj was ideological. His elaboration of the Aryan conceptualization of the past counteracted Western scholarly interpretation of the Vedic period as well as orthodox views of traditional Hinduism. In addition, he carried on Dayanand's struggle with Christian missionaries and criticized Sikh leaders and Sikh ideology. Guru Datt became the leader of a devoted and worshipful group who accepted him as their spiritual guide. These disciples—socially radical and religiously militant—soon began to press for changes in both the direction and methods of the Samaj.

The second figure in this group of radicals, Lala Munshi Ram, was born in Jullunder District in 1856. Young Munshi Ram came to Lahore in 1882, to study for the law examinations, accepted Guru Datt's leadership and, in 1885, joined the Arya Samaj. Munshi Ram returned to Jullundur and became president of the local Arya Samaj. This Samaj provided him with a base of power and strength for the next two decades. Munshi Ram, like Guru Datt was a religious militant and, as such, soon experimented with new methods to promote Samaj ideology. Under Munshi Ram's leadership the Jullundur Samaj pioneered in missionary work. Money was collected through the sale of surplus grain, donated by each Arya household, *Nagar Kirtan* or street processions accompanied by devotional singing were instituted, and

Aryas, including Munshi Ram, began to travel to the surrounding villages in search of converts. At the Hindu celebration of *Dussehra* the Jullundur Samaj publicly challenged the Christian missionaries with lectures and an open display of Samaj symbols. Munshi Ram reports that "Intense propaganda was carried on there on behalf of the Arya Samaj....Even the sons of Zamindars and Sowcars who were wasting their lives in vice were moved by our lectures. The two or three Hindu boys who were attending Christian lectures also came of their own accord to our camp. That year's Christian propaganda was a distinct failure."

In 1888-1889 Munshi Ram took two important steps towards more effective propaganda of Arya Samaj ideology. He founded the *Sat Dharam Pracharak (Herald of the True Religion)*, an Urdu weekly , and toward the end of 1889 he started the Doab Updeshak Mandal (Doab Missionary Circle). Munshi Ram also advocated the use of *Shuddi*-a form of traditional purification ceremony—to reconvert Hindus from Islam or Christianity. The activities of both Guru Datt and Munshi Ram came increasingly into conflict with the more conservative members of the Samaj. The conservatives were primarily interested in the educational movement begun in 1883. By 1886 the Samaj had succeeded in opening a high school in Lahore and three years later college classes were added. This was the basis for the Dayanand Anglo-Vedic educational movement that spread throughout northern India and as far south as Maharashtra. Both "radicals" and "conservatives" participated in this movement, but gradually the Lala Hans Raj-Lajpat Rai faction gained control and the radicals found themselves gradually excluded from positions of leadership in educational affairs.

A third leader of this group of young radicals was Pandit Lekh Ram. Born in the village of Sayydpur in the district of Jhelum, educated there and later in Rawalpindi, he did not share in the Western education that was typical of most Samaj leaders, nor did he travel to Lahore and partake of the new culture developing in that city. He became interested in the Arya Samaj while living in Peshawar and in 1880 travelled to Ajmer to meet Dayanand. Bold, aggressive, outspoken, Lekh Ram knew both Persian and Arabic which he used with deadly effect in his later career. Unlike Dayanand or Guru Datt, his prime opponent was not orthodox Hinduism or Christianity, but Islam. Growing up in a Muslim area and serving under Muslim officers in the police, Lekh Ram reacted by becoming self-consciously and militantly Hindu. From the beginning he entered into activities which were either directly or indirectly anti-Muslim. When he joined the Samaj in 1880 he took up three causes: (1) cow protection (2) the advocacy of Hindi as a medium of instruction for government schools, and, (3) anti-Ahmadiya propaganda. In 1884 he left the police service in order to devote his full time to the Samaj, and soon afterward he came into conflict with Mirza Ghulam Ahmad, founder of the Ahmadiyas.

The Ahmadiya movement has many close parallels with the Arya Samaj. It too was concerned with modernizing and reinterpreting a religious tradition, this time Islam, and it too became involved in serious competition with orthodox Islam, with the Christian missionaries and with a variety of reformist societies in all three religious communities. Mirza Ghulam Ahmad proclaimed himself both the Mahdi of Islam and the Messiah of Christianity. He began to proselytize in 1879 but did not become prominent until the later eighteen eighties. It was inevitable that an aggressive Islamic movement would clash severely with both Christians and Aryas, but the struggle that developed between Lekh Ram and Mirza Ghulam took a personal quality that went beyond ideological animosity. Their conflict took the form of a pamphlet war, a war maintained with increasing violence until Lekh Ram's death in 1897. In 1885 Lekh Ram visited Qadian, the home of the Ahmadiya movement. Here he preached publicly against the Ahmadiyas and managed to found a branch of the Arya Samaj. In 1887 he accepted the editorship of the Urdu paper, the *Arya Gazette* published in Ferozepore. For two years he remained as editor and during this period became known throughout the Arya Samaj for his writings as a combative exponent of Arya tenets.

By 1888 the militant wing of the Arya Samaj intensified its criticism of the three great enemies: the "Kernanis", "Kuranis", and— "Puranis", Christians, Muslims and orthodox Hindus. In addition, there was considerable anti-Sikh agitation throughout the late eighteen eighties. Pandit Guru Datt chose the eleventh anniversary celebration of the Lahore Samaj to publicly attack Sikhism. His speech met with approval of the majority, but resulted in immediate loss of Sikh support for the Arya Samaj. Bhai Jawahi Singh, Vice President of the Lahore Samaj, Bhai Dit Singh Gyani and Bhai Maya Singh left and later joined the Singh Sabha movement. Competition between the Arya Samaj and Singh Sabhas for the commitment of Sikh intellectuals developed and is reminiscent of the earlier struggle between the Brahmo Samaj and the

Arya Samaj. In 1889 Radha Kishen, a prominent Arya, published *Granthiphobia*, a highly critical review of Sikhism, while Lekh Ram and Guru Datt continued these attacks, using the newspapers they controlled as effective means of expression. Street preaching, in which the Sikh Gurus were denounced as "illiterate, self-conceited and hypocritical", did much to embitter relations between Aryas and Sikhs. Yet in the later years there was often close cooperation between Sikh and Arya organisations and the total picture of Sikh-Arya relations, as with the problem of overall relations between Sikhs and Hindus, is still unclear; however, relations between Aryas and other groups were quite explicit.

The eighteen eighties saw a gradual worsening of relations between Hindus and Muslims, between Aryas and non-Aryas. Modern methods of communication and organization, coupled with rising literacy, created an increased potentiality for ideological debate. The printing press became a major weapon of religious controversy. Books, pamphlets and periodicals appeared in a widening stream which carried in it the rising consciousness of communal identity. The Arya Samaj participated in this revolution of communications. Aryas founded a series of newspapers, as did their opponents. Samaj missionaries and volunteers proclaimed the new gospel in the cities and towns of the province. They preached in the bazaars and on street corners, marched with songs and banners throughout towns and cities, and publicly debated with their critics at religious fairs wherever they were held. Arya aggressiveness met with opposition from protective associations of Muslims, orthodox Hindus and Sikhs, as well as from aggressive sects, such as the Dev Samaj, and the Ahmadiyas.

During the period from 1889 to 1891 the Samaj, led by Munshi Ram, began to consider using a new type of institution, *shuddhi,* or purification. In its earliest forms *shuddhi* was aimed at reconverting Hindus from either Christianity or Islam. Later it was broadened to include the conversion of non-Hindus and even those whose ancestors had never been Hindu. Also, it was used as an institution for caste reform. Outcaste groups could, through *shuddhi*, be purified and raised to the level of the twice-born, or pure caste Hindus. Although earlier cases of *shuddhi* occurred, it was not until 1891 that regular reports began to appear. At this time the institution was still new and no standard ceremony had been created. Many of the more conservative leaders within the Samaj were reluctant to sponsor *shuddhis,* and many in the Samaj itself felt too insecure to challenge the orthodox community. By 1893, the Samaj showed a new confidence and dared in one *shuddhi* ceremony to have the newly purified Hindu distribute sweets which were accepted by all present. By this time the Samaj was cooperating with the Singh Sabhas in the performance of *shuddhi* ceremonies.

The growing militancy apparent in Samaj relations with other organizations was echoed by growing strain within the Arya Samaj, between those who advocated this militancy and those who were more concerned with education, who were less emotional and less religious about the whole Samaj programme. In 1888 the two groups clashed over the presidency of the new Dayanand Anglo-Vedic College. At this time the conservatives, led by Lala Sain Das, Lala Hans Raj and Lala Lajpat Rai, won—but the Guru Datt-Munshi Ram faction continued to advocate their own programme. This internal competition subsided somewhat with the death of Guru Datt in 1890 but was revived again as Lala Munshi Ram took the position of leadership left vacant on Guru Datt's death. Tensions within the Samaj broke into an open struggle for power in 1893, with the conservative wing retaining control over the college movement, its organizational structure and physical assets, while the radicals, led by Lala Munshi Ram and Pandit Lekh Ram, captured the provincial organization, the Ayra Pratinidhi Sabha of the Punjab, and a majority of the local Samaj branches.

With this split two important developments took place. First, the radical wing was freed to follow their own policies and was no longer restrained by the more conservative elements, elements now almost solely concerned with the Dayanand Anglo-Vedic College movement. Second, the radicals, after deciding to end their support of the college, needed to find new avenues of activity. They came out of the contest with an organization but no cause to take up the energies and resources of that organization. As victors, they possessed an organization without a cause, resources without goals. The resulting vacuum was filled by *Ved Prachar,* the preaching of the Vedas, and missionary work replaced education as the major goal of the radicals. In June 1894 the Arya Pratinidhi Sabha, now under radical control officially, decided to cease supporting the Dayanand Anglo-Vedic College movement. A *Ved Prachar* committee and fund were begun. The casual sending of *updeshaks* (missionaries) was now organized and put on a systematic basis. By 1895-1896 the entire province, plus Sind and Baluchistan, had been divided into Mandals (Circles) with an officer-in-charge and paid ministers for each circle. Every *updeshak* was expected to make a ten-month circuit of his *mandal,* visiting all towns and cities in it. The officer-in-charge reported to the Arya Pratinidhi Sabha which places were visited and when. It was the duty of the ministers to aid the local Samajes and particularly to be available to refute and hold public discussions with missionaries of other religions. Also, he was to aid in performing *shuddhi* ceremonies, since some of the smaller Samajes did not have the resources of confidence to engage in this activity.

This system was difficult to maintain, and the elaborate organizational structure created by Samaj planners was never fully translated into reality. Thirty full-time ministers were needed, plus extensive funds and supporting activities. While the ideal number of missionaries could not be found, the Samaj did provide a core of professionals whose effectiveness was argumented by considerable volunteer and part-time work. Money was collected for the Ved Prachar Fund, using the skill and sophistication developed previously in the Dayanand Anglo-Vedic College movement. The radicals opened a central tract department to supply Arya missionaries with a wide variety of literature, adopting successfully the patterns of organization introduced by the Christian mission. Although few in number, the Samaj missionaries spread throughout the province. They toured branch societies, appeared at religious fairs, participated in public debates, and preached in bazaars and in the streets, providing an expertise and presence that greatly strengthened the entire sphere of Arya activities.

The emphasis on proselytizing resulted in the establishment of new branch samajes and in the rise of the number of *shuddhis* performed. With the division of the Arya Samaj the debate over *shuddhi* had ended and, after 1893, reconversion became one of the major activities of the radical wing. The Aryas were not alone in their desire to protect themselves from Christian and Islamic campaigns of conversion. Allies appeared from within the Sikh community. During the early eighteen nineties a Shuddhi Sabha had been founded in Lahore by both Sikhs and Aryas. This organization, along with the Samaj and the Singh Sabhas, performed a growing number of purifications. The Lahore *Tribune* reported two *shuddhis* in 1891 and two in 1892. The number rose slowly to nine in 1894, 14 in 1895, and then to 226 in 1896. The sudden increase in 1896 grew out of the change from individual to group reconversions. The Shuddhi Sabha of Lahore purified several small groups, five in March, six in April, and nine in June. Then in August it took the radical step of purifying a family of over two hundred outcaste Sikhs. Henceforth Shuddhi functioned both as a weapon of conversion and a method of social reform. Because the Shuddhi Sabha and the Singh Sabhas were largely under Sikh control, the Arya Samaj lessened its cooperation with time. More and more the Samaj acted on its own in an attempt to insure that the reconverted would themselves become Samaj members.

Growing Samaj independence within the *shuddhi* movement contributed to rising Sikh self-consciousness. In 1900 the Arya Samaj purified a group of outcaste Rahtia Sikhs and as part of the ceremony shaved their heads and beards, transforming them into pure caste Hindus. Many in the Sikh community now saw Aryan reconversion as a direct threat, potentially as dangerous as Christian or Islamic conversion. Disillusionment with the Arya Samaj paralleled Sikh questioning of their identity vis-a-vis Hinduism. Beginning in 1897 letters appeared in the Lahore *Tribune* which raised the question of "Are Sikhs Hindus?" A public debate ensued which generated a series of books, pamphlets and letters supporting a wide variety of opinions on Sikh-Hindu relations. No consensus was reached, but by 1900 Sikhs were less and less willing to class themselves automatically with the Hindu community.

The *shuddhi* movement acted on relations between Hindus and Muslims, not to clarify overlapping identities, as with Hindus and Sikhs, but to reinforce existing communal separatism. The record of individual *shuddhis* illustrates a preponderance of reconversions from Islam. In 1893 thirteen were reconverted from Islam, two from Christianity. As Samaj attention focussed on the purification of outcastes a vast section of the Islamic community became available for proselytization and reconversion. The rising radicalism of the Samaj, plus its growing organizational strength, combined to turn Arya against Muslim, and to reinforce existing communal divisions.

The Arya contributions to the worsening of inter-communal relations can be illustrated best by Pandit Lekh Ram's career as a militant defender of the new Aryan faith. Beginning with a strongly anti-Muslim bias, Lekh Ram made a career of his prejudice. During his life he wrote 32 books and pamphlets on religious subjects, many of which were violently critical of Islam. Examples can be seen in his *Takzib-e-Burahin Ahmadiya (Refutation of the Ahmadiya Arguments)*;

Volume I subtitled "A Gun-fire to break the flanks and tyranny of Mohammad's Islam." *Takzib-e-Burahin* was published in response to a book authored by Mirza Ghulam Ahmad, and was the beginning of a lengthy pamphlet debate between the two religious leaders. Lekh Ram also wrote *Nuskha-e-Khabt-e-Ahmadiya (A Prescription for the Madness of Ahmadiyas), Radd-e-Khilaat-e-Islam (Rejection of the Islamic Robe of Honour), Ibtal-e-Bashart Ahmadiya (Refutation of Ahmadiya Statements),* and his most famous anti-Islamic work, *Jihad or the Basis of Mohammadi Religion.* In *Jihad* Lekh Ram maintained that Islam was a religion of violence and tyranny, which engaged in holy war only as an excuse for the seizure of booty, women, children and slaves. He traced the rise of Islam throughout the world and particularly in India, seeing it as a bloody tale of slaughter and destruction.

The activities of Lekh Ram outraged all segments of the Muslim community—orthodox, Ahmadiya, and reform. He was threatened with law suits by Muslims from Bombay and Lahore, and was attacked in Muslim, Sikh and Christian newspapers. He was accused again and again of using insulting and vile language in referring to Islam. The threat of legal action and public criticisms of Lekh Ram did not intimidate him and in 1896 a court case lodged against him by several Muslims was dismissed. There appeared no legal way of silencing his constant attacks, but one method did bring an end to his career, violence; on March 6, 1897, while staying in Lahore, Pandit Lekh Ram was assassinated.

The next few months saw the welling up of hatreds and fears usually hidden below the surface of normal life. Within three days of Lekh Ram's assassination, Lala Rala Ram, an Arya Samaj leader in Peshawar, was reported murdered. Rumors spread throughout the province that all leading Aryas would be assassinated and that Muslims were conspiring to kill Sikh and Hindu leaders of the Shuddhi Sabha. Reports from both the Hindu and Muslim communities exacerbated the tense situation. Mirza Ghulam Ahmad, who had predicted that Lekh Ram would die a sudden death, was stated to be jubilant over the fulfilment of his prophecy. Rumours of impending Hindu revenge spread rapidly and were accompanied by instances of violence. On March 27, a Muslim meeting hall was burnt, Muslim editors were threatened and a growing number of poisoning cases reported, usually poisoning of Muslims by Hindu food vendors. Both communities urged their members to cut all economic relations with the opposing community. There was a sudden rending of the social fabric by a deliberate move toward communal independence and self-sufficiency.

Within three months, the more violent passions had quieted and on the surface life returned once more to its normal channels. Yet the assassination was not forgotten. Rumors continued and in November, when Lekh Ram's assassin was supposedly arrested, signs of unrest returned in an aftershock to the earlier quake. For the Samaj and particularly the radical section, Lekh Ram was a martyr. He was the latest in a long list of Hindus who had fallen fighting the arch enemy, Islam. His memory was revered and his communal aggressiveness carefully maintained. The legacy of Pandit Lekh Ram left a permanent anti-Muslim bias in the Arya Samaj, a bias that was to find added justification in the coming years. The Arya-Muslim clashes of the eighteen eighties and eighteen nineties were seen, in retrospect, as forerunners of the Hindu-Muslim struggles of the twentieth century. The divisions within British India that were stimulated in part by Arya Samaj activity returned to legitimize Samaj attitudes underlying those same divisions. Because the Arya Samaj helped to set Hindus against Muslims, later Hindu-Muslim rivalry proved the correctness of Aryan attitudes. The spiral of growing communal tension had begun and once in existence tended to feed on itself.

The Arya Samaj contribution to this climate of communalism was immense and varied. The Samaj provided an ideology of militant Hinduism that had a wide appeal to Punjabi Hindus. As a minority community who, in the past, experienced Muslim and Sikh rule and who suffered from the effects of proselytization by Muslims, Sikhs and Christians, Punjabi Hindus needed a new ideology to unify and defend their community. The aggressive stance of the Arya Samaj, its insistence on the unique and superior qualities of Hinduism, and its willingness to do battle for acceptance of these claims provided such an ideology. The Samaj differed sharply in these qualities from the syncretistic and overtly Western Brahmo Samaj, a difference which accounts for the rapid decline of the Punjabi Brahmo Samaj after 1877.

Building on the techniques of Christian missionaries, of the Brahmo Samaj, and on elements of traditional culture, the Arya Samaj added a new and extremely significant dimension to the Hindu religion. Hinduism became a *pracharak-dharm*, a conversion religion. No longer did the Hindu community face threats of conversion empty handed. *Shuddhi* provided the capacity for defence and offence. Aryan efforts to proselytize, convert, educate and reform were supported by a variety of modern and traditional techniques. Contemporary forms of communications, sophisticated methods of fund raising and organization enabled the Samaj to effectively mobilize support for its programmes. The Samaj stood boldly in defence of Hinduism, but only in its Aryan reinterpretation.

The initial Samaj impact on the Hindu community was divisive, pitting militant reformers against the orthodoxy. But with the increasing polarization of the Indian world between Hindus and Muslims, the Samaj moved closer to its past enemies. *Shuddhi* received tacit approval of the pandits, Samaj insistence on the glories of *Arya Bhasha* (Hindi) and *Ved Bhasha* (Sanskrit) was echoed by leading orthodox figures, while many of the reforms demanded by Aryas were in later years accepted. Writing in 1939, Ganga Prasad, a leading Arya, commented that, "Forty years ago the Arya Samaj was looked upon as a great defiler of the Hindu religion by bringing in an alloy from outside. Today the Arya Samajist is counted as a great defender of the faith." With the blending of Aryas and orthodox, the forces of Hindu communalism possessed a modernized identity based on a reinterpreted tradition. This new consciousness possessed a variety of techniques to defend and maintain itself from external challenges. The concepts and forms that appealed to a defensive Hindu minority of the Punjab found acceptance throughout much of north India among both reform and orthodox-minded Hindus who shared a similar Islamic past and Christian present.

While Arya Samaj ideology and techniques were exported from the Punjab, within that province communal identity was greatly strengthened by Samaj activities. By the eighteen nineties, the Punjab possessed an impressive array of societies, sects, and organizations— Hindu, Muslim, and Sikh—orthodox, heterodox, and reform, each with its own ideology and programme, each caught up in a struggle with one or more opponents. These organizations were fully equipped with newspapers, tracts and ministers to publicize their programmes, to seek converts, and to condemn their opponents. Modern communications and organizational techniques had been widely accepted and, with this acceptance, came a hardening of religious divisions. Doctrinaire controversy rapidly increased throughout the province.

The three major communities exhibited a growing insistence on their "rights", such as the "right" to kill cows or to play music anywhere at any time. Activities in the past which had sporadically resulted in violence were now openly practised and even flaunted before the opposing community. Offence was intended and was taken. Converts and reconverts represented victories over an opponent and each was celebrated with due publicity. This attitude of provocation and retaliation resulted in a steady rise in communal violence and, by 1897, the divisions between Hindus and Muslims had hardened. Patterns of conflict became institutionalized; provocation produced set responses. What had been implicit in the nature of Punjab society now became explicit. Tensions might increase or decrease, but beneath the surface fears, suspicions and hatreds remained. The existent divisions of Punjab society between religion, language, and script were deepened. By 1900 communalism became the dominant form of identity in Punjab. This does not mean that one form of identity dominated a religious community, that all Hindus were Aryas, or all Muslims Ahmadiyas, but that in one form or another religious identification tended to receive greater loyalty than any type of secular identity. The resulting religious competition so pre-empted the consciousness and energy of Punjabis that external issues received little attention and little commitment. Religious identity dominated and Punjabis became lost in a world of their own creation, emerging only when an overriding national issue penetrated their communal consciousness.

14

*Among Muslims accommodation to the new colonial order involved
at once a re-valuation of their own heritage as Muslims and the
creation of new institutions. Among the latter were not only schools
that taught Western knowledge, such as the famous Aligarh
College, but others that taught traditional subjects in new ways to
fit their students for the new world of colonial India. In the process
these schools, by enhancing a shared sense of Muslim identity
among a wide circle of students and supporters, laid the foundation
for the growth of Muslim political consciousness in the twentieth
century.*

The Madrasa at Deoband:
A Model for Religious Education in
Modern India

BARBARA METCALF

A recent conference of specialists on the study of Muslims in South
Asia identified as one of the neglected areas of their field the study of
traditional religious institutions in the modern period. Such institutions
as the sufi orders, the religious schools, and the system of pious
endowments have been treated, if at all, only in their relation to political
developments. Thus the leading theological academy of modern India,
the Dar ul 'Ulum of Deoband, has been studied because many of its
ulama played an important role in nationalist politics in India and
opposed the foundation of Pakistan. That motive for study has seriously
distorted the treatment of the nineteenth-century history of the school,
endowing it with an anti-British and revolutionary character when, in
fact, the school's concerns were totally a-political. An investigation of
the early history of the school suggests many other significant historical
themes, notably an important incipient trend towards a formal
bureaucratization of the ulama and their institutions. Studies of
religious institutions outside India such as Gilsenan's study of the
Hamidiya Shadhiliya order in modern Egypt and Roff's study of the
Majlis Ugama in Malaysia suggest that successful functioning in the

modern period has required such a transformation in organizational structure. This article describes the organization of Deoband in its initial decades.

THE ORGANIZATION OF DEOBAND

The madrasa at Deoband began modestly in 1867 in an old mosque, the Chatta Masjid, under a spreading pomegranate tree which still stands. The first teacher and the first pupil, in a coincidence deemed auspicious, were both named Mahmud: Mulla Mahmud, the teacher, and Mahmud Husan, the pupil, who was later to become the school's most famous teacher. Despite the timeless atmosphere surrounding its inauguration, however, the school from its inception was unlike earlier madrasas. The founders emulated the British bureaucratic style for educational institutions instead of the informal familial pattern of schools then prevalent in India. The school was, in fact, so unusual that the annual printed report, itself an innovation, made continuing efforts to explain the organization of the novel system. The school was, notably, a distinct institution, not an adjunct to a mosque or home. As soon as possible, it acquired classrooms and a central library. It was run by a professional staff and its students were admitted for a fixed course of study and required to take examinations for which due prizes were awarded at a yearly public convocation. A series of affiliated colleges was even set up, many ultimately staffed by the school's own graduates and their students examined by visiting Deobandis. Financially, the school was wholly dependent on public contributions, mostly in the form of annual pledges, not on fixed holdings of *waqf*, pious endowments contributed by noble patrons.

In older schools, like the famous Farangi Mahall in Lucknow, family members taught students in their own homes: there was not central library, no course required of each student, no series of examinations. After a student had read a certain book with his teacher, he would receive a certificate, a *sanad*, testifying to his accomplishment, then seek another teacher or return home. The Farangi Mahall family depended primarily on revenue from their endowments and on the largesse of princes. The ulama of the school cultivated intellectual interests and trained students to become government servants. The Deobandi ulama, in contrast, sought to create a body of religious leaders able to serve the daily legal and spiritual needs of their fellow Muslims apart from government ties.

The structure of the school encouraged the effective pursuit of such a goal and the opportunity for influence over a wide geographic area. The founders had seen the efficiency of a variety of British institutions in pursuing specific goals. Many of them, including three Deputy Inspectors of the Education Department, were government servants; some had attended schools like the Delhi College; and now all confronted with concern the influential missionary societies. In dealing with these institutions, they learned their methods and chose to compete with them on equivalent terms. They were familiar as well with a system of formal structure from the days of the Mughals. Then, however, the court had provided a framework of patronage and responsibility for the judical and educational work of the ulama. Now the ulama had to create a structure themselves. In doing so successfully, they laid a foundation for effective influence in a modern society. The school produced ulama, recruited from a widespread area, who disseminated a uniform religious ideology to many Muslims who welcomed teachings that emphasized common bonds among Muslims rather than local ones.

In setting up the school on a formal basis, the founders faced two critical problems: the definition of a rationale for relations among members and the establishment of a secure system of financing. One of the leading founders, Maulana Muhammad Qasim, enunciated eight fundamental principles dealing with these issues for the guidance of the initial members of the school. The relations of those associated with the school called for special attention since the school was not in the hands of a single family, subject to the understood and accepted norms of kin behaviour. The personnel consisted of the teaching staff, the administrators, and a consultative council. The staff comprised about a dozen members, ranked by learning with the entire Arabic faculty given precedence over the Persian. There were three administrators: the *sarparast*, the rector, the patron and guide of the institution; the *mohtamim*, the chancellor, the chief administrative officer; and the *sadr modarris*, the chief teacher or principal, the person responsible for instruction. In 1892 a fourth administrator, the *mufti*, was added to supervise the dispensation of judicial opinions on behalf of the school. The consultative council was composed of the administrators and seven additional members.

The rules called on all to subordinate personal interests in striving for common goals. Members were to demonstrate openness and tolerance in dealing with each other, engaging in mutual consultation not on the basis of position but on that of the value of their ideas. The principles were as follows:

> The councillors of the madrasa should always keep in mind its well-being. There should be no rigidity of views, and for this reason it is important that they never hesitate to express an opinion and that listeners hear it with an open mind. So...if we understand another's idea [to be better], even if it is against us, we will accept it wholly....For this same reason it is necessary that the *mohtamim* always seek advice of councillors, whether those who are the permanent councillors of the madrasa or others who possess wisdom and understanding and are well-wishers of the school...Let no individual be unhappy if on a certain occasion he is not asked for advice...If, however, the *mohtamim* asks no one, all the councillors should object.

> It is essential that the teachers of the madrasa be in accord and, unlike the worldly ulama, not be selfish and intolerant of others.

> Instruction should be that already agreed on, or later agreed on by consultation...

The last principle was particularly significant, asking the teachers to forego individual inclinations in the interest of a common programme.

Rafi ud-Din, *mohtamim* from 1872 to 1889, further formalized Muhammad Qasim's guidelines for the institution by giving precedence to the council over staff and administration. He insisted that grievances be presented to the council directly. Moreover, he urged that the power of the *mohtamim* be limited by curtailing the amount of money available for use at his discretion. In 1887 he wrote: "All decisions are made by the consultative council. Even I, though the *mohtamim*, present here in the school for twenty years, will be removed if they see fit." By having the council so central, the school was freed of both instability and personal whim. No one person either by virtue of his administrative position or by his seniority within the family, was to dominate the school.

A second cluster of principles dealt with the new system of financing. The system arose in part because the founders had no option but to find an alternative to the increasingly insecure princely grants. Muslim princes of states like Hyderabad, Bhopal and Rampur did, to be sure, patronize learning and extend their bounty across the border to their fellows in British India. Large landlords in an area like the United Provinces did dispense some of their wealth for religious causes. But such contributions could never be as substantial as those of the days of Mughal rule, nor could they be as certain in a period of economic, social, and administrative flux. Nor were the ulama willing to accept British grants-in-aid, for such help was precarious and carried as well the taint of its non-Muslim source. Therefore, the Deobandis solicited annual pledges from their supporters, a method learned from missionary associations. The system was complex, requiring careful records and dependent on the new facilities of postal service, money orders, and even the printing press. Thanks to the last, the annual proceedings were able to publish widely the list of donors who thus received recognition for their generosity. The donors were listed in the order of the size of their gift, but even the humblest contributor was included. The Deobandis also encouraged single gifts in both cash and kind. Especially in the early days of the school people donated books, food for the students, and household items to furnish the school. Groups of people also organized collections of hides of animals left from the Id sacrifice, selling them and sending the proceeds to the school. People were encouraged to designate their contributions as *zakat*, the obligatory alms which in other eras was collected by the state. The resultant network of donors formed a base not only for financial support but for dissemination of Deobandi teachings.

Five of Muhammad Qasim's eight principles dealt with this new financial arrangement. They stressed the obligation of all associated with the school to encourage donations of cash and food. They also pointed out the spiritual advantage of poverty in fostering unity by drawing the personnel of the school together.

First, the workers of the madrasa should, as best they can, keep in view the increase of donations; and should encourage others to share this same concern..

The well-wishers of the madrasa should always make efforts to secure the provision of food for the students, indeed, they should try to increase the food.

As long as the madrasa has no fixed sources of income, it will, God willing, operate as desired. And if it gains any fixed income, like *jagir* holdings, factories, trading interests or pledges from nobles, then the madrasa will lose the fear and hope which inspire submission to God and will lose His hidden help. Disputes will begin among the workers. In matters of income and buildings.. let there be a sort of deprivation.

The participation of government and wealthy is harmful.

The contributions of those who expect no fame from their gifts is a source of blessing. The honesty of such contributors is a source of stability.

In fact, many wealthy people were among the donors and many, no doubt, did expect and receive recognition in return. Still, the system of popular support was effective, both financially and symbolically, and became a model for new religious schools. Other schools, like Farangi Mahall, which clung to support from landed wealth, have in part for this reason disappeared.

The formal organization of the school was supplemented by associational ties of origin, family, and educational experience. Such ties were not incompatible with a formal system, for in India informal patronage and apprenticeship were characteristic of both the Mughal and the British bureaucracy at least until the end of the nineteenth century. The formal organization of posts does not wholly reveal the lines of influence at Deoband.

The two dominant figures in the school's first decades were Muhammad Qasim and Rashid Ahmad, both of leading *shaikh* families of the area, sometime students together in Delhi, and common disciples of Hajji Imdadullah in the Chisht order. Muhammad Qasim was *sarparast* until his death in 1879, but shunned an active administrative role for fear of tainting the school's reputation because of his participation in the Mutiny. For the first three years of the school, he did not even come to Deoband but stayed at his printing work in Meerut. None the less his influence was central. Rafi ud-Din, the *mohtamim*, said: "There was such closeness between Muhammad Qasim and myself that whatever was in his heart, I knew....I did what was revealed to him." Rashid Ahmad did not initially hold any formal post but was absent in Gangoh, occupied as sufi shaikh, teacher of hadith, and jurist. However, he, too, was a great force in organizing and shaping the school.

A special bond existed between many because of common allegiance to a sufi order, particularly so for the many who were disciples of Imdadullah. In general, allegiance to the Chisht order predominated at the school. Moreover, most were *shaikh* in family and many closely related to each other. Muhammad Yaqub Nanautawi, the first principal (1867-96)and Zulfaqar Ali, Deputy Inspector in the Education Department and a member of the council for forty years, were brothers and cousins of Muhammad Qasim. Muhammad Munir Nanautawi, who served as *mohtamim* for one year, 1894-5, was also a cousin of this family, as was Mahtab Ali, a resident, a ra'is and scholar of Deoband descended from the Mughal diwan Shaikh Lutfullah was also a member of the council. His sister was married to Muhammad Qasim and he himself married Qasim's elder sister in order to set an example of widow remarriage. Fazl-i Haqq, a member of the council and briefly *mohtamim,* was a cousin of Saiyid Abid Husain, a revered elder of Deoband and the first *mohtamim.* In a society where family and clan were so important, such relationships among members of a common enterprise were typical. At Deoband, however, they were to give way to greater diversity in geographic and social origin and to ties based not on kin but on personal achievement and interest. Such a development was implicit in the organization of the school.

THE SYSTEM OF INSTRUCTION

The goal of the school was to train well-educated ulama dedicated to scriptural Islam. Such ulama would become prayer leaders, writers, preachers, and teachers and thus disseminate their learning in turn. To this end the school set formal requirements for admission and matriculation. Local students were admitted to study Persian or Qur'an, but the Arabic students, roughly three-quarters of the whole, were required to have already studied Persian to the level of the *Gulistan,* to have completed the Qur'an, and to pass an examination. Only half of those examined were admitted. There were seventy-eight students in the first year, rapidly increasing to a constant two to three hundred for the rest of the century.

Students were expected to study a fixed and comprehensive body of learning in the course of a programme of studies originally scheduled for ten years, later reduced to six. They were not to come informally, sit at the feet of a particular teacher, then move on to another master and another centre of learning. Rather, in this one place, the school claimed, students would be trained in the specialties of the three great intellectual centres of North India: *manqulat,* the revealed studies of hadith or tradition and Qur'an associated with Delhi; and *ma'qulat,* the rational studies of *fiqh* or law, logic and philosophy associated with the two Eastern cities of Lucknow and Khairabad. Basically, the school taught the *dars-i nizami,* the curriculum evolved at Farangi Mahall in the eighteenth century that spread throughout India. They made, however, important modifications, particularly in their emphasis on the two subjects of hadith the *fiqh.* These were to be the basis of their popular teaching. In law they stressed not jurisprudence but correct performance of ritual and ceremonial duties. In hadith they greatly expanded the offerings of the Nizami curriculum. Instead of requiring only a summary (the Mishkat ul-Masabih of al-Ghazali), they included in their entirety the six classical collections of the precedents of the Prophet. They deemed hadith, the basis of correct practice and belief, the crowning subject. The most influential teacher was the *shaikh ul-hadith* at the school; and only good students were encouraged to study the subject. "Once a follower asked Rashid Ahmad to inaugurate a student's study of Tirmizi... for the student's understanding was deficient. Rashid Ahmad answered: 'When that is the case, teach a student *fiqh* or Urdu or Persian [but not hadith].' " Moreover, the school de-emphasized the so-called rational sciences, logic and philosophy, that had been the chief distinction of the Nizami teaching.

There was actual opposition led by Rashid Ahmad to teaching these rational sciences at all. He felt that the subjects were a waste of time and that the only merit in studying them was preparation for their refutation. Muhammad Qasim, in sympathy with this position, felt that students should study, if anything, the 'new philosophy' of the West, not that derived from the Greeks. Rashid Ahmad even argued that philosophy was opposed to the sharia, but he primarily emphasized that such study was trivial in contrast to study embodying the revealed truth of religion. Many of the staff and council were cautious, however, and wanted students to read the books of logic and philosophy to ensure their getting jobs. Despite Rashid Ahmad's indignant response—'Would you clean latrines to get a job'?—the books that had initially been eliminated from the curriculum did gradually creep back.

There were no spokesmen for including English or Western subjects. Muhammad Qasim insisted that the school was not opposed to such study, but simply wanted to avoid duplication of government efforts. Students could, he insisted, continue in government schools after completing their studies at Deoband, but even when the curriculum was reduced to six years, few continued beyond that long course. Thus with no new subjects and philosophy gradually restored, the curriculum was not dramatically innovative. It was, however, to become famous for its emphasis on hadith, a subject that provided material for popular teaching and influence.

In technique of instruction there were modifications. Indeed, many thought the school to be a continuation of the old Delhi College, not only because of the continuity of personnel and the modern organization of the school, but also because of the style of teaching. The technique of Arabic instruction, for example, was the British one of translation into Urdu and from Urdu into Arabic. Later, the exercise of monthly compositions written in Arabic was added in order to improve fluency and command of the language. Most important, the school continued the use of Urdu, not Persian, as a medium of instruction and thus shared in the general trend of the times toward the development of the modern vernaculars. Students came even within the first years of the school's existence, from places as distant as Afghanistan and Chittagong, Patna and Madras, but all were of return with a common language in Urdu. Even those who were of North India often spoke a dialect in their homes and now acquired a standard form of the language. Like the Westernizing college at Aligarh, Deoband was instrumental in establishing Urdu as a language of communication among the Muslims of India. Such a change was obviously central to enhanced bonds among the ulama and between them and their followers.

An abortive innovation on the part of the school was the inclusion of training in crafts and trades. There was hope that students, thus trained, could support themseves in villages and small towns and, simultaneously, share the benefits of their religious training with their neighbours. This would, no doubt, have furthered the influence of the ulama, but the plan came to nought because the students deemed such work unsuitable. There was also talk of teaching surveying and cartography in order to provide students with skills for jobs with the expanded public works department of the government. But even this plan did not materialize. The preference for intellectual work and its concomitant status was too strong. Only two kinds of vocational training had any place at the school: calligraphy and *tibb* or *yunani* medicine. Both were considered suitable activities for the ulama, related to the religious activities of copying manuscripts and healing their followers. In 1873 a skilled calligrapher joined the staff to train students for work at the increasingly important lithographic presses. As for *tibb,* some, like Rashid Ahmad, opposed its inclusion, for they saw it, like philosophy, as distraction from more important matters. However, the school did make *tibb* a part of its curriculum at the end of the century. It was the religious science, unchanged in substance, which the school primarily taught.

Students were tested on the results of their study. The examinations were an innovation in Arabic madrasas and hence extensively described in the school's annual reports. During a student's first two years, they were simply oral; in the subsequent four years, they were written. The staff took pride in the difficulty of the exams, for there were no optional questions, only five required ones on each book with each answer accorded twenty points. The students were supervised to prevent cheating and identified their examination by number only to ensure objectivity on the part of the examiners. The school was not organized by classes, but by books, so that if a student failed one book he would repeat that but not the others. The students, in fact, did well in their exams and few failed.

At an annual convocation, prizes were awarded to those with the highest grades. *Sanads* were also distributed, describing the books each student had completed during the year, and commenting on the character, capacity, and skill of the student as well. Those who had completed the entire course and were considered truly outstanding were sometimes awarded a *dastar,* a turban, which was wound on their head by the *sarparast.* The granting of turbans took place on only four occasions, at irregular intervals, and was finally given up after 1909. Those who received turbans were considered to possess both brilliance and exemplary personal qualities, including mastery of cultured language.

As the criteria for distinction indicate, the school sought to shape the character as well as the intellect of the students. A regimen was instituted for their personal lives. They were required to promise that they would be devoted to their studies and obedient to their teachers. Should they none the less miss classes, they were deprived of food and if they generally failed to work, they were simply expelled. John Palmer, a government official who toured the school in 1875, reported that teachers treated their students with severity but was impressed by the explanation that the staff deemed it beneficial to train students while young to have a sense of work. Except for the Friday holiday and one month each year, the students did indeed work continually.

They were expected to live respectably but modestly. The school provided not only books and instruction free of charge but a collection of necessities for each boy as well: four suits of clothes each year; two pairs of shoes; a cotton quilt; money for laundry; oil and matches for light; and medicine and care when sick. At the end of the century the school established a boarding house. Previously, students had lodged in homes and mosques and received food from individuals or from the residents of a *mohalla* jointly. In the boarding house, modelled on those newly established at Aligarh and the government schools, their daily life was put under the close supervision of the staff. In that setting, moreover, the students formed close bonds with each other.Such bonds transcended those of kin and locality and prepared the students for mutual cooperation and participation not only in religious activities but in government, voluntary associations, and politics.

The faculty was, of course the chief influence on the students. They were as a group dedicated to their work. Almost all of the leading teachers were offered positions in princely states or government service, but stayed at the school in return for small salaries of ten or fifteen rupees each month. In 1872, a year of few contributions, the teachers simply reduced their salaries and advanced students voluntarily took on the burden of aiding them with lessons. Not all the teachers were of equal skill, and those entrusted with the rational sciences—not surprisingly, given the emphasis of the school—tended to be less distinguished. Logic was taught for many years by an Afghan, Maulana Ghulam Rasul, whom the students claimed to be unable to understand. But there were always a few outstanding teachers. Among them in the early years was Rashid Ahmad who taught hadith to students in Gangoh.

He was the true successor of Shah Waliullah and people came from places like Bengal, Madras and Punjab to study from him. He would begin his teaching of hadith with Tirmizi and impress on each student the interpretation and meaning of the work in simple words. He was very patient, and often repeated his explanations. For example, he would take a simple word like *attarah,* perfumer's wife, which I recall him defining three times for an Afghan student, each time in simpler language. He always taught after ablution and required the same of his students. If they got tired he would amuse them with jokes and anecdotes until their stomachs hurt. Then, refreshed, they would be able to go on. He would tell a story so seriously that others laughed the more. Then he would become formal again, maintaining that respect and awe necessary for a teacher. His teaching was unique in that he spoke in accordance with each student's capacity...His memory was so extraordinary that he could cite the page of a relevant hadith in the *sahih* collections....His students became his lovers, but he considered himself nothing.

After Muhammad Qasim's death, Rashid Ahmad became *sarparast* of both Deoband and its sister school, the Mazahir ul-Ulum in Saharanpur. Like the other great elders of the school, despite his eminence he was known for his kindness to the students and was not above chiding those he felt did not treat the students generously.

A second great teacher long associated with the school was Maulana Mahmud Hasan. He had sought out Muhammad Qasim in the printing houses of Meerut and Delhi in order to be one of the few to undergo his demanding teaching of hadith. When Mahmud Hasan completed his education in 1873 he joined the staff of the school and for the next forty years was a dominating influence in its teaching and administration. He was a man of extraordinary energy, teaching ten lessons each day, writing, caring for Muhammad Qasim in his final illness. He was devoted to the school and resisted all invitations to leave it. His fame was especially in hadith; and, his biographer notes, in the course of his career he taught over a thousand students from such distant places as Kabul, Qandahar, Balkh, Bukhara, Mecca, Medina, and Yeman. Among them were Anwar Shah Kashmiri, Shabir Ahmad Osmani and Hafiz Muhammad Ahmad, the leaders of the third generation of ulama at the school.

For the students the years at the school were intensive and formative, providing them not only with intellectual skill, but shaping their personalities and relationships. Husain Ahmad Madani, a student at the school at the end of the century, wrote a description of his experiences:

> I took up residence with my brothers in a room near the home of Maulana Mahmud Hasan. My brothers asked him to initiate my studies as a blessing; and he, assembling a group of ulama, directed Maulana Khalil Ahmad to begin my instruction. I was then in my twelfth year, but I was very small. Because a boy so small, from

such a distance, was unusual, I was treated with great kindness. I would go to my teachers' houses to help with writing and accounts and received great kindness from the wife of Mahmud Husan in particular.

But whatever small freedom I had at home was now gone. My eldest brother beat me often, and never showed me even the occasional kindness my father had. My brother taught me Persian and I also studied from Maulana Mahmud Hasan after hours.

I rapidly advanced beyond those in my classes. During the years from 1890 to 1898 I studied from Maulanas Zulfaqar Ali, Abd ul-'Ali, Khalil Ahmad, Mahmud Hasan, Mufti Aziz ur-Rahman, Ghulam Rasul, Manfa at Ali, and Habib ur-Rahman. We studied the books of the *dars-i Nizami* ....which was used in the Arabic schools of Hindustan. There were some books of literature, mathematics and medicine which I could not complete because of our departure for Medina.

I never had much enthusiasm for study and would not review my books. I did well in the beginning books on which there was only an oral exam, but did not do so well in the later written ones... The night before the exam I would study the whole book, drinking tea and having snacks whenever I felt sleepy; for I always needed much sleep, and especially felt sleepy when reading. After my first failure, I did better, and I often attained distinguished marks. The exams were very hard in comparison with those of the government schools where there was a choice. Deoband was unique among the Arabic schools in enforcing such a high standard, supervising exams to see that a student had no help....Unfortunately the education in many of the other schools was defective. When students from here entered other institutions or studied English they were always most distinguished.

Although I never liked work, gradually my intellectual inclination and balance of character grew. At first my interest was logic and philosophy, then literature, and finally hadith.

This account tells much about student life. There appears to have been a closeness between teachers and students, illustrated by the attention of teachers to their students' well-being and, in this case, by the services rendered to the teachers by the students. There was, moreover, a sense of being unique, of being in a school that was better than the others, harder even than the English schools. From this closeness and discipline, Husain Ahmad indicates, he was encouraged to shape his intellectual interests in the direction of those dominant at the school.

At the school, moreover, he received his first spiritual training, asking a member of the staff as guide. Both he and his eldest brother were disciples of Rashid Ahmad; his other brother, of Mahmud Hasan. In later years all three would return to the school from Medina whenever they came to India in search of brides or in connection with other family business and would always seek advice from their sufi shaikhs and even undertake further study. Husain Ahmad went on to be a pillar of the school, a distinguished scholar, and a leading figure in nationalist politics. In ulama like him the school fulfilled its goal of preserving the learned tradition and providing a structure of religious leadership for Muslims without the support of the state.

TWO CONTROVERSIES

Despite such success on the part of the school, there were people who opposed its style of organization. As a result, two major crises arose in the initial decades of the school's existence. The first, in 1876, concerned the issue of erecting separate buildings for the school; the second, in 1895, of opposition to the school's administrative personnel. Both, generally speaking, were resolved in favour of those who supported the original bureaucratic conception of the institution.

At issue in the first quarrel was the question of the school's existence as a distinct institution. At first it did operate in mosques and rented buildings. But the founders—or most of them—held to the idea that the school should have a building of its own. The idea was a new one, and even Muhammad Qasim initially felt that a fine building might encourage pride. He was ultimately persuaded of the value of a separate building by the insistence of his teacher, Maulana Ahmad Ali Saharanpuri, that it would be conducive to the independence and efficient running of the school. Muhammad Qasim himself recognized the problems of lodging students in mosques when there were hundreds of them, not just an occasional few. The *qaum* of students, he noted, was a free one, and there would be endless complaints of broken vessels, lost lanterns, and other such problems.

Practical considerations aside, there was a symbolic motive in establishing separate buildings for the school. With Mughal decline there were no princes to construct the grand tombs, city mosques, ceremonial gateways and forts which had been the material statement on the physical landscape of the existence of Muslim culture and society. Rather, through the efforts of the ulama and other pious people, madrasas and mosques became not only the loci of the organization of their religious life but also the concrete evidence of the Muslim presence. Separate madrasas had heretofore not been characteristic of Muslim architecture in India, perhaps because the ulama and their law schools had not been central in organizing Muslim communal life. Now schools like Deoband served that function and symbolized Muslim culture. The early buildings at Deoband were domed and arched in the style of imperial structures. Early in this century, for example, the school used money donated by the Amir of Afghanistan to construct a grand ceremonial outer gate which particularly evoked an imperial motif.

The leading opponent of constructing the first building was Saiyid Abid Husain, the first *mohtimim* and a man of such great influence that one associate observed that even the sultan of the Turks could not control Deoband without his aid; and another suspected that even the jinn obeyed him. He preferred an informal associational style of education, with no formal buildings. He mainly argued that a separate building would be too expensive and urged instead the building of additional cells, *hujras*, in the new Jami' Masjid. In 1871 when he returned from hajj he took up the supervision of the building of that mosque instead of his previous post of *mohtamim*. He used this position to build *hujras*, despite the decision of the council in favour of a proper building. He thus differed with the council not only on a matter of substance but on the legitimacy of their authority to make binding decisions on all associated with the school.

A contemporaneous account claimed that Hajji Abid had the support of the townspeople in this dispute. The nature of this support is difficult to analyze since, the account continued, because of Muhammad Qasim's stature "even though peoples' faces changed, they said nothing." Presumably Hajji Abid's support was based on his deep personal influence and not on the issue itself. Those active in the dispute, however, were united by a position of principle, not by kin or personal ties. The entire administration supported the cause of a new building. Rafi ud-Din even dreamed of divine indications of the precise spot where it should be built.

Finally, in 1876 Muhammad Qasim announced that there would be a new building without indicating whether it would be separate or part of the Jami Masjid. He hoped that once the announcement was made Hajji Abid would accept its being separate. Muhammad Qasim set the date for the foundation stone to be laid after a Friday congregational prayer at which he would preach. At the end of his sermon he announced that the school had purchased the *maidan* in front of the *mahall-i diwan* and that the new building would be built there. Hajji Abid cried out in shock. Muhammad Qasim, insisting that the decision was a correct one, urged him to join the throng which was then moving to the *maidan* to lay the foundation stone. But Hajji Sahib left, enraged, and retired to the Chattah Masjid. Muhammad Qasim followed him there, touched his feet with his hands, and said to him, "You are our elder, and we, your younger. You cannot leave us, nor we, you." Both wept. Reconciled by Muhammad Qasim's moving act of personal humility and by the inevitability of the new building, Hajji 'Abid agreed to attend the ceremony. Three distinguished elders then laid the foundation stone: Hazrat Miyanji Mune Shah, a revered *saiyid* and elder; Maulana Ahmad Ali, the great hadith scholar of Saharanpur; and Hajji Abid himself, as representative of the council. The decision made and the work begun, "everyone's heart felt a strange joy", concluded a historian of the event.

This first building was completed within five years. Like many later buildings, it was financed by a special group of donors, in this case one organized in Hyderabad. The mosque was the special contribution of a wealthy trader, Seth Ghulam Muhammad Azam. The hostel, completed in 1898, was built through the support of the princes of Hyderabad, Chattari, and Bhopal. Hajji Abid and the people of the town came to accept and take pride in these buildings. There were other occasions when Hajji Abid differed with other members of the school. The annual reports account for his occasional withdrawal from the school by his preoccupation with his many followers. In fact, he long failed to appreciate the formal, modern format of the school and its extra-local character

These issues reappeared in the dispute of 1895, a crisis that lasted longer and was of potentially greater danger to the school. The opponents in this case were leaders of the town whose attempts to gain control of the school were perhaps not unexpected. Muhammad Qasim had early set the rule that the councillors should be ulama and not 'respectable people', *arbab-i wijahat*, in order to ensure that the religious quality of the school would be preserved and that the school itself would not merely be an institution of the town, subject to its local problems and constraints.

Internal problems gave the townsmen an opportunity to criticize the school. In 1892 Hajji Abid Husain, again unwilling to accept a decision of the council, resigned from his post as *mohtimim*. He objected on this occasion to the decision to reduce the pay of a recalcitrant teacher who was felt to compromise the school by resorting to government courts. He also used the occasion to argue in vain that most of the dozen teachers at the school should be fired and only two or three of the very good ones kept. Mahmud Hasan, who, by this time, was clearly the school's best teacher, supported the continuation of a proper staff and simply insisted that if anyone went it would be he. New crises built on this one.

The council next appointed Maulana Fazl-i Haqq Nanautawi, an original member of the council and Abid's sometime aide, as the new *mohtimim*. He was discovered shortly after his appointment to have been guilty of a minor embezzlement of some seventy rupees. Rashid Ahmad, as member of the council and *sarparast*, prevailed in his opinion that whatever the repercussions, he be asked to resign. The campaign of the dissidents then began with letters to Rashid Ahmad objecting to Fazl-i Haqq's removal. Rashid Ahmad answered them by explaining that he was answerable only to the contributors, an assertion of the non-local character of the school.

Once Fazl-i Haqq had resigned, the council appointed the venerable Maulana Munir Nanautawi, of Muhammad Qasim's family, to take his place. They also added two new members to the council: Muhammad Ahsan Nanautawi, the teacher and publisher who was also a member of the family, and Hajji Shaikh Zahur ud-Din Deobandi, a favoured disciple of Muhammad Qasim. They joined two others who had been appointed during the previous decade, Maulana Ziya ud-Din Rampuri, a revered shaikh, and Hakim Mushtaq Ahmad of Deoband. Despite the presence of such distinguished elders, the dissidents continued to speak of the school's decline and bad management. Not surprisingly, active among the critics were relatives of Fazl-i-Haqq, prominent citizens of the town who chafed at his disgrace.

The opposition crystallized in the formation of 'The Reform

Committee of the Arabic Madrasa of Deoband' which sent out five hundred copies of a complaint against the school which invited supporters to be present at a meeting. It charged that the 'waqf' of Deoband had become the private property of the council members who included two brothers as members and four of their sons as teachers at the school. The pamphlet argued that by the standard of either the sharia or of the government such nepotism was inappropriate. They reminded their readers of the importance Muhammad Qasim had attached to the cooperation of the people of the town, for whom they claimed to be the spokesmen, and insisted that they had no personal antagonism to the school. The statement had twenty-six signatures, headed by three members of the 'municipality', i.e. men who had attained influence through the new local government institutions inaugurated by the British. Two were wakils, one a former revenue official, another a ziladar. One identified himself as a maulavi, three as *hafiz* who had memorized the Qur'an, and four as *hajji*. Eight began their names with *shaikh*. The group was thus, presumably, drawn from the most influential of the town's residents, led by men who filled the local councils set up by the British.

Among those who attended the meeting were a dozen men from Delhi, Meerut and Muzaffarnagar, who were staunch defenders of the school; and they, in the end, dominated the meeting. They accused the critics of seeking their own personal goals against the welfare of the school and of engaging in such despicable tactics as going from *mohalla to mohalla* to encourage the townsmen to stop their contributions for the students. They also accused them of spreading reports against the school in the newspapers, as indeed, one extant item in the *Tuti-yi-Hind* of Meerut confirms. In it was reported a sermon given in the Jami Masjid by Munshi Abd ur-Razzaq, a member of the municipality and signatory of the circular, who claimed that Hajji Abid had severed his connection with the school and asked that the government intervene in the interests of reform. The defenders also accused the critics of circulating a false announcement in Saharanpur that Rashid Ahmad had resigned and that contributions should now be sent to Abd ur-Razzaq as the new *mohtamim*. When this failed, the critics had distributed an announcement entitled 'For the Attention of the Government', a scurrilous attack which claimed that the school educated students for religious warfare and drew students from the frontier particularly for this purpose.

The school's defenders answered these charges of resignations, nepotism, and disloyalty. They were quick to emphasize the influence of Rashid Ahmad and said of Abid Husain, as Muhammad Qasim had said twenty years earlier, "he cannot leave us, nor we him." Mohi ud-Din Moradabadi, an important support of the school, argued that the familial links among the school's members were a virtue and stressed that members were 'united and the same sort of people'. He emphasized that appointments were made by the whole council and that the qualifications of a teacher like Mahmud Hasan, the son of a council member, were outstanding. He cited the important precedent of the Prophet who did not hesitate to appoint his own relatives.

Maulana Zulfaqar Ali in particular addressed himself to the charge of disloyalty. He declared that as a 'salt-eater' of the government, he personally took responsiblity for the school's loyalty. The district collector, Mr. Irwin, was invited to the school to confirm its integrity. He did come, and offered an Urdu speech in its praise. Janab Babu Raja Lal, a former tahsildar, was asked to investigate the school and subsequently worked for several months, making inquiries in Nanauta, Rampur, and elsewhere. In conclusion he denied the critics' claims and in particular praised the fine students and Zulfaqar Ali, a man who had been honoured at the Queen's durbar with chair and robe of honour. Local newspapers reported these two investigations and concluded that the charges of the 'malcontents' had been finally laid to rest.

Meanwhile, supporters of the school hastened to testify to their confidence in the school's administration. Their letters reveal the wide range of support the school now had. The association formed in Hyderabad to raise funds, consisting of princely employees, a publisher of religious books, and a religious teacher, used this occasion to declare its opposition to the residents and to send an additional contribution. Fifteen contributors from Bijnur sent a petition of support. A head maulavi in a government school in Banda in the east wrote an appreciation of the school. High officials from the state of Bhopal, including a wakil at the high court and the city munsif, who was from Deoband, added their support. Forty-seven contributors wrote from the qasba of Tandah, in Oudh, where most of them were posted in connection with government service. Other letters came from a wakil in Jaunpur and the Deputy Collector of Eta.

So serious a dispute could not be resolved by a simple personal act like that of Muhammad Qasim's in 1875. The council did not, however, propose arbitration or compromise with their opponents, but rather, unilaterally, rallied support for themselves. In addition to the testimonials from presumably impartial Hindu and British officials and from the loyal donors, they summoned four of the most influential figures associated with the school to render a final opinion. They were Rashid Ahmad, *sarparast*; the Nawab of Chattari, the philanthropist Shaikh Basharat Ali, a former deputy collector; and Maulavi Muhammad Ismail, the successor of the revered Maulana Muzaffar Husain Kandhlavi. The great *sarparast*, the influential landholder and benefactor, and the representatives of the government bureaucracy, and sufi piety respectively, together inspected the school's finances and records and asserted emphatically that all was in excellent order. Then Rashid Ahmad, with the agreement of the council, expanded its membership. The six new members were all from outside Deoband and all known for their learning. The 'respectable people' of the city who had sought places were thus defeated.

The council then appointed a new *mohtamim* to replace Maulana Munir Nanautawi. The proceedings reported that he had resigned because of his brother Ahsan's death, but, in fact, he had never been a strong administrator. Maulana Hafiz Muhammad Ahmad, Muhammad Qasim's son, took his place, there to remain for forty years. He was, at times, a figure of controversy because of his willingness to jeopardize the school's well-being by political involvement, but he was, unquestionably, a strong and effective administrator. Moreover, his position as the son of the founder of the school was of great importance in establishing his claim to authority.

The controversy resolved, the school held its annual prize distribution and convocation, meeting for the first time not in the Jami Masjid of the town but, significantly, in the school itself. The people of the town were invited on the day before the ceremonies for special speeches. Zulfaqar Ali and Hajji Abid himself presided. And the ceremonies closed with prayers for the wealth and spiritual well-being of the people of the town Deoband.

The dispute had been more ideological than personal. There were, to be sure, a cluster of relatives on each side. And personal ties certainly played a part in shaping the loyalties of some. One supporter of the administration, for example, simply wrote, "What can I say, he [Rashid Ahmad] is my *murshid* [sufi preceptor] and guide." But kin did not wholly account for people's allegiances and some participants explicitly denied its importance. An official from Bhopal mocked the dissidents for sending their announcement to Fazl-i Haqq's brothers... "because they assumed that he would be in opposition.... He is not such a man." Place of origin did not define the two sides, since many residents of the town supported the administration. Nor did social differences, since both groups were composed of respectable people, largely *shaikh*, many of them associated with government and educated in religious studies.

The sides were, however, united by different positions. The opponents were not committed to the bureaucratic organization of the school and its concomitant broad network of support. Ironically, they, who accused the administration of nepotism, in fact wanted to make the school parochial by putting its control in the hands of townsmen instead of in those of the far-flung contributors and councillors. Most wanted a share in a successful enterprise without understanding the basis of its success. Some few, like Hajji Abid with his proposal to eliminate most of the staff, felt a modest, old-fashioned school sufficient for the town.

The dissidents, moreover, seem not to have subscribed to the scripturalist reform that defined the teachings of the school. A former revenue official, sometimes tahsildar in Deoband wrote:

> I got the announcement [of the meeting], I suppose, because I am of their *qaum*. I am; and I am well acquainted with all the gentlemen and *shaikhs* of Deoband. And I don't know who the people are who signed it. Look at them—'Deputy', 'Babu', 'Municipality',—not such as are involved in the work of God and his Prophet. Let them give their age, occupation and whether they fast and pray. I recognized the first two names. I think one of them is some relation of mine. The other carried a *tazya* [Shia effigy] in the Muharram celebration.

Even Hajji Abid, however beloved, was less committed to reform than the other Deobandis. Although he had been influenced by Imdadullah to give up practices of extreme mortification and to be faithful to his religious duties, he never took the active stance of some of the others. His resignation on this occasion, for example, suggests his lack of interest in the reformist cause of adherence to the judicial opinions of the ulama instead of the use of government courts.

Those who supported the administration favoured a form of organization that de-emphasized purely local ties in favour of the separate unity and identity of the whole group of Deobandis, whatever their geographic origin. At the same time, they fostered a style of Islam that preferred universal practices and beliefs to local cults and customs. They were inspired by a belief in continuing divine sanction to their work and felt that sanction confirmed by their record of training some six hundred ulama by the time of the dispute. Against such success the opposition could make little headway.

THE SPREAD OF DEOBANDI MADRASAS

The success of the school was measured not only by events at the mother school but by the spread of Deobandi teachings through similar schools. The ulama of Deoband early tried to establish a system of branch schools which were to follow the pattern of British universities with their affiliating colleges and be subject to control of both curriculum and administration. The ulama were familiar with examples of such institutions, set up in India pursuant to the Wood Dispatch of 1854; and they, in turn set up a somewhat similar system of education. They founded many schools, particularly in the Doab and Rohilkhund, which had much the same goals as the mother school: the propagation of reformed religious knowledge and the training of young men for professional religious careers. The schools often submitted their records to Deoband for inspection, sought its approval of major decisions, and received. its ulama as both external examiners and distinguished visitors. But they were never formally and fully integrated into a single educational system, largely because personal ties were so effective in maintaining contacts. A proposal to appoint an inspector of schools in the British style was considered from time to time but simply deemed unnecessary.

In their first dozen or so years, the Deobandi proceedings included discussions of many of these schools, ranging in administration from one at Thana Bhawan, whose staff for a time was even paid from Deoband, to one at Lucknow which was 'like Deoband'. Many of these smaller schools were the work of a single patron in cooperation with a Deoband graduate while others had complex administrations modelled on the mother school. Among the latter was the large and successful Mazahir-i Ulum in Saharanpur. There was never any claim that it was a branch of Deoband, for in size and influence, it was to be second only to Deoband, itself in the entire subcontinent. Founded only six months after Deoband, it explicitly modelled itself on the nearby school.

Leading Deobandis contributed to the school, presided at prize distribution, and gave examinations. Rashid Ahmad was *sarparast* of both institutions at the end of the century and many of the staff moved from one school to the other. The school was more locally based than Deoband. In a dispute similar to the one over control of Deoband, the city leaders of Saharanpur received some recognition of their responsibility for general administrative decisions and fund raising. The role of people of the city in financing the school was also more marked than at Deoband. The school also adhered longer and more consistently to family connections in making appointments. In part because of its more parochial style, its ulama in this century have not played the role in politics that the Deobandis have. Whatever difference of emphasis, the Mazahir-i Ulum called itself Deobandi.

Increasingly, the name of Deoband came to represent a distinct style, a *maslak*, of Indian Islam that emphasized the diffusion of scripturalist practices and the cultivation of an inner spiritual life. By roughly 1880 there were over a dozen Deobandi schools; by the end of the century, at least three times that many, some in places as distant as Chittagong, Madras, and Peshawar. Deoband had pioneered a non-governmental style of formal organization for madrasa education in India. Thanks to that structure, the school succeeded in training a large number of ulama in its reformist ideology and in establishing a network of ancillary schools further disseminating that teaching. Deoband thus offers a striking and successful example of the bureaucratization of traditional religious institutions that has made them effective in the modern world.

The Sense of the Future

As Western-educated Indians grew in number and sophistication, they became increasingly restive under the constraints of British rule, with its foreign monopoly of all important posts and its aura of racist paternalism. By the 1880's these Indians were looking toward the future—to an India that would be master of its own destiny. Before independence arrived, however, many visions of the future were to be put forward and many different paths tried in the effort to attain it.

The early nationalists, imbued with the constitutional liberalism of mid-Victorian Britain, confined their political activity to respectful petitioning. They urged the admission of more Indians to the civil service and the legislative councils, and an end to the "drain" of wealth to England. In the early years of the twentieth century, dissatisfied with the slow pace of reform, many turned to more extreme tactics, among them vilification of the British and the throwing of bombs. This new emotional nationalism found sustenance in the past glories of Hindu India and, for the people of Bengal and Maharashtra, in a lyrical evocation of their regional heritage.

PART IV

The Sense of the Future

15

Although little known and rarely studied in the West, extremist nationalism exercised a powerful attraction upon the educated youth of India for several decades. At the same time it contributed much to that growing Hindu communal sentiment which helped make a united India unpalatable to the Muslims. In the following autobiographical memoir the brilliant, if sometimes eccentric, Bengali scholar Nirad Chaudhuri looks back upon his own youth in the years just after Lord Curzon's 1905 partition of Bengal, when nationalist excitement was at its height.

FROM

The Autobiography of an Unknown Indian: Chapter III, "Enter Nationalism"

NIRAD CHAUDHURI

It was in October 1905 that we had our formal initiation into the nationalist movement. The previous year, after coming back from Calcutta, we had heard that Lord Curzon had been at Mymensingh and made a speech there, which our elders discussed with great vehemence and some amusement. It had something to do with the proposed partition of Bengal. In 1905 the partition came and with it the nationalist agitation. Our opposition to the division of Bengal was fierce.

The same class of Hindu Bengalis who opposed Lord Curzon's partition of Bengal have now themselves brought about a second partition of their country—a good illustration perhaps of the inconsistency which is inseparable from the method of arriving at political decisions by the assertion of collective whim. This politically incompetent and emotionally unstable class is having its post-partition heart-searchings. But these are caused less by any qualms that a mistake may have been committed in 1947 than by the difficulty of proving that the Bengali Hindu has been as right in 1947 as he was in 1905, for there

Reprinted by permission from Nirad Chaudhuri, *The Autobiography of an Unknown Indian,* London: John Farquharson Ltd., pp. 218-32 and 240-244.

is nothing he cares for more than his reputation for superlative cleverness which, he thinks, makes everybody else look a blinking fool by his side. But at the time of the first partition we did not have this quandary before us, and the Press, that kept woman of Demos, egged us on against the partition as on the recent occasion it egged on packs of craven dotards and barbarised youngsters in favour of another partition. I still remember a cartoon in a Bengali newspaper in those far off anti-partition days which showed Lord Curzon sawing a live woman. I am living away from Bengal now and never see any Bengali newspapers. But I should think they must have been, with their normal crudity, representing Lord Mountbatten as a midwife attending the confinement of an elderly woman and holding up a promising little one-armed and one-legged baby to the world.

But I should not anticipate matters. For the moment I am concerned only with the first observance by us of the partition day, when a gentleman called at our house with a bundle of silk threads and my father asked us to have a bath in the river first and then in a state of cleanness tie the thread round our wrists as a token of the brotherhood of all Bengalis. We were to observe that day as a day of national mourning and fasting. We also put away all our clothes manufactured in England and put on *dhotis* made in the Indian mills, which at first were as coarse, heavy, and thick as sackcloth.

OUR POLITICAL IDEAS

I was, however, too young at the time to have an understanding of the intellectual content of the new nationalism. But I did share the twin sentiment which with the boys of my generation was the nearest approach to a political concept. We had already acquired a genuine passion for personal freedom, and any suggestion that we could not hold whatever political, religious, or moral convictions our conscience prompted us to adopt, or that we could not give free expression to them, would have been resented even by the boys that we were as a monstrous tyranny. With this feeling for freedom and impatience of outside compulsion went a very idealistic and fervent republicanism. We unquestioningly assumed that there was some inherent virtue in the removal of an absolute monarch, or even in a partial reduction of his powers. Harmodius and Aristogeiton and Lucius Junius Brutus were as much our heroes as the heroes of the Athenians and Romans. In fact, Greek and Roman republicanism had cast its spell as decisively on us as on the makers of the French Revolution, and under its influence we seemed always to feel on our shoulders the weight of an unseen toga. In the actual unfolding of contemporary history it made us read with delight and high hopes the news of the political revolutions of our youthful days—the Russian Revolution of 1905, the Young Turk Revolution of 1909, and the Chinese Revolution of 1911. We invariably identified political freedom with two things: the absence of an absolute monarch and the presence of an assembly of representatives of the people. But we never worked out the relationship between these representatives and the general mass of the population of a country.

Certain modern personalities and movements contributed powerfully to our political consciousness, of which there were two clearly discernible facets. The first and rational facet was indoctrinated by Burke and Mill, but shaped in its practical expression by the liberalism of Gladstone and Lincoln. The second facet was purely emotional, and its inspiration was furnished by Rousseau and Mazzini besides the Ancients. The methods of political action were suggested by the leaders of the American Revolution, the Italian Risorgimento— particularly Garibaldi—and the Irish Nationalists. The entire course of English constitutional history and, more especially, the turmoils of the seventeenth century, together with the American, French, Italian, and Irish movements were freely drawn upon for precedents and also for operational hints. Of course, it was sometime before we the boys could mix our political physic ourselves. For the time being it was dispensed to us by the grown ups. But eclectic as they and we were, the German nationalism of the nineteenth century, curiously enough, did not influence us. This appears surprising in view of the close resemblance to Nazism that Indian nationalism came to bear later, but it is also perfectly intelligible, because the German nationalist movement of the nineteenth century was not like the nationalism of Italy or of Ireland, the nationalism of a subject people. The other fact that we were not influenced by the nationalism of the Balkan people appears stranger, and is only to be accounted for by our ignorance of it. For when in later life I read Professor Seton-Watson's works and also Miss Rebecca West's *Black Lamb and Grey Falcon* I found the nationalist emotions and impulses described in these books to be very similar to those we felt between 1908 and 1919.

We went no further in comprehending the intellectual content of the nationalist movement. But we were swept by its emotional fervour. The first element in this emotion was an intense, almost religious, hopefulness. We believed in the second advent of our country and nation with a firmness of conviction which nothing could shake. We knew that our present condition was pitiable: we were poor, subjugated and oppressed, and even degenerate in certain respects; but we were great once and should be even greater in the future. This amazing faith, running counter to all the known facts of history which go to prove that a nation overtaken by decline after once creating a great civilization never rises again, was to us justified by itself and needed no evidence of validity external to itself. If any proofs at all were needed, we could point to the fact that while every other ancient nation which had created a civilization—the Egyptians, Chaldeans, the ancient Greeks, the Romans—had disappeared, we, the Hindus, had survived; this could only mean that we were a chosen people who were destined, or rather ordained, to have a future more glorious than even their past.

The faith was fixed in our mind by a large number of patriotic songs whose single theme was that our country would be great again. When I was a boy I was once told that the regimental band was the most important part of a regiment, for the men fought only as long as the band urged them on to fight with music and as soon as the music ceased the fighting spirit of the men also disappeared. I was further told that for this reason the enemy always tried to pick off the bandsmen first. If not true of soldiers, that was certainly true of us, for I am quite sure that all our patriotic fervour would have vanished but for the songs. St. Paul declared that without charity he was as sounding brass or a tinkling cymbal; we should have been without charity even for our mother country without the sounding brass and tinkling cymbal.

To begin with, however, we had wood-winds rather than a brass band. When the anti-partition agitation began there were no readymade songs embodying the sense of grievance created by Lord Curzon's administrative measure, and no songs crackling with the anger of the hour. We had to fall back on the patriotic songs composed in the preceding era, many of which were by Tagore and breathed a lyrical love for our country, both India and Bengal. This patriotic lyricism was the second note in the emotion we felt at the coming of the nationalist agitation, and its poignancy lay in the continuous evocation of the beauties of nature: the waters, the green grass, and the golden cornfield of Bengal, the fragrance of the mango blossom in the spring; while on a grander level we had the snows of the Himalayas and the waves of the Indian Ocean. Even now I cannot read the words of these songs, far less whistle the tunes, without instantly bringing back to my ears and eyes all the sounds from the soft rumble of the rain on our corrugated-iron roofs to the bamboo pipe of the cowherds, and all the sights from the sails of the boats on our great rivers to the spreading banyan tree—the sounds and sights which embody for me the idea of Bengal.

An eagerness to serve and sacrifice ourselves, was the third element in our patriotic emotion. Henceforward, we thought, we had no right to live any other life but a dedicated life. Our country was waiting for us to rescue and redeem her. She could be only what our faith and effort would make her. The sense of the demand made on us by our country was so real that it seemed as if actual calls of distress from some living person were reaching us, and we felt guilty if we could not show some activity at every hour of the day which could be interpreted as the service, direct or indirect, of our country. It was living with an all-consuming intensity; but even with that strain it was delightful: if I were to say,

> Bliss was it in that dawn to be alive
> But to be young was very heaven!

—that would not be mere, and rather threadbare, rhetoric.

Gradually, however, as the agitation became more intense and heated, other feelings began to take possession of us. Our messianic faith in the future of our country was filled out with a definitely Hindu content; to our lyrical love for our country was added a fierce hatred of the English; the spirit of self-sacrifice and dedication found its natural, but always fatal, complement of fanaticism. When in later life I read Sir Valentine Chirol's *Indian Unrest*—we had been taught to hate him and his book equally well—and compared what he had written with my own recollections, I found that he had been wholly correct in his estimate of the Swadeshi movement, in representing it as being essentially a movement of Hindu revival. It was not the liberal political thought of the organizers of the Indian National Congress, but the Hindu revivalism of the last quarter of the nineteenth century—a movement which previously had been almost wholly confined to the field of religion—which was the driving force behind the anti-partition agitation of 1905 and subsequent years. This movement was bound sooner or later to clash with liberalism, and the clash which occurred at Surat in 1907 was only superficially a quarrel between the Moderates and the Extremists; in essence it was the manifestation of the irreconcilability of liberal nationalism and Hindu nationalism.

In demagogic politics the less extreme never has any chance against the more extreme. There is a Gresham's Law as much in politics as in economics, and therefore the liberal form of nationalism began to lose not only support but also reputation. We always turned up our noses at the mere mention of the Moderates, and even before we had begun to air our contempt for them a complete transformation had come over our spirit. We found the older patriotic songs very tame and uninspiring. They seemed to contain very namby-pamby sentiments. Inevitably, new songs began to make their appearance to cater for the new spirit. It is significant that one of the new songs, and one of the most popular, was composed by a journalist of the orthodox Hindu school, a man who had once been sentenced to imprisonment for a dishonourable libel on the wife of a distinguished Brahmo. Some of the lines of this song were:

> If I should die,
> By our Mother, let me die,
> Fighting for my land
> The cops in blue and red
> A little blood may shed;
> The more our blood shall flow
> The stronger should we grow;
> Bogey's had his day,
> To him we will pay
> The tribute of a pie.
> Even if I die
> By our Mother, I shall die
> Fighting for my land.

We were highly taken with this song, and we thought it very much better than the Tagore songs we formely used to sing. On the second or the third anniversary day of the partition we were going round the town singing patriotic songs, and when we came near the Government treasury we stopped at a distance of about fifty feet from the armed sentry, singing with the greatest imaginable gusto: "The cops in blue and red..." We snapped our fingers at him and yelled and danced in cannibalic exultation, with the poor fellow looking on helplessly, perhaps all the time feeling more and more guilty of his unpatriotic employment.

A year or two later we went further and adopted an even more uncompromising Hindu song, one stanza of which called on the goddess Kali to come to our aid. We sang:

O Great Mother, now descend
With your looks that horror shed;
Also all your witches send,
Who the burning-ghat do tread.

The help was asked of course to drive out the English. My brothers and I often sang the song, because it was a great favourite. I still remember the evening when my elder brother and I, having been sent to do some shopping, went along singing this ultra-Hindu song at the top of our voices, singing it even more lustily when we were before the police-station and the Kali temple, both of which were on the main road adjacent to each other. Two clear young voices sent the terrible invocation ringing through the stillness of the evening. It was dark, and the street was very poorly lighted, so nobody could identify us.

Not less significant as an indication of the change that was coming over us was the fact that after a little while we ceased, when we playfully charged one another, to give our childish and unmeaning yells. We rushed on our momentary enemies, sometimes with awful seriousness and sometimes by way of horseplay repeating the Maratha war-cry—"Hara, Hara, Mahadeo!" Perhaps equally significant was the adoption in our family of the *Basumati*, the organ of orthodox Hinduism, as our daily newspaper, instead of the *Sanjivani*, which was liberal, although the Brahmo editor of the *Sanjivani* was one of the famous nine to be deported under the notorious Regulation III of 1818.

One destructive form of patriotism, however, we avoided in our family. There were only too many who did not feel that they had made their final choice for nationalism, and burnt their boats behind them, until they had also literally burnt their clothes of English manufacture. Neither my father nor my mother saw any sense in this demonstrative exuberance. They put away our old clothes and made us put on Indian clothes, and they also used nothing but Indian clothes. Even so, the patriotic fury touched my mother once, illustrating the extreme emotional instability which the nationalist agitation had generated in us. The result was the unnecessary destruction of a poor glass waterjug in 1909, after it had survived the emotional storms of the first four years of the Swadeshi movement. My mother was coming from Kalikutch to

Banagram, and she was travelling in a palanquin for a part of the way. When not very far from our village she felt thirsty and asked for some water. The water was brought to her in the glass jug. Suddenly she took a violent dislike to the vessel as a foreign article, and told my brother— the brother next to me who was called madcap and who was always ready for feats of this kind—to break it. The boy was overjoyed and smashed the jug against a tree.

HINDU-MUSLIM ENMITY

I can throw a collateral beam on the character of our nationalism by describing what we felt about the Muslims. When I see the gigantic catastrophe of Hindu-Muslim discord of these days I am not surprised, because we as children held the tiny mustard seed in our hands and sowed it very diligently. In fact, this conflict was implicit in the very unfolding of our history, and could hardly be avoided. Heaven preserve me from the dishonesty, so general among Indians, of attributing this conflict to British rule, however much the foreign rulers might have profited by it. Indeed they would have been excusable only as gods, and not as man the political animal, had they made no use of the weapon so assiduously manufactured by us, and by us also put into their hands. But even then they did not make use of it to the extent they might easily have done. This, I know, is a very controversial thesis, but it can be easily proved if we do not turn a blind eye to the facts of our history.

When we were very young, that is to say when the Swadeshi movement had not coloured our attitude to the Muslims, we presented four distinct aspects in our attitude towards them as it was shaped by tradition. In the first place, we felt a retrospective hostility towards the Muslims for their one-time domination of us, the Hindus; secondly, on the plane of thought we were utterly indifferent to the Muslims as an element in contemporary society; thirdly, we had friendliness for the Muslims of our own economic and social status with whom we came into personal contact; our fourth feeling was mixed concern and contempt for the Muslim peasant, whom we saw in the same light as we saw our low-caste Hindu tenants, or, in other words, as our livestock. Of these four modes of feeling the first was very positive and well-organized intellectually; the rest were mere habits, not possessing very deep roots.

Nothing was more natural for us than to feel about the Muslims in the way we did. Even before we could read we had been told that the

Muslims had ruled and oppressed us, that they had spread their religion in India with the Koran in one hand and the sword in the other, that the Muslim rulers had abducted our women, destroyed our temples, polluted our sacred places. As we grew older we read about the wars of the Rajputs, the Marathas, and the Sikhs against the Muslims, and of the intolerance and oppressions of Aurangzeb. In nineteenth-century Bengali literature the Muslims were always referred to under the contemptuous epithet of Yavana. The historical romances of Bankim Chandra Chatterji and Ramesh Chandra Dutt glorified Hindu rebellion against Muslim rule and showed the Muslims in a correspondingly poor light. Chatterji was positively and fiercely anti-Muslim. We were eager readers of these romances and we readily absorbed their spirit.

Our attitude to the Muslims whom we saw around us was also influenced, if not by the positive utterances, at all events by the silences, of our nineteenth-century writers. In them the hatred of the Muslim was the hatred of the Muslim in history. It operated, as I have said, retrospectively. Of Muslims as contemporaries they were almost totally oblivious; and when they were not forgetful they were indifferent. British rule in itself was a factor which discouraged the cultivation of Islamic culture and sympathies by the Hindus, and to British rule was added the far stronger influence of the discovery of the ancient Indian civilization. The very first result of this renaissance was a progressive de-Islamization of the Hindus of India and a corresponding revival of Hindu traditions. Throughout the nineteenth century the culture of the Hindus of India was taken back to its ancient Sanskritic foundations. The only non-Hindu influences which it recognized and tried to assimilate were European. All the thinkers and reformers of modern India from Ram Mohan Roy to Rabindranath Tagore based their life-work on the formula of a synthesis, by which they understood a synthesis of Hindu and European currents. Islamic trends and traditions did not touch even the arc of their consciousness.

Thus the new Indian culture of the nineteenth century built a perimeter of its own and put specifically Muslim influences and aspirations beyond the pale. In relation to it the Muslims stood outside as an external proletariat, and if the Muslims wanted to come into its world they could come only after giving up all their Islamic values and traditions. The modern Hindu did indeed send many invitations to the Muslims:

Will you, won't you, will you, won't you, will you join the dance?
Will you, won't you, will you, won't you, won't you join the
dance?

The modern Hindu also felt very aggrieved when the Muslim did
not show any alacrity to accept their invitations. But the Muslim was
perfectly clear-sighted and sensible:

Said he thanked the whiting kindly, but he would not join the
dance.
Would not, could not, would not, could not, would not join the
dance.

When the Muslims were invited to join the Congress on its very
inception their leaders very politely but firmly declined, and one of the
greatest of them said shrewdly that the Muslims, "tied to the wheels of
the Juggernaut of majority, would be in the end crushed out of all
semblance of nationality." The so-called two-nation theory was
formulated long before Mr. Jinnah or the Muslim League: in truth, it
was not a theory at all; it was a fact of history. Everybody knew this as
early as the turn of the century. Even as children we knew it from before
the Swadeshi movement.

The nationalist movement brought about an accentuation of the
difference. Theoretically it preached Hindu-Muslim unity. We sang
quite a number of songs which taught us that the Hindu and the Muslim
were brothers. But against that unconvincing preaching was to be set the
definite inculcation of an anti-Muslim doctrine, which took two forms.
In one of its aspects it was a further perfection of the historical enmity.
Nationalism cannot flourish in the abstract: Indian nationalism had to be
correlated to the facts of the political history of India; and in bringing
about this necessary correlation the Hindu nationalists showed
themselves to be highly selective. Even the theoretician of the Swadeshi
movement, Bepin Chandra Pal, wrote: "If the Moslem leaders tried to
wipe out the memories of the Sikhs and the Mahrattas, the Hindu
nationalist leaders sought to revive them. It was no doubt a supreme
psychological need of nationalist propaganda; and so far as these
memories were revived to recreate the self-confidence of a people
suffering from a state of hopeless and listless inertia, they did only good
and no harm." But even Pal had to admit: "It gradually awoke, at least in
a section of the nationalists, the foolish and suicidal ambition of once
more re-establishing either a single Hindu state or a confederacy of
Hindu states in India."

The other and the more dangerous form of the aggravation of Hindu Muslim antagonism by the Swadeshi movement was that this hostility was not brought down from the historical to the contemporary plane, and converted from a retrospective hatred to a current hatred. For this the Muslims were as responsible as the Hindus, although, as I see it, they could hardly have acted otherwise than they did without abandoning their group consciousness as Muslims. With the prospect of a transfer of political power from British to Indian hands the old Hindu-Muslim political rivalry was bound to be resuscitated. It was; and to begin with, the Muslims showed themselves as the allies of the British and opponents of the nationalists. It was in two districts adjacent to my own that this new form of antagonism first made its appearance. My early memories are crowded with the incidents of this clash and the conversations arising out of it. The Muslim League was formed at Dacca, and one of the earliest Hindu-Muslim clashes with a purely political complexion took place in the chief town of my mother's district, Comilla.

I shall cease generalizing at this point and relate some of the experiences of my boyhood. When living in Calcutta, as I have done for the greater part of my life, I hardly met any Muslims and became intimate with none. There I found an arrogant contempt for the Muslims and a deep-seated hostility towards them, which could have been produced only by a complete insulation of the two communities and absence of personal relations between their members. This inhuman antagonism could not exist in East Bengal, where owing to the number of the Muslims and also to the fact that they were Bengali-speaking, the economic and social life of the two communities was interwoven. Even when there was no unity of moral and religious outlook, as for the most part there was not, the mere physical contiguity could not be avoided; and when one has to meet another person at all times of the day on personal business, it is very difficult to visit on him the wrath generated by the supposed historical injuries inflicted by his community. The most serious and tragic aspect of the Hindu-Muslim discord in India today is the creation of a moral atmosphere in which it has become possible to extend the rancorous hatred which one can feel only for an abstract entity, or only for the foe who is of one's household, to the relations between man and man, neighbour and neighbour, friend and friend, playfellow and playfellow, fellow-worker and fellow-worker, when they happen to be of rival faiths. We began without this hatred.

There were a number of Muslim lawyers in our street, whom we respected as much as any other colleague of my father. With their sons and nephews we were as friendly as with the children of our Hindu neighbours, and two boys, Akhtar and Karim, were my particular friends. A very large number of our school-fellows were Muslim, and in the whole school there were at least as many Muslim boys as Hindu. We worked, talked, and played with them quite naturally. We never associated them with the abstract entity labelled Muslim, existing in our historical consciousness, for which we had such hatred, and it never occurred to us that anything could happen which could make us modify our behaviour towards our Muslim neighbours in the light of collective emotions generated by collective rivalries.

But the change inevitably came, and came very early. It was from the end of 1906 that we became conscious of a new kind of hatred for the Muslims, which sprang out of the present and showed signs of poisoning our personal relations with our Muslim neighbours and school-fellows. If the sprouting enmity did not go to the length of inducing us to give up all intercourse with them, it made us at all events treat them with a marked decline of cordiality. We began to hear angry comment in the mouths of the elders that the Muslims were coming out quite openly in favour of partition and on the side of the English. Nawab Salimullah of Dacca, the protagonist of the Muslim League and new Muslim politics, became our particular *bete noire*—and we contemptuously called him "The One-eyed." We also noticed that our Muslim school-fellows were beginning to air the fact of their being Muslims rather more consciously than before and with a touch of assertiveness. Its first expression in our school was the protest of the Muslim students against acting certain scenes from a Bengali drama on the school anniversary day. We had always acted these scenes and saw no justification for the protest, but the Muslim boys said that the speeches were offensive to Muslim feeling, which of course they were, because no Bengali historical play written by a Hindu is complimentary to the former Muslim rulers of the country. The school authorities stopped the anniversary celebrations altogether, and we waited long in the hope of their revising their decision. But they did not, and we came back home almost in tears, leaving all the decorations of the hall, over which we had spent so much labour, as if the performance were to take place in the evening.

At about the same time we heard of the rioting in the town of Comilla, occasioned by the visit of the Nawab of Dacca. The conversation of the elders gave us the impression that although the troubles had been provoked and started by the Muslims, they, and more particularly their Nawab, had not come out of the affair with flying colours. The elders related with contemptuous amusement that as soon as a gun had been fired at the Nawab from a Hindu house, he had run for dear life to Dacca. That was our version of the events, and we, the children, discussed with glee the flight and loss of face of Salimullah the One-eyed.

But the next Hindu-Muslim episode gave us a sense of frustration. Late in the spring of 1907, at the time of the Hindu festival of Vasanti Puja, the image of the goddess Durga was desecrated; in fact, broken to pieces by a Muslim mob at Jamalpur, one of the subdivisional headquarters of Mymensingh district. We were furious, and we heard with still greater fury that the magistrate of Mymensingh, Mr. Clarke, had prevented the volunteers of the Suhrid and Sadhana Samitis from going to Jamalpur to help the Hindus there. Had they been allowed to go, we felt certain they would have taught the Muslims a lesson which they would not have soon forgotten. It appeared that Muslims were doing for the British the dirty work of suppressing the nationalist movement by terrorizing the Hindus in general, and we could not get at them on account of their powerful protectors. Mr. Clarke, the magistrate, was already very unpopular with us as a violent opponent of the Swadeshi movement. He used to fly into a rage, and the most undignified rage, at the mere cry of *Vande Mataram,* and mischievous little boys let go no opportunity of annoying him and watching the fun by shouting *Vande Mataram* from behind walls and hedges when they saw him passing. After the Jamalpur affair both he and the Muslims became even more unpopular with us.

It was just after this incident that we heard Kishorganj people talking with some excitement and panic of the possibility of the coming of Nawab Nawab Ali Chaudhuri, a well-known Muslim zamindar, to our town. Thought not hated as much as the Nawab of Dacca, he too was suspect in our eyes, and people felt that if he came to the town serious trouble would follow. My mother and we, the children, were then getting ready to go away to Kalikutch, and we did not pay much attention to the rumours, nor did it strike us, as I have already said, that the possibility of a Hindu-Muslim riot in the town had anything to do with our going. At Kalikutch people surprised us by asking whether we had come away on account of the likelihood of trouble at Kishorganj. We pooh-poohed the idea, but when we came back to Kishorganj we were told, very definitely by our school-fellows that my father had sent us away to be out of harm's way, should anything have happened at Kishorganj. But, actually, Nawab Nawab Ali Chaudhuri had not come. Most probably he had been advised not to, in view of the Hindu-Muslim tension throughout the district. The year 1907 was a year of very bad feelings between Hindu and Muslim. At Kalikutch we heard ceaseless talk about the possibility of attacks on us by the Muslims, and at Kishorganj, too, these rumours were persistent. Even friends, when they belonged to the rival communities, kept discreetly aloof for the time being. The Nawab came to Kishorganj a year later and was given a tremendous reception by the Muslims. The high feeling had by that time subsided, and there was no incident. On the contrary, we rather admired the Muslim procession and thought they were making quite a good show of it. This was all the more of a surprise because the Muslims were not as practised in public demonstrations as we Hindus were.

Many years afterwards my father told me the whole story of our going away to Kalikutch. It was indeed due partly to the expectation of Hindu-Muslim trouble. In recent years, wherever Hindu-Muslim rioting took place in Bengal over large tracts of the countryside, the men were seen to run away leaving their women folk and children behind. But in our childhood this was not considered to be quite creditable on the part of the men, and my father particularly was a believer in the English method of putting women and children out of the way when he wanted to fight. He told me that very thorough preparations had been made by the Hindus to meet possible Muslim attacks. Trunkfuls of pistols and ammunition had been passed from house to house; swords, spears, and even bows and arrows had been collected in large quantities. Every Hindu house would have been defended by men practised in arms, and blood would have flowed had there been a clash. At the same time, my father also told me that he had got the Muslim version from a close friend of his, who was a notable Muslim gentleman from the village of Baulai, near Kishorganj. This friend told him some months afterwards, when they could exchange notes, that, all along, the Muslims of Kishorganj on their part had been anticipating Hindu attacks on themselves in retaliation for what had happened at Jamalpur and had made their defensive preparations. To fear the worst and be prepared for it is always very dangerous game, and when during the recent riots in Delhi in 1947 I heard the Hindu chatter that the Muslims had made extensive preparations for attacking the Hindus, I naturally recalled the story of the Hindu preparations and Muslim counter-preparations, or if one wants to have it put differently, of the Muslim preparations and Hindu counter-preparations at Kishorganj in 1907 in the now forgotten epoch of the Swadeshi movement, and I thought that there was no new thing under the sun.

Although open clashes were avoided, the year left a permanent legacy of estrangement. A cold dislike for the Muslim settled down in our hearts, putting an end to all real intimacy of relationship. Curiously enough, with us, the boys of Kishorganj, it found visible expression in the division of our class into two sections, one composed purely of Hindus and the other of Muslims. We never came to know all the circumstances of this division. Whether or not the Muslim boys had also expressed unwillingness to sit with us, for sometime past we, the Hindu boys, had been clamouring that we did not want to sit with the Muslim boys, because they smelt of onions. The authorities of the school may have heard of this. It is also possible that they acted on their own initiative. A third possibility is that they received instructions from the Inspector of Schools. In any case, they carried out a change of deep significance. Compartmentization by communities came into our education before it was introduced into our politics. Nobody seemed to be sorry. On the other hand we were as pleased with the division as were quite a respectable number of high placed and low-placed imbeciles at the division of India in 1947...

THE PROBLEM OF POLITICAL ACTION

... The problem of political action exercised us from the very beginning. The meetings, processions, demonstrations, and the boycott were good enough as the means of expressing our discontent, but even as children we felt that they were not to be identified with true political action and could not by themselves bring us liberation from foreign domination. At best they offered us openings for suffering for our cause, and we were prepared to suffer because we knew unless we went through suffering we could develop neither will nor character. None the less, we almost instinctively felt that the most effective kind of effort could not come unless we were given a method containing the possibility of going over to the offensive, wresting the initiative from the English. This, in the ultimate analysis, we could think of as nothing but armed rebellion.

From the outset we judged all political action by the criterion of insurrection. We took it as an axiom that only military power, actual or potential, could drive out the English. This idea obtained a lodgment not only in the minds of us, the young, but fantastic as it may sound, in those of our elders as well. I can cite a casual remark of my mother to illustrate this point. One day a school-fellow of mine and I had a great argument whether we should or should not be able to keep our independence if we won it. We carried the dispute to my mother. She heard us and then made a very brief remark, "If you are able to win your independence from the English by driving them out of the country, you will also be able to keep it." I was not more than ten years old when my mother told me this. But her remark made an deep impression on me. Of course, at the time, neither we nor our parents could conceive of a situation in which, in less than fifty years, the English power in India would come to an end of its one inanition without our acquiring in the process of extorting our independence that strength which would be adequate to preserve it. We never thought we could secure independence, or even gain it, without military power, and therefore military power was to us the key to the political problem. All our thoughts and efforts converged on the task, however small to begin with, of creating military power.

The first step towards this end was to set up physical-culture clubs. These became a feature of the nationalist agitation of 1905. They were not pure and simple institutions of physical culture, but were, like the Prussian gymnastic clubs organized by the poet Jahn before the war of liberation against Napoleon, institutions for giving training in patriotism, collective discipline, and the ethics of nationalism, with the ultimate object of raising a national army to overthrow British rule. There were two such clubs at Kalikutch. One of them was conducted by Mahendra Babu and the other run by a young gentleman of the same clan whose name was Rasik Nandi. His associate and right-hand man was the husband of my Aunt Sushila of Banagram, the same man who had abandoned her and his two children. His name was Prakash Chaudhuri. Neither of the men had any education, and therefore their club was on a lower ideological plane compared with Mahendra Babu's. But they had enthusiasm.

We frequented their club, not Mahendra Babu's. Almost every afternoon for some weeks we went there as the tomtoms began to beat, and watched the display. The greatest emphasis was placed on fencing with singlesticks. Rasik Nandi and Prakash Chaudhuri led like the most important couple at a ball. In this case the partners stood facing each other from the opposite ends of the lawn, their *dhotis* tucked high, the stick in right hand, and the cane buckler in the left. They glared at each other and gave the traditional war cry of the Bengal dacoit and fighter— *ha re re re re-e-e-e-e-e-e!*" In actual fact the first teachers in these physical culture clubs were the hereditary Mussalman retainers who were kept by the zamindars in their employ to do all their violent work and had the craft handed down from father to son.

After the opening shout the fighters began to advance towards each other, making figures on the ground which were as elaborate and complicated as those of a dance. As they closed up there commenced a tense struggle in which each tried to hit the other, and the field rang with the raps of sticks on bucklers. But as soon as one of the men thought he had had enough he relaxed his grimace and began to fall back, making the same complex figures and fighting back against the vigorous pursuit of his opponent.

The excitement spread to us, and soon we began to practise on our own. Our teacher was an old but immensely powerful fisherman, Golak by name, who was also in the habit of holding forth on the motive behind all this practice as he understood that motive. "Don't worry", he assured us almost everyday, "if the Mussalmans come we'll fight like this." Golak made long bamboo spears for us and put us through the practice of thrusting and counter-thrusting with them. One day while practising I wounded my sister, and after that we were forbidden to handle spears. But the stick practice was kept up.

The military cast of my political thought was hardened by the drills and physical exercises I went through, by the inculcation in all of us of the habit of implicit obedience to our leaders, and the preaching of an impossible ideal of discipline. But there could not be, of course, any open preparation for military action, not even talk about it. Thus from the very beginning our military thought fell under the shadow of conspiratorial methods. I discovered later that from the outset many of the organizers of the secret conspiratorial societies had contemplated a quite different method of political action—assassination, in imitation of the Russian revolutionists. But for a long time I did not realize this, and when at last I perceived in what direction the revolutionary movement was going I lost much of my sympathy for it. But that is a later story. At the beginning even the outrages on individuals—the attempt to blow up the train of the Lieutenant-Governor of Bengal, the murder of Mr. Allen at Goalundo, the explosion at Muzzafarpore of a bomb which was meant for Mr. Kingsford, the judge, but succeeded only in killing two English women, all examples of that side of the conspiratorial method which relies on the assassination of officials and terrorization of the governing class—were interpreted by me as experiments in insurrection. I even glorified the dacoity of Barha, the first, and still the most sensational, political dacoity in Bengal.

In the light of these early feelings the men of the Maniktallah Bomb Case, who were the organizers of the Muzzafarpore outrage, became our heroes instantly. They were all arrested in May 1908, and in the weeks following my brother and I were almost always engaged in manufacturing make-believe bombs of coconut shell with charcoal, kerosene and other combustible substances inside them. One day a friend of my father saw us at work and remarked to him that quite a new mood was coming over the country, so that even small boys, instead of being frightened by the arrests, had been prompted by the account of the activities of the Maniktallah conspirators to imitate them. But even then I could not make a hero of Praphulla Chaki, one of the young men who had killed the Kennedys and had escaped arrest only by committing suicide. Nor could I share the apotheosis of Khudiram Bose, the other young man responsible for the Muzzafarpore outrage. I felt that there was something repelling in the glorification of mere murder. Pictures showing the dead body of Praphulla Chaki tied to a frame and portraits of Khudiram Bose were circulating in large numbers at the time. I never could bear to look at them, far less take them home and keep them religiously in our boxes. As the revolutionary movement tended more and more towards the method of murder and robbery I began to feel an emotional revulsion from it. In this my mother's attitude influenced me very strongly. From the very beginning she came out very decidedly against murder and dacoity. She refused to concede that the end justified the means. Her mind never succumbed to the casuistry which became all too prevalent amongst us.

In spite of the utter impracticability of the military method my mind remained permanently militarized in regard to politics. In other words, it remained wedded to a vision. War to me always was, and with qualifications still is, the ultimate and supreme resource of policy. This bent was confirmed in me by the spectacle of military drill and military smartness presented by the volunteers of the Sadhana and Suhrid

Samitis at the time of the political conference at Kishorganj. After the conference I was always drilling my brothers, and one day our nephew Rajendra, seeing me doing this and absorbing how faithfully I was copying the drill of the volunteers, made me the captain of a small team, in which there were not only my brothers, but also all the boys of our side of the town. He told me that I was their captain, and would drill them everyday, and that they were to obey me implicitly. It speaks volumes for the sense of discipline that was coming over that very indisciplined people, the Bengalis, under the stimulus and influence of the Swadeshi movement, that even boys who were older than I or considerably stronger never demurred to my orders. It was almost like the young and slight Napoleon cowing down the Massénas and Augereaus.

I drilled the boys throughout the summer, sometimes making them go down to the edge of the river and lie down in the mud. We built a small redoubt behind our study and bedroom in two floors, and stored in it not only mud shells but also bamboo and wooden spears, which in the hands of small and irresponsible boys could easily prove lethal; and one day an incident did happen that led to the demolition of the structure and confiscation of the arms. As I was leading a storming party after bombarding the fort, the garrison, which had had to endure a shower of lumps of earth for some time, went for the attackers with their spears. One of these, in the hands of my fiery younger brother, hit the head of one of the boys on my side and made a flesh wound. We were terribly frightened, and my mother hearing of it came running and bandaged the boy's head. After that she ordered the immediate destruction of the redoubt.

The permanent result in me of this early initiation in military ways was the development of a taste for the study of military history and art of warfare, which enabled me at a considerably later period of my life to earn my living as a commentator on the operations of the Second World War. But something was absorbed also by my moral being. I could and can never think of any collective action, and more especially political action, except as the calm and resolute action of formed bodies of men. The vision of valiant warriors in uniform marching under the complete control of their leaders, who can urge or check them by a sign of the hand, keeps rising before my eyes. For this reason the course of political agitation in India has been one of the greatest mortifications of my life. I have been compelled to look on spectacles of simian gesticulation and

chatter by ragged and wild mobs and read or hear them glorified as
rebellion or revolution. Even when my heart was wholly in the
nationalist movement I could never endure that sight, nor tolerate that
misrepresentation...

16

Romantic evocation of past greatness and an appeal to Hindu and regional sentiments greatly enhanced the attraction of nationalism. The Bengal partition agitation of 1905-1907 was the first genuinely populist upheaval of the national struggle. But it left the movement fragmented and leaderless. In similar fashion conspiratorial terrorism, although emotionally satisfying, held out no hope of moving the British, whose military strength was overwhelming and whose conscience was not troubled by the repression of violence. Into this scene emerged the figure of Mohandas K. Gandhi. A man of intense moral conviction and shrewd political sense, Gandhi transformed India's sense of weakness from a liability into an asset. Self-suffering he argued, if undertaken with ethically pure motives and on a large scale, could bring both personal strength and national renewal. In the following study of Gandhi's background and upbringing Susanne Rudolph shows how he developed his unique programme of satyagraha, or non-violent non-cooperation, and how it fitted the needs of India at the time.

The New Courage: An Essay on Gandhi's Psychology

SUSANNE HOEBER RUDOLPH

In an era that takes matters of religious faith lightly, it becomes difficult to consider thoughtfully a man who is suspected of saintliness. The task is particularly vexing for Americans, who have no feudal historic memories to remind them that saints were once important people. The obvious solution is to avoid the issue of saintliness altogether—to avoid, for example, questions about whether Gandhi's political shrewdness was compatible with the essential innocence of heart that one asks of saints; above all, to avoid trying to satisfy a generation of ambivalent skeptics who in one breath deny that saints exist and in the next maintain that Gandhi could not have been one because he did not meet such and such criterion of saintliness. The issue of saintliness is a diversion from a serious consideration of Gandhi's contribution.

Reprinted by permission from *World Politics*, Vol. XVI, No. 1 (October, 1963), pp. 98-117. Footnotes omitted.

The matter of Gandhi's role in speeding England's exit from India provides another distraction. It can be argued plausibly that England would have departed from the subcontinent in or around 1947 whether or not Gandhi had lived and acted. The question of Gandhi's success or failure in his stated political objective fails to touch what may turn out to be the most important contribution of his career—what he did for Indians, rather than what he did to Englishmen. Like sit-ins in the American South, which appear to have a significant subjective effect on the self-estimation and sense of potency of their Negro participants—to some extent regardless of whether they "succeed" or "fail" objectively—Gandhi's nationalism provided an opportunity for Indians to act in ways which would repair wounds in the nation's self-esteem inflicted by 150 years of imperialized existence—regardless of the short-term political consequences of his nationalism.

Like so many thinkers and actors in the Indian tradition, Gandhi cared more for men's inner environment than their outer and was highly self-conscious about the effect his method would have on how Indians felt about themselves. The young Nehru, who often doubted that the Mahatma's political tactics were the most efficacious, concedes this effect on the nationalist generation again and again: "Much that he said we only partially accepted or sometimes did not accept at all. But all this was secondary. The essence of his teaching was fearlessness and truth and action allied to these....So, suddenly as it were, that black pall of fear was lifted from the people's shoulders, not wholly, of course, but to an amazing degree....It was a psychological change, almost as if some expert in psychoanalytic method had probed deep into the patient's past, found out the origins of his complexes, exposed them to his view, and thus rid him of that burden."

The portrait of Gandhi probing the nation's historical subconscious is not inept. Gandhi had a unique sensibility both for the nightmare terrors of the Indian psyche and for its commonplace daytime self-doubts. He understood both the fundamental fear of Indians that those Englishmen who judged them as lacking in basic components of moral worth—like courage—might be right, and their more superficial doubts as to their technical ability to do anything about removing the *raj*. The nightmare fears he understood in party by analogy with his own personal terrors, terrors involving especially the issue of courage. The shape which he gave to the national movement—above all, the technique of *satyagraha,* or non-violent resistance—had much more than strategic significance; it provided a path of action which "solved" some problems of Indian self-esteem arising from acceptance of the negative judgments of Englishmen.

The things that Englishmen had to say about India in the nineteenth century varied so widely that any attempt to distill their judgments seems wildly rash. And yet, in the second half of the nineteenth century and at the turning of the twentieth, even as the nationalist movement was gathering strength and new policy decisions by Englishmen carried India further toward self-government, certain distinctive themes in English judgments of India emerged. These judgments distinguished between certain categories of Indians, especially between "masculine" and "feminine" races; between the "natural" Indian leaders and the unrepresentative *babus* "posing" as leaders; and between the "real" Indians and the *assimiladoes*. In each case, the categories carried their own implications as to who was on the side of the angels. These themes are to be found more in the pronouncements of men like Lytton, Fitzjames Stephens, John Strachey and Curzon, hostile to Indian self-rule,than Ripon or Allen Octavian Hume, sanguine on the same topic. And it is difficult to say whether the judgments were a product of the belief that India should not rule herself, or whether the judgments produced that belief. In any case, the themes became a conventional part of the unsystematic theory which rationalized the maintenance of Empire.

The distinctions between masculine and feminine races is an especially pervasive theme in this unsystematic imperialist theory and appeared most frequently in connection with the Bengalis, whom most Englishmen knew best and who had most swiftly responded to English culture. The late Joseph Schumpeter remarked in his account of imperialism that the imperialists were feudal atavists, men whose hunger for the chivalric life could not be accommodated by the middle-class civilization of nineteenth-century Europe, and who turned to the new frontiers of the colonies for the challenge they could not find at home. The picture one has of the pre-competition *wallahs,* the early nineteenth-century administrators in India, clodhopping Collectors with their trusty rifles slung over their shoulders and their boar spears in their left hand, confirms this view. Such men would have felt impatience with the unathletic Bengali, and admiration for the muscular and venturesome tribal people of the North-west. When Kipling declared that "East is East and West is West and never the twain shall meet," he added that there was indeed *one* equalizer of national difference: courage. The frontier Pathan and the English soldier of his ballad could understand one another as warriors: "But there is neither East nor West, Border, nor Breed, nor Birth, when two strong men stand face to face, though they come from the ends of the earth." But, unfortunately; Englishmen fancied that this levelling element was available only among a limited number of Indians. By the second half of the century, adventurous Englishmen went to Africa as often as to India; and if men of Strachey's and Curzon's era speak with contempt of Bengali "feminism", it is more with the ambivalent masculinity produced by *fin de siecle* British public-school training. Much of Indian society, particularly that made up of the non-martial twice-born castes, does seem to tolerate a larger component of feminine qualities in its men than most Western societies do even though homosexuality appears to be a less significant issue in India than in more masculine countries. In any case, a substantial group of English felt ill at ease in a culture where the demand for overt signs of martial, leatherfaced masculinity was not very strong, and a much more gentle, even effete, masculinity was understood to be compatible with being an effective man. They much preferred the "races"—like the Sikhs and Muslims and Rajputs and Pathans—that exhibited a more familiar aggressive spirit.

For a passage that exhibits this particular theme, one may turn to John Strachey's book *India,* which is dedicated to Fitzjames Stephens, and represented a usual training assignment for Indian Civil Service probationers just before the turn of the century. Describing the diverse races of India, it begins with a quote from Macaulay concerning the Bengalis: "The physical organisation of the Bengali is feeble even to effeminacy. He lives in a constant vapour bath. His pursuits are sedentary, his limbs delicate, his movements languid. During many ages he has been trampled upon by men of bolder and more hardy breeds....His mind bears a singular analogy to his body. It is weak even to helplessness for purposes of manly resistance; but its suppleness and its tact move the children of sterner climates to admiration not unmingled with contempt...."

Strachey proceeded to distinguish the more vigorous Muslims from the feeble Bengalis—presumably Hindu Bengalis—only to be drawn back in a kind of horrified fascination to his previous subject: "The Mohammedan peasantry of the eastern portion of the province are men of robuster character....It has often been said, and it is probably true,

that Bengal is the only country in the world where you can find a great
population among whom personal cowardice is looked upon as in no
way disgraceful. This is no invention of their enemies; the Bengalis
have themselves no shame or scruple in declaring it to be a fact ....It is
for such reasons that Englishmen who know Bengal, and the
extraordinary effeminacy of its people, find it difficult to treat seriously
many of the political declamations in which the English-speaking
Bengalis are often fond of indulging." The contrast to these supple,
vapour-bathed creatures was to be found among the "martial" races, the
Sikhs, Pathans, Rajputs, and Muslims, people who by either caste ethic,
religion, or geographic circumstance adhered to a more aggressive
world view.

The distinction between the martial and non-martial was no
invention of the English. It had accumulated ethical and historical
meaning in Hindu caste structure, which inculcated a non-violent
perspective in some castes and an aggressive one in others. But in
English minds at the end of the century, the distinction was stressed as
much for its instrumental utility in the imperialist theory as for its
academic interest as a description of caste or regional character. The
"martial" races for the most part adhered to the British *raj*, not because
they were martial—the unlikely collaboration of the Pathans with
Gandhi must have come as a fearful shock to many Englishmen—but
for political considerations: the Rajputs because they were the princes
of states whose autonomy would be threatened by a self-ruled India, the
Muslims because they feared a Hindu majority in an independent India.
The non-martial races, on the other hand, produced nationalism, the
non-violent Brahmans and Kayasths providing shock troops of the pen
to launch nationalist polemics in dailies and pamphlets, and speakers in
legislatures who attacked the government with the Mill and Mazzini
discovered in Anglicized university classes." They produced it
especially in Bengal, where the English influence was oldest. Since the
capital was then at Calcutta, and many secretariat-centred Englishmen
therefore imagined Bengal was India, the non-martial epithet could be
freely generalized to Indian nationalism as a whole, without too much
care for the obvious anomaly in applying it to nationalist Chitpavan
Brahmans who spoke for a Maharashtra that had given English much
pain on the field of battle.

The masculine-feminine distinction overlapped with the "natural"
leader versus "unnatural" *babu* category as well as with the "real"

Indian-*assimiladoes* distinction. What could be more "natural" in a leadership position than a sturdy Rajput, whose fighting arm had given him dominion over the land of his fathers, and who stood in paternal and autocratic relationship to traditional followers? What less "natural" than the socially mobile men seeking to add political power to traditional priestly and literary power, the non-martial Brahmans and Kayasths whose new status was often a product of the opportunities England had created, and who claimed now to lead a rural India with which they had no long-inherited traditional leadership ties? To cap it, these *nouveaux arrivés* politicians and thinkers were no longer "real" Indians. They were men who had cut themselves off from India by successfully embracing the gifts of Western, or more particularly English culture. Englishmen greeted their success with the special brutality reserved by aristocracies for new men: if they failed to emulate, they showed their incapacity to appreciate and strive for higher ideals; if they successfully modelled themselves on their betters, they lost their integrity by trying to be something they "really" were not.

What is most significant about these distinctions, and what makes them relevant to the consideration of Gandhi, is that nationalist Indians half-accepted them. They half-accepted the implication that they were as impotent as women, and that on that account they somehow lacked moral worth as well. As the young Gandhi put it, "It must at the outset be admitted that the Hindus as a rule are notoriously weak." Why the fact of inferiority in arms, general technology, and effective political and administrative organization should persuade colonial people that they are morally and culturally inferior is not clear, but most of them seem to arrive at this conclusion. It is probably the most degrading and tragic consequence of colonialism. This state of mind—a sense of importence, combined with a fear of moral unworthiness arising from impotence—is not unique to India. It provided a central theme in other nationalist movements and led to attempts—to use the Chinese nationalist phrase—at self-strengthening. The fear that this impotence was innate in Indians was fed by the scientism of post-Darwinian race theory in the late nineteenth century. Ethnologists, particularly ethnologists of India, were fond of imputing a biological fixity to culturally transmitted traits. Further, men of the nationalist generation were by no means sure that they were "natural" leaders, or that they were still Indians. A good bit of the Hindu fundamentalism that suddenly inflamed men like Sri Aurobindo, raised in an emphatic Western tradition, may be related to this quest to be "really" Indian.

One of the first items on the agenda of nationalism, once it stepped beyond the peaceable, intelligent, and ineffectual parliamentarism of the early nationalists and began to grapple with the moral and emotional issues of Indian self-definition, was the creation of an answer to the charge of national impotence. A veriety of answers were formulated— among them the calisthenic muscle-building and aggressive Hindu spirit-building launched by the gymnastic societies of militant Mahrattas at Poona. "Our young men must be strong," Swami Vivekananda urged a generation. "Religion will come afterwards... You will be nearer to Heaven through football than through the study of the Gita." Then there was the ascetic soldiery of the novel *Ananda Math*, training in a forest Ashram, brave, sturdy, disciplined; and the blood deeds of a terrorist generation in Bengal and the Punjab. Indeed, there seems to have been some perverse historical dialectic in violent Bengali nationalism: as though the young men of Calcutta were saying "No" to Macaulay's and Strachey's assertions of their physical ineffectualness. But their no's failed to convince: England could in good conscience manage young men who threw bombs, especially if they threw them at ladies on a Sunday afternoon, and violence did not in fact turn out to be an effective basis for rallying a mass Indian nationalism—except in some areas. These proofs of courage helped, but they did not help most people, and they did not help in the long run to build a sense of national self-esteem. For this, another formulation of the issue of courage was required, a formulation which had to speak to the other two issues as well.

Two of the issues of self-esteem which afflicted Indian nationalism—that of strength and weakness and that of cultural integrity—afflicted Gandhi personally. For him, they were connected: he was prepared to embrace any tradition, Indian or foreign, that would strengthen him. He confronted these issues over a period of some thirty-five years before he solved them for himself, but the solution that he then found helped his generation to deal with them as well. He resolved the issues of courage and of cultural integrity in connection with one another: much of his early life was spent deciding whether he could best master himself and his environment by following an English or quasi-English life path or by committing himself to a certain kind of Indian way. The dilemmas of the young Gandhi in many ways approximated those of his generation, and to grasp them one must turn to his autobiography, a document which makes it clear that he meant to be judged privately and publicly simultaneously. The autobiography must be read with a particularly sensitive ear, one that "hears" what he has to say concerning his diet, or his passion for his wife, considers what this might mean for his political style, and does not relegate these remarks to the category of personal foibles and curiosities that constitute the small talk rather than the significant statements of a great man.

The small princely state of Porbander, in Kathiawad, where he was born in 1869, lies on the Sea of Oman, in the centre of an area which has always been open to the trade of Iran, Arabia, and Africa on the one hand, and the interior of India on the other. He was born to the Modh Banya caste, a trading caste which has flourished in that region owing to the hospitable conditions for commerce. His grandfather, whose memories had taken on mythical grandeur by the time Gandhi was a child, served, as members of trading castes often did in Western India, as Prime Minister of a princely state. Gandhi's father did the same, though probably with less dash than the grandfather, who served before princely states had fallen into decay. Gandhi grew up in the midst of non-violent and ascetic influences. The Modh Banyas, like other merchant castes, held to a non-violent ethic suited to commerce, and to ascetic standards which often supplied the moral equivalent of a Protestant ethic for Indian merchant castes. Kathiawad was strongly influenced by the Vaishnavites, with additional influences from Jainism—the most non-violent of Indian sects. Nor were the Gandhis indifferent practitioners of the sectarian and caste ethic. They regularly visited the temple, even had their own temple. During the three years as an invalid which preceded his death Gandhi's father seems to have been most attentive to religious matters. Gandhi's mother painstakingly observed the more rigorous demands of her faith. Her strong ascetic demands on herself—"self-suffering", as Gandhi was to call it when he made it part of his political method—seem to have been a central virtue in the Gandhi home. Mrs. Gandhi fasted frequently and practised other austerities. "During the four months of *Chaturmas* Putlibai lived on one meal a day and fasted on every alternate day." "Self-suffering" was important in other ways to the family. If one member of the household was angry with another, he would punish him by imposing some penalty on himself. Thus young Gandhi angry because his family failed to summon to dinner a friend whom he wished to invite—it may have been a Muslim friend, with whom the family could not dine without transgressing the caste ethic—ceased to eat mangoes for the season, though it was his favourite fruit. The family was duly distressed. On another occasion, Gandhi, finding difficulty in confessing a minor theft to his father, wrote him a note. "In this note not only did I confess my guilt, but I asked adequate punishment for it, and closed with a request to him not to punish himself for my offence." It was the father's self-suffering, not punishment, that he claims to have feared most. Gandhi's father, in turn, had used self-punishment in his relations with the ruler he served by vowing to go without food and drink until arrangements were made for his transport out of the state when his master was reluctant to accept his resignation.

Gandhi himself was a shy, fearful, and pathetic child. "I used to be haunted by the fear of thieves, ghosts, and serpents. I did not dare stir out of doors at night." He feared school and his school fellows: "I used to be very shy and avoided all company. My books and my lessons were my sole companions. To be at school at the stroke of the hour and to run back home as soon as school closed—that was my daily habit. I literally ran back, because I could not bear to talk to anybody. I was even afraid lest anyone should poke fun at me." He shunned the actively virile and competitive sports, enjoying neither cricket nor gymnastics, which his headmaster made compulsory in line with English public-school models. Gandhi's father, entertaining a rather different idea of what was good for the character of a young man, had his son exempted from sports so the boy might come home and nurse him. It was uncompetitive, unassertive walking which the young man learned to like. His wife Kasturba whom he married at the age of thirteen, was no help in enhancing the self-esteem of a fearful child. She was willful and self-assertive, did not reciprocate his passion, and resolutely refused to be the deferential Hindu wife he had hoped for, adding to his sense that he could not command where others had traditionally done so. He describes himself at thirteen or fourteen as a boy who had failed to develop a sense of personal competence in any area.

To judge from his subsequent actions, one must conclude that Gandhi found very little support in his immediate environment for solving the issue of personal competence. He felt himself insufficiently strong and courageous, and longed to be brave and aggressive. He had an inexhaustible fund of energy from the time he was quite small, but seems not to have known how to convert it into assertiveness. The caste ethic of the Modh Banyas and Vaishnavite asceticism both discouraged all overt aspects of an aggressive, masculine assertiveness. *Ahimsa,* harmlessness, crucial to the doctrine of Gandhi as a mature leader, dictated meekness in almost all situations—though it should be added that Indian merchant castes often express a good many aggressive instincts in the practice of trade. Sexual expression, although formally sanctioned, was frowned upon. What one might call culinary masculinity, the eating of meat, was equally discouraged in a society which was vegetarian.

Gandhi staged a massive revolt against his family, caste, and religious ethic in an effort to gain a more helpful perspective. Between the ages of thirteen and sixteen, he undertook a resolute programme of transgressing every article of the codes which mattered to those around him. His counsellor in revolt was Sheikh Mehtab—a Muslim, significantly enough—representing an ethic totally different from his own, the ethic of one of the "martial" races. The friendship was the most significant and enduring of Gandhi's youth, lasting well into his South African years. Mehtab came to live with him there until, discovering his friend was bringing home prostitutes, Gandhi threw him out. It is usual among Gandhi's biographers to endorse the Mahatma's description of the relationship, that he took up Mehtab in order to reform him. In fact, on the evidence of Gandhi's own words, Mehtab was a model, and one from whom he only gradually liberated himself. Mehtab was everything Gandhi was not—strong, athletic, self-confident, lusty, bold. As Gandhi writes, he was "...hardier, physically stronger, and more daring.... He could run long distances and extraordinarily fast. He was an adept in high and long jumping. He could put up with any amount of corporal punishment. He would often display his exploits to me and, as one is always dazzled when he sees in others the qualities he lacks himself, I was dazzled..." Mehtab encouraged Gandhi to eat meat, urging that it would have a physiological effect in lending him new strength. "You know how hardy I am," he said, "and how great a runner too. It is because I am a meat-eater." But there was a larger social context to the meat-eating issue. It had become attached to the problem of cultural virility for people other than Gandhi. Many people in Kathiawad, according to Gandhi, thought meat-eating was, so to speak, responsible for British imperialism, being the essence that made the Englishman strong. "Behold the mighty Englishman! He rules the Indian small; because being a meat-eater, he is five cubits tall!" went the ditty of Gandhi's schooldays. "I wished to be strong and daring and wanted my countrymen also to be such, so that we might defeat the English and make India free." Actually, Gandhi did not have to look to British culture to discover that meat-eating "produced" courage. The fighting castes of India, particularly the Kshatriyas, have always eaten meat, and it has always been thought to contribute to their strength. But meat-eating was not the only kind of demonstration of strength in which Mehtab supported Gandhi. There was also a brothel episode, presumably meant to lead Gandhi to a more zestful lustiness than the guilty pleasures of his legitimate bed. Gandhi suffered a Holden Caulfieldesque experience of tentative approach and horrified retreat.

The primary intention of this effort at rebellion was a search for courage and competence, to overcome fearfulness and shyness through following an ethic other than the one to which he had been born, an ethic practised by Englishmen and the "martial" races. But it should be pointed out that the search for courage itself exacted courage of another kind. To revolt in secret against strongly held family prejudices over a period of three years required considerable inner strength, strength of the kind the mature Gandhi would have approved, though in the service of other objectives. He demonstrated the same kind of courage, although he described himself as still a coward, when at the age of nineteen, after his father's death, he decided to go to England for an education. He was obliged to confront the opposition of the caste council at Bombay. In an open meeting where he appears to have been afflicted by little of the shyness he always attributed to himself, he faced the elders who forbade his English trip and threatened him with all the sanctions of outcasting if he defied their verdict. "I am helpless," he told them.

In some respects, the English experience, during which Gandhi studied for the matriculation exam and was eventually admitted to the bar, represented an attempt to solve the issue of self-esteem by acquiring a new cultural style and by escaping ties which he still deemed in some way responsible for his incompetence and weakness. For three months after his arrival, he dedicated himself to a systematic effort to become an English gentleman, ordering clothing of the correct cut in the Army and Navy Stores and evening clothes in Bond Street, worrying about his unruly hair which defied the civilising brush, unhappy perhaps that his prominent ears prevented his cultivating a suitably dashing appearance, spending time before the mirror in the morning tying his cravat, taking dancing lessons so that he might be fit for elegant social intercourse, and violin lessons to cultivate an ear for

Western music so he might hear the rhythm, which escaped him when dancing. In the hope of overcoming his incapacity to communicate effectively, he took elocution lessons, only to find that they helped him in neither public nor private speaking.

Some aspects of this systematic attempt to approximate urbane English manners remained with him for a long time: the pictures of the young Gandhi, as a lawyer earning thirty thousand dollars a year in the South Africa of 1900—one is apt to forget that he was capable of that kind of worldly success—presenting a late Edwardian appearance, bear witness to the experience. So did his English which, after three years in South Africa, bore the marks of relatively cool English understatement. The writings of his early maturity strike quite a different note from the un-English moralising of the *Autobiography,* written after he had become the Mahatma and returned to more Indian modes in all respects. But the attempt at Anglicisation apparently failed to satisfy Gandhi, partly because he could not always make a go of it, partly because it didn't "feel" right to him when he could. Besides, the England he encountered was not the England of public schools and playing fields, of clubs and sporting society, but an England closer to Kathiawad, an England of vegetarian Evangelicals and Theosophical reformers, an England suffering like Kathiawad from the effects of industrialization. After three months he gave up much of the Anglicization effort, and began a gradual return to a personal style of life more in line with the ascetic, self-denying, and non-violent ethic which he had left behind when he began his rebellion at home almost seven years before.

Gandhi now started to live very thriftily, partly through economic necessity, partly because the change "harmonized my inward and outward life." He had restricted himself to vegetarian restaurants because of a vow to his mother but had remained committed to meat-eating in theory in the interest of reforming the Indian character. Now he embraced vegetarianism by choice, in a spirit which stressed a different kind of strength than that which meat promised. He began to rejoice in the effort of denying himself, in the strength of mastering his pleasures. He walked rather than rode to his studies, and took up moral and philosophic writing seriously for the first time, although more in the spirit of one seeking confirmation than of one seeking. He was moved by the Biblical exhortation. "That ye resist not evil", and by passages urging self-suffering as a mode of conversion. He noted passages in the

Gita condemning the senses, and concluded that "renunciation was the highest form of religion."

In this period lay the beginning—it took another two decades to complete the process—of a rejection of any solutions to his personal dilemmas which were radically foreign to the Gujarat cultural setting in which he was born, solutions drawn primarily either from England or from various features of Indian culture which were closer to English culture. In this period also lay the beginning of his construction of an Indian solution for himself, a solution which finally produced the Gandhi who in 1906 began political action in South Africa, and who in 1920 took over the Indian nationalist movement. In the long run, these new experiments led to the development of a personal style in line with traditional Indian models rather than with the London-touched barrister style to which some other Indian nationalists adapted much more readily. The early experiments in vegetarian restaurants and the considered return to an un-English asceticism were not unrelated to the later techinques of agitation and appeals in line with traditional Indian sensibilities and perceptions.

But while, by the end of the English experience, Gandhi had learned to understand that the English solution was not the one which would meet the personal dilemmas he had taken to England with him, the man who returned to India, and spent several years in practice there, felt himself still a failure. "But notwithstanding my study, there was no end to my helplessness and fear." Though he was a barrister-at-law, more highly qualfied than a great many of the traditional *vakils* who had no such elevated training, he knew little Indian law and could not even master the fundamental skill of the courtroom lawyer—public speaking. In England, he had made several attempts to give public speeches, generally at vegetarian societies. Each time he failed. On one occasion, to encourage himself, he decided to tell an anecdote about Addison, as diffident as Gandhi, who rose on the floor of Commons and tried to open his speech by saying, "I conceive." Three times the unfortunate man uttered the same phrase, but could get no further. A wag rose and said: "The gentleman conceived thrice but brought forth nothing." Gandhi thought the story amusing; unfortunately, in his recitation of the anecdote he too got stuck, and had to sit down abruptly.

His first court case in India was a disaster; obliged to cross-examine plaintiff's witness in a petty case, he was unable to bring himself to open his mouth. "My head was reeling and I felt as though the whole court was doing likewise. I could think of no question to ask. The judge must have laughed, and the *vakils* no doubt enjoyed the spectacle." He retreated from court work altogether to return, more or less defeated, to Kathiawad, where he took up briefing cases for other lawyers, earning a respectable 300 rupees per month, but feeling that he would get nowhere at this rate. It is worth pointing out that a twenty-three year old Indian in 1892 who considered himself a failure at Rs. 300 per month had high standards. At twenty-four a personal tiff with the Political Agent—an Englishman—at Porbandar caused him to decide that he had no future there, and he determined to retreat from the Indian situation. "I wanted somehow to leave India." The flight seems to have come at the lowest moment of his life.

The low point was also the turning point. His first experiences in South Africa, where he went as a barrister for a Muslim firm, persuaded him that the lot of Indians in South Africa was a humiliating and opressed one. He was discriminated against on trains, beaten by low-class white men who laughed at his legalistic insistence upon his rights. Discussing his experience with other Indians, he discovered that the South African Indian community had suffered such humiliations for many years, pocketing insults as part of the conditions of trade. The discovery had a curious effect on his outlook. He recognized—rather suddenly, it seems from the autobiography-that the skills which he had acquired in recent years, particularly a facile use of English, a familiarity with legal codes and processes, and a belief that English justice must be enforced, were desperately needed and lacking among the Indian community. The South African Indians consisted of a merchant community and a much larger group of Tamil indentured labourers. Both lacked political sense and were ineffectual at dealing with any part of their environment that transcended business. In this setting Gandhi, as the only Indian barrister, found himself to be *the* Indian professional middle class. Skills which in India had seemed ordinary here seemed extraordinary and strengthened Gandhi's self-estimate with an apocalyptic abruptness. Within three weeks of his arrival in South Africa, the shy boy of twenty-four suddenly called a public meeting of all Indians in Pretoria for the common discussion of their wrongs and oppressions in the Transvsaal. With a new-found authority, the man who had been unable to speak in public rose to sum up the problems of the community and propose an agenda for their future actions. One has the sense that the overwhelming humiliations of the community around him suddenly transported him beyond the self-consciousness of his own failings, in a manner reminiscent of the stutterer in *He Who Must Die*. While speaking in court was an exercise which would show whether he measured up to the standard set by a famous barrister like Pherozeshah Mehta, a performance profoundly disturbing to a precarious ego, this speech had, ostensibly, nothing to do with his own standing. The new context, service, seems to have made it possible for the young man to do what he could not do where his own reputation was at stake. The fact that service could lend him the effectiveness and potency he otherwise lacked must have had much to do with the life path he chose. Away from home and the omnipresent reminders of early failure, and performing a new task, he felt, "I acquired some measure of my capacity." The South African experience added to his previous recognition that he must search for solutions compatible with the traditional Indian outlook and ways, the further recognition that his personal salvation lay in devoting himself to solving the problems of those who were more helpless than he.

But most crucial for Gandhi's history as an Indian leader, and for the issue of Indian courage generally, is not the mere fact that he found himself able, that he mastered his self-doubts and created a personal courage, but the kind of techniques in which he found his new competence and the style of leadership of which he found himself capable. He found his competence in techniques which rallied Indians to refute English imputations of their lack of courage, without, however, repairing to the standard of courage which Englishmen had in mind.

The prevailing Western definitions of courage, as well as definitions embracing what Englishmen called the "martial" races of India, have generally stressed masterful aggressiveness, based on the classic military model of the soldier willing and eager to charge a numerically superior enemy, bayonet in hand, in a heroic act of self-assertion. The military analogy is merely the most extreme symbolic expression of a whole set of cultural attitudes: an aggressive, "meat-eating', masterful personal style, overt self-expressiveness, self-confident lustiness, which go well beyond military achievement. Its opposite, the quality of courage cultivated by the explicitly and self-consciously non-martial classes of Indian society, draws more on self-punishing strivings, less on qualities of mastering, more on virtues of receiving, submitting, suffering. It is a non-aggressive, internalised courage, involving the capacity to suffer pain without retaliation, not to retreat but to stay and suffer more. It relies for its effectiveness on the moral sensibilities, or at least guilt capacity, of the aggressor, using his conscience as the weapon with which to "beat" him. (Gandhi was aware of the psychological aggression which self-suffering could involve, and hoped to train his followers to purge the technique of this aspect.) Thus Gandhi defined *Satyagraha*—technically "truth-force", but in fact his name for non-violent resistance—as "the vindication of truth not by infliction of suffering on the opponent but on oneself".

This kind of courage tends to go with other cultural attitudes— vegetarianism, asceticism, self-control rather than self-expression. If the more aggressive style of courage is no monopoly of the West, but has its counterpart in the ethic of certain Indian castes, the self-suffering style also has its Western equivalents. The Christian directive to turn the other cheek is a compelling Western version of self-suffering and it is no accident that this line of the Gospel impressed Gandhi more deeply than any other. This style of courage has been common in Indian tradition among the non-fighting twice-born, among the Brahmans and Kayasthas and Vaishyas with whom Gandhi was most familiar, and who provided the core of nationalist leadership in India. Self-suffering was a traditional weapon of the Brahman, whose protest against oppressive rule was often fasting, self-injury, or even suicide, drawing upon the oppressor the supernatural sanctions of having caused the death of a Brahman. The technique was and is used in Indian homes, not merely in Gandhi's. Members of the family express protest by abstaining from meals. One need only recall the significance attached to mother's cooking in American homes that preserve strong ethnic traditions to imagine the potential effectiveness of the weapon. When Indian journals carry advertisements calling for an errant son to return home, as they often do, warning him that "mother will not take food" until he returns, the message conveys a form of pressure, not merely a loss of appetite.

But beyond the distinction between English and Indian definitions of courage lie some cultural differences concerning the honourable and "moral" way to resolve conflict in general. The belief that conflicts are best resolved through the frank confrontation of alternatives, the clear articulation of opposites, their clash and the victory of one alternative over the other, is embodied, at least in theory, in much of the adversary legal tradition of the West, and in its political life. Traditional Indian ideas of conflict resolution in both politics and law tend to stress arbitration, compromise, and the de-emphasis of overt clashes and victories or defeats. The rhetoric, if not always the practice, of Indian foreign policy, the continued striving for consensus processes in village affairs, and the opposition to partisanship as evil are only are few modern Indian expressions of this traditional feeling. These approaches are in line with the preference for meekness and harmlessness as against aggressive self-assertion.

Gandhi began to translate these convictions concerning courage and conflict resolution into techniques of action as he worked toward an approach to action for his fellow Indians. Concluding his first big case in South Africa, the one that had called him there, he believed he had found the path to his future work. The case had been settled by arbitration out of court and, further, he had persuaded his client to take payment in instalments from the loser in order not to ruin him. Both actions could have been justified on the ground of ordinary legal or business prudence, but Gandhi did not choose to view the settlement in that light: "My joy was boundless. I had learnt the true practice of law. I had learnt to find out the better side of human nature and to enter men's hearts. I realized that the true function of a lawyer was to unite parties driven asunder." Adversary proceedings, the principle that out of the conflict of two parties, each of whom tries to score as many points as possible, justice would emerge, seemed to him a doubtful doctrine. "The counsel on both sides were bound to rake up points of law in support of their own clients," he complained. Solutions based on compromise seemed happier to him, because they rested on mutual confidence rather than instituionalized conflict. Essentially, as a more mature Gandhi would formulate the issue, such solutions arose out of the doctrine of harmlessness, *ahimsa*, non-violence translated into opposition to conflict in general, not merely to physical violence. Had Gandhi developed a different, more aggressive cultural style, had he been bolder in court and public, he might have taken a different view of the issue of courage, and of the adversary mode. As it was, he turned into a virtue and into an effective political weapon what he once considered a failing in himself: his incapacity for aggressiveness. For Gandhi, these solutions were of a piece with his renewed concern for the ethic of harmlessness of his youth, as against the aggressive self-assertion which he had attempted and rejected.

What Gandhi concluded about the law, he applied thereafter to all other situations of dispute, including his struggles in South Africa and in India. The thread of compromise, of avoiding conflict, of finding areas of agreement which would produce settlement, remained central to his technique, sometimes to the despair of his followers, some of whom wanted a more definitive opposition. To it, he added as a technique of pressure the self-suffering which had been a coercive measure in his home, and which was resonant with traditional methods of the non-martial Indian classes. And if any wished to assert that this technique was "unmanly", Gandhi reformulated the imputation. When Indians practised non-violence, they would not be as impotent as woman; they would be as potent as woman. "Has she not greater intuition, is she not more self-sacrificing, has she not greater powers of endurance, has she not greater courage?" And the technique was, moreover, apt. England had the necessary conscience. "Self-suffering" would move Englishmen, as it might not some other imperial powers.

In finding the technique which he contributed to Indian nationalism, Gandhi in some ways did no more than return to the mild, non-violent, but ascetic and self-suffering ethic of his Gujarat youth. And yet he returned not so much as one who comes back unselfconsciously to revel in what is comfortable and well-known. He came as one who, like many of his countrymen, had attempted other alternatives bacause the culturally given way seemed inadequate. When he returned, because the alternatives too proved inadequate, and because he could not manage them, he revalued and gave a new formulation to the familiar, asserting its dignity and moral worth in a way which persuaded both himself and many of his fellows. Their situation and ethical background resembled his own; as Indians they now had an approach to protest which was as effective as the path of aggressive self-assertion.

The Gandhi who had eaten goat with Sheikh Mehtab and envied his friend's muscles had experienced the attempt of a generation to equal Englishmen and oust them by discovering and developing the qualities that made Englishmen strong. When he ceased to eat meat and returned to vegetarianism, and when he began the slow return from his other attempts to acquire English manners, he approximated the experience of a generation which had been unable or unwilling to manage the alternative model. When he turned to *satyagraha* and *ahimsa,* he proposed to re-embrace the traditional concept of courage, in which non-violence and self-suffering were central, and which Englishmen had persuaded Indians was not courage.

Like others of his era, but for personal reasons as well as historical or cultural ones, he had sought to strengthen himself by repairing to another cultural style, including a different cultural style of courage. But it had failed to bring him strength; to his sense of insufficiency, it had added the belief that he had abandoned his cultural integrity. Thus Gandhi taught his countrymen no new path to courage. He resurrected an old and familiar one, one that had always been significant to the twice-born castes, that had fallen into disrepute. By giving it new toughness and discipline in action, by stressing the sacrifice and self-control which it required, by making it an effective device of mass action, by involving millions in it, he reasserted its worth with an effectiveness that convinced his countrymen. He allowed them to embrace an approach that was familiar, emphasizing its moral superiority to the desperate assertions of Bengali assassins, and took from them the fear that the familiar attitude was both cowardly and ineffectual. In the process of mastering his own fear and weakness, he reassured several generations that they need not fear those who had conquered them, and, more important, that Strachey and Macaulay had been wrong, that the Indians, were not cowards. As Nehru wrote: "He had instilled courage and manhood in [India's] people.... Courage is the one sure foundation of character, he had said; without courage there is no morality, no religion, no love."

17

As Gandhi set out to rally the Indian people to his programme of non-violent non-cooperation, the peasantry made of him a "mahatma" whose power and influence far outran his own chosen role. In this selection Shahid Amin shows how the peasantry created the Gandhi they wanted, a man who could work miracles, and how in the process they used his name to sustain campaigns of direct action, often marked by violence, that Gandhi would himself have disavowed.

Gandhi as Mahatma: Gorakhpur District, Eastern UP, 1921-1922

SHAHID AMIN

"Many miracles were previous to this affair [the riot at Chauri Chaura], sedulously circulated by the designing crowd, and firmly believed by the ignorant crowd, of the Non-cooperation world of this district.

-M.B. Dixit, Committing Magistrate,
Chauri Chaura Trials.

I

Gandhi visited the district of Gorakhpur in eastern UP on 8 February 1921, addressed a monster meeting variously estimated at between 1 lakh and 2.5 lakhs and returned the same evening to Benaras. He was accorded a tumultuous welcome in the district, but unlike in Champaran and Kheda he did not stay in Gorakhpur for any length of time to lead or influence a political movement of the peasantry. Gandhi, the person, was in this particular locality for less than a day, but the 'Mahatma' as an 'idea' was thought out and reworked in popular imagination in subsequent months. Even in the eyes of some local Congressmen this 'deification'—'unofficial canonization' as the *Pioneer* put it-assumed dangerously distended proportions by April-May 1921.

In following the career of the Mahatma in one limited area over a short period, this essay seeks to place the relationship between Gandhi and the peasants in a perspective somewhat different from the view usually taken of this grand subject. We are not concerned with analyzing the attributes of his charisma but with how this registered in peasant consciousness. We are also constrained by our primary documentation from looking at the image of Gandhi in Gorakhpur historically—at the ideas and beliefs about the Mahatma that percolated into the region before his visit and the transformations, if any, that image underwent as a result of his visit. Most of the rumours about the Mahatma's *pratap* (power/glory) were reported in the local press between February and May 1921. And as our sample of fifty fairly elaborate 'stories' spans this rather brief period, we cannot fully indicate what happens to the 'deified' image after the rioting at Chauri Chaura in early 1922 and the subsequent withdrawal of the Non-Cooperation movement. The aim of the present exercise is then the limited one of taking a close look at peasant perceptions of Gandhi by focussing on the trail of stories that marked his passage through the district. The location of the Mahatma image within existing patterns of popular beliefs and the way it informed direct action, often at variance with the standard interpretations of the Congress creed, are the main issues discussed in this essay.

In a number of contemporary nationalist writings peasant perceptions of and beliefs about Gandhi figure as incidents of homage and offering. Touching instances of devotion and childlike manifestations of affection are highlighted in the narratives of his tour in northern India during the winter of 1920-2. And if this spectacle of popular regard gets out of hand, it is read as a sign of the mule-like obstinacy (*bathagraha*) of simple, guileless *kisans*. The sight and sound of uncouth peasants invading the train carrying Gandhi, rending the sky with cries of '*jai*' and demanding *darshan* at an unearthly hour, could be annoying and unnerving. But all was not yet lost because local Congress leaders could be counted on to restrain the militant exuberance of lathi-wielding, torch-bearing enthusiasts. A passage titled 'Boundless Love' from the tour diary of his secretary is representative of how peasant attitudes towards Gandhi have been written about in nationalist narratives:

It is impossible to put in language the exuberance of love which Gandhiji and Shaukat Ali experienced in Bihar. Our train on the

B.N.W. Railway line stopped at all stations and there was not a single station which was not crowded with hundreds of people at that time. Even women, who never stir out of their homes, did not fail to present themselves so that they could see and hear him. A huge concourse of students would everywhere smother Gandhiji with their enthusiasm. If at some place a sister would take off her coral necklace and tell him, "I give this specially for you to wear", at some other, *sanyasis* would come and leave their rosaries on his lap. If beautiful sheets of handspun and hand-woven cloth, many yards long, would be presented at one place, at some other place would turn up a loving villager from the woods, boastful of his trophy, saying, "Maharaj (an address of reverence) this is my feat of strength. The tiger was a terror to our people; I am giving the skin to you." At some places, guns normally used as fog-signals were fired in his honour. At some others, we came across railway officers who would not give the green flag, when our train came within their jurisdiction, in order to have and let others have Gandhiji's *darshan*. Not minding the fact that our 'Special' was certain to pass by them in terrific speed, people were seen at some places, standing along the railway lines in distant hope of having just a glimpse of Gandhiji or at least of making their loud shouts of 'Gandhi-Shaukat Ali-ki-jai' reach his ear. We have met with even policemen who had the courage to approach Gandhiji to salute him or touch his hand, and and CID's [*sic*] also who would plaintively say, "We have taken to this dirty work for the sake of the sinning flesh, but please do accept these five rupees."

Examples of such darshan-seeking scenes could be multiplied, and we shall come back to them in our account of Gandhi's passage through Gorakhpur. It is worth stressing here that the Gandhi-darshan motif in nationalist discourse reveals a specific attitude towards the subalterns—the *sadharan janta* or ordinary people as they are referred to in the nationalist Hindi press. To behold the Mahatma in person and become his devotees were the only roles assigned to them, while it was for the urban intelligentsia and full-time party activists to convert this groundswell of popular feeling into an organized movement. Thus it would appear that even in the relationship between peasant devotees and *their* Mahatma there was room for political mediation by the economically better off and socially more powerful followers....

II

The spread of Gaurakshini Sabhas (Cow Protection Leagues) in the 1890's and the subsequent growth of the Nagri movement, Hindi journalism and Hindu social reform in the 1910's appear to have been the important landmarks in the political history of Gorakhpur in the period up to 1919-20. These saw the involvement of a wide range of the district's population. Former *Pargana* chiefs—rajas and ranis, members of the dominant landed lineages, schoolmasters, postmasters and *naib-tahsildars,* middle-caste Ahir and Kurmi tenants—all "rallied round the Cow" (although the last two did so with ideas quite different from the rest). The developments in the first twenty years of the present century relied on *rausa* and trader support but drew in the intelligentsia, religious preachers and sections of the rural population as well. Gorakhpur neither witnessed widespread agitation against the Rowlatt Acts, as had happened in the Punjab, nor did a Kisan Sabha movement of the Awadh type develop in this region.

The Gaurakshini Sabhas of Gorakhpur in their attempt at selective social reform anticipated the 'Sewa Samitis' and 'Hitkarini Sabhas'—Social Service Leagues—of the early twentieth century. A mammoth meeting of the Gorakhpur sabha held at Lar on 18 March 1893 laid down rules for different castes regarding the maximum number of *baratis* (members of the bridegroom's party) to be entertained at a wedding and the amount of money to be spent on the *tilak* ceremony—all in an effort to cut down 'foolish expenditure on marriages'. Observance of proper high-caste rituals was also stressed. Thus it was made obligatory for "all *dwija* castes (i.e.Brahmins, Kshatriyas and Vaishyas)... to recite the *gayatri mantra* at the three divisions of the day", and he who failed in this was to "be expelled from the brotherhood". Contributions "for the protection of the Gao Mata" (Mother Cow) were also made compulsory for every Hindu household on pain of exclusion from caste. Rule 4 of the Lar sabha stated that "each household [should], everyday contribute from its food supply one *chutki* [handful], equivalent to one *paisa,* per member," and that "the eating of food without setting apart the *chutki* [should] be an offence equal to that of eating a cow's flesh." Women were tobe "instructed as to the contribution of *chutki* in proper fashion with due regard to *pardah.*"

Again, the power of panchayats was brought to bear upon 'remorselessly [to] boycott' those who sold cows or bullocks to

Muslims or butchers. It seems that these panchayats were of two kinds. In the 'Cow Courts' of Azamgarh "whose proceedings...were a somewhat flattering imitation of the proceedings in the Magistrate's Courts" it was generally the zamindars who acted as judges. In certain other cases, as in that of a 'respectable Hindu farmer' of Sagri pargana of that district in June 1893, a less formal and more militant boycott was undertaken by the peasants themselves. To quote Gyan Pandey:

> Villagers gathered at...[the house of Lakshman Paure], pulled down tiles from the roof, smashed his earthen vessels, stopped the irrigation of his sugarcane field, prohibited Kahars from carrying sweets which were needed for his daughter's entry into her bridegroom's house and slapped Lakshman, adding the threat that the house would be looted and he himself killed if he did not get the bullock back.

The 'Gandhi Panchayats' of the early 1920's organized by local volunteers meted out punishment similar to what Lakshman Paure of the village of Pande Kunda had received in 1893. However, in the spring of 1921 when all was charged with magic, any mental or physical affliction (*kasht*) suffered by persons found guilty of violating panchayat decisions adopted in Gorakhpur villages in the Mahatma's name was often perceived as evidence of Gandhi's extraordinary powers, indeed as something providential and supernatural rather than as a form of chastisement devised by a human agency.

Hindi was officially adopted as the language of the courts of law in UP in 1900. Soon after, the *Nagri pracharini* (Hindi propagation) movement began to pick up momentum in Gorakhpur as well. In 1913 the local branch of the sabha agitated successfully for judicial forms to be printed in Hindi, and in September 1914 *Gyan Shakti*, a literary journal devoted to 'Hindi and Hindu *dharma prachar*', was published by a pro-government Sanskrit scholar with financial support from the rajas of Padrauna, Tamkuhi and Majhauli, as well as some from the prominent rausa of Gorakhpur. In the following year Gauri Shankar Misra, who was later to be an important figure in the UP Kisan Sabha, brought out a new monthly—*Prabhakar*—from Gorakhpur. Its object was to 'serve the cause (*sewa*) of Hindi, Hindu and Hindustan', However, the journal ceased publication within a year, only *Gyan Skakti* remained, and even this closed down between August 1916 and June 1917. The full impact of Hindi journalism was not felt in Gorakhpur unitl 1919. In April and August of that year two important papers—the weekly *Swadesh* and the monthly *Kavi*—made their appearance. These, especially Dasrath Dwivedi's *Swadesh*, were to exercize an important influence in spreading the message of Gandhi over the region.

In the 1910's movements and organizations of Hindi, Hindu culture and social reform—'nagri sabhas', 'pathshalas' (vernacular schools), 'gaushalas' (asylums for cattle), 'sewa samitis' (social service leagues) and 'sudharak sabhas' (reform associations) of various sorts provided the support and cover for nationalist activity in Gorakhpur. Each type of these socio-political movements served nationalism in its own way; but there was a considerable amount of overlapping in their functions and interests. In August 1919 a branch of the Bhartiya Sewa Samiti which had M.M. Malaviya for its head was established in Deoria. A number of 'sudharak' and 'gram hitkarini sabhas' (village betterment societies) and subsidiary branches of the sewa samities were established in the smaller towns and bigger villages of the region during 1919-20. The inspiration usually came from the local notables and pleaders at the tahsil and pargana headquarters, though sometimes appeals in the *Swadesh* for the setting up of community organizations also bore fruit. At these sabhas, heads of Hindu religious trusts (*mahants*) and celibates (*brahmacharis*) from nearby *ashrams* or itinerant preachers (*pracharks*) from neighbouring districts and from Benaras discoursed on the Hindu way of life and its rituals. *Yagya* (sacrifice) was performed; a Sanskrit pathshala and a gaushala endowed with financial support from traders, arrangements made for the orderly running of Ramilias and *melas*, and panchayats set up for the arbitration of disputes....

Caste sabhas could undergo interesting transformations as well. Thus on 12 December 1920 a Bhumihar Ramlila Mandal was established at Bhiti village in the Bansgaon tahsil of Gorakhpur; its "object was to encourage unity and propagate satyagraha by revealing the [true] character of Sri Ramchandraji." Similarly in a great many cases lower and middle-caste panchayats imposed novel dietary taboos as a part of the widespread movement of self-assertion which was also exemplified by acts such as the refusal of their women to work as housemaids or the withholding of *begar* (forced labour) both from the *sarkar* and the zamindar.

III

Gorakhpur in 1920 was no stronghold of the Congress or the independent Kisan Sabhas. In fact the relative backwardness of the entire region comprising Gorakhpur, Basti and Azamgarh districts was lamented repeatedly by the editor of the Congress weekly, *Swadesh*, and the main reason for this was thought to be the absence of an effective and dedicated leadership. Political meetings in Gorakhpur city and in important market towns like Deoria and Barhaj Bazar picked up from July-August 1920, as the campaign for council elections by the rajas, rausa and *vakla* was sought to be countered by challenging the bona fides of 'oppressive landlords' and 'self-seeking pleaders'. Open letters appeared in the columns of *Swadesh* highlighting the oppression suffered by peasants in the bigger zamindaris and challenging the presumption of the rajas to be the natural spokesmen of their *praja* (subjects). At a public meeting of the newly-formed Voters' Association in Deoria the representative of a landlord candidate was faced with the charge that his patron's command of English was inadequate for him to follow the proceedings of the legislative council. But increasingly, the boycott of council elections, and, after the Nagpur Congress (December 1920) the propagation of Non-Cooperation, was being written up and broadcast as a part of the spiritual biography of Mahatma Gandhi. In a powerful editorial, prominently displayed by *Swadesh* on the front page on 11 November and reprinted the next week, Dasrath Dwivedi appealed to the local electorate in bold typeface:

OH YOU VOTERS OF THE GORAKHPUR DIVISION! HAVE SOME SELF RESPECT. BEWARE OF THE OBSEQUIOUS STOOGES! BE SURE WHO IS YOUR GENUINE WELL WISHER! MAHATMA GANDHI, PT MOTILAL NEHRU, PT MALVIYAJI or those who are now running after you, begging for your votes? Think for yourself; what good have the latter done for you so far that you may now expect them to help remove your sorrows and sufferings from inside the Council. Now cast your eyes towards Mahatma Gandhi. This pure soul (*pavitra murti*) has sacrificed everything for you (*tan-man-dhan....arpan kar diya hai*). It is for your good that he has taken the vow of renunciation (*sanyas-vrat*), gone to jail and encountered many a difficulty and suffering. Despite being ill, he is at this moment wandering all over [the country] in the service of your cause. It is the *updesh* of this

same Mahatma Gandhi that you should not vote. And you should not vote, because approximately thirty thousand of your unarmed Punjabi brethren were fired upon in Amritsar, people were made to crawl on their bellies, and despite the hue and cry for justice you were shooed away like dogs *(tumhen dutkar diya gaya tha)* And no heed was paid whatsoever. Look out. Beware.
DO NOT VOTE FOR ANYBODY.

In this text, which may be regarded as representative of the local nationalist discourse on council boycott the 'Punjab Wrongs' and the callous indifference of the British are no doubt mentioned as reasons for not voting; but it is hard to miss the person of a saintly Gandhi, resplendent in his suffering for the people, and, in turn, requiring and even demanding their obedience to his injunctions. Perceived thus the boycott of elections and the rejection of loyalist candidates appear as a kind of religiously prescribed abstinence from the polling booth, analogous to the observance of proper Hindu rituals and self-purification which was being propagated by many of the nationalist religious preachers and taken by certain low-caste panchayats as well. It was to such a region, which was not unaware of the peasant rioting in southern Awadh in January 1921 but had not yet developed any comparable peasant movement of its own, that Gandhi came on 8 February 1921.

The decision to invite Gandhi was taken at a public meeting held in Gorakhpur city on 17 October 1920. Maulvi Maqsood Ali Fyzabadi presided over it and Gauri Shankar Misra was the main speaker. The meeting resolved to support the cause of those arrested in connection with the Khilafat agitation, pronounced *asahyog* (Non-Cooperation) to be *uchit* (proper) and decided to send a telegraphic invitation to Gandhi and the Ali brothers to visit Gorakhpur at an early date. Gandhi was also approached by the Gorakhpur delegates (prominent amongst whom was Baba Raghav Das, successor to the spiritual *gaddi*—seat—of Anant Mahaprabhu and founder of the Paramahansa Ashram, Barhaj) at the Nagpur Congress and he told them that he would visit the district sometime in late January or early February. To the creed of *asahyog* that Raghav Das and Dasrath Dwivedi brought with them from Nagpur was added mounting excitement at the prospect of its author's advent. Propagation of the politics of Non-Cooperation in the Gorakhpur countryside in early 1921 had elements of a celebratory exordium, a preparing of the district for the Big Event. The peregrinations of Raghav

Das and his branmachari followers around their ashram in Barhaj, the 'melodious Gandhi-*bhajans*' sung by Changur Tripathi to a peasant assembly at Kuin nearby and the 'poetical effusions' in the first issue of a rejuvenated *kavi* magazine—'written with the set purpose of arousing in the masses and classes alike a yearning for the quick descent of Krishna, the Messiah—are the few surviving fragments of this picture of enthusiasm and expectation in Gorakhpur at that time.

An index of this popular expectation was the increase in the number of rumours which assigned various imaginary dates to Gandhi's visit. By the first week of January the news of his arrival had 'spread like wildfire'.

Meanwhile the District Congress Committee (DCC) geared itself into action. It had been decided to get a national school inaugurated by Gandhi, and the DCC was active on this front. Advance parties of lecturers (*vyakhyandata*) announcing his arrival were to be dispatched to the tahsil headquarters and to Barhalganj, Dhakwa and Gola in the densely populated southern tahsil of Bansgaon; to Rudarpur and Captainganj in the central tract of Hata; to the railway towns and marts of Deoria, Salempur, Majhauli, Lar, Bhatpar and Barhaj Bazar to the south-east, and to Padrauna in the North-east. Within the sparsely populated northern tashil of Maharajganj, Peppeganj and Campierganj—seats of European zamindaris—and Siswa Bazaar, the important entrepôt of gur and rice, were to be the target points. At meetings held at these places, the visiting lecturers were to preach the doctrine of the Congress and ask for contributions to the National School Fund. In their turn the local residents were to ensure that people within a radius of ten miles attended these public discourses on the philosophy and advent of Gandhi. The massive attendance at the Gorakhpur sabha on 8 February and the crowds that thronged the five stations on the fifty-mile railway strip between Bhatni and Gorakhpur city suggest that the news had spread widely enough.

On 30 January the *Swadesh* announced that the probable date was now 8 February and requested the people of Gorakhpur to seek the Mahatma's darshan and bring their donations with them. It also wrote about the need for more Congress workers to come forward and help in supervising the arrangements.

An editorial which appeared in the columns of that newspaper on 6 February announcing the impending arrival is a significant text. Besides illustrating how the image of the distinguished visitor was projected in Gorakhpur by local Congressmen, it is also representative of nationalist understanding of the relationship between the subaltern masses, the elite leadership and Gandhi himself. Dasrath Dwivedi, the young author of this text, had been trained as a journalist on the staff of the *Pratap* in Kanpur and on Ganesh Vidayarthi's advice had come back to his home district in 1919 to start his own *Swadesh*. The editorial, 'The Great Fortune of Gorakhpur', was written by one who was obviously an ardent nationalist disappointed at the political stupor prevailing in the region, and who felt as if his dream of Gandhi bringing about a transformation was soon to be fulfilled. Addressed basically to lawyers and students whom it urges to cast off sloth, it is also significant in its attitude towards the common people:

> Our plea is that the common people (*sadharan janta*) of Gorakhpur are only anxiously awaiting for the darshan of the Mahatma. The Mahatma will arrive, the public will have darshan and will be eternally greatful for it. There will be no end to the joy of the people when they are able to feast their eyes on the Mahatma.

> But what about those who are openly cooperating with the government ....don't they have some duty at this juncture....? A voice from the heart says 'Of course! ...*They should kneel before Mahatma Gandhi and pray to the Almighty for courage to enable them to row their boats out of the present whirlpool and into safety....For Mahatma Gandhi to appear [avteern: from avtar] before us in these difficult times is a tremendous boon, for us, over society and our country....* Don't vacillate, arise now to serve the oppressed brothers of your district. Blow the *shankh* (conchshell) of Swaraj...This movement is an elixir (*amrit-bati*) for you. Mahatma Gandhi is offering it to you.

How the common people and the elite should respond to Gandhi's visit is thus clearly laid out. The task of the janta is to congregate in large numbers, 'feast their eyes on the Mahatma', count themselves lucky, and after such brief taste of bliss return to their inert and oppressed existence. So far as they are concerned the Mahatma is to be in Gorakhpur for no other purpose than to offer them darshan. They are not expected to proclaim the cause of *swaraj* on their own. The clarion call (written metaphorically, as *shankhnaad*, after the blast of conchshells used for Hindu sacred rituals) of swaraj in villages requires only the power of elite lungs: for that rallying blast the 'oppressed brothers' of Gorakhpur must rely on the initiative of the elite followers of the Mahatma. The implication is that the peasants' pilgrimage to Gorakhpur and the mufassil stations will be useless for a nationalist perspective unless 'leaders' step in to channel the goodwill generated in the villages as a result of Gandhi's darshan. That such a journey, made often in defiance of landlord opposition, could in itself be a political act and that Gandhi's message might be decoded by the common villager on his own, without prompting by outsiders, were possibilities not entertained by Dasrath Dwivedi at this time. Yet a perusal of local news published by him in subsequent months shows that these were the lines along which popular response to the Mahatma's visit expressed itself.

Apart from this the imagery, feeling and metaphors used by Dwivedi to convince educated waverers about the greatness of Gandhi and convert them to his cause are of interest in themselves. At this level there is no significant difference between the religiosity informing the peasants and the attitude Dwivedi wants the intelligentsia to adopt towards Gandhi; the language of belief seems to be the same in both instances with merely some variations in tone and accent. The italicized portions of the extract quoted above testify to the religious, indeed devotional nature of Dwivedi's writings. The boat and boatman imagery occurs frequently in rural and urban devotional songs. As Susan Wadley notes in her study of popular religion in a village in western UP, "many ...devotional songs use the whirlpool analogy for a crisis situation, along with other nautical imagery (the ocean of existence, boat, boatman, ferry across, the far side, etc.)."

Gandhi's visit to Gorakhpur was well organized and the gatherings of people on that occasion were truly phenomenal. An advance party of Gorakhpur Congressmen had been sent to Bhatni junction at the south-eastern edge of the district, and the train by which he travelled made its way very slowly through, stopping at every railway station where people had assembled for darshan. As Shyam Dhar Misra who led the reception party reported in *Swadesh:*

At Bhatni Gandhiji addressed (*updesh diya*) the local public and then the train started for Gorakhpur. There were not less than 15 to 20,000 people at Nunkhar, Deoria, Gauri Bazaar, Chauri Chaura and Kusmhi [stations]....At Deoria there were about 35-40,000 people. Mahatmaji was very pleased to witness the scene at Kusmhi, as despite the fact that the station is in the middle of a jungle there were not less than 10,000 people even here. Some, overcome with their love, were seen to be crying. At Deoria people wanted to give *bhent* [donations] to Gandhiji, but he asked them to give these at Gorakhpur. But at Chauri Chaura one Marwari gentleman managed to hand something over to him. Then there was no stopping. A sheet was spread and currency notes and coins started raining. It was a sight...Outside the Gorakhpur station the Mahatma was stood on a high carriage and people had a good darshan of him for a couple of minutes.

IV

If this was the way in which the peasants reacted to Gandhi, how was his message understood by them? Were there any ambiguities in what Gandhi said or was believed to have said? If so, what implications did these have for peasant beliefs about Gandhi as revealed in the 'stories' about his power?

The main thrust of Gandhi's speeches at the 'massive gatherings of peasants' in Fyzabad and Gorakhpur was to condemn the recent acts of peasant violence and rioting in southern Awadh.

What happened in Fyzabad? What happened in Rae Bareli? We should know these things. By doing what we have done with our own hands we have committed a wrong, a great wrong. By raising the *lakri* [i.e.lathi] we have done a bad thing. By looting haats and shops we have committed a wrong. We can't get swaraj by using the lakri. We cannot get swaraj by pitting our own devilishness (*shaitaniyat*) against the satanic government. Our 30 crore lakris are no match against their aeroplanes and guns; even if if they are, even then we shall not raise our lakris. The Quran says so. Brother Mohammad Ali tells me that [according to the Quran] as long as the raising of the stick is unnecessary we cannot do so...

Our kisan brothers have committed a mistake. They have caused great anguish to my brother Jawahar Lal. If further difficulties [of this sort] are put in our way then you shall see that that very day it would become impossible for Gandhi to live in Hindustan. I shall have to do penance—this is a peaceful struggle. Only after I retire to the Himalayas can it become a violent struggle. Our fight should be like the one put up by our Sikh brethren in Taran Taran ....They did not seek revenge against their oppressors.... This is our way, this the *asahyog dharma*, this is real *Brahmacharya*. This is *kshatriya dharma*. And today this is the dharma of the Musalmans. To go against it is to commit a sin....

Right now we should forget about 'social boycott'. The time has not yet arrived for such actions. Nobody should prevent any brother from going to the burial ground, nobody is to prevent anybody from the use of the services of barbers or to have *chilum* [i.e.ganja] and liquor. In fact we want to rid everybody of chilum and booze (*daru*). If all of you give up [these things] today then we shall attain swaraj straightway....

[Congratulating Gorakhpur on its organization of this meeting Gandhi continued] The real result of your organizational abilities and your work would be seen when in Gorakhpur lawyers give up their practice, schools no longer remain sarkari [i.e.affiliated to the government], titles are given up, no drinkers, no whoremongers, no gamblers remain in your district. When every house has a *charkha* and all the *julahas* of Gorakhpur start weaving [hand-spun yarn]... You should produce so much khaddar in Gorakhpur that you people don't have to go to Ahmedabad, to Bombay or Kanpur [for your cloth]...

I would request you to be patient and listen to Maulana Mohammad Ali's speech and carry on donating money to the volunteers. Please refrain from being noisy. I want to tell you, if you follow my programme—I want to assure [you] if you do as I tell you, we shall get swaraj by the end of september. We could also get the Khilafat and the Punjab Wrongs undone by the sarkar. But this is the right [task] of only those who accept the things discussed at the Nagpur Congress. This is not the business of those who are not with us in our work... From those who are not with us, but still come to our meetings, I expect that they will at least keep the peace—we can attain swaraj by end September if God grants us peace; if all of us Indians have the spirit of self-sacrifice and self-purification then 30 crore people can achieve just about anything.

The main constitutive elements—*baat* in the indigenous parlance—of Gandhi's message to the Gorakhpur kisans could be arranged as follows:

1. Hindu-Muslims unity or *ekta*.
2. What people should *not* do on their own: use lathis; loot bazaars and haats; enforce social boycott (*naudhobi band*).
3. What the Mahatma wants his true followers to do: stop gambling ganja-smoking, drinking and whoring.

4. Lawyers should give up their practice; government schools should be boycotted; official title should be given up.
5. People should take up spinning and weavers should accept hand-spun yarn.
6. Imminence of swaraj: its realization conditional on innate strength of numbers when matched with peace, grace of God, self-sacrifice and self-purification.

This sequential summary of Gandhi's speech is an attempt to reconstruct the way in which his utterances might have been discussed in the villages of Gorakhpur. It is reasonable to assume that such discussions would proceed by breaking up his message into its major ideological constituents. If the practice, which is current even today, of communicating printed news in the countryside is any guide, then in all likelihood the main points of that speech summarized from the version published in *Swadesh* was conveyed to the illiterate peasants in the local dialect.

It will not be seen that baat No.4 does not greatly concern the peasants. No. 1 is very general and figures only marginally in the Gandhi 'stories'. Baat no. 5 is, in part, far too specific as an instruction addressed exclusively to weavers, while the advice in favour of spinning might thave sounded rather too general, lacking as it did an infrastructure to make it feasible at this stage. It is the conflation of baats no. 3 and no. 6, and its contexualisation within the existing ideas about 'power' and magic, which lay at the root of some of the 'stories' relating to the Mahatma in Gorakhpur. It seems that the complementarity of his negative advice with regard to popular militancy (baat no.2) and the positive actions enjoined on the 'true followers' (beat no 3)—the complimentarity, so to say, of the do's and don'ts in these particular messages, was (*pace* Mahadev Desai) largely lost on his rustic audience. On the other hand baats no. 3 and 6 came to be associated in the popular mind as a linked set of spiritual commandments issued by a god-like personage. As such these were consistent with those legends about his 'divinity' which circulated at the time. The enforcement of social boycott was not widespread yet; it was to pick up only from late 1921. Meanwhile, that is immediately in the wake of Gandhi's visit, people, acting on their own or through their panchayats and sabhas, were still involved in efforts at self-purification, extending and transforming his message on this theme. It is with the intervention of the supernatural in this process and the Mahatma's role in it that most of the Gorakhpur 'stories' are concerned.

V

The enthusiasm Gandhi generated, the expectations he aroused and the attack he launched on British authority had all combined to initiate the very first moments of a process which, given other factors, could help the peasant to conceptualize the turning of his world upside down. This was an incipient political consciousness called upon, for the very first time, to reflect—albeit vaguely and intermittently—on the possibility of an inversion of many of those power relations deemed inviolable until then, such as British/Indian, landlord / peasant, high-caste / low-caste, etc. This process of conceptualization was set in train that spring in Gorakhpur by a clash between the ordinary and the extraordinary, between the habitual and the contingent—a clash triggered off directly by the Mahatma's visit.

VI

Stories about Gandhi's occult powers first appeared in the local press in late January 1921. An issue of *Swadesh* which announced his arrival in the district also carried a report under the heading: "Gandhi in dream: Englishmen run away naked." A loco-driver—presumably an Anglo-Indian—who had dozed off while reading a newspaper at Kasganj railway station in Etah district woke up from a nightmare at 11 p.m. and ran towards a cluster of bungalows occupied by the English and some Indian railway officers shouting: "Man, run, man! Gandhi is marching at the head of several strong Indians decimating the English." This caused a panic and all the local white population emerged from their bedrooms in a state of undress and ran towards the station. The key to the armoury at the station was asked for, but could not be found as the officer-in-charge was away. English women were locked up in boxes and almirahs, and some Englishmen were heard saying, "Man! The cries of *'jai jai'* are still reaching our ears. We shall not go back to our bungalows." In the morning Indians who heard of this incident in the city had a good laugh at this example of English self-confidence *(atmikbal)*. This story, first published in the Benaras daily *Aaj* and then in *Swadesh,* is illustrative of the wider tendency of the times to berate British power and boost Indian prowess by contrast. The British emerge in tales of this kind as a weak-kneed race, mortally afraid of the non-violent Mahatma.

Other stories to appear in the press just prior to and immediately after his arrival were about a lawyer of Deoria who was cursed by a follower of Gandhi for going back on his promise to give up legal practice and had his house polluted with shit; about a high-caste woman who suffered the same polluting fate after she had denied a young boy a blanket to protect him from the cold when he wanted to go to the station at night to seek darshan; about a Kahar who tried to test the Mahatma's power with a foolish wish and came out the worse for it; and about a Pandit who sought to defy Gandhi by insisting on eating fish only to find it crawling with worms. These stories have the same sequential and structural characteristics as many others reported from Gorakhpur. Taken together and classified according to their motifs, they may be said to fall into four fairly distinct groups. I am aware that these stories can well be classified differently, and that a particular story can be grouped under more than one category. However, I have found the following classification useful for the purposes of the present discussion.

A. Testing the power of the Mahatma.
B. Opposing the Mahatma.
C. Opposing the Gandhian creed in general and with respect to dietary, drinking and smoking taboos.
D. Boons granted and / or miracles performed in the form of recovery of things lost and regeneration of trees and wells.

A. *Testing the Power of the Mahatma*

1. Sikandar Sahu of *thana* Mansurganj, mauza Mahuawa (Dist. Basti) said on 15 February that he would believe in the Mahatmaji when the *karah* (boiling pan) full of cane-juice in his *karkhana* split into two. The karah split into two in the middle!

2. On 18 February a Kahar (domestic servant; palanquin bearer) from Basantpur said that he would be prepared to believe in Mahatmaji's authenticity (*sacha manoonga*) only when the thatched roof of his house was raised. The roof lifted ten cubits above the wall, and fell back to its original position only when he cried and folded his hands in surrender and submission.

3. On 15 March a cultivator in mauza Sohraghat (Azamgarh) said that he would believe in the Mahatmaji's authenticity (*sacha jaane*) if sesamum sprouted on 1.5 *bighas* of his field. Next day all the wheat in that field became sesamum. "I have seen this with my own eyes at the house of Pt Brijwasi vakil," wrote a correspondent. "The ears look like that of wheat, but on rubbing with hand, grains of sesamum come out of them."

4. Babu Bir Bahadur Sahi of mauza Reaon was getting his fields harvested on 15 March. In order to test the Mahatma's powers he wished for some sweets. Suddenly sweets fell on his body. Half of the sweets he distributed among the labourers and the rest he kept for himself.

5. On 13 April a *karahi* was being set up as an offering to the Mahatma. The wife of one thakur saheb said that she would offer karahi to the Matatmaji only if there were some miracles performed. Suddenly a dhoti hanging on a peg caught fire and was reduced to ashes, although there was no smell of burning whatsoever. "I have seen this with my own eyes."

6. A reader of *Swadesh* from Barhaj wrote: 'Two chamars while digging were having a discussion about the *murti* (idol, image) that had emerged in Bhore village (Saran). One of them ..said ... "only if a murti emerges at that site as well will I accept that the one at Bhore is calling out for Gandhi." By a coincidence, while digging, a murti of Mahadev came out. On hearing the news people rushed for darshan, and *puja-paath* was done and offerings made. People are of the opinion that the cash offered should be sent to the National School [fund]."

7. A similar incident was reported to have happened at the well of Babu Shiv Partap Singh of Gaura [adjacent to Barhaj]. But it was said that as soon as people rushed to get the murti out of the well, it disappeared.

8. A Brahman of mauza Rudrapur (Post Office Kamasi) had the habit of stealing grass. People tried their best to convince him that Mahatma Gandhi had forbidden such evil deeds. He replied, "I shall believe in Gandhiji if when I go stealing grass at night someone catches me, or I fall ill, go mad, or start eating *gobar* (cow dung)." Strange are the ways of God: all these things happened .While stealing grass he started shouting that someone was coming to catch him. He fainted. He ran a high fever. People got hold of him and took him to his house. Soon after he ran out and started eating gobar. When after three days his family members took the *manauti* [i.e.pledged to propitiate Gandhi if the patient recovered], he started feeling better. "As a result of this people in the village and its neighbourhood have given up theft etc. completely."

9. Shri Balram Das of the Gorakhpur School reported, "On February 26th I had gone to the Rudrapur village in Maharajganj

tahsil to give a lecture. Everybody agreed to follow the ways of Mahatma Gandhi. But one character did not give up his [old] habit and went to cut grass. On his return he went mad. He broke and smashed things around him. When he offered Rs 5 in the name of Mahatmaji he quietened down *(shanti hui)."*

Even a cursory reading of these 'stories' suggests that two obvious processes are at work here. First, the rumours are indicative of a considerable discussion about Gandhi in the villages of Gorakhpur in spring 1921. The recurring phrase, "I shall believe in Mahatmaji only in the event of such an extraordinary happening", should be read as an index of a dialogue between sceptics and firm believers. It makes sense only in the context of such a discussion.

Secondly, this crucial phrase also suggests that what people thought of the Mahatma were projections of the existing patterns of popular beliefs about the 'worship of the worthies' in rural north India. As Willim Crooke has observed, the deification of such 'worthies' was based among other things, on the purity of the life they had led and on 'approved thaumaturgic powers'. The first of these conditions Gandhi amply satisfied by all those signs of saintliness which a god-fearing rural populace was prone to recognise in his appearance as well as in his public conduct. As for thaumaturgy, the stories mentioned above attribute to him magical and miraculous powers which, in the eyes of villagers nurtured on the lore of Salim Chishti and Sheikh Burhan, put him on a par with other mortals on whom peasant imagination had conferred godliness.

Turning to the stories themselves we find that they are developments of the basic idea of the genuineness of the Mahatma as revealed through various tests. In its simple version a test is set in the context of the immediate activity or environment of the person concerned, or there is the fulfilment of an expressed wish. The conditions are met and the story or the rumour connected with it goes no further . Examples of this are to be found in Nos. 1, 3 and 4, and to a lesser degree in No. 5 as well. In some of the other instances a further development takes place: the person who sets the test submits to the Mahatma's power. Thus the Kahar of Basantpur in No. 2 gets the roof of his hut back in position only after he makes amends for questioning the saint's authority by tearful repentance.

A clearer example of the power of rumours in spreading the name of Gandhi in villages and reorienting normal ritual actions towards nationalist goals is contained in story No. 6. Of the two Chamars, one evidently believed in the rumour from Saran district in Bihar. But the other made his acceptance conditional on an extraordinary occurrence taking place in the context of his immediate activity—digging. When as a result of coincidence his spade brought out a murti from the ground, the Chamar (perhaps convinced of the power of the Mahatma) retired as the subject of the narrative. Now others, who also had heard this particular rumour (futher proof of which had been unearthed in their own area), entered the scene and propitiated the image of Mahadev in the usual way by having darshan and making offerings of flowers and money. But it is significant that the money which would otherwise have gone towards the construction of a concrete platform at that site was earmarked as a contribution to the National School Fund, a project with which Gandhi was directly associated in Gorakhpur.

The story about finding a murti in Barhaj (No.7) follows the line of popular interpretation adopted for the previous anecdote. That this particular rumour might have been spread deliberately by someone, and that the idol had 'disappeared' by the time people rushed to the scene, is immaterial for the purposes of the present discussion. What is important is that a series of 'extraordinary occurrences' in the villages of Gorakhpur were being read in a familiar way, that is according to the conventions of reading the episodes in a sacred text but with their religiosity overdetermined by an incipient political consciousness.

There is an element which story No. 2 shares with No.5—where the *thakurain* makes her offering to the Mahatma conditional on the occurrence of a miracle and where this happens in the form of a dhoti bursting into flames. In both stories it is fear which imposes faith on non-believers. This penal motif recurs frequently in many religious ballads in eastern India. The doubting woman and the sceptical Kahar are persuaded to join the devotees—and do so ritually in the karahi episode—in the same way as a forceful display of an offended godling's wrathful power breaks the resistance of a non-conformist in a *vratkatha* or *panchali*.

This motif is made explicit in No.8 and its variation No.9, by the challenge to the Mahatma's power and the manner in which the latter is seen to triumph. The Brahman thief of Rudrapur village is representative not just of the ordinary village sceptic but of high-caste opposition to the Gandhian creed. His resistance questions by implication the conformism of the rest of the village see the modified version in No.9). But he pays for this by being subjected to physical and mental suffering. Only when his family relents on his behalf, joins the Mahatma's devotees by taking a vow in the latter's name and makes an offering does the man's condition improve. It is hard to miss the similarity between this and many other stories of opposition to the Gandhian creed, and between their predictable outcomes. The ending— "as a result of this particular occurrence people in the village and its neighbourhood have given up theft/drinking/gambling, etc."— announces in each instance the victory of the new moral authority which is made all the more resplendent by the fact of having been deified at the outset....

[Categories B and C, together with stories 10 through 27, are omitted here.]

D.   *Boons granted and/or miracles performed in the form of manauti and the recovery of things lost.*

28.   Pandit Jiwnandan Pathak from mauza Devkali, PO Bhagalpur wrote, "As a result of manauti of Mahatmaji a vessel of a Musalman which had fallen into a well six months ago came up on its own."

29.   In Naipura village (Azamgarh), the long-lost calf of Dalku Ahir returned to its peg as a result of the manauti of Mahatmaji. Dalku Ahir has contributed the one rupee of the manauti to the Swaraj Fund.

30.   A gentleman from Ballia district wrote, "In mauza Rustampur a *thaili* (purse) of a gwala-sadhu containing Rs 90 had disappeared from his hut. When he took manauti of Mahatmaji, he found it back in his hut, and the money was intact."

31.   A well-known zamindar of mauza Samogar (tahsil Deoria) had taken a *minnat* [manauti] of Bhagwatiji and offered a goat as a sacrifice. Many took the meat as *prasad*. After sometime the son of the zamindar found his hands stuck to his chest and his wife went mad. It was only when the zamindar vowed to contribute the price of the sacrificial goat to the National School Fund and feast Brahmans that both the son and the daughter-in-law began to feel well.

Boons granted and/or miracles performed in the form of regeneration of trees and wells.

32. "In mohalla Humayunpur, Gorakhpur city, two dead trees which had fallen in the garden of Babu Yugal Kishore, vakil, have planted themselves back! Many believe that this is due to the grace of Mahatmaji. This, because the person who cut the trees said that if *pratap* (spiritual power) of Mahatmaji was *saccha* (genuine) the trees would stand up on their own! Thousands gather at this site everyday and *batashas* (a kind of sweetmeat), money and ornaments are offered by men and women alike. It is said that the proceeds will be donated to the Swarajya ashram and the Tilak Swaraj Fund"....
     [Numbers 33 and 34 are omitted here.]

35. "In Basti town there lives a widow of Sri Raghubar Kasaudhan. She had a son who died three years ago. Her late husband had planted two mango trees; one was cut down sometime back and the other dried up a year ago. Fifteen days ago it began sprouting fresh leaves. The old woman maintains that she had taken a manauti of Mahatmaji: 'This tree is the only *nishani* (sign) of my late husband, let this tree live.' A large crowd gathers at this site as well".

36. "Last Saturday smoke started coming out of four or five wells in Gorakhpur city. People exclaimed that the water had caught fire. The whole city rushed to the spot. Some people drew water from one well: it had the fragrance of keora *(pandanus odaratissimus)*. It is believed that this is also due to the 'pratap' of the Mahatma! Some money etc. has also been offered to the well."

37. "Some days ago a major fire broke out in a village near the Gorakhpur Civil Courts. The entire village was burnt down. There is *a nala* (open drain) nearby. People started digging a *chaunra* (*katcha* well) in the nala to get some wet clay and water, but water was not struck even after digging several cubits. It is said that in the end one person took the manauti of the Mahatma. After this such a huge jet of water gushed out that not only was the 16-17 cubit deep well filled up, but also the two adjacent *garhas* (depressions) were also submerged. Since then thousands of men and women gather at the site. Flowers, batashas and money are offered, they bathe and wash their faces there and some even carry the water back to their homes."
     [Number 38 omitted here.]

39. "The *bhakts* (devotees) have... offered Rs23-8-12 in Mirzapur Bazaar where water had come out on its own. Sri Chedi Lal has arranged for this sum to be sent to the Gorakhpur Swaraj Fund."

40. The water of a well in Bikramjit Bazaar, tappa Belwa (Basti) had a very foul smell. Two *mahajans* took a manauti of the Mahatmaji. By morning the water had become pure.

41. "Plague was raging through Sonaura village. People were living in [outlying] huts. The water in a well at this place was so shallow on 27 April that even a small drinking vessel *(lota)* could not be fully submerged in it. Seeing this, one Misrji offered to distribute Rs 5 in the name of Gandhiji. Subsequently, water began to rise slowly. By the afternoon of 28 April the well had filled up to five cubits, the next day it was eleven cubits deep."

Once again we have in these stories the suggestion that the Mahatma's image takes form within pre-existing patterns of popular belief, and ritual action corresponding to these. In Nos. 28-30, Gandhi is fitted into the widespread practice of taking a vow (manuati) addressed to a god, a local godling or a saint on condition of the removal of an affliction or the fulfilment of a wish. In No. 31 we have an interesting development of this idea. Here the sacrifice of a goat in accordance with a manauti to Bhagwatiji boomerangs—it brings physical and mental suffering to the high-caste household of the zamindar of Samogar. The penance required is not limited to the traditional feasting of Brahmans; it now includes the donation of an amount equivalent to the cost of the sacrificial goat to the National School Fund.

The stories connected with wells (Nos. 36-41) which underline their importance for irrigation and even more for supplies of drinking water, call for some additional comments. The two major themes here are, first the taking of a manauti by a banker or a high-caste person (usually a landlord) for the purification of drinking water (Nos. 40 and 41), and secondly, the more common offering of flowers, batasha and money to wells where water has appeared miraculously. Both these are readily understandable once it is realized that it was generally the bigger zamindars and bankers who invested in the expensive construction of pukka (masonry) wells. This was a highly ritualised activity in Gorakhpur and was described thus by a local ethnographer towards the end of the nineteenth century:

When a man intends to sink a well he enquires an auspicious moment from the Pandit to commence it. When that hour comes, he worships Gauri, Ganesh, Shesh Nag, earth, the *kudari* (spade), and the nine planets. After worshipping these deities the person himself begins to dig with the *kudan* five times, facing the direction the Pandit has prescribed. Then the labourers begin their work. When they have sunk, so far as to make water appear, an auspicious moment is obtained to put the *jamuat* or wooden support on whom *[sic]* the brick structure of the well rests in the well. At the auspicious moment the person to whom the well belongs smears the *jamuat* with red powder in five places and ties grass (*dub*) and thread (*raksha*) on it, and then it is lowered down in the well. On this occasion a fire sacrifice (*homa/hawan*) is performed and Brahmans are fed. When the well had been sunk, cowdung, cow-milk, cow-urine, cow-ghee, Ganges water, leaves of tulsi plant and honey are put in it before its water is made use of. Then a fire sacrifice (*homa*) is performed and Brahmans are fed.

In Gorakhpur, according to the same informant, a mango tree was usually 'married' to a well. Accounts from neighbouring Basti district suggest that the construction of a pukka well was both a communal and a ritual act. Neighbouring zamindars sent men, women and children to collect wood for the firing and baking of bricks, and the *sattu,* gur and liquor received by them were regarded "in the light rather of a marriage feast than of remuneration." The 'marriage' of the well to an image (*jalotsarg*) was preceded by the carpenter spreading a *chaddar* (sheet) on the wooden frame. Into this the members of the brotherhood would throw coins of various denomination ranging from one paisa to one rupee, depending on their means and liberality. It was a measure of the importance of ritual in the consecration of pukka wells in this region that the 'regular cost' of constructing a well, eight feet wide and nineteen feet deep, was reckoned to have been Rs 43 in the 1860's, while nearly twice as much was spent on ceremonial expenses. As the settlement officer reported from Rasulpur Ghaus, Basti, "On account of the expense the ceremony is often delayed one or two years, during which time the family of the builder makes no use of the water."

With this kind of worshipful attitude towards the construction of masonry wells, the offerings of flowers and money to those spots where water had appeared miraculously in the spring of 1921 and the transference of these offerings to a nationalist fund appear as an elaboration of existing ideas in a novel context. The practice of Gandhi *manauti*, of his *vrat* and *aradhana* (fast and worship), and of women begging alms in his name and making offerings of cooked food (*karahi charana)*, as noticed in some of the earlier stories, can all be adduced as further instances of this process at work.

VII

Taken together, these stories indicate how ideas about Gandhi's *pratap* and the appreciation of his message derived from popular Hindu beliefs and practices and the material culture of the peasantry. Does not the fact of the reporting of these rumours in the local nationalist weekly suggest that these were actively spread by interested parties? It is true that such rumours enter our sources at the point where a correspondent communicates them to the *Swadesh*. But that need not be taken to mean that these did not exist prior to and independent of their publication. Their generalized circulation in the villages of Gorakhpur is also attested by their being reported and denied in the local anti-nationalist monthly, *Gyan Shakti*.

There can be no doubt that the reporting of these rumours in the local paper, *Swadesh*, must have added to their circulation and even to their authenticity. Lefebvre in his study of rural panic in revolutionary France observes how journalists imbued rumours "with a new strength by putting... them into print." However it seems unlikely that printing could have changed the character of these rumours to any significant degree; it merely increased their effectiveness as oral and unauthored speech. People in the Gorakhpur countryside believed in these not out of any unquestioning trust in the weekly newspaper but because they accorded with existing beliefs about marvels and miracles, about right and wrong.

In Indian villages even printed texts often revert to their oral characteristics in the very process of communication. It has been noted that newspapers, pamphlets, etc., are made intelligible to the illiterate population in the countryside by reading aloud, paraphrasing the text in the rustic dialect and commenting on it. In 'advanced cultural communities', Vachek notes, written texts are taken "as a sign of the first order (i.e. the sign of an outside world)," the deciphering of which requires "no detour by way of spoken language." It seems that one of the reasons for the reading aloud of newspapers in Indian villages is that even for a large part of the technically literate population printed texts can be deciphered only by a detour through the spoken language. In such readings, it seems reasonable to suggest, a story acquires its authentication from its motif and the name of its place of origin rather than from the authority of the correspondent. It then spreads by word of mouth, and derives its credibility from any association, real or imaginary, it might have with place-names familiar to the local population.

How did the local Congress leadership react to the spread of these stories? Maulvi Subhanullah, the DCC President, while recounting some of these to the Sessions Judge in June 1922, admitted that "no attempt was made by the Congress or Khilafat to prevent [the] public from believing in them." *Swadesh,* the newspaper which published these stories under the sanctimonious rubric *bhakton ki bhavnain—* 'beliefs of the devotees'—adopted a double-edged policy in this regard. On the one hand it published a note every now and then debunking some of the more fanciful stories and also let its satirist, Mannan Dwivedi, poke fun at them. On the other hand when attacked by the *Pioneer,* it came up with a spirited defence of its policy of printing these stories.

In March 1921 some people used the services of public criers to announce that "Mahatmaji had emerged from fire [unhurt] and that Swaraj had been established." They went so far as to swear by the truth of such statements. The editor of *Swadesh* promptly denounced this as an irresponsible act which had no sanction from the Mahatma. However, the same issue of the journal contained two columns of Gandhi stories under the heading 'strange happenings'. Elsewhere in the same issue Mannan Dwivedi, writing under the pen-name Shriyut Muchandar Nath, satirised some of these as follows:

> It is true that a felled tree in the front of Babu Yugal Kishore's garden has planted itself back and even sprouted leaves due to the grace of Mahatmaji. [See No. 32]. Every day lakhs of people come to see this [miracle], as a result of which crores of rupees are being collected. Therefore, due to the efforts of Babu Krishna Prasad, neither will postal rates go up nor will there be a deficit in the budget this year...

> It was rumoured that a well in Gorakhpur was smelling of keora. [See No. 36]. Now it has been confirmed by the Khilafat Committee that Sri Shiv Mangal Gandhi had emptied his karahs full of keora into the well, as it is said that he is going to perform the

last rites for his Sundar Shringar Karyalay [a perfumery in the city]
and is shortly to take up the running of a [nationalist] press.

It is doubtful how many outside the city of Gorakhpur would have
understood Mannan Dwivedi's allusions or allowed satire to get the
better of belief. Even the editor of *Swadesh,* when pressed, could write
an impassioned defence of the peasant's acceptance of these stories:

> We do not consider...*Swadesh* to be the property (*miras*) of its
> editor. Therefore, we consider it as part of our duty to report the
> thoughts and feelings current among the people (janta), whether
> right or wrong, in our paper... It is possible that some people might
> doubt these strange happenings, but the janta does not consider
> them so [improbable]. And there is a reason for this. It is because
> Hinduism has placed faith and belief (*shraddha aur vishwas*) on a
> high footing. It is because of this that those who worship stone
> images have their prayers answered. It is because of this that people
> take a dip in the holy waters of Gangaji and think that their sins
> have been washed away. In every age and country, every now and
> then, such things have happened. Even in the time of the Buddha,
> Mohammad and Christ such miracles were supposed to have taken
> place. Then we see no reason why miracles (*chamatkar*) should not
> be associated with Mahatma Gandhi whose name is perhaps even
> better known in India than that of Ram and Sita. Faith yields fruit.

The editor of *Swadesh,* who had himself sought to inculcate an
attitude of devotion in the district towards the Mahatma, had thus no
hesitation in printing rumours about the latter's pratap. It was only when
these appeared to instigate dangerous beliefs and actions, such as those
concerning demands for the abolition of zamindari, reduction of rents or
enforcement of just price at the bazaars, that the journal came out with
prompt disclaimers.

VIII

Just as the Mahatma was associated in Gorakhpur with a variety of
miraculous occurrences, so did his name lend itself as a label for all
sorts of public meetings, pamphlets—and of course for that polysemic
word Swaraj. Surveying the background to the Chauri Chaura riot, the
judges of the Allahabad High Court found it "remarkable... how this
name of 'Swaraj' was linked, in the minds of the peasantry of
Gorakhpur, with the name of Mr. Gandhi. Everywhere in the evidence
and in statements made... by various accused persons," they found that

"it was 'Gandhiji's Swaraj', or the 'Mahatmaji's Swaraj' for which they [i.e. the peasants] were looking." 'Announcements in Urdu' were sold by Lal Mohammad, one of the principal accused in the Chauri Chaura case, as 'Gandhi papers' which were to be preserved and produced "when Gandhiji asked for... [them]." The receipt for donations to the Khilafat fund, which bore a superficial resemblance to a one-rupee bank note, was referred to as a 'Gandhi note' by the peasants of Gorakhpur. The editor of *Gyan Shakti,* to whom we owe this information, alleged that villagers interpreted its non-acceptance (as legal tender?) as an act of opposition to the Mahatma. Whether peasants genuinely failed to recognize the difference (as officials in some Awadh districts implied), or whether this was just a conscious manipulation of an ambiguous printed paper to force non-believers into acceptance, we do not know for certain. What is clear, however, is that we have in the 'Gandhi note' an index of the popular tendency to look upon the Mahatma as an alternative source of authority. We have it on local testimony that peasant volunteers proceeding to a *sabha* at Dumri on the morning of 4 February 1922 (hours before the historic clash with the police was to occur at the Chaura thana a couple of miles away), claimed that they were "going to hold a Gandhi Mahatma Sabha" which would bring about 'Gandhi Swaraj'.

The popular notion of 'Gandhiji's Swaraj' in Gorakhpur appears to have taken shape quite independently of the district leadership of the Congress party. As the High Court judges observed, the local peasantry "perceived of it [Swaraj] as a millennium in which taxation would be limited to the collection of small cash contributions or dues in kind from fields and threshing floors, and [in] which the cultivators would hold their lands at little more than nominal rents." During the course of the trial the district Congress and Khilafat leadership repeatedly denied having propagated any such ideas in the villages. In fact there is evidence that as early as March 1921 public proclamations about the advent of Swaraj were being made in the Gorakhpur countryside. These, as we have noted above, were denounced by the Congress paper *Swadesh.* The pro-landlord *Gyan Shakti* drew pointed attention to such occurrences as ominous signs which boded ill for all concerned:

> One night people from all the villages [!] kept awake and roamed over five villages each. That night it was impossible to get any sleep. They were shouting 'Gandhiji ki jai'. They had *dhol, tasa, jhal, majiras* (kettledrums and cymbals) with them. The din thus

caused was unbearable. People were shouting, this is the drum of swaraj *(swaraj ka danka)*. Swaraj has been attained. The English had taken a bet with Gandhiji that they would grant Sawraj if Gandhiji could come out of fire [unhurt]. Gandhiji took hold of the tail of a calf and went through fire. Now Swaraj has been attained. It was also announced that now only four annas or eight annas a bigha would have to be paid in rent. We have also heard that some peasants are insisting that they will not pay more than eight annas a bigha as rent.

These rumours are signs of an impending clash between the peasants and the landlords. As a result of this both parties shall suffer. Sensible *(parhe-likhe)* peasants, landlords and the government should ·refute such rumours. Remember this! If ordinary people retain their belief in such rumours and persist in their quest for the chimerical then the attainment of Swaraj will become increasingly distant. Peasants are now refusing to obey their landlords, or work for them. This is not a good sign for the country.

Quite clearly this was a miracle (Gandhi's passage through fire) consistent with the existing level of peasant consciousness and its foil in utopian hopes for a world free of rents—a far cry these from official Congress policy—which marked the irruption of Swaraj that night in Gorakhpur villages. However, as local-level volunteer activity entered a more militant phase in late 1921, the coming of Swaraj was perceived—contrary to anything the Congress stood for at that time—in terms of the direct supplanting of the authority of the police (just as the earlier notion of divine punishment for opposition to the Gandhian creed was replaced by the idea that it was for the panchayats themselves to dispense justice in such cases). Thus Sarju Kahar, the personal servant of the murdered thanedar of Chaura, testified that "two or four days before the affair [he] had heard that Gandhi Mahatma's Swaraj had been established, that the Chaura thana would be abolished, and that the volunteers would set up their own thana." According to Harbans Kurmi of Mangapatti, Narayan, Baleshar and Chamru of his village said on their return from the riot that "they had burnt and thrown away and Swaraj had come." Or as Phenku Chamar told the Sessions Judge in August 1922:

Bipat Kahar, Sarup Bhar and Mahadeo Bhuj were coming along calling out 'Gandhi Maharaj Gandhi Maharaj' from the north, the direction of Chaura, to [the] south, the direction of Barhampur. I asked why they were calling out 'Gandhi Maharaj' and they said the thana of Chaura had been burnt and razed to the ground [by them] and the Maharaj's swaraj had come.

IX

Corresponding to this dramatic change in the manifestation of 'Gandhiji's Swaraj', there was for the peasant volunteers of Chauri Chaura a transformation in the spirit of that ubiquitous cry, 'Gandhi Maharaj ki jai', as well. We have noticed how this cry had assumed an audacious overtone during Gandhi's return journey from Gorakpur in February 1921. Within a month, the 'Swaraj ka danka' episode suggests, the *jaikar* of Gandhi had become a militant avowal of the organized strength of peasant volunteers, a cry which mobilized and struck terror in the hearts of waverers and enemies alike. For the peasants of north India this had ceased in effect to be a Gandhian cry; it was now a cry with which an attack on a market or a thana was announced. 'Mahatma Gandhi ki jai' had, in this context, assumed the function of such traditional war cries as 'Jai Mababir' or 'Bam Bam Mahadeo'. An interesting case of such a transformation is provided by the following intelligence report from Bara Banki:

> The big Mahadeo Fair near Ramnagar passed off quietly, though the extensive substitution of Gandhi ki jai for the orthodox Bam Bam Mahadeo was noticeable even when there were no government officer [s] present.

The crowd of Badhiks (a so-called 'criminal tribe') that looted the Tinkonia Bazaar in Gorakhpur on 15 February 1921, did so to the cry of 'Mahatma Gandhi ki jai'. In a small fair at Auraneshwarghat in Bara Banki a dispute with *halwai* (confectioners) on 22 February 1922 led to the upsetting and looting of sweatmeat and other stalls "to the accompaniments of shouts of *Mahatma Gandhi ki jai aur mithai le leu."*

Thus a 'jaikar' of adoration and adulation had become the rallying cry for direct action. While such action sought to justify itself by a reference to the Mahatma, the Gandhi of its rustic protagonists was not as he really was, but as they had thought him up. Though deriving their legitimacy from the supposed orders of Gandhi, peasant actions in such cases were framed in terms of what was popularly regarded to be just, fair and possible. As an official reply to the question of haat-looting in north Bihar in the winter of 1921 stated:

The evidence in the possession of the Government leaves no doubt that the haat-looting was directly connected with the state of excitement and unrest produced by the non-cooperation agitation. The persons who started the loot first of all asked the price of rice, or cloth or vegetables or whatever the particular article might be, and when the price was mentioned, alleged that Gandhi had given the order that the price should be so much, usually a quarter of the current market rate. When the shopkeepers refused to sell at lower prices, they were abused and beaten and their shops were looted.

There was thus no single authorized version of the Mahatma to which the peasants of eastern UP and north Bihar may be said to have subscribed in 1921. Indeed their ideas about Gandhi's 'orders' and powers' were often at variance with those of the local Congress-Khilafat leadership and clashed with the basic tenets of Gandhism itself. The violence at Chauri Chaura was rooted in this paradox.

18

*Much of the credit for the founding of Pakistan must inevitably go
to Mahomed Ali Jinnah, who fought unswervingly for its creation,
despite intense opposition not only in the Congress but among
many of India's Muslims. This selection examines how Jinnah first
secured the support of the Muslim League for the idea of Pakistan,
and then kept that vision alive throughout the intricate
constitutional negotiations of the 1940's. In the end, Moore
concludes, though the state of Pakistan was not as large as Jinnah
would have wished, it still embodied the ideal of a Muslim
homeland in South Asia.*

Jinnah and the Pakistan Demand

R.J. MOORE

ENIGMA

In an age sceptical of the historic role of great men there is universal
agreement that Mahomed Ali Jinnah was central to the Muslim
League's emergence after 1937 as the voice of a Muslim nation; to its
articulation in March 1940 of the Pakistan demand for separate statehood for the Muslim majority provinces of north-western and eastern
India; and to its achievement in August 1947 of the separate but
truncated state of Pakistan by the Partition of India. Subcontinental
judgements of Jinnah are bound to be *parti pris* and to exaggerate his
individual importance. While Pakistanis generally see him as the
Quaid-i-Azam, Great Leader, or father of their nation, Indians often
regard him as the Lucifer who tempted his people into the unforgivable
sin against their nationalist faith. Among distinguished foreign scholars
unbiased by national commitment, his stature is similarly elevated. Sir
Penderel Moon has written:

> There is, I believe, no historical parallel for a single individual
> effecting such a political revolution; and his achievement is a
> striking refutation of the theory that in the making of history the
> individual is of little or no significance. It was Mr Jinnah who
> created Pakistan and undoubtedly made history.

Professor Lawrence Ziring believes that Jinnah's "personality ...made Pakistan possible" and that "it would not have emerged without him." Sir Cyril Philips has argued that without Jinnah's leadership regionalism would probably have competed seriously with Muslim nationalism as the aim of the Muslim majority provinces. Professor Nicholas Mansergh looks to Jinnah for "the classic exposition of the two-nation theory" in his March 1940 address prefiguring the Pakistan resolution and revises sharply upwards the determining influence of the concept upon the interplay of men and events that culminated in the Partition of India.

Yet the relation of Jinnah to the rise of the League and its demand and movement for Pakistan is still obscure. Eminent contemporaries were puzzled by the sources of his apparent power. For example, as last Viceroy, Lord Mountbatten thought the idea of Pakistan 'sheer madness' and wrote of Jinnah in bewilderment: "I regard Jinnah as a psychopathic case; in fact until I had met him I would not have thought it possible that a man with such a complete lack of administrative knowledge or sense of responsibility could achieve or hold down so powerful a position." Mountbatten saw Jinnah as a leader whose 'megalomania' was so 'chronic' that he pursued his own power to the material detriment of his misguided followers. British statesmen and officials and Congress leaders alike attached immense significance to vanity and pride in Jinnah's quest for Pakistan and their views continue to influence the historiography of the Partition.

In a perceptive analysis Professor Khalid Bin Sayeed seeks the key to the relationship between Jinnah's personality and the Pakistan movement in the 'congruence' between the ambition of Jinnah, a domineering man whom reverses in life had made desperate, and the needs and characteristics of his people "a community...looking for a great saviour....who was prepared to unite the community and bring earthly glory to Islam." Nevertheless, for Sayeed "it continues to be an enigma how these people followed a leader who was so austere and so remote from them." The link, he speculates, was "that this power-conscious man promised to them the political power which the Qur'an had promised to them and which their forbears had wielded in India."

Historians have also emphasized the enigmatic nature of Jinnah's 'promise'—the vagueness of the Pakistan demand and the variety of constitutional forms that Jinnah seemed willing to accept in satisfaction of it. Some have sought to resolve the paradox by construing the demand as a bargaining counter, whereby Jinnah sought to enhance the power of the League and himself within a united free India. Others have argued that Jinnah was 'hoist with his own petard': he fell captive to his promise of separate statehood for six provinces and was left by the Partition with the truncated state that was alone consistent with the concept of a nation defined by the religious map of the subcontinent.

The following analysis seeks to clarify the relation between Jinnah and the Pakistan movement during the decade preceding Partition, in terms of both his charisma and his constitutionl strategy, but not, it should be stressed, in terms of party organization and political mobilization, on which much more work remains to be done.

SOURCES OF CHARISMA

Jinnah was born on Christmas day 1876 in a tenement house in Karachi. He was to be the eldest of seven children of a hide merchant, whose modest means confined the family's living space to two rooms but somehow sufficed to despatch Jinnah at the age of sixteen direct from the Sind Madrasa to Lincoln's Inn. The exemplary pupil qualified for the Bar precociously young, but during his short four-year absence his mother and child-wife died and his father suffered financial ruin. He chose to make his way at the Bombay Bar. After three briefless and penurious years his powers of application, analysis, and advocacy brought him rapid success and wealth, the springboard to his political career. By the age of forty he had been prominent in the Indian National Congress, toured Europe with Gokhale, represented the Muslims of Bombay in the Imperial Legislative Council, and acted as principal negotiator of the Lucknow Pact for Congress-Muslim League unity. When Edwin Montagu visited India in 1917 he recorded meeting this "young, perfectly mannered, impressive-looking... very clever man", who, "armed to the teeth with dialectics" tied the Viceroy up in verbal knots.

By the standards of his gilded youth the next twenty years of Jinnah's life were leaden. Poised to scale political heights he fell and suffered disappointment. Gandhi's Congress-Khilafat non-cooperation movement, which was inimical to his constitutionalist style, was partly responsible for his eclipse, but perhaps as important was the shift that the dyarchical provincial councils effected in Muslim politics. Given the realities of office and patronage the Punjab Unionist Party became the powerhouse of Muslim policy. Confronted with Congress initiatives to inherit the central government of India, the All-India Muslim Conference, led from the Punjab by Mian Fazl-i-Husain, espoused schemes for entrenching the Muslims in quasi-sovereign provinces, yielding to a federal centre only such powers as they chose and given effective safeguards for Muslim interests. Jinnah remained a leader of the League and a member of the Central Legislature but the action had moved elsewhere. In 1928 he was worsted by the forces of Hindu orthodoxy when he sought accommodation with Congress on an all-parties constitutional scheme. At the Round Table Conference he was suspected by the dominant Muslim delegates as an unreliable conciliator, and he seemed to speak for no-one but himself. For three or four years he turned his back on India and tried to settle in London, living in Hampstead and practising at the Privy Council Bar. When he returned to India in 1936 to set up the League's Parliamentary Board to contest the 1936 elections under the India Act of 1935's provisions for provincial autonomy, he was shunned by the Punjab Unionists. He remained hopeful of achieving an all-India Hindu-Muslim settlement under a Congress-League *rapprochement* until, after its electoral triumph, Congress made it apparent that its terms were the League's capitulation.

Jinnah's personality and experience disposed him to feel bitterly the Congress denial of the Muslims' political identity. Lacking inherited status, from an early age his place in the world had rested wholly upon his own efforts. By observing a regimen of discipline and self-denial he had earned a place of dignity in Indian politics. The single-minded pursuit of professional and political success left him little opportunity to cultivate a private life that might mitigate the sense of public rejection. The exaggerated refinement of the English dress and personal style that he adopted seem more like carapaces than indulgences. The political reverses of middle-age were unrelieved by any of the usual pleasures of personal or domestic life. His marriage at the age of forty-two to the eighteen-year-old daughter of a Parsi friend had, after several unhappy years, finally collapsed in 1928. Her death soon afterwards left him bereaved and with a sense of guilt. For the rest of his life his sole companion was his loyal sister Fatima, who from living with it daily, came to share his acute sense of persecution.

Like Jinnah's personal standing the status that the Muslims had achieved by 1937 had been hard won. Latecomers to western education, official employment and party politics, they had, as collaborators of the

British Raj, advanced rapidly in the twentieth century. In the United Provinces they had consolidated their tenure of land and won weightage well beyond their numbers in councils and government service. Since the first elections to the Montford councils they had succeeded to decades of Congress ascendancy in Bengal and won office in Punjab. The All-India Muslim Conference had defended separate electorates in both majority provinces and applied a strategy of 'provincial balance' to secure the separation of Sind from Bombay and its elevation, together with that of the North-West Frontier Province, to full provincial status. In 1936, the last year of his life, Fazl-i-Husain could reflect that the Muslim position was now 'adequately safe- guarded'. The sense of achieved security owed much to checks that the India Act of 1935 seemed to place on the power of the Congress, for in its contemplated all-India federation a third of the seats were reserved to the Muslims and a third to nominees of the Indian princes. The emergence of Congress dominance in 1937 changed all that.

In March 1937, when Nehru remarked that the Congress and the Raj were the only two parties in India, Jinnah replied to the rebuff by claiming the Muslim League as a third, a rightful 'equal partner' of the Congress. It was the Muslims of the Congress provinces who first apprehended the dangers of Hindu ascendancy under a Congress Raj and reacted with a sense of persecution. Muslim grandees in the United Provinces grew anxious when Congress denied them a share in government and threatened their culture, property and prospects of public employment. In Muslim minority provinces it seemed that under responsible government the Congress could withhold their participation in office permanently. In Muslim majority provinces Congress sought power through alignments with Muslim factions. Rajendra Prasad commented:

> The attempt of our party in most [of these] provinces had constantly been to win over members of the government party and thus secure a majority for itself, so that is may form a ministry. In effect its action has been not so much to consider the criticised government measures on their merit and secure the adoption of its own programme by the government, but to try somehow or other to oust the party in power. The result... has been to create much bitterness against the Congress....

At the all-India level the Congress High Command pursued its advantage by pressing the princes to fill their federal seats by election instead of nomination, which would open the prospect of sufficient Congress victories to destroy the statutory check upon its power. Jinnah became convinced that parliamentary government would mean Congress 'totalitarianism' in India. The only safeguard of equal rights to India's Muslims lay in their achievement of equality of power through their solidarity within the All-India Muslim League. Under his organization the League's membership grew from a few thousand to several hundred thousand in 1937-38.

Jinnah harped on the theme of equality. At the League's annual session at Lucknow in October 1937 he insisted that "an honourable settlement can only be achieved between equals." He demanded of Nehru that Congress must recognize the League "on a footing of perfect equality. He internalized the Muslims' sense of 'suffering and sacrifice' from the 'fire of persecution'. He expressed himself with personal conviction: "I have got as much right to share in the government of this country as any Hindu;" and "I must have [an] equal real and effective share in the power." The appeal was underpinned by an assertion that Islamic society was based on the equality of man.

The essential link between Jinnah's leadership and the emergence of a Muslim national consciousness was that Jinnah personified the sense of persecution felt by Muslims—more precisely, Urdu-speaking Muslims—at the Congress denial of their achieved status. The widespread assumption that vanity, pride, ambition and megalomania were the dominant facets of his personality has masked it. In a similar way, the extension of impressions of his personality to generalizations about his political style has exaggerated the intellectual distance between the leader and his followers, obscuring the doctrinal cut and thrust from which emerged the constitutional strategy that would afford a refuge from persecution.

FROM KARACHI TO LAHORE

Almost all who observed Jinnah described him as reserved, remote, aloof and, above all, lonely. His remoteness in later life was caused partly by his chronic bronchial infection, which had probably appeared in 1936, and from July 1943 partly by the precautionary measures of up to three official bodyguards who were assigned to him after he was attacked by an assassin. But clearly he did not enjoy physical contact and kept the world at a distance. The famous monocle and frequent changes of clothing seem, like his aversion to shaking hands and travelling by train unless in a first class coupé, expressions of immaculacy. When Sir Stafford Cripps visited him in December 1939 he noted: "Altogether he gave me the impression of an intensely lonely man in prepetual conflict with himself and with no-one in whom he could confide or who could give him reliable advice, but he put his case with great ability and clarity." In January 1942 Sir Reginald Coupland visited him at his new house on Malabar Hill and was struck by the "great forensic ability... admirable lucidity... and clear conclusions" of this "very able advocate". His notes suggest Jinnah's clinical detachment and self-sufficiency, living and working in a mansion with "beautiful rooms, lavishly furnished, and a most attractive curving marble terrace, with lawn beneath it sloping to a belt of trees with a gap in it through which the sea..." Jinnah plied him with League literature "largely reprints of his own speeches". A few weeks later Coupland described Jinnah as 'virtually dictator' of the League, a judgement that A. V. Alexander echoed at the time of the Cabinet Mission: "Mr Jinnah, the so-called Man of Destiny of the Muslim League [is] a clever lawyer... and I should think in his own way pretty near to being a complete dictator." Mountbatten believed that "the only adviser that Jinnah listens to is Jinnah."

Yet in the crucial eighteen months preceding the proclamation of the Pakistan demand at Lahore Jinnah's role in the formation and expression of constitutional thought and strategy was certainly not that of an isolated, lonely and self-sufficient leader.

In October 1938 Jinnah returned to a king's welcome in the city of his birth, Karachi, for a conference of the Sind branch of the All-India Muslim League. He rode from the railway station in an open limousine at the head of a procession three miles long. Some 20,000 delegates were assembled, among them the provincial premiers Sir Sikander Hayat Khan (Punjab) and Sir Fazlul Haq (Bengal), the U.P. leaders Liaquat Ali Khan (Secretary of the League), the Raja of Mahmudabad and Chaudhry Khaliquzzaman, the old Khilafat leader Shaukat Ali, and prominent Sindhis. The main object of the Sindhis in organizing the conference was to bring to bear upon the province's faction-ridden Muslim establishment the unifying influence of the national body. The benefits of the separation from Bombay of this majority province had been squandered by the recourse of its Muslim premiers to Hindus for their survival. In July 1937 M.H. Gazdar (a future mayor of Karachi) had written to Jinnah in disgust at the state of Sind politics and proposed the creation of an independent Muslim state comprising the four north-western provinces. The initiator and reception committee chairman of the conference was Sir Abdoola Haroon, a self-made merchant and industrialist prince of Karachi, campaigner for the separation of Sind, member of the Central Legislature (1926-42), founder of the Sind United Party on the model of the Punjab Unionists, and member of the League's Working Committee. In his opening address he focussed attention upon the need for an all-India Hindu-Muslim settlement, failing which Muslims may need "to seek their salvation in their own way in an independent federation of Muslim states," in the division of Hindu India and Muslim India 'under separate federations'.

Haroon was moving further and faster towards a separatist objective than Jinnah, who emphasized the primary need to consolidate Muslims to resist Congress oppression. Fourteen months later Jinnah was still professing to be as much an Indian nationalist as Nehru, and in January 1940 he could still write of India as the 'common motherland' of Muslims and Hindus. He was disquieted when Haroon incorporated the goal of an independent Muslim state in a resolution:

> The Sindh Provincial Muslim League Conference considers it absolutely essential in the interests of an abiding peace of the vast Indian continent and in the interests of unhampered cultural development, the economic and social betterment and political self-determination of the two nations, known as Hindus and Muslims, that India may be divided into federations, namely, the federation of Muslim States and the federation of non-Muslim States. This conference therefore recommends to the All India Muslim League to devise a scheme of constitution under which Muslim-majority-provinces Muslim Indian States and areas inhabited by a majority of Muslims may attain full independence in the form of a federation of their own...

Jinnah is reported to have entered a caveat: "The Government is still in the hands of the British. Let us not forget it. You must see ahead and work for the ideal that you think will arise 25 years hence." Next day, with his tacit consent, Haroon's draft was passed thus modified:

> This conference considers it absolutely essential, in the interests of an abiding peace of the vast Indian continent and in the interests of unhampered cultural development, the economic and social betterment and political self-determination of the two nations,

known as Hindus and Muslims, to recommend to the All-India
Muslim League to review and revise the entire conception of what
should be the suitable constitution for India which will secure
honourable and legitimate status to them.

While the two nations theory now became the League's creed it was
clearly not synonymous with separatism. Even the mover of Haroon's
original resolution, Shaikh Abdul Majid, expected that the Hindu and
Muslim federations would be linked by a common centre for foreign
affairs, defence and the settlement of disputes. Clearly, too, Jinnah was
drawn this far by the initiative of the Sindhis and the need to
accommodate policy to it in the interests of solidarity.

Jinnah was unwell during the following weeks and made no
speeches until 26 December at the League's annual session at Patna,
when he spoke impromptu. He then observed the awakening of a
"national consciousness among the Muslims" comparable to that of the
Hindus, but warned that a "national self and national individuality" had
yet to be developed. The session authorised him to explore suitable
constitutional alternatives to the 1935 Act, and the following March the
Working Committee set up a committee to examine those that had
already appeared and others that might emerge. Jinnah was to head the
committee and eight others, including Haroon, Liaquat, Sikander,
Nazimuddin (Bengal), and Aurangzeb Khan (N.W.F.P) were
empanelled. Next month Jinnah intimated that several schemes were
before the committee, including one for dividing the country into Hindu
and Muslim India. In fact the committee never met and the initiative
remained in Haroon's hands.

During the interim between the Karachi and Patna conferences
Haroon took a number of steps to advance the general cause of a
separate federation of Muslim provinces and states. His resolve was
strengthened by Congress activities in the states towards the end of the
year. He failed in an attempt to enlist the support of the Aga Khan.
However, the Council of the League now established a Foreign and
Inland Deputations subcommittee, and Haroon became its chairman. It
was to send deputations abroad, to explain the views of Muslim India
and counter Congress allegations that the Muslims were reactionary and
unpatriotic, and from the Muslim majority to the minority provinces, to
consolidate links between their organizations. The committee
performed some of the functions appropriate to offices for foreign
affairs and propaganda. Haroon also involved it in planning when he

asked Dr Syed Abdul Latif to meet in Lahore in January 1939 to discuss
his ideas for the recognition of the two nations by the redistribution of
India into cultural zones. Though Latif's approach was to accommodate
the two nations within a 'common motherland' under a single federal
authority, rather than to pursue the separate federations that he himself
favoured, Haroon advanced Rs 2,000 for the publication and foreign
distribution of Latif's scheme in expanded booklet form. The
circulation of Latif's views in 1938-39, in pamphlets, the newspapers
and the booklet, stimulated controversy over the constiutional future of
Muslim India.

Much of the constitutional planning occurred in the Punjab, where
there was already a significant legacy of separatist thought. As
president of the League in 1930 the philosopher-poet of Lahore, Sir
Muhammad Iqbal, had called for the amalgamation of the four north-
western provinces, less some non-Muslim districts, into "a Muslim
India within India". As the religious units of India had never been
inclined to sacrifice, their individualities in a larger whole "the unity of
an Indian nation must be sought, not in negation, but in mutual harmony
and cooperation." The "effective principle of cooperation" in India was
the recognition of 'homelands' in which the Muslim might enjoy "full
and free development on the lines of his own culture and tradition." In
1933 the Cambridge student Rahmat Ali, the Punjab coiner of the name
'Pakistan', proposed the separation from India of a Muslim state
embracing the four provinces and Kashmir, and soon afterwards
launched the Pakistan National Movement. During the year preceding
his death in April 1938 Iqbal's opposition to a single Indian federation
had hardened and he had urged Jinnah to demand one or more separate
Muslim states, though he was silent as to their relations with the rest of
India.

In March 1939 the fact that the League Working Committee had
Latif's scheme before it provoked Ahmad Bashir, secretary of the
youthful and intellectual Pakistan Majlis, Lahore, to petition Jinnah,
Liaquat, Harooon, Fazlul Haq and Sikander. Latif's scheme would
prejudice the political and economic integrity of Pakistan by casting the
eastern tracts of the Punjab and Kashmir into a Hindu-Sikh zone:

As the scheme is likely to influence the natural boundaries of
Pakistan I feel the interest of Pakistan and the Movement started
towards the creation of an independent state in the North-West of
India comprising the whole of the Punjab, Kashmir, the North

Western Frontier Province, Sind and Baluchistan would materially suffer if the Cultural Zones Scheme is extended towards the North West of India.....The Pakistan mind is slowly believing in its physical whole and any attempt to disintegrate this natural geographical identity will certainly be detrimental to the cause of Muslim India.

The references to the Pakistan Movement and the claim to the full four north-western provinces plus Kashmir suggest the influence of Rahmat Ali on the Pakistan Majlis of Lahore. However, they also drew on Iqbal's ideas. The Majlis' full title, 'Majlis-i-Kabir Pakistan, Lahore', suggested its reverence for the saintly poet who was also the prophet of Indian unity. In the spirit of Iqbal, Ahmad Bashir wrote to Jinnah: "Nobody questions India's unity but how that unity can be achieved is a matter that deserves special attention of all the parties concerned. It is a matter...[that] must be given precedence to everything else." The recognition of "separate homelands by dividing India into autonomous homogeneous states" was "the one and the only way to India's Unity". Ahmad Bashir was to supply Jinnah with ringing passages for his inspiring Lahore presidential address.

In summer 1939 the alternatives open to the League were clarified by Sikander's formulation of a scheme for a loose all-India federation of zones including provinces and states, and its rejection first by Ahmad Bashir and then by scholars at Aligarh. The latter favoured the division of British India into "three wholly independent and sovereign states". Two Aligarh authors, Professor Syed Zafarul Hasan and Dr M.A.H. Qadri, insisted that the Muslims of India, "a nation by themselves", must not be "enslaved into a single all-India federaiton with an overwhelming Hindu majority in the Centre." The three sovereign states of British India would be North-West India or Pakistan, Bengal, and Hindustan. The principalities within these states or exclusively on the frontier of one of them would be attached automatically, while those adjoining more than one state might choose their attachment. But Hyderabad must recover Berar and the Carnatic and become a fourth sovereign state, "the southern wing of Muslim India". Pakistan would include the four north-western provinces, Kashmir and other adjacent states. Bengal would embrace the existing province less the districts of Howrah, Midnapur and Darjeeling, but plus the district of Purnea (in Bihar) and Sylhet (in Assam). Both Pakistan and Bengal would be Muslim states. Hindustan would comprise the rest of India but within it two new autonomous provinces—Delhi and Malabar—should be formed, with strong Muslim minorities. The three states would have separate treaties of alliance with Britain and should join together in a defensive and offensive alliance. The Hasan-Qadri scheme was commended warmly by eight Aligarh scholars who, at the same time, deplored Latif's proposals. The scholars claimed to have discussed 'the Aligarh scheme' with its authors in principle and detail and were convinced that it went as far as possible to meet the just claims of the 'two nations'.

By September 1939, when Britain shelved the paper federation of the 1935 Act, Muslim constitutional thought was certainly turning against the federal principle, even as expressed in the zonal schemes of Latif and Sikander. A year after the adoption at Karachi of the two nations theory its practical application was a live issue. On 18 October, when Lord Linlithgow spoke of India's destiny in terms of unity, Ahmad Bashir protested to Jinnah at his blunt rejection of "the national demand of the Muslims regarding the recognition of their separate national status". Next month the Aligarh group was provoked when Gandhi attacked the theory of separate Muslim nationahood. On 15 November Professor Hasan, together with Dr Zaki Uddin and Dr Burhan Ahmad (two of the eight who commended the Aligarh scheme), and Ubaid Ullah Durrani, petitioned Jinnah at length upon the matter. They concluded: "Neither the fear of British bayonets nor the prospects of a bloody civil war can discourage [the Muslims] in their will to achieve free Muslim states in those parts of india where they are in majority." Soon afterwards the several Muslim authors of constitutional plans met for ten days "to evolve a consolidated scheme", which they sent to Jinnah confidentially. This "fresh plan on the basis that Moslems are a separate Nation" so constituted Muslim zones in the north and the east as to include seventy-two per cent of the total Muslim population of India. A Delhi province was added to the nothern zone and all of Assam to the eastern. A third of the land mass of India was claimed.

On 1 Feburary 1940 Haroon presided at New Delhi over a joint meeting of his Foreign Commitee and the authors of schemes. It resolved to recommend that the Working Committee "state its mind in unequivocal language with regard to the future of the Indian Moslem Nation." India's Muslims were a separate nation entitled to self-determination. In order to make that right effective "the Moslems shall have separate National Home in the shape of an autonomous state." The meeting's resolutions were sent to Liaquat (as League secretary) and to Jinnah on 2 February. Two days later the Working Committee adopted the nub of them which was, of course, expressed in the Lahore resolution's call for independent Muslim states in the north-western and eastern zones of India.

The Lahore expression of the two nations theory as a demand for separate Muslim statehood was thus the culmination of eighteen months of controversy. The variety of its analogues goes far to explain the vagueness of the resolution over the delineation of the contiguous Muslim regions of north-western and eastern India and the contemplated relations between them. The notoriously obscure provision for 'territorial readjustments' was clearly a holdall for additions to, as well as reductions of, existing provinces. Doubts about the desirable relations between the regions are revealed by the authorization of the Working Committee to frame a scheme providing "for the assumption finally, by the respective regions, of all powers" such as "defence, external affairs, communications, customs and such other matters as may be necessary." Again, 'finally' suggests an antithesis to an interim period of coordination by a common authority, such, perhaps, as the resolution's seconder, Khaliquzzaman, favoured. However, it is clear that by its separatist emphasis the resolution marked the firm rejection of Sikander's view that Muslim India's national destiny might be achieved within an all-India federation. He indeed acknowledged that his own preferred resolution was lost. One possibility left open was that of an independent Bengal nation, the destiny most favoured by the resolution's proposer, Fazlul Haq.

No more than the resolution itself was Jinnah's Lahore address the achievement of the Quaid unaided. The most remembered passages in his speech were drawn essentially unchanged from the representations of Ahmad Bashir and the Aligarh group. After roundly condemning the 1935 Act as unsuitable to India he followed Hasan and Qadri in quoting for criticism a London *Times* leader of 1 April 1937 that had consigned the difference between Hindus and Muslims to the realm of transient 'superstition', no real impediment to the emergence of a single nation. He then took his reputation of British views from Ahmad Bashir's condemnation of Linlithgow's statement of 18 October 1939:

Ahmad Bashir

His Excellency the Viceroy thinks that this unity can be achieved with the working of the constitution as envisaged in Government of India Act, 1935. He hopes that the passage of time will harmonise the inconsistent elements in India. Maybe, he holds this view with sincerity, but it is in flagrant disregard to the past history of the sub-continent as well as to the Islamic conception of society. The nationalities which, notwith-standing thousand years of close contact, are as divergent as ever, can never be expected to transform into one nationality merely by being subject to the same constitution. What the *Unitary* Government in India has failed to bring about cannot be achieved by the imposition of the *Federal* Government.

It is, however, satisfying to note that His Excellency the Viceroy and the Secretary of State along with the House of Lords are fully alive to the fundamental differences between the peoples of the Indian continent. Yet unfortunately, they are uwilling to recognise their separate national status. It is more than truism to say that the Hindus and Muslims represent two distinct nationalities. Therefore, any attempt to dissolve their present differences which disregards this vital fact is doomed to precipitate. Hindu-Mulsim problem is not an intercommunal issue and will

Jinnah

So according to the *London Times* the only difficulties are superstitions. These fundamental and deep-rooted differences, spiritual, economic, cultural, social and political have been euphemised as mere 'superstitions'. But surely, it is flagrant disregard of the past history of the subcontinent of India as well as the fundamental Islamic conception of society *vis-a-vis* that of Hinduism to characterise them as mere 'superstitions'. Notwithstanding thousand years of close contact, nationalities which are as divergent today as ever, cannot at any time be expected to transform themselves into one nation merely by means of subjecting them to a democratic constitution and holding them forcibly together by unnatural and artificial methods of British Parliamentary Statutes. What the unitary government of India for 150 years had failed to achieve, cannot be realised by the imposition of a central federal government. It is inconceivable that the fiat or the writ of a government so constituted can ever command a willing and loyal obedience throughout the subcontinent by various nationalities except by means of armed force behind it.

The problem in India is not of an intercommunal but manifestly never be solved on inter-communal lines. It is manifestly an international problem and therefore it must be treated as such. It will submit itself to a permanent solution on that basis alone. Any constitution be it in the form of Dominion Status or even 'Complete Independence', which disregards this basic truth, while destructive for the Muslims cannot but be harmful to the British and Hindus.

If the British Government is really serious and sincere in bringing about peace in the sub-continent, it should not only appreciate the difference but also allow the two nationalities separate homelands by dividing India into autonomous homogeneous states. These states shall not be antagonistic to each other, they on the other hand, will be friendly and sympathetic to one another; and by an international pact of mutual goodwill and assistance they can be just as united and harmonious as today are France and Great Britain. This is the one and the only way to India's Unity.

We are confident that it shall ensure eternal harmony, calm and friendliness between the Hindus and Muslims and materially accelerate the progress of the sub-continent.

If this method for the salvation of India's problems is not adopted the fate of the Muslims as a nation is sealed in India' and no revolution of stars and no rotation of the earth would resuscitate them.

of an international character and it must be treated as such. So long as this basic and fundamental truth is not realised, any consititution that may be built will result in disaster and will prove destructive and harmful not only to the Mussalmans, but also to the British and Hindus. If the British Government are really in earnest and sincere to secure peace and happiness of the people of this subcontinent, the only course open to us all is to allow the major nations separate homelands by dividing India into 'autonomous national states'. There is no reason why these States should be antagonistic to each other. On the other hand the rivalry and the natural desire and efforts on the part of the one to dominate the social order and establish political supremacy over the other in the government of the country, will disappear. It will lead more towards natural goodwill by international pacts between them, and they can live in complete harmony with their neighbours. This will lead further to a friendly settlement all the more easily with regard to minorities by reciprocal arrangements and adjustments between the Muslim India and the Hindu India, which will far more adequately and effectively safeguard the rights and interests of Muslims and various other minorities.

The Ahmad Bashir text was thus the source of Jinnah's 'quiet assertion' of the international status of the Indian problem that Mansergh has held to be 'the essence of his case'. Jinnah notably dropped the emphasis (following Iqbal) upon present division as 'the only way to India's Unity' in future. He continued by drawing upon the Aligarh petition of 15 November 1939 to fill out the rhetoric of his 'classic exposition of the two-nation theory'. Again, where the scholars' target was specifically Gandhi, Jinnah's is more generally the Hindus:

Aligarh Scholars

It is extremely difficult to explain Mr.Gandhi failing to appreciate and understand the real nature of Islam and Hinduism. Islam as well as Hinduism are not only religions in stricter sense of the word, but are in reality different and distinct social orders governing practically every individual and social aspect of their adherents. It should be clear beyond doubt that Hindus and Muslims cannot evolve a common nationality. A few following arguments must convince Mr. Gandhi on this issue.

1. That the Hindus and Muslims belong to two different cultures. They have totally different religious philosophies, social customs, laws and literature. They neither intermarry nor interdine together and, indeed, belong to two different civilizations which are in many aspects based on conflicting ideas and conceptions....

2 That the Hindus and Muslims drive [sic] their inspiration from different sources of history. They have different epics, different

Jinnah

It is extremely difficult to appreciate why our Hindu friends fail to understand the real nature of Islam and Hinduism. They are not religions in the strict sense of the word, but are, in fact, different and distinct social order and it is a dream that the Hindus and Muslims can ever evolve a common nationality, and this misconception of one Indian nation has gone far beyond the limits and is the cause of most of our troubles and will lead India to destruction if we fail to revise our notions in time. The Hindus and Muslims belong to two different religious philosophies, social customs, and literature. They neither inter-marry, nor interdine together and indeed they belong to two different civilizations which are based mainly on conflicting ideas and conceptions. Their aspects on life and of life are different. It is quite clear that Hindus and Mussalmans drive [sic] their inspiration from different sources of history. They have different epics, their heroes

heroes and different episodes. Very often a hero of one is a foe of the other and likewise, their victories and defeats overlap.....

The above facts must convince everybody that all those ties which hold people together as one social unit (Nation) are entirely wanting in the case of Hindus and Muslims of India. Nor there is any possibility of their ever being created here.

Mr Gandhi and other Congress leaders stress the significance of a common country and cite the examples of Egypt, Turkey and Persia. They only state a half truth in this argument. Egypt, Turkey and Persia are wholly Muslim countries and the Muslims there are naturally free to determine their own future.

A discontent is bound to occur wherever two different people are yoked under a single state, one as minority and the other as majority. A number of instances like those of Great Britain and Ireland, Czechoslovakia and Poland can exemplify the above. Further it is also too well known that many Geographical tracts which otherwise should have been called as one country, much smaller than the Indian sub-continent have been divided into as many states as are the nations inhabiting them. The Balkan Peninsula comprises as many as eight sovereign states. The Iberian peninsula is also

are different, and they have different episodes. Very often the hero of one is a foe of the other and likewise their victories and defeats overlap. To yoke together two such nations under a single state, one as a numerical minority and the other as a majority must lead to growing discontent and final destruction of any fabric that may be so built up for the government of such a state.

History had presented to us many examples such as the Union of Great Britain and Ireland, of Czechoslovakia and Poland. History has also shown to us many geographical tracts, much smaller than the subcontinent of India, which otherwise might have been called one country but which have been divided into as many states as there are nations inhabiting them. Balkan Peninsula comprises as many as 7 or 8 sovereign states. Likewise, the Portuguese and the Spanish stand divided in the Iberian Peninsula. Whereas under the plea of unity of India and one nation, which does not exist, it is sought to pursue here the line of one Central Government when, we know that the history of the last 12 hundred years, has failed to achieve unity and has witnessed during the ages, India always divided into Hindu India and Muslim India. The present likewise divided between the Portuguese and the Spaniards.

Mr. Gandhi stresses the historical unity of India even during the days of Muslim kings. We cannot accept his contention. No student of history can deny the fact that all along the last 12 hundred years India has always been divided into a Hindu India and a Muslim India. The extent of one or the other might have been varying from time to time, but the fact remains untarnished that Hindu and Muslim Indias have always been co-existing. The present unity of India dates back only to the British conquest...

We want to assure Mr. Gandhi that the ideal of having free sovereign Muslim states in India which now inspires a very large number of Muslims is not actuated by a spirit of hatred or revenge. It is initiated by an earnest desire of solving Hindu Muslims problem on an equitable basis and epitomises the natural desire of Muslims of India to determine their future independently in the light of their own cultures and history.

artificial unity of India dates back only to the British conquest and is maintained by the British bayonet, but the termination of the British regime, which is implicit in the recent declaration of His majesty's Government, will be the herald of the entire break-up with worse disaster than has ever taken place during the last one thousand years under the Muslims.

Jinnah was carried to Karachi on the shoulders of his fellow Sindhis and soared to Lahore on the wings of young intellectuals of the city and scholars of Aligarh. The Great Leader who personified Muslim apprehensions synthesized plans to assuage them in acceptable formulations of Muslim nationalism (the two nations theory) and separatism (the Pakistan demand).

THE MEANING OF 'TWO NATIONS'

In October 1939, when Lord Linlithgow called Jinnah into discussions with the Congress leaders about participation in government during the war, he was certainly recognising him as the Muslim leader *par excellence*. But in large measure Jinnah had earned the status by the solidarity that the League had then achieved. In May 1939 Sikander, the senior Muslim premier, had observed publicly that Jinnah had answered for Muslims the question: "Are we content to lose out identity and to be relegated to the position of political pariahs?" Jinnah's mobilisation of the League in reaction to Congress "totalitarianism" under the 1935 Act had made it the voice of the putative nation. In December 1939 Liaquat estimated that it had over three million two-anna members. In the early wartime negotiations Jinnah could, pursuant to the two nations theory, make acceptance of the League's status as sole Muslim spokesman the precondition of cooperation with government or Congress, thereby outflanking dissidents (be they even premiers) by appeals to the national will. It was another corollary of his theory that as one of the two nations Muslim India must be treated as the co-equal of Hindu or Congress India. In consequence, the League called for the right to consultation prior to any British statement about India's constitutional future and to veto any scheme. By November, Rajendra Prasad (now Congress President) shrewdly perceived that Jinnah's insistence upon the League's equality with Congress would mean not only "equality in the matter of negotiations" but also "division of power in equal shares between the Congress and the League or between Hindus and Muslims, irrespective of population or any other consideration."

The meaning of the two nations theory and its implications for Jinnah's leadership became manifest in League Working Committee resolutions in June 1940. In any wartime reconstruction of the central or provincial governments the League must receive half of the seats (more if the Congress was non-cooperating), Jinnah alone might negotiate with Viceroy or Congress, and without his consent no League member might serve on war committees. The resolutions were a rebuff for Sikander, who, appalled at the grave implications for India of the allies' defeats in Europe, was negotiating with Congress leaders for a constitutional settlement. In August a British statement, efffectively according the Muslims a veto on any constitutional scheme, seemed to remove the danger of a Hindu raj. Here was a major victory for the two nations theory. Another was soon to follow.

Leading Muslim politicians including the premiers, were now prepared to join war committees on a basis short of parity. By so doing they would, in effect, be compromising the cause of Muslim equality embodied in the two nations theory. In summer 1941 Jinnah brought the theory to bear in order to force their resignations from the Viceroy's Defence Council. That this was no mere exercise of personal power but rather the execution of essential League policy is revealed by Liaquat's advice to Jinnah a month before the Working Committee met to consider the matter. Liaquat advised that Jinnah's condemnation of the collaborators had "given expression to the feelings of a vast majority of Musalmans on the subject." The question now was "whether the disciplinary action... should be taken by you or by the Working Committee and the Council" (an elected body of 465 members). Liaquat strongly advised the latter course:

> Let us put up an imposing show and I think the people will appreciate [it] if the Council is given an opportunity of expressing its views on the conduct of those who have let down the League... Let it not be said that the decision is of only one individual or a few persons. Let the whole Council which is the most representative body of the League give its verdict and I have no doubt as to what the verdict will be....

On 24 August the Working Committee demanded the collaborators' resignations from the Defence Council and expelled from the League those who resisted the verdict. The Council did not meet to ratify the action for two months but its attitude was not in doubt. Jinnah was, of course, aware of allegations that he was a dictator. The two nations theory enabled him plausibly to brand as 'traitors' Muslims who collaborated with the Raj on a basis short of parity. As national leader he saw it as his duty to identify their 'mistakes', leaving the Working Committee and the Council to determine their punishment.

By applying the theory vigorously Jinnah engineered the nationalization of Muslim politics throughout the war. The theory's meaning was revealed most dramatically at Simla in June 1945, when Jinnah demanded not only Hindu-Muslim parity in the Viceroy's executive but also that all the Muslim members must be League nominees. The demand destroyed Lord Wavell's attempt to reconstruct his government on the basis of party representation.

DEFINING 'PAKISTAN'

In February 1941 Jinnah explained the meaning of 'Pakistan', for the term had not been used at Lahore.

Some confusion prevails in the minds of some individuals in regard to the use of the word 'Pakistan'. This word has become synonymous with the Lahore resolution owing to the fact that it is a convenient and compendious method of describing [it]... For this reason the British and Indian newspapers generally have adopted the word 'Pakistan' to describe the Moslem demand as embodied in the Lahore resolution. I really see no objection to it...

But the resolution was obscure on the demarcation of the Pakistan regions, their relation to each other, and any interim constitutinal rearrangement prior to their 'finally' assuming such powers as defence, foreign affairs, communications and customs. While Jinnah demanded parity as the basis of participation in government, the vagueness of 'Pakistan' was such as to make impracticable its acceptance by the Raj a precondition of cooperation. He did, however, insist that no constitutional scheme that was inconsistent with its eventual achievement must be imposed. The 'Pakistan' demand meant that Muslim India's right to national self-determination must not be transgressed, not that separate statehood must be embodied in a constitutional settlement. Jinnah drew the distinction explicitly in his speeches. The diversity of the schemes embodying 'Pakistan' that were extant in March 1940 helps to explain the obscurity of the Lahore resolution. Any precise scheme must surely divide the League. However, the resolution did provide for the Working Committee to prepare a particular scheme. Haroon's Foreign Committee seems to have continued to discharge the primary planning function.

In Februrary 1941 a scheme recommended by the Haroon committee was leaked to the press. Consistently with the direction pursued by the Aligarh scholars and the assemblage of authors during winter 1939-40, it delineated sovereign Muslim states: the four north-western provinces plus a Delhi province; and Bengal (save Bankura and Midnapur districts) plus Assam. The principalities adjoining them might federate with them, and Hyderabad would become a separate sovereign state. For a transitional period the four powers listed at Lahore for assumption finally by the regions would be exercised by a coordinating central agency. Jinnah denied that the Working Committee had adopted the scheme and on 22 February it merely reaffirmed the Lahore resolution. The main effect of the leakage was to draw from Sikander a long, reasoned denunciation of 'Pakistan', if it meant separatism.

In his presidential address to the League's session at Madras in April 1941 Jinnah emphasized the goal of "completely Independent States in the North-Western and Eastern zones of India, with full control of Defence, Foreign Affairs, Communications, Customs, Currency, Exchange etc." The League would "never agree" to an all-India constitution "with one Government at the Centre". As if to suggest that the two nations theory did not restrict future development to the emergence of only two states he explained that in Hindu India there was a Dravidian nation, Dravidistan, to which the Muslims would stretch their 'hands of friendship'. In amplification of this trend in his thinking he told the Governor of Madras that he envisaged four regions— Dravidistan, Hindustan, Bengalistan, and the north-west Muslim provinces. They would be separate self-governing dominions, each with its own governor-general controlling its foreign affairs and defence and responsible to the British parliament through the secretary of state. Here was a scheme for subordinate dominions, with princely states joining them and remaining apart under a Crown Representative. It bore some resemblance to Haroon's leaked scheme.

In February 1942 Khaliquzzaman explained a similar proposal to Coupland:

> The Moslem demand is that Britian, after the war, should by Act of Parliament, establish the zonal system, before considering further Swaraj. British control would be still required at the Centre— apparently for an indefinite period—since Defence and Foreign Policy (which is practically all the Centre would deal with) should still be in British hands. The zones would have fiscal autonomy. If they couldn't agree on tariff policy, the British at the Centre would settle it. Pakistan, moreover, would require British aid and capital for its development before it would be able to stand alone.

Khaliquzzaman seemed to be saying that in the event of a complete British withdrawal the Muslims would accept nothing short of sovereign Pakistan; but that they would welcome a protracted British presence—in effect, Indian unity under the Crown, with the sub-national zones standing as recognition of Muslim nationhood. Unlike Jinnah he was opposed to the session of the non-Muslim districts of Punjab (Ambala division) and Bengal (Burdwan division).

On the eve of Cripps's arrival in India Coupland analysed Jinnah's position on the Pakistan demand:

(i)   While claiming Dominion status for Pakistan, Jinnah has more than once intimated that it need not be full Dominion status and that he would like Foreign Affairs and Defence to remain, at least for the time being, in British hands; and

(ii) he has never asked that H.M.G. should accept Pakistan, but only that it should not be ruled out of discussion nor the chances of its adoption prejudiced by the form of an interim constitutional system. Nevertheless, *Pakistanism might triumph as a counsel of despair*.

The Cripps declaration proposed Dominion status for a Union of India, but though it did not accept Pakistan it did accord provinces the right to secede from the Union and become separate dominions. Jinnah and the League saw it as recognising the principle of Pakistan. From the notes of Coupland, Cripps and the Intelligence Department there can be no doubt that Jinnah and the League were disposed to accept the offer.

On 28 March 1942 Jinnah "stated [to Cripps] the League's acceptance of the Declaration." On 7 April he intimated that "he must hold back the League's acceptance till after the Congress has accepted." Coupland foresaw that if Congress rejected the offer the League would follow suit, "so wording their rejection as to obtain some British and world support without losing face as Indian patriots." On 9 April, when Congress seemed posed to accept, Jinnah was reported as saying "that Pakistan could be shelved," given a satisfactory position in the Viceroy's executive and a suitable procedure for the secession of provinces. When Congress rejected the declaration the League did likewise, deprecating H.M.G.'s objective of Union, the provision for a single constituent assembly in the first instance, and the eligibility of non-Muslims to participate in the Muslim provinces' decisions on secession.

In February 1944 Jinnah stated that Britian "should now frame a new constitution dividing India into two sovereign nations," Pakistan and Hindustan, with "a transitional period for settlement and adjustment" during which British authority over defence and foreign affairs would remain. The length of the period would depend upon the speed with which the two peoples and Britian adjusted to the new constitution. Though the statement clearly contemplated continued subordination to Britain it is too vague to be read as a shift from the notion of zonal dominions. In September 1944 the Gandhi-Jinnah talks concentrated attention on the precise meaning of the Pakistan demand. The Bengal Provincial League now wanted "a sovereign state in N.-E.India that will be independent of the rest of India," though it was divided over the cession of the Burdwan districts, with some members arguing that their retention would win Hindu approval. The talks themselves did little to clarify Jinnah's conception of Pakistan but he reiterated that for the regions in which the Muslims predominated it was they alone who must determine their future. Jinnah also spoke now of Pakistan as a single state.

Throughout the war Jinnah contemplated the post-war emergence of one or two Pakistan 'dominions', co-existing with one or two Hindustan 'dominions' and the princely states, and with Britain retaining power over defence and foreign affairs. The separateness and equality of the Pakistan Hindustan 'dominions' would be a recognition of the validity of the two nations theory and of their right to eventual sovereign independence. The conception resembled that which some British Conservatives formed at the time of the Cripps mission and espoused until the eve of the transfer of power.

DEFINITION BY CIRCUMSTANCE

With Labour's assumption of office in July 1945 it was soon apparent that there was not to be a gradual demission of power by stages but an early and complete withdrawal. Jinnah now became adamant that there must be a state of Pakistan and the League fought the elections of 1945-46 on that platform. The announcement in February 1946 of the imminent despatch of a Cabinet Mission on 4 April confirmed that Labour was in a hurry. Fortified by the League's electoral triumph, on 7 April Jinnah led a convention of 470 League members of the central and provincial legislatures to an unequivocal resolution in favour of "a sovereign independent state comprising Bengal and Assam in the North-East zone and the Punjab, North-West Frontier Province, Sind and Baluchistan in the North-West zone." Acceptance of this precise demand for Pakistan and its implementation without delay, by the creation of a Pakistan Constituent Assembly, was made the *sine qua non* for the League's participation in an Interim Government. The opening of the imperial endgame had precipitated an immediate and full-blooded definition of the Pakistan demand.

By 10 April Cripps had prepared a draft proposal for discussion with the Indian leaders and a few days later the Mission confronted

Jinnah with two alternative approaches that it advocated: either a truncated Pakistan, independent and fully sovereign but limited to the Muslim majority areas, and thus short of far more of the territories of Punjab, Bengal and Assam than the League had contemplated; or the grouping together of the whole of the six claimed provinces, beside a Hindustan group, within a union exercising power over defence, foreign affairs and communications. When Jinnah refused to choose either alternative Cripps prepared a draft that rejected a fully independent Pakistan. But it proposed a powerful subnational Pakistan, with its own flag, forces to maintain internal order, and enjoying parity with Hindustan in an all-India government. The League would draft its constitution and join with Congress on the basis of parity to draft the Union constitution. The Mission was willing to concede its right to secede from the Union after fifteen years. This remarkable scheme was the furthest that H.M.G. ever went towards accepting the full Pakistan demand.

It is scarcely surprising that Jinnah and the League were drawn into negotiations on the basis of this scheme, though some Leaguers speculated that Jinnah's departure from the legislators' full-blooded resolution evidenced vacillation among 'weak-kneed' members of the Working Committee. During the subsequent month of negotiations the Mission reduced the concessions to the demand in order to woo Congress, so that when its scheme was published on 16 May it was far less attractive to the League. It split the six 'Pakistan' provinces into two groups, the formation of which was to depend upon the voluntary accession of each province to its assigned group. It abandoned parity in the making of the Union constitution, enlarged the Union's power to include finance, and failed to provide for the secession of groups or provinces from the Union. Though some Leaguers feared that the Union's powers would enable Congress to abort the emergence of Pakistan, the counsels that prevailed were that the Cabinet Mission's scheme met "the substance of the demand for Pakistan". First, it provided that the provinces must enter constitution-making 'sections' that were co-terminous with the groups. Secondly, the section constitution-making procedure was to precede Union constitution-making. Thirdly, the Working Committee assumed, on the basis of discussions that Jinnah had had with the Viceroy, that the League would enjoy parity with Congress in an Interim Government, which seemed a tacit admission of Pakistan's right to separate nationhood.

Jinnah received written letters of advice from Aurangzeb Khan and Jamil-ud-din Ahmad that emphasized the advantages of accepting the Mission's scheme. Ahmad, then Convenor of the League's Committee of Writers, expressed the 'prudent' strategy vigorously. The League should

> work the Plan up to the Group stage and then create a situation to force the hands of the Hindus and the British to concede Pakistan of our conception... [We should] make known in most emphatic terms our objections to the Plan specially with regard to the Centre and declare that we will... not be bound to submit to a Union Centre which does not accord us a position of equality. We [should] give a chance to the Hindu majority to accommodate us at the Centre.... After we have made the constitutions of Groups B and C according to our wishes our position will be stronger than what it is now if we use our opportunities properly. We will have some foothold. When we reassemble in the Union Constituent Assembly we can create deadlocks on really important issues....If the worst comes to the worst and the Hindu majority shows no willingness to compromise we can withdraw from the Assembly in a body, and refuse to honour its decisions. Ours will be a solid block as there won't be more than two or three non-League Muslims in the Assembly... We will be on strong ground morally and politically because firstly we will have previously declared that we can never acquiesce in any Centre which reduces us to a subordinate position and secondly we will be in power in the Groups, and will be better able to resist the imposition of an unwanted Centre.

In the spirit of this advice the League resolved that:

> ....inasmuch as the basis and the foundation of Pakistan are inherent in the Mission's plan by virtue of the compulsory grouping of the six Muslim Provinces in Sections B and C, [it] is willing to cooperate with the constitution-making machinery proposed in the scheme outlined by the Mission, in the hope that it would ultimately result in the establishment of complete sovereign Pakistan...

Jinnah was authorized to negotiate for the entry of the League to the Interim Government. He wrote to Wavell to emphasize that his assurance of parity therein had been 'the turning point' in the League Council's acceptance.

The League's strategy was destroyed by the Congress's refusal to contemplate parity in the Interim Government or the compulsory grouping of provinces for constitution-making, together with H.M.G.'s conviction that Congress goodwill was vital for a peaceful transfer of power. In August 1946 Jinnah was driven to a course of 'direct action' by his mistrust of the Congress and H.M.G.'s infirmity. Certainly, by December, when he and Nehru were called to London in a desperate attempt to secure agreement on sectional procedure, Jinnah had abandoned his mid-year hopes of realizing Pakistan through the Mission's scheme. He now reverted to the notion of a Pakistan dominion and rehearsed it not only with Attlee and the Cabinet Mission ministers but also with British Opposition leaders. Churchill, for whom a secret telegraphic address was established, assured him that the Pakistan areas could not be turned out of the Commonwealth as part of an Indian republic. Indeed, in parliamentary debate Churchill affirmed that Muslim India and the princes should be accorded Commonwealth membership. That winter Jinnah sought assurances that other Conservatives would support Pakistan dominionhood. His inquiries converged with intrigues for separate princely dominions, to which he gave his blessing.

Jinnah welcomed the prospects of a transfer of power on a provincial basis that Attlee's time-limit statement of 20 February 1947 foreshadowed. In his first discussions with Moutbatten he sought a Pakistan dominion comprising the full six provinces, but he did not oppose the option of separate sovereign provinces that the 'Dickie-bird' or Ismay plan ('Plan Balkan') offered. His objection to Plan Balkan was that it envisaged the severance from Punjab and Bengal of their non-Muslim areas. When he first saw the Plan he argued "that power should be transferred to provinces as they exist today. They can then group together or remain separate as they wish." When Mountbatten asked his views on H.S. Suhrawardy's proposal for "keeping Bengal united at the price of its remaining outside Pakistan", he replied: "I should be delighted. What is the use of Bengal without Calcutta; they had much better remain united and independent; I am sure they would be on friendly terms with us."

Whereas in 1946 Jinnah had been prepared to find the Pakistan demand realized, at least temporarily, by the grouping of the six provinces within the Union of India, in 1947 he was willing to see it satisfied by the separate dominionhood of provinces. Now again he was frustrated by Congress, which was no less opposed to the instant loss to India of non-Muslim areas of provinces than it had been to their distant loss by secession from the Union. The outcome of negotiations in 1947, a dual transfer of power to a single truncated Pakistan dominion and a single Indian dominion (to one of which the states were obliged to accede), flowed from Congress policy and H.M.G.'s acquiescence in it. Given the reversals that he suffered in the three-sided discussions from April 1946 to May 1947 it is scarcely surprising that Jinnah eschewed the prolongation of triangularity implied in proposals for Mountbatten to become Governor-General of both dominions and the retention of a Joint Defence Council. However, at the end of the Raj he still acknowledged Pakistan's need for British agency. The retention by Pakistan of British governors, chiefs of staff and civil and military officers was consistent with his expectation that the transfer of power would be a phased process.

MAN AND MOVEMENT

At the age of sixty Jinnah made the cause of Muslim India his life. An extraordinary match of man and movement followed. Ambition, pride and vanity were less important to it than his refined sense of Muslim injury under Congress rule and his capacity to express the hurt and specify the cure. Like Gandhi he evoked national consciousness in opposition to felt wrongs. While Gandhi had experienced India's emasculation by British imperialism Jinnah felt the impotence of Muslim India under Congress totalitarianism. Jannah articulated not the Koran's promise of political power nor memories of the Mughals but the Muslim's sense of persecution at the sudden threat to all that he had achieved in the twentieth century. When the Congress governments resigned in November 1939 he rallied Muslims to celebrate their "deliverance from tyranny, oppression and injustice." Jinnah's constitutinal remedies were not of his own making. The Pakistan demand was no pet scheme of which he dreamed alone but an ideal to which he was converted by others, colleagues of long-standing like Haroon, thinkers in the line of Iqbal, scholars of the Aligarh school. His very formulation of the two nations theory drew upon their thoughts and words. His amplification of the theory into a demand for parity was a brilliant tactical manoeuvre, but its effectiveness rested on the willing support of the League, most notably when Linlithgow set up his Defence Council and Wavell attempted to reconstruct his executive. The tactic consolidated the League as the microcosm of the Muslim nation and Jinnah as its leader.

It is a paradox that the demand for separate Muslim statehood based on the existing Muslim provinces with territorial adjustments should finally have found recognition in a Pakistan truncated to a degree never envisaged by Jinnah and the League. It is inconceivable that they did not realize that the truncation was a logical corollary of the distribution of the peoples of the two nations. The arguments that they adduced to resist it could scarcely be accepted with justice by a departing Raj, whether they emphasized the need for hostages, or for matching minority populations for exchange in case of need, or for non-Muslim territories to make Pakistan viable economically. The incorporation of the full six provinces in Muslim zones could only have been secured by British award, and it seems most likely that Jinnah envisaged such an award as a line of advance consistent with Britain's continuing presence in her own interests. In other words, he probably assumed a British withdrawal by stages, at the first of which the Pakistan Zones would receive subordinate dominionhood, secured like the princely states by H.M.G.'s continuing control over defence and foreign affairs (as the 1935 Act had stipulated). His reference in October 1938 to a further twenty-five years of imperial rule, the Lahore resolution's emphasis upon all powers 'finally' passing to independent states, his wartime comments, his play for Pakistan dominionhood from December 1946, his reliance on British agency after August 1947, all support such a thesis. His acceptance of the Cabinet Mission's scheme might be seen similarly as evidence of a readiness to postpone full sovereign statehood, provided that the conditions of its eventual emergence were safeguarded, that is Muslim zones and parity in government. He was willing to associate the Muslim nation with central government on the basis of parity but he doubted that such a government could endure. He told Coupland as much:

> Assume a 50:50 basis... The central questions are just those on which Moslems and Hindus must disagree: e.g. (a) Defence: Hindu Ministers will at once want to Indianize in communal proportions... (b) Tariff: Hindu ministers will want high protection for industries, which are mainly in Hindu hands, to the detriment of the Moslems who are more confined to poor agriculturalists than the Hindus.

Such caveats were urged upon Jinnah in May 1946, when he judged the disadvantages of a temporary union to be worth the prize of a safe passage through grouping to an eventual six-province fully sovereign Pakistan.

Jinnah's planning was undermined by the Labour Government's belief that Britain's post-war interests would be best served by immediate withdrawal, and that an orderly retreat and sound post-imperial relations with the sub-continent would alike be best achieved by enlisting Congress cooperation. His hopes of obtaining more than a truncated Pakistan depended upon an extended imperial presence of some sort. That they were no mere illusions is revealed by the sympathies of some leading British Conservatives and Liberals. As late as May 1947 Mountbatten's staff and the India Committee of Attlee's Cabinet espoused a scheme that permitted an independent India of many nations while the Chiefs of Staff advised that if Congress rejected Dominion status then Commonwealth membership might be accorded severally to West Pakistan, united Bengal, and even to a maritime state such as Travancore.

Jinnah's readiness to accept, from time to time, quite different constitutional forms as consistent with the Pakistan demand flowed in part from the necessities of a dynamic situation, but in part, too, from the advice proffered by colleagues. In April 1946, 470 Muslim legislators voted for a single sovereign Pakistan of six full provinces; a few weeks later the Working Committee and the Council accepted a scheme for a Union of India; in April 1947 Jinnah endorsed Suhrawardy's plan for a 'Free State of Bengal'; two months later he accepted 'moth-eaten' Pakistan. Yet the essence of the Pakistan demand—the right to a territorial asylum, to the self-determination of the Muslim nation in the north-western and eastern regions of India— was never compromised. Certainly, Jinnah planned that the regions should include virtually the whole of six provinces, whereas in the circumstances of 1947 he was left with a Pakistan defined by religious distribution district by district. Yet that outcome lends no support to speculation that the Pakistan demand was Jinnah's barganing counter for power in a united India, or that the partition hoisted him with his own petard.

19

Ultimately victorious in gaining India its independence in 1947, the Congress under Jawaharlal Nehru went on to provide the new state with leadership during the critical years of transition. Subsequently it became an ordinary political party among others, though usually more successful, contesting elections and forming ministries. Under Nehru's daughter Indira Gandhi and her son Rajiv Gandhi, India's government, apart from a brief Emergency during the mid-1970's, has worked within the framework of a parliamentary system, modelled largely on British precedents and regulated by a written constitution. This modern system is, however, only one level of the Indian body politic. Beneath it is a world where the enduring values of caste, community, and region form the language of political discourse. Apart from both is a "saintly" mode of politics, associated with Gandhi's name and idealism. This concluding essay shows how secular ideals for the future, the customs and ties of the past, and a sense of urgency which echoes a deeply felt desire for a better standard of living, combine to give the subcontinent's largest state its distinctive political identity.

India's Political Idioms

W. H. MORRIS-JONES

The study of the politics of a society undergoing transformation is indeed as difficult as it is important and exciting. All these qualities are enhanced when the transformation is being effected not by an outside power (as in India under British rule or in Tibet today) nor by a single coherent political force (as in China), but by a variety of internal pressures and pulls. One of the best entrances into an understanding of Indian politics may be through a discussion of the difficulty of its study.

One very general way of putting the problem is to point out that the student of Indian political institutions soon forms the impression that the main thing he has to learn is that nothing is ever quite what it seems or what it presents itself as being. At first he may put this down to his own faulty vision, to his unavoidable tendency to try to fit new things

From C.H. Philips, ed., *Politics and Society in India*, London: George Allen & Unwin, Ltd., 1963, pp. 133-154, with omission. Reprinted by permission of George Allen & Unwin, Ltd., London, and Frederick A. Praeger, New York.

into categories which he has brought with him. But later he realizes that the matter is not so simple; there are different categories operative within the Indian context itself. Perhaps this should not surprise us. Indeed, it would be odd if it were otherwise. Everyone knows that in India's economic life whole European centuries co-exist within the present moment, and in her social life too. The bus-ride from the airport to city centre announces this enormous fact even to the passing traveller. Why then should we expect her politics to belong to any single simple style?

Yet while the complexity of styles should not surprise us, it is nevertheless worth emphasizing that for most students of politics this phenomenon is unusual and for that reason at first baffling to the understanding. Of course the idiom in which political activity is conducted certainly varies from country to country. The Britisher who seeks to understand American politics knows that he must master a new idiom—one which is dictated by the size of the country, the peculiar character of the nation-building process which has taken place there, the separation of powers, and so on. But at least it is, by and large, just one idiom. The regional variations are related to the main theme. The conversation of American politics may be 'tapped' at any level and any place and the language will remain the same. And I should say that this is true of most countries whose study has figures prominently in the development of political science.

It may be argued that the matter is one of degree only—but then the range is very wide. We may concede at one end that even in the socially tight little island of the United Kingdom politics looks rather different according as to whether it is seen in Whitehall or in a miners' lodge. But the differences are, as it were, of tone and volume, not of basic language. For all participants have shares in a common culture. In some other countries of Western Europe, such as Belgium and France perhaps, the variety of political styles may be more marked: it may be a long way from Clochemerle to Paris. Further along this scale would come a country like Italy where culture contrasts between the South and the North are pronounced. But even there—with the exception of Sicily's Mafia—politics could be said to be in one language with several dialects.

The case of Communist regimes seems different in an emphatic way; if we are to speak of differences only of degree, then at least we must say that here is a sizable jump along the scale. For in Communist countries it seems that an idiom of politics derived from Marxism is found along with a primarily national idiom; the two may not mix in such a thorough way as to form a coherent new language. The observer of the political life of such a state may easily get the impression that things are not what they seem. The confusion or incoherence is in the situation itself and can express itself in different ways. Men may act in one political fashion but give an account of their acts in another set of terms. Or some men may act more or less fully in one political manner while others of their countrymen, within the same political institutions, act more or less thoroughly in another manner. Or it could be that the same men act in different styles according to occasion and context.

This way of putting things may or may not be helpful in understanding Communist political life, but it certainly proves an aid to probing the nature of Indian politics. Tentatively I would distinguish three main languages in which political life in India is conducted. The least inappropriate of a poor set of labels for them would be 'modern', 'traditional' and 'saintly'.

It may have been already noticed that I speak of these as 'languages' and 'idioms' while also referring to 'manners', 'styles', 'fashions'. Perhaps all these terms indicate a particular view of politics. Perhaps they all seem ambiguous and unclear. Some of the ambiguity attaching in particular to the word 'language' is, however, quite fitting. As already suggested, I wish to talk both about behaviour and accounts of behaviour and I intend to use the same term to extend over both. I am content to do this partly because there is a similarity between learning or acquiring a language and adopting a way of behaviour, partly because it may be useful to emphasize the close interacting relation between practical behaviour and descriptions of behaviour.

It can be argued—and indeed the point has been put to me in discussion—that this talk of languages of politics is unnecessarily confusing and that the contrast between modern and traditional in particular is rather a contrast between the political institutions of a nation state and the structure of an ancient society. There is some force in this view. Certainly I am only too pleased to emphasize that the key to Indian politics today is the meeting of these two as strangers. Political system and social structure, so far from having grown up together, have only just been introduced to each other. Before Independence, limited franchise and alien rule kept them apart. Even the great national movement for all its long history and wide appeal seems in retrospect to have skated quite lightly over the surface of Indian social relations, cutting it up as it were only in one or two patches such as Gandhi's untouchability campaigns. With the disappearance of the white outcastes and the introduction of adult suffrage, 'politics' and 'society' come to meet. However, to speak of languages of politics still seems valuable. First, it serves to stress that no social relations—however ancient and no matter how far bound up with religious ritual—are devoid of political content. Traditional India is not non-political, only it contains a different kind of politics from that of the 'modern' state. Second, this way of putting the matter makes it easier to bring out the peculiar third language of saintly politics.

The language of modern politics is undoubtedly important in India—more so than perhaps in most other parts of Asia. This is less on account of the long period of British rule than because of the existence for nearly one hundred years of an Indian *elite* steeped in its grammar and masters of its accents. Members of this *elite* were not only the agents of much of the administrative and economic development of the country; they also provided the leadership of some of the more important movements of social reform and of the nationalist movement itself. It is true that an important change came over the nationalist movement with the impact of Gandhi's leadership after 1917, but it would be a mistake to imagine that Gandhi did not employ the modern idiom; he combined it with another, but by no means abandoned it or prevented its continuous development.

This language is so widespread in India that it has seemed possible to give a well-nigh comprehensive account of Indian political life without moving outside its terms. That indeed is what we political scientists have been doing. We have found so much modern behaviour and so much modern talk about the behaviour that we hardly found our own language of description deficient. This modern language of politics is the language of the Indian Constitution and the Courts; of parliamentary debate; of the higher administration; of the upper levels of all the main political parties; of the entire English press and much of the Indian languages press. It is a language which speaks of policies and interests, programmes and plans. It expresses itself in arguments and representations, discussions and demonstrations, deliberations and decisions.

Within this idiom are conducted several momentous conflicts of principle and tussles of interests. These are so wide-ranging that observers could be forgiven for greeting this Indian politics as a well-recognized familiar friend and assuming that this is the whole of Indian politics, the complete story. For what more could one ask? One kind of 'debate', for instance, is that which is carried on—partly within the Congress party, partly between it and the Swatantra Party on the 'right' and the Socialist and Communist Parties on the 'left'—about the size of the public sector of the economy, the degree and forms of governmental controls and the direction and pace of land reform. This looks very like some of our doctrine-and-interest conflicts. Another 'argument'—still conducted within the modern idiom—relates to the 'federal' theme, and will also sound familiar to western ears. Here men will discuss the relative roles of centre and state governments, the impact of the Planning Commission on the federal structure, the Supreme Court's influence on the federal balance through its interpretation of the Constitution, and so on. (The whole range of disputes between India's linguistic units concerning the division and boundaries of territories—the splitting of Madras and Bombay, the demands of the Sikhs, the violent hostility between Bengalis and Assamese—can up to a point be regarded as falling within this category; but, as we shall see, only up to a point; to get full meaning we have to move into a different language for the reason that those involved are operating in a different language. The same is the case with the strictly linguistic tussles between Hindi and the regional languages and between both and English.) A third example of 'debate' within the modern idiom would be mostly discussion about forms of political organization and relations between organizations. Here one would place conflicts between party organs and party groups in legislatures; relations between Ministers and backbenchers and between Ministers and civil servants; the composition and powers of the Planning Commission; relations between governments and opposition parties.

Most evidently, then, this is an important language of politics, covering most of what is to be expected as politics. A good index to a book written in these terms on Indian political life would bear comparison with a standard work on Britain or the United State. This is not to say that there would be no items peculiar to India; nor that many of the apparently familiar items would on closer examination prove so readily recognizable. It is only to say that if this modern language comprehended the whole of Indian politics, then as a subject it would for all its distinctiveness be susceptible to analysis by the same methods as French or Dutch politics.

But this is not the case. The observer of Indian politics will not look at his subject for long before he gets the feeling that he is missing something. This feeling can perhaps be described only by metaphors. The actors on a stage do not know why the audience should laugh just then, because they have not seen the cat which is playing with the stage curtains. Of, again, the audience may detect an awkward pause, but they do not know that the actors are preoccupied because the hero's make-up is coming apart. Such a feeling with regard to Indian politics is perfectly justified; what the observer has so far not taken into account is a play within the play.

Indian politics is in part conducted in a very different language. The traditional idiom is that which social anthropologists and sociologists in India are busy discovering or rediscovering for us at the present time. In its purest form it is spoken in rural India. It knows little or nothing of the problems of anything as big as India and its vocabulary scarcely includes policies and Plans. One way of indicating how different it is would be to use the term 'feudal', for this word, although in some ways misleading and inexact, would at least put us at an appropriate distance from idiom. 'Tribal' might also do the trick and would not be without some justification.

This language of politics is that of a particular kind of highly developed status society. It is far more important as a manner of behaviour than as a language of description; it is acted upon more than it is spoken about. It is the chief source of the contrast between the inside and outside stories of Indian politics, even of the gap between practice and profession which is a striking feature of Indian life.

Caste (or subcaste or 'community') is the core of traditional politics. To it belongs a complete social ethos. It embraces all and is all-embracing. Every man is born into a particular communal or caste group and with it inherits a place and a station in society from which his whole behaviour and outlook may be said, in idea at least, to be derived: his occupation, the range from which his parents will choose to negotiate for his bride, his fairly precise standing in terms of privileges and obligations to members of his own and other caste groups, his attitude towards them. For this reason, caste cannot easily be assimilated within the world of modern politics. It is seldom *merely* a group operating as a unit within a modern whole—as perhaps the Roman Catholics in Australian politics or the Irish in parts of earlier U.S.politics. When it comes into politics it comes not with a list of demands but with a way of life.

But that is already an over-simplification. For that way of life is itself undergoing change. Indeed, the presence of organized caste pressures within Indian political life is itself a sign of the changing of traditional India; this is behaviour unbecoming to units of a status society. It is easy for the modern eye to see caste as a recalcitrant and limited focus of loyalty in stubborn competition with 'the state'. But this tends to overlook the rather different role of caste in the proper setting of its own society. There it contributes to social cohesion, it organizes the parts into the maintenance of a whole local community, the village. The allocation of privileges and obligations between the parts is such as to serve and permit the survival of the whole. Internal disturbance through fresh claims and sectional demands are as much to be resisted as impacts from outside. Coherence is maintained or restored by the preservation or re-settlement of status.

Although caste and its world have been under slow erosion—by improvements in communications and education—for a hundred years, their massive importance was only slightly touched. But the impact of caste on political life was restrained, first by the presence of alien rulers, second by the movement of nationalism, above all by the fact that even after Gandhi's arrival so much of the initiating, positive politics of India belonged to a fairly restricted *elite*. Now this has changed. From the traditional society, itself changing, caste moves out into politics. At the same time mass politics means new political invasions of traditional society. To these new encounters, caste brings as part of its way of life certain attitudes of special relevance to politics. Of these the central one concerns the nature of political authority. In the traditional idiom political authority is of course an extension of a certain general status; it has its natural, substantially hereditary seats. In most regions of India there appears to be a particular local caste which is 'dominant'. In each village within that region the natural repositories of authority will be men of certain families within the caste. (Economic status seems to have some, rather variable, part to play in this matter of dominance.) Other castes will have their own leaders but they will be no more than spokesmen for partial groups. The political leadership of the whole little community will be provided by those who have this task as one of their recognised functions, part of the contribution they are expected to render to the system of carefully graded privileges and obligations which they uphold and which upholds them. Political authority is thus taken as naturally determined and given, not a question of choice, election and wills. (Plato would have understood.)

The manner in which they will normally exercise authority is determined by the simple twofold political need of an Indian village: it requires leadership partly for the resolution and settlement of internal disputes, partly for the task of interceding with the outside world and its *Raj*. So the leaders must be good at reconciliation and the production of a 'consensus' and, secondly, they must be successful in 'securing favours' from the 'powers that be' outside.

The third language of saintly politics is to be found 'at the margin' of Indian politics. By this I certainly mean that it is in some quantitative sense relatively unimportant, spoken only by a few and occupying a definitely subsidiary place on the political page. But I would also be content to be taken to mean 'margin' to have something of the importance given to that term in economics: there may be few or none actually at the margin but location of the point has an effect on all operators as a kind of reference mark. In other words, saintly politics is important as a language of comment rather than of description or practical behaviour. The outstanding figure of nation-wide importance in this idiom is Vinoba Bhave, the 'Saint on the March' who tours India on foot preaching the path of self-sacrifice and love and polity without power. His effective active followers may not be many but his own activities and pronouncements are reported week by week, almost day by day, in the press. The direct impact of Bhave is a matter of some uncertainty and dispute. The startling initial success of his call for donations of land for distribution to the landless prompted all political parties to pay tribute to him and accord him respectful recognition. Subsequently, doubts about the motives of land donors and a certain ineffectiveness in the distribution programme have lowered the temperature of enthusiasm. More recently, there has taken place the experiment of taking Bhave's help in dealing with the dacoit menace in the region south of Delhi; police action was called off while Bhave went in to talk to the brigand gang leader; the present impression is that the dacoits were keen to benefit more from the withdrawal of police attention than from the message of Bhave.

But the direct effects of Bhave are less important than the indirect. This language has a widespread appeal to all sections in India. For many people it is identified with the political style of Gandhi. This is a bad over-simplification: for one thing this was only one of Gandhi's styles; for another, this idiom was already present in Indian society before Gandhi undertook its systematic and organized development. I do not know if in European history there are any even remote parallels to this kind of influence: possibly the sort of direction in which one might look would be that of the early Christian Church or some of the monastic orders. Be that as it may, the influence of 'saintly' policies in India cannot be ignored. Admittedly it affects men's actual behaviour very little; remarkably few men engaged in political activity within the other two idioms are striving to be saintly. Its influence is rather on the standards habitually used by the people at large for judging the performance of politicians. In men's minds there is an ideal of disinterested selflessness by contrast with which almost all normal conduct can seem very shabby. I do not imply that such a standard is applied continuously or to the exclusion of other standards. I would argue, however, that it contributes powerfully to several very prevalent attitudes to be found in Indian political life: to a certain withholding of full approval from even the most popular leaders; to a stronger feeling of distrust of and disgust with persons and institutions of authority; finally, to profoundly violent and desperate moods of cynicism and frustration. I repeat that I am not making 'saintly' politics a sole cause of these sentiments; I am only indicating how it can add, as it were, a certain bitterness and 'edge' to them. I would also (much more tentatively, for I do not know what social psychologist would say) suggest that the existence of this standard may if anything affect actual behaviour in a morally adverse manner: if the only really good life is one which seems to belong to a world beyond reach then a man might as well not strain too hard in that direction and indeed might as well be hung for a whole big black market sheep as for a little irregular lamb.

That I consider saintly politics worth listing as a third idiom does not imply that I see it as wholly unrelated to the other two. In curious ways which there is here no room to examine, it takes in much from both; indeed, in this lies much of its power. A Bhave talking of the corruption of party politics appeals at once to the modern notions of public spirit and civic conscience and the traditional ideas of non-competitive accepted authority working through a general 'consensus'. Similarly and even more conspicuously, a Narayan speaking of public 'participation' in a 'communitarian' democracy stirs the imagination of the advanced radical and the conservative traditionalist alike.

The tale of three idioms is one to be put to work, for it may help us to understand certain both general and particular aspects of Indian political life. Consider, for instance, this matter of the gap between profession and practice, the difference between the way things really get done and the way in which they are presented as being done. Of course, this kind of contrast happens everywhere: in England, for example, different sorts of 'old boy networks' are to be found smoothing the course of politics in city council, parliament and Whitehall alike. There is a cement of informality that holds together the formal bricks. But this is not the same as the mixing of entire political styles that happens in India. It is not simply that these people whom a foreigner is likely to question will reply in the 'Western' idiom for his benefit—though this certainly happens. It is also that such people will in any case habitually use that idiom when explaining things to each other. That is to say, Indian political life becomes explicit and self-conscious only through the 'Western' idiom, that is practically the only language in which the activity of description, giving an account of matters, will normally take place. But this does not prevent actual behaviour from following a different path. This situation is a course to be found in many spheres besides the strictly 'political'. "Applications for scholarships will be considered by the Committee on the basis of recommendations submitted by the Head of the Department," but the natural tendency will be for the aspirant to tackle this problem in terms of 'favours' and 'influences'. Likewise with such matters political as the casting of votes, the selection of candidates and distribution of portfolios, and with such matters of administration as the siting of a new school or the granting of an industrial licence. One must be careful not to exaggerate and careful not to imply that in English local government or in American party organization everything is as in the textbooks. But I believe there is a substantial difference.

The gap between supposed and real patterns of behaviour is a much wider matter than corruption, but the two are yet closely related. Corruption—the fact itself but, even more important, the talk about it—occupies a great place in Indian politics. It is of two kinds. Much of what is called corruption is no more than behaviour conducted in terms of one idiom being looked at in terms of another. Anyone holding any kind of position of power may be inclined to regard that position in both modern and traditional terms. Even if he is himself peculiarly free from the grip of traditional categories and loyalties, he will be subjected to steady pressures framed in those terms—and it will be very difficult not to give in. Of course, the proportions in which modern and traditional are mixed will very greatly: there may be 100 per cent modernism in the

Planning Commission and 90 per cent traditionalism is a Mandal Congress Committee in Madhya Pradesh. But at most levels two mainly antagonistic sets of standards will be in competition for the power to control a man's conduct. Equally important, these two sets will also be employed—frequently by the same persons—for judging his conduct. The behaviour which the traditional language holds to be irresponsible is for the modern idiom responsible and that which the modern regards as irresponsible is for the other the very opposite.

This type of contrast can be greatly sharpened when the third idiom is present. This will happen more often than one might imagine. This is not simply because of the personal influence of Bhave or the traditional appeal of those ideas or even because of memories of the saintly aspect of Gandhi. It is also on account of the actual experience of many people in the nationalist movement. That movement did bring out of ordinary men and women a remarkable standard of behaviour. From a sense of dedication or merely from sheer excitement and exhilaration men forgot about themselves and thought only of the cause. There is perhaps a tendency today to exaggerate this in retrospective glances at the golden age, but there is a big element of truth in it. There is a natural unwillingness to accept that period as exceptional and therefore a strong inclination to be severely critical about the decline in standards.

The second kind of corruption is in a way the opposite of the first. The first is a demonstration of the power of the traditional idiom; the second is a sign of its weakness. When a man 'fixes' applications and licences in disregard of merit but in accordance with group loyalties he is obeying a law of social conduct more ancient than that of the upstart state. But when a man puts into his own pocket moneys intended for some organization, when he relentlessly exploits every situation for perfectly private gain, this is not obedience to the rule of any traditional society. No doubt in every society some men have been very selfish when opportunity was provided. But within a compact and tightly knit social unit of India's traditional kind, the checks on anti-social selfishness would be very strong indeed, the sanctions against it awesome. There can be little doubt that much present corruption in India is the work of men not long released from one set of firm social bonds, not yet submissive to a new set. Both corruptions can flourish side by side for two social processes are contemporaneous: the intrusion of caste into the new fields (mainly of regional and even national politics) and the erosion of caste as a feature of social life as a whole.

Corruption is at once what one political language calls the other and what happens when one is displacing the other.

Related to this is a further striking general feature of Indian political life—and again it is a feature rather of social life which politics shares: a certain caution and distrust in relations between people. In the Courts a man in India is innocent until he is proved guilty, but in social and political life the position tends to be reversed. One has noticed the wariness with which people encounter each other and the relative difficulty of establishing friendships except within 'community' groups. In politics this has its equivalent in the extraordinary extent to which the other man's motives are suspect, the difficulty of concerted action and so on. Myron Weiner had already discussed one aspect of this in the *Party Politics in India:* the resistance to unification on the part of political groups with almost identical policies and the readiness in many groups to split and break away. He offered the explanation that in many cases party has become a substitute for a community group and that the members demand the snug and reassuring coherence of a unit in which there are no strangers or outsiders. A more general (though not incompatible) explanation would be that even in the sophisticated world of urban party politics men have not wholly shed the traditional attitudes. No one can be regarded as an individual, taken as he stands; he is always to be 'placed' in terms of the group to which he 'belongs'. This makes complete frankness and trust difficult. Shils had put the point very well when speaking of the Indian intellectual. "If Indian intellectuals are 'cut off from the people' the caste system must take some of the blame....The alienation a the intellectual from Indian society is probably in fact less pronounced than is the alienation of most other Indians from Indian society." The intellectual's alienation may be in fact less pronounced but its impact is more agonizing for, as Shils goes on to say, the ideal of national unity is more real for the intellectual. He feels that something of this has been lost since the independence movement and he feels a resentment against the barriers that separate man for man—while himself remaining in some measure a victim of such attitudes.

Thus man as man, man as clerk in an office, employee in a factory, even student in a college, is placed at a distance from his fellows; indeed, it is not easy to recognize the other as fellow. But this is not all. Present day India strikes many observers as a ruthless and unkind society—and this by way of contrast with the recent past. This may seem strange in view of the well-known efforts of the present regime to establish a welfare state and raise the living standards of the impoverished masses. Yet the impression has some basis. As the status society slowly crumbles, personal ambitions are released and new men press hard on the traditional holders of authority. Perhaps it is to be expected that men escaping from a world of set status may for a while swing violently to the opposite extreme of competitive struggle for all kinds of power. To caution and distrust of the other man there comes to be added disregard. This tendency, already present before independence, was somewhat held in check by the spirit of fellowship in the freedom movement; it has now been let loose.

It is, then, the meeting, the mixing, the confrontation of political idioms which dominates the Indian political scene and gives it distinctive tone. The 'pure' expressions of each language occupy certain areas but these are less significant than the areas of co-habitation. But what is happening in this great encounter? Does one language gain over the others?

The different views on this question have something to do with the professional interests of the observer. In particular social anthropologists and political scientists have seemed to be giving different answers, Indian politics becoming a battlefield in the process. The former has set out from his base in caste and kinship groups and found himself drawn towards the area of political behaviour; the latter, encamped in parliament and party, has had to reconnoitre the regions of social background. This is as it should be, for such movements only correspond to the changes actually taking place in Indian life.

The social anthropologist has put a strong and clear case. With the coming of independence (which incidentally made the serious study of caste possible and no longer an unpatriotic betrayal of the nationalist cause!), a wholly Indian administration and parliamentary democracy, caste and community has been able to move out of the villages and penetrated further towards the centre than ever before. The modern *elite* is no longer protected from the influence of traditional politics by the triple bulwarks of British administrative overseers (who mostly kept out of the caste network), the Indian national movement and a restricted electorate. The Constitution and the national leaders proclaim the goal of a casteless society and hardly a day passes without the vigorous condemnation by Nehru or one of his colleagues of the divisive forces of casteism, linguism, and the like. But these are the only terms in which the newly enfranchised masses know how to operate. And so, in the middle and lower reaches of the parties and the administration, realistic men learn that they must also talk that language if they are to be understood and if they are to be effective. What sounds good up in the Delhi Parliament or for the newspaper-reading public will cut no ice at the grassroots. Nor should it be imagind that caste has stopped at the city limits. It is true that the long run effects of urban life may lead to a weakening of its hold, but there appears to be sufficient evidence that in the shorter run caste not only continues to prevail in city life (caste members often settle in the same localities within the city; immigrants from rural areas keep very close economic and social ties with their village bases), but under urban conditions finds it desirable and possible to attain a higher level of organization than in rural India.

Work already done or in progress indicates clearly enough the pattern of sociological interpretation of Indian politics. Behind the voting figures there is revealed the work of intermediaries who secure the votes of their group for a given candidate. Behind the choice of candidates is discovered careful calculation of caste appeal. The whole shape of Mysore politics, which a political scientist might have been content to describe in terms of relations between parties and between the parliamentary and organizational wings of the major party, is shown to be determined by an age-old rivalry between two powerful castes in that region. Orissa's interesting political history of the last dozen years is likewise explained in terms of shifting caste positions and alignments. The working in practice of much of the movements of 'democratic decentralization' and community development is shown to be conditioned and /or distorted by traditional politics' powerful grip.

However, what the anthropologist may miss—and what political scientists have not been very effective in demonstrating—is that all this, although true and important, is only one part of a double process. For the modern idiom is also moving out of its base in the *elite* just as surely as the traditional idiom is emerging from its hidden habitat. Therefore the attempt to show how modern political institutions are open to manipulation and exploitation by traditional social forces should be accompanied by equivalent attention to the way in which such institutions by their existence constitute modern social forces.

Take, for instance, the Congress Party, probably the most important single political institution in India today. It certainly displays within itself most of the important features of Indian political life, while its present role and future development in great measure determine the course of Indian politics....

In terms of our analysis, the Congress is a crucial meeting ground of the three languages of politics. Within the party are to be found many men who speak the modern idiom—most of them with skill and polish, some of them even with love. Most of the internal party debates would seem to be conducted in this language; for instance, the arguments between the 'right-wingers' (supposedly, for example, Desai, Pant) and the left (Menon and members of the one or two 'ginger groups') on the size of the public sector, the seriousness with which land reforms are to be tackled, the tone of voice to be adopted when speaking to China and the U.S. When commentators talk of the wide range of opinion held together by Nehru, it is a range within this one language which they have in mind. (The same range is to be found, though more obscurely, in the top administration.) The 'federal' tussles within the party are also for the most part in the modern idiom—the location of new steel mills and the choice of ports for development.

At the other end of the machine, so to speak, there is to be found a very different kind of person engaged in a very different kind of operation; the Mandal and District party leaders. Now I am aware that local party secretaries in England and ward bosses in the U.S. are concerned with rather different issues from those which preoccupy the parliamentary and senate leaders. The difference to which I refer in India is, however, a sentate leaders. The difference to which I refer in India is, however, a profounder one of the very manner and style of behaviour; the difference in social setting imposes quite different techniques and is associated with quite different values and standards. The Congress worker in 'rural' India (I use the quotes since the term has to be taken to include sections of cities too) has to operate in the traditional language. But who is the present-day Congress worker?

Most observers would agree that some change has taken place since independence in the character of the men who do Congress politics at the lower levels. Older party workers will often explain with regret and scorn how new men of the wrong kind have got into the organization. The voice of saintly politics is often heard in this strain. But the point has some validity. Of course, the motives which impelled a man to join and work for Congress in re-independence days were more numerous and varied than the old-timers would have us believe, and 'national sentiment' no doubt covered a mutlitude of different characters. But the new men are indeed different.

Some investigators seem to have found two kinds of new men inside the Congress machine. First, there are the leaders of the new village establishment. Until the introduction of adult franchise, the politically active sections of rural India were generally men of higher castes than the peasants and for this reason even a mass party like Congress was manned by Brahmins and other high caste men out of proportion to their numbers. The politics of adult franchise has in many regions raised the influence of the non-Brahmin middle peasants who are at once numerous and—as compared with the hardly less numerous untouchables—economically substantial. Men from these groups seem to be more prominent in Congress than before. The opponents of the party cry out that Congress is courting and capturing the influential leaders of rural life. Of course it is. But is is equally true that such leaders have in their own ways been courting and capturing Congress. Village India, playing its own game of politics in relation to outside *Raj*, has been adjusting itself to Congress power. The men who for economic and electoral reasons count in any area naturally regard it as one of their functions to get to positions from which they can do what is expected of them by their clients and dependants.

Secondly, however, there may have arisen an even newer kind of local Congressman—the man who relies not on his local social status as a member of a dominant caste but solely on his political skill in the new politics. Whereas the first type would operate in the traditional idiom as a matter of course, this second brand of newcomer is really a modern who is simply able to exploit that idiom. (In addition to both these, there naturally continue to be many party workers who belong to those sections who, while numerically and even economically weak, provided social and intellectual leadership in the past.)

Thus Congress is one of the great meeting-places of the three languages of politics. That the party has in some measure gone traditional under the impact of mass electorate politics seems clear. But it must not be forgotten that a political party *as such*—its very organization, as well as the character of Congress national leadership and the fact of its governmental responsibilities—is a modernizing influence. So which language wins? The question remains—and must do so until we know more about Congress. But at least we know what we need to know: the procedures by which Congress' internal elections take place; the negotiations leading to the choice of Parlimentary and, even more important, State Legislature candidates; the relations between Pradesh Congress Committees and Congress State Ministries; the character of the agitations and campaigns on liguistic and communal (e.g., reservation of posts for scheduled castes) issues; the extent and character of party pressures on State Congress Governments in relation to land legislation. On each topic there would be at least two main futures to examine. First, the extent to which community and caste considerations were present and influential; second; the extent to which the exercise and reception of authority was conducted in modern terms of theinstitutions and offices or in traditional terms of social status and customary respect. Lest it be thought that all this is in some derogatory sense academic, let it be said that the battles being conducted within the modern idiom as between 'right' and 'left', 'centralist' and 'statist' will be most significantly influenced by the outcome of the underlying conflict between the two languages. The traditional way points to the right and points away from the centre.

Consider also India's representative institutions. In this world too, as in the world of party, the two idioms meet (with the third idiom again keeping up, as it were, an influential running commentary on the proceedings). There is general agreement that the central Parliament in New Delhi is a powerful instrument of political education for members and public alike. The education it conveys is almost entirely in the modern idiom; this is certainly true of the debates on the floor of the House, in all the parliamentary committees and in some party committees; it is less certainly so in the case of certain other party committees and in regard to general lobby conversation. The members are powerfully influenced by its atmosphare and they are under that influence for by far the greater part of the year. The public that reads papers is also accustomed to watch it closely—so large is the space devoted by the press to its proceedings. The talk is all of issues and problems and programmes and the scale is emphatically all-India. As Asoka Mehta strikingly said recently, Parliament is the great unifier of the nation. This is true; it has taken over that role in large measure from the freedom movement. (I find the parallel with the Tudor parliaments very close and instructive: Nehru is the Queen in Parliament; in no other place does he "stand so high in his estate royal"; and through Parliament the feudal powers in their country seats are kept relatively subdued and in order.)

Much less clear is the character of the State Legislative Assemblies. Students have already pointed out that the members of these bodies are drawn from layers much closer to those of traditional politics. Also they are in the Assemblies for quite a short part of the year; the rest of the time they will be in their home districts which are, increasingly, their constituencies. No one can visit the lobbies of a State Assembly without realising quite vividly that the M.L.A. is 'in touch with' constituents; the corridors are full of them, some still bearing the dust of the village tracks if not the earth of the fields themselves. The M.L.A. is thus another critical point in the drama of Indian politics: which language of politics does he speak? He is himself undergoing 'modern' education from his seniors on the front benches, but the 'courses' are shorter and of a fairly 'elementary' nature. Still he learns to think of his state (even if not yet of India) and to talk of power projects (even if the big decisions are taken in Delhi). At the other end there are the pressures from home and in the corridors—to remember that he comes from the Vidarbha part of Maharashtra , or that he is a Mahar or that he must please those who count in his district party. So evidently he becomes 'bilingual'. But we would still like to know in which language he does his thinking and his dreaming. And anyone anxious to secure the victory of the modern language over the traditional would do well to concentrate on the M.L.A. and should presumably try to strengthen the links that join him to circles where the modern idiom is spoken. The M.L.A. is one of the great 'gap-closers' in Indian politics but we do not yet know whether he is achieving this in ways favourable to the modern or to the traditional style.

Even State Ministers have to operate in the two languages. Indeed, one might say that the successful Chief Ministers are those who are equally skilled in both idioms. Chavan of Bombay may be a good exmple of this kind. But in at least one state, Madras, there was a fascinating division of labour between the Chief Minister, who speaks little or no English but manages the 'informal politics', and a colleague who handles the policy questions and converses with New Delhi.

The combination, the containment in peaceful interpenetrating, of these diverse and in principle competitive languages of politics is the great achievement of political life in independent India. Vast social and economic changes are being accomplished steadily and without obvious drama and are being accommodated and digested by and within a political structure which is successfully flexible, 'politically multi-lingual'. The instruments of this achievement are, first, the two great legacies which India inherited from the days before 1947: the

Government and the Movement, a stable administrative structure and a capacious political organization, both equipped with able leadership. To these must be added India's parlimentary institutions—in many respects a development of independence politics, yet owing much of their present success to earlier beginnings.

Yet the enterprise is not without its grave difficulties. Some of these may be indicated by turning attention to what is perhaps the really threatening force in Indian political life: the discontent of the educated middle classes. (None of the popularly supposed threats to democracy in India—a failure sufficiently to increase agricultural production, a slower rate of economic growth than China, etc.—has any political significance except in so far as it can operate through the opinions of this section of the population. And these opinions can be affected by many things besides economic statistics.) This discontent is as it were not in the direct line of fire between the modern and traditional idioms, but it is greatly influenced by factors arising out of that conflict.

The present mood of the educated mainly urban middle classes is dictated by those of its less successful members. There are many men (and an increasing number of women) who are in secure and satisfying employment in the services and in industrial and commercial enterprises—as technicians, administrators, educators and entrepreneurs . And it is of course true that they are relatively contented with their own lives. Yet it is striking to note the extent to which even such people will speak of India's political life in terms which seem to belong more appropriately to those of their fellows who are unemployed, mal-employed or insecurely employed. The general attitude is one of deep disgust with those in power and profound scepticism about the effectiveness or suitability of existing political institutions. The fact that much of the criticism is based on very great ignorance of what is actually going on does not lessen its significance. There is a conviction that all holders of political power—great and small alike—are abusing their positions for illegitimate ends. These may be personal or family or group. There are no men of 'public spirit' in public life, no disinterested politicians of pure motives.

In other words, this influential section of the public is engaged in a continuous complaint about political life in India. Too modern to be able to operate traditional politics, they are at the same time sufficiently sympathetic to certain idealized features of traditional society to be very ready to condemn modern ways of politics as unsuited to India's genius. They enjoy exposing the way in which institutions of modern politics are at the mercy of older systems and pressures. They learn easily the language of saintly politics—not necessarily directly, as preached by Bhave and Narayan, but as mediated to them through experience or impressions of the great days of the national movement. Eager to take part in politics, they find there is little room for them.

This explains in part the enthusiasm with which linguistic agitations are supported and even led by these elements. Their energies find release in these campaigns, for here an attractive common ground between traditional and modern politics is provided. The young student cannot hope to overcome his supposed alienation from the masses by raising and developing issues of, say, public economic policy. So he mainly neglects such questions. But if inter-group tensions develop, he will be there and so also will be the new caste leaders; the latter can rise to the level of such issues, while the student or clerk finds it no effort to come down to meet them, for part of him is already there. In the Assamese-Bengali killings, in the turbulent struggles for Maharashtra or Andhra, culture-gaps closed wonderfully; men from the worlds of both languages join hands. There may be an element of direct class interest involved in these cases—a belief that, for instance, the Bengalis are keeping you out of a decent job or the Gujaratis are not giving the others a chance. But these agitations, though evidently most satisfying emotionally—even recapturing the thrill of the freedom struggle—are, alas, mainly irrelevant to the main needs of the frustrated urban moderns. It is doubtful if they can for long give even emotional satisfaction.

Perhaps the central problem is that suitable channels for political action seem to be fewer than the demand for them. India's is an underdeveloped polity from the point of view of the needs of its educated middle class. It is shaped like a narrow pole rather than a solid pyramid. It is not exactly that there are no organizations and associations at a convenient level ('infra-structure'?), but rather that most of these are talking the wrong language. There are plenty of caste organizations, but few lively professional bodies or opinion-propagating societies. It may be that the middle-class feeling of wanting to 'participate' is abnormally developed (a hangover from the national movement where all were excitingly employed, a sign of lack of absorption in their own jobs, a genuine misunderstanding of the meaning of democracy—some of all these things and no doubt more), but there is certainly no room on the narrow pole for all who seem to want a place there.

The structure of 'modern' political institutions is not only frustratingly narrow—limited to legislatures and parties. There is also the difficulty that that structure is itself dominated by one organization, the Congress Party. And there is very little that the middle classes can do about this in the short run. They might organize other parties, and indeed have of course done so—P.S.P. Jan Singh Swatantra. But how can such parties make any impression on the solid base of the Congress which is located in the world of 'traditional' politics where Swatantra and P.S.P. alike hardly know how to walk? (The Communists have sometimes done better by exploiting caste blocs—as in Andhra and Kerala. Even Swatantra is learning, from some of its new-found allies of the 1962 elections.) In any case, in the world of 'traditional' politics, governments are not changed or chosen so much as used or evaded. The circle is a most vicious one: you can't be taken seriously by the local men who matter until you are the government, but you can't be the government until you have been taken seriously. It is interesting to reflect that nothing but adult franchise could have secured Congress rule with such certain stability; a more restricted franchise would have meant the conduct of politics in much more purely 'modern' terms, and that would have permitted a much greater 'openness of texture' and flexibility.

Thus, the vital educated middle classes are politically quite frustrated. They have no liking or trust or confidence in Congress, but they cannot budge it because the levers are not in their hands. So the 'modern' opposition remains puny, the 'traditional' 'opposition' works in other ways, and the student masses (the jargon seems correct in India's case) become a shade more cynical and despairing as each year passes. Of course, a dozen years of stable government in the wake of independence and partition is no mean blessing, as every administrator in India knows. Yet the disadvantages are now beginning to become substantial. The icepack is forming and the ship of state may soon be crushed. The most obvious dynamite available to break the ice and permit free political navigation is the withdrawal of Nehru. If that were to happen, Congress would less easily hold together. (No one else has such wide and varies appeal. No one else is so regularly forgiven. No one else has his ability and dedication. No one else could confuse the issues and blur the distinctions to the degree that Congress leadership demands.) In that case—and despite the temptation for all factions to stay under the Congress shelter—struggle could become more open. There would be awful dangers and great losses but there are days when these seem to be less terrifying than those entailed in getting frozen up.

Index